Library of
Davidson College

Library of
Davidson College

MICROPROCESSOR DATA BOOK

MICROPROCESSOR DATA BOOK

S. A. Money
T Eng (CEI), MITE, MBCS

McGraw-Hill Book Company
New York St. Louis San Francisco Auckland
Bogotá Hamburg Johannesburg London Madrid
Mexico Montreal New Delhi Panama Paris
São Paulo Singapore Sydney Tokyo Toronto

Library of Congress Cataloging in Publication Data
Money, Steve A.
    Microprocessor data book.

    1.Microprocessors.   2.Microcomputers.
I.Title.
QA76.5.M549   1982   001.64   82-14053
ISBN 0-07-042706-2

Copyright © 1982 by S.A. Money. All rights reserved. Printed in the United States of America. Except as permitted under the United States Copyright Act of 1976, no part of this publication may be reproduced or distributed in any form or by any means, or stored in a data base or retrieval system, without the prior written permission of the publisher.

234567890   HDHD   89876543

ISBN 0-07-042706-2

CONTENTS

Preface	vii

1 INTRODUCTION	1

Architecture. Bus systems. CPU control. CPU execution. Subroutines and stacks. Interrupts. Memory. Input–output. Word length. Types of device. Fabrication technology. Choosing a microprocessor or microcomputer. Microprocessor prices.

2 4-BIT MICROPROCESSORS AND MICROCOMPUTERS	11
AMD Am2900 series	16
AMI 2000 series	19
Hitachi HMCS40 series	21
Matsushita MN1400/1500 series	23
Motorola MC10800 series	24
National COPS2 series	26
N.E.C. μCOM40 series	28
OKI Series 40	31
Rockwell PPS4/1 series	34
Texas Instruments TMS1000 series	36

3 8-BIT MICROPROCESSORS AND MICROCOMPUTERS	39
Fairchild F8 family	45
General Instrument PIC1650 series	48
Intel 8048 series	50
Intel 8051 series	54
Intel 8080A	57
Intel 8085A	60
Mostek 3870 series	63
Motorola MC6800 series	66
Motorola MC6801 and MC6803 series	69
Motorola MC6802 series	73
Motorola MC6805 series	77
Motorola MC6809 series	79
Motorola MC146805 series	82
Mullard MAB8400 series	85
National 8060/8070 series	88
National NSC800	90
MOS Technology MCS6502 series	93
N.E.C. μPD7801 microcomputer	96
RCA 1800 series	98
Rockwell R6500/1 series	102
Signetics 8X300	105
Signetics 2650A	107
Zilog Z8	110
Zilog Z80	113

4 16-BIT MICROPROCESSORS AND MICROCOMPUTERS	117
AMD Am29116	121
Fairchild Microflame 9440/45	123
Ferranti F100L	125
General Instrument CP1600	127
Intel iAPX86 series	129
Intel iAPX88 series	132
Motorola MC68000 series	136
National NS16000 series	139
Texas Instruments TMS9900	141
Texas Instruments TMS9940 and 9985	144
Texas Instruments TMS9980	147
Texas Instruments TMS9995	150
Western Digital Pascal Microengine	152
Zilog Z8000 series	154

5 OTHER MICROPROCESSOR TYPES	157
Intel 2920 Analogue Signal Processor	159
Intersil IM6100	162

6 PARALLEL I/O DEVICES	165
Principles	167
IEEE488 Interface Bus	168
Intel 8255 PPI	169
Motorola MC6821 PIA	170
Zilog Z80-PIO	171
Intel 8291 GPIB listener-talker	172
Intel 8292 GPIB controller	173
Motorola MC68488 GPIB interface	174
Texas Instruments TMS9914 GPIB adapter	175

7 SERIAL I/O DEVICES	177
Principles	179
Intel 8251A PCI	181
Intel 8273 PDLC	182
Intersil IM6402 UART	183
Motorola MC6850 ACIA	184
Motorola MC6852 SSDA	186
Motorola MC6854 ADLC	187
N.E.C. μPD379 USRT	188
Signetic 2651 PCI	189
Synertek SY6551 ACIA	190
Signetics 2661	191
Texas Instruments TMS9902 ACC	192
Texas Instruments TMS9903 SCC	193
Zilog Z80-SIO	194

8 MEMORY DEVICES	195
Introduction	197

2101/11/12 series 1k bit static RAM	199
2102 series 1k bit static RAM	201
256 × 4 bit CMOS static RAM	203
2114 series 1k × 4 bit static RAM	205
256 × 8 bit erasable nMOS PROM	207
512 × 8 bit nMOS erasable PROM	209
2708 series 8192 bit nMOS erasable PROM	211
2716 series 16k bit erasable PROM	213
2532/2732 type 32k bit erasable PROM	215
64k bit dynamic RAM	217

9 PERIPHERAL DEVICE CONTROLLERS — 219

Visual display controllers	221
Motorola MC6845	224
Motorola MC6847	226
Thomson EFCIS EF9365/6	228
Thomson EFCIS 96364	230
Floppy disk controllers	231
Disk controller data	232

10 OTHER SUPPORT DEVICES — 233

Intel 8252 Timer	238
Motorola MC6840	239
Zilog Z80 CTC	240
Analogue converter device data	241
Analogue device manufacturers	242

11 DEVELOPMENT AIDS — 245

Evaluation boards	247
Full development systems	248

12 DIRECTORY OF MANUFACTURERS — 251

13 GLOSSARY OF MICROPROCESSOR TERMS — 259

PREFACE

Advances in the techniques for manufacturing large scale integrated (LSI) circuits have, in recent years, made it feasible to incorporate most, or in some cases all, of the complex logic required for a small digital computer system on to a single silicon chip. One example of the application of these LSI techniques is in the familiar digital pocket calculator, which is in fact a specialised digital computer. In these devices all of the electronic logic is contained in a single integrated circuit package.

In designing modern electronic systems the engineer must now take into account the ready availability of microcomputer and microprocessor devices which can simplify design, making the end product more versatile or more economical to produce.

One problem which faces the designer planning to use a microprocessor is the great multiplicity of devices that have become available. Choosing a suitable microprocessor could involve collecting together and searching through a mountain of different data sheets and manuals.

In this book condensed data have been provided for most of the available types of microprocessor and microcomputer device. For each major type or series a description is given of the internal architecture, instruction set, main electrical data and package details.

Most of the popular devices are manufactured by several different suppliers, and a list of alternative sources and type numbers have been included in the data for each type. Support chips designed for that processor have also been listed.

For convenience the devices have been divided into groups covering 4, 8 and 16-bit types and other processors. It would not be practical to include full details of each type, but it is hoped that sufficient information has been provided to allow the designer to narrow down his choice to perhaps one or two types. The manufacturer's data sheets or manuals may then be consulted for more detailed operating and application information.

In order to choose a processor for a project some knowledge of the basic principles of the devices is required, and this has been covered in the introductory chapter. A general guide has also been included on the factors involved when a processor type is chosen.

A complete system normally consists of a microprocessor together with a selection of supporting devices to handle input–output, external device control and to provide memory. The number of support devices available is even greater than that of microprocessor types, so no attempt has been made to include details of all of these. Some descriptions have been included covering the major support device functions, and data have been included on some of the more popular types as a guide to the facilities provided by such devices.

At the end of the book a directory of microprocessor manufacturers has been included and there is also a glossary of some of the terminology used in the microprocessor field.

It is hoped that the information given in this book will assist designers in choosing suitable devices and that it will be generally useful to those engaged in designing or planning microprocessor based products.

Finally, I would like to express my thanks to all those manufacturers and distributors who supplied the data and other information which made it possible to compile this book.

1 INTRODUCTION

In recent years the advent of microprocessors and microcomputers has revolutionised the whole process of digital system design. Projects which, a few years ago, might have required tens or hundreds of digital logic devices can today be implemented by using perhaps one or two LSI circuits. Of course, LSI circuits have been around for some years, but economic considerations have usually limited their use to applications, such as digital calculators, where high volume production is possible and high design costs can be recovered quickly. The advantage of the microprocessor is that a standard device can be used for many applications by merely altering the program of instructions held in its memory. Thus design costs can be reduced and a variety of products may be built using perhaps a standard circuit board.

Microcomputers, however, bring with them a number of new design concepts which may be unfamiliar to the system designer used to working with conventional digital logic systems. In this introductory section we shall examine the internal organisation of microcomputer systems and their general principles of operation. Later we shall consider the various factors that are involved in choosing a suitable type of microprocessor for a design project.

ARCHITECTURE

The general organisation or architecture of a digital computer, whether it be a mainframe, a minicomputer or a microcomputer, follows the basic arrangement shown in fig. 1.1.

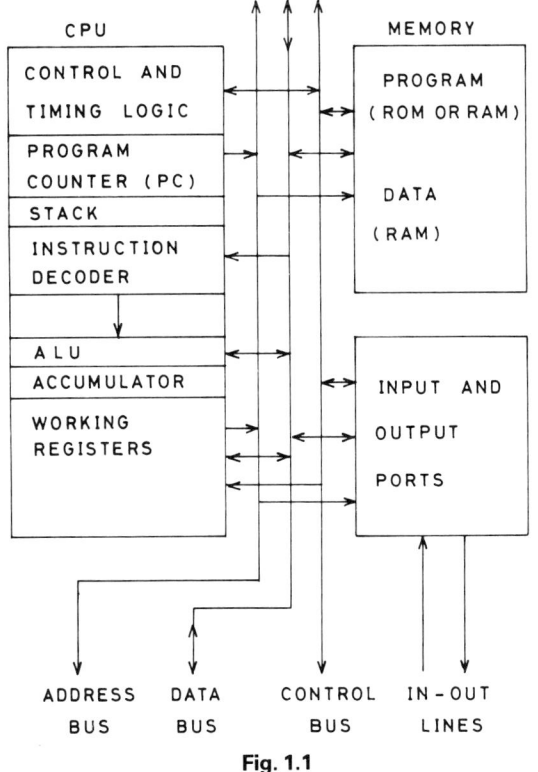

Fig. 1.1

At the heart of the system is the *central processor unit*, generally referred to as the CPU. Functionally the CPU can be broken down into two subsections, one of which is used to control the timing and sequence of operations in the system, whilst the other executes the required arithmetic and logical functions and handles the data being processed. A memory system is connected to the CPU and is used to store the list of instructions to be executed, known as the *program*, and the data being processed. In some types the data and program memories are separated but for most of the general purpose microprocessors a common memory is used. Communication with the outside world is handled by two further sections, known as the *input* and *output* ports, which allow data to be transferred to and from external devices such as keyboards, display units and printers. The various components of the microcomputer system are tied together by a system of bus lines which are common to all units. This is of course a very much simplified description of a microcomputer system and we shall now go on to look at each section in more detail.

BUS SYSTEMS

Data is transferred between the various units of the system over sets of parallel wires known as *buses*. Normally there are three buses, one for data, one for addresses and the third for control signals.

The data bus allows data to be transferred between the CPU and the memory or input–output lines. This bus is in fact bidirectional and controlled by the CPU. A read–write line, which forms part of the control bus, determines the direction of data flow along the data bus. This signal is generated by the CPU and if set to *write* allows data to be output from the CPU to other parts of the system. When the control line is set to *read* the CPU accepts data which have been placed on the data bus by one of the other units in the system. The bus may only be driven by one device at a time, although all of the other devices may read data from the bus simultaneously.

The address bus is used to provide an address signal for the memory to select one particular location within the memory for connection to the data bus. Normally the address bus is an output from the CPU and data always travels from the CPU to the memory. The address bus may also be used to select individual input or output channels when there are several of these connected to the data bus. Some of the smaller processors may have separate address lines for program memory and data memory.

The control bus provides a selection of control signals to and from the CPU to govern timing and control of transfers of data on the other bus lines. Among these may be signals for halting the operation of the CPU and perhaps disconnecting it from the bus system. The address and data buses are normally tri-state in operation. Apart from the normal 0 and 1 states the CPU, or memory, may be switched into a high impedance state which effectively disconnects it from the bus. This facility may be used when it is desired to have another device take over control of the bus system. Typical applications are in multiprocessor systems where a bus is shared between two or more CPUs, only one of which may access the bus at a time.

In a large system the output drivers of the CPU and other devices may not be capable of driving all of the loads on the bus. In such cases bus drivers or bus transceivers would be used where each device connects to the bus system. In some such systems the data signals on the data bus may be inverted by the transceivers or buffers.

CPU CONTROL

Apart from system timing and control logic the control part of the CPU normally contains a register called the *program counter*, an address register, an instruction decoder, a stack or stack pointer register and some interrupt logic.

Instructions making up the program to be executed are stored in the memory and are normally called up in sequence for execution. The function of the program counter is to give the memory address of the next instruction to be executed. At the start of a program the program counter will be loaded with the memory address of the first instruction. When the system starts running this address will be transferred to the address bus and the instruction code will be read in from memory. One part of the instruction is called the operation code or *opcode* and determines the type of operation to be performed. Typical operations might be ADD, SUBTRACT or AND, each of which will have a different opcode pattern. The opcode data read in from memory are passed to the instruction decoder, which then sets up all of the logic linkages required within the CPU to perform the desired operation. At this point the contents of the program counter will be updated to give the address of the next opcode in the memory. Some operations will require data, as well as an instruction code, and for these one or two additional words of data may follow the opcode in the memory. These data words will be dealt with as the instruction is executed. When such data exist the contents of the program counter may be incremented by two or three to provide the correct address for the next opcode. This updating is governed by the instruction decoder according to the type of opcode detected.

A typical instruction execution sequence consists of one or more instruction cycles. The first cycle normally calls in the opcode from memory and is called the *instruction fetch cycle*. On simple instructions this will be followed by an execution cycle, when the required operation is carried out. If data are required extra cycles are required to read in the data words following the opcode. In some cases these words may be a memory address, and once in the CPU will be transferred to the address register and address bus during the execution cycle.

Timing varies from one type of processor to another. In some types, such as the 6800 and 6502 series the timing is relatively simple with each instruction cycle divided into a pair of time periods called $\phi 1$ and $\phi 2$. Internal CPU functions occur during $\phi 1$, such as execution, and memory access occurs during $\phi 2$. Thus a simple instruction calls in the opcode on $\phi 2$ and executes the instruction during the following $\phi 1$ cycle. Other processors may divide up the instruction cycle into many different time periods, which may vary according to the type of operation being performed. Manufacturer's data sheets should be consulted for detailed instruction timing for any given processor type.

We shall look at the stack and interrupt functions in more detail later. The timing clock for the CPU will often be a multiphase type, but in many of the newer types of device it will be generated by an on-chip oscillator which merely needs an external quartz crystal for timing. Older types often do require multiphase clocks but usually a special clock chip is available to generate these, using a crystal for timing. In some cases the system clock will also be needed to control the timing of the memory and input–output channels.

CPU EXECUTION

In the execution section of a microcomputer CPU there will be an arithmetic and logic unit or *ALU*, which is a complex logic array to carry out the desired arithmetic or logic function. Associated with the ALU is a special register called the *accumulator*. Normally the ALU has two data inputs and one output which may each be 4, 8 or 16 bits wide. Data for one of the ALU inputs are provided by the accumulator and the results of the operation are placed in the accumulator after execution.

Apart from the ALU and the accumulator the execution unit may also contain a number of general storage registers, which may be used to hold data or intermediate results. In some types of processor these additional general purpose registers may be used as accumulators. Data may be transferred to and from the accumulator, ALU input and general registers and memory via the data bus.

Using the internal registers for data storage can speed up the operation of the program, since these registers can be specified by the opcode, thus avoiding the need for extra memory access cycles when the instruction is executed. Some CPUs, such as the 6800 and 6500 series, use memory locations as general purpose registers allowing operations such as shifts and incrementing or complementing of data directly within the memory.

Many CPUs have data pointer or index registers within the register bank. These registers may be used to hold memory addresses rather than data and for certain instructions their contents may be placed on the address bus to select data in the memory. Such registers may be incremented or decremented to allow tables of data to be handled in the memory.

Typical functions provided by the ALU and accumulator are ADD, SUBTRACT, AND, OR, EXCLUSIVE OR, complement and clear. It is also possible to shift data left or right by one bit in the registers and to rotate data where the bit pushed out at one end of the register may be inserted again at the other end to give a continuous loop of data moving through the register. Other operations include incrementing and decrementing contents of registers. Normally arithmetic uses pure binary numbers, but for some applications binary coded decimal (BCD) format may be used where groups of four binary bits are used to represent decimal digits.

On a few more sophisticated processors multiplication and division instructions may be provided, but for most types these operations must be implemented by a small sequence of instructions. Many processors with a multiply or divide will use an internally stored program to carry out the operation which will be relatively slow to execute. Some types, however, use a hardware logic array within the chip to give very fast multiplication execution times.

A very important facility in microprocessors is the

ability of the CPU to test the results of an operation and to take alternative courses of action depending upon those results. Typical tests provided are zero, minus, carry and overflow. Carry indicates that a carry out of the accumulator was generated by the operation and overflow indicates that the result is a number larger than the register can handle. As a result of these tests the CPU may be made to skip, branch or jump instead of executing the next instruction.

A skip operation causes the CPU to skip over the next instruction in sequence and execute the following one. In a branch or jump instruction a new value is placed in the program counter and execution is transferred to another point in the program. For jumps the new instruction address follows the jump instruction as data in memory. Branch instructions often use relative addressing, where the data following the branch instruction are added to the current contents of the program counter to generate the new instruction address. In a conditional branch the program will branch to a new point if the condition of the branch is true, whilst execution will continue with the next instruction if the condition is not true. When an unconditional branch or jump occurs the program will always go to the new point specified by the branch or jump.

Typical branch conditions are Branch if Zero, Branch if Not Zero, Branch if Plus, Branch if Minus and so on. Results of the various tests are normally stored as flag bits in a status register. Often these flags can be manipulated by the program so that if desired the carry bit could be set or reset directly by the program.

SUBROUTINES AND STACKS

Often there will be frequently repeated sequences of instructions in a program. Typical of these might be the set of instructions to read data from a keyboard or to carry out a multiplication. Whilst these instructions could simply be repeated as desired throughout the program a more convenient technique is to make use of a subroutine. In a subroutine the small sequence of instructions is treated as a small separate sub-program and is stored once in the memory. When the subroutine is to be used a special jump to subroutine or CALL instruction is used. This causes the contents of the program counter to be temporarily stored away and then a jump is made to the start of the subroutine instructions. At the end of the subroutine a RETURN instruction is executed which causes the old program counter contents to be restored and the program will then continue to execute with the instruction immediately after the CALL.

In simple processors a single temporary register is used for saving the program counter, but with such a scheme it will not be possible to call a subroutine from within another subroutine. Some processors may have several save registers, which are called the *stack*, and as each register is filled a new one is selected for loading. In such a system the last register loaded will be the first to be read out, and this type of memory is sometimes called a first in last out or FILO type. In computers this type of memory arrangement is called a stack and in most of the general purpose processors the stack is built up in the main memory. To keep track of the current stack top location a data pointer register known as the *stack pointer* is used and this is normally part of the CPU control section. On each subroutine call the contents of the program counter are written to the top of the stack in memory and the stack pointer is automatically updated to point to the next free location in the stack. On a return from subroutine the stack pointer is moved down to point to the last data written to the stack and then those data are transferred to the program counter. Most general purpose processors will allow data to be moved to and from the stack by using PUSH and PULL (or POP) instructions with the stack pointer being updated as required. Some of the more advanced processors have two stack pointers, one for storage of subroutine addresses and generally called the *system* or *supervisor stack*, whilst the other may be used for data storage and is called the *user stack*.

When a stack is implemented in memory subroutines may call other subroutines, a process known as *nesting*. As the inner subroutines complete execution the program transfers to the next subroutine up until eventually a return is made to the main program. When nesting is used the size of the stack space available will determine the number of levels to which subroutines may be nested. In some processors the return from a subroutine may be made conditional so that returns may be made from different points in a subroutine, according to the results of operations carried out within the subroutine.

Sometimes it may be desirable to transfer data from the main program into a subroutine. This can be done by pushing the data on to the stack before the subroutine call. Once inside the subroutine the stack pointer may be manipulated to allow access to the data and perhaps to replace them with data to be transferred back to the main program. The only critical point here is that the stack pointer must be restored to its proper position pointing to the return address before the return from subroutine is executed.

INTERRUPTS

When communicating with the outside world there will often be occasions where the processor is ready to transfer data but the external device isn't or *vice versa*. These situations can be overcome by placing the processor in a testing loop, where it waits for a ready signal from the external device. This is inefficient, however, since the processor is not processing data whilst it is waiting for the external device. A technique for overcoming this problem is to use an interrupt system. In an interrupt system the external device applies a pulse to a special interrupt request input on the CPU, and this sets a flip flop within the CPU. When an interrupt occurs the CPU will complete the execution of the current instruction and then branch to an interrupt service routine which will deal with the external device. The service routine is in fact very much like a subroutine. When the interrupt is acted upon the contents of the program counter are stored as for a subroutine, but usually the status register contents will also be saved on the stack as well. Some processors, such as the Motorola 6800, will save the contents of all of the internal registers when an interrupt occurs. As with a subroutine at the end of the interrupt service routine the program counter and any other saved registers will have their contents restored and program execution continues with the next instruction in the program.

The simple interrupt described above is usually called a *non-masked interrupt* or NMI. For some purposes it is useful to be able to inhibit interrupts and this can be done by using a maskable interrupt. By setting or resetting a bit in the status register the interrupt may be inhibited or activated as desired. Interrupts may be nested as for subroutines if desired.

A further type of interrupt is the software interrupt, which is triggered by an instruction rather than by a pulse from external hardware. This type of interrupt is generally used for debugging programs, but may also be used to indicate a fault condition thrown up by a program test.

Most processors have only one interrupt request (IRQ) line for masked interrupts and one for non-masked interrupts. Normally the non-masked and software interrupts will have priority over masked interrupts and are thus dealt with first if both types occur together. There may be several external devices sharing the common interrupt line, and some form of priority of service may be desired between the various devices. In such cases priority will usually be determined by external logic, but some processors such as the Texas 9900 series do allow for priority decoding within the CPU.

Most general purpose processors use what are known as *vectored interrupts*. Here each type of interrupt will cause the CPU to go to a different address which will contain the interrupt vector which is the start address for the service routine corresponding to that particular interrupt. In some types the vector address of the service routine must be fed in via the data bus from the external interrupting device when the CPU acknowledges acceptance of the interrupt.

Power on reset or initialisation sequence is a special form of interrupt. Normally this causes the program counter to be loaded from either the top location in the memory or from the bottom location. The CPU then executes a start up routine which resets the internal logic and starts execution of the program at the reset vector address stored at the top or bottom of memory.

MEMORY

The microcomputer memory is used to store both program and data. Characteristics of various types of memory device are discussed in Section 8. Normally the program will be held in some form of read only memory for a dedicated system, whilst the data are held in read–write memory, often referred to as RAM. Some data, such as constants, may be stored in ROM along with the program. In a general purpose computer system, such as a development system or a personal computer, the user program will often be stored in RAM but the operating system and its associated programs are often stored in ROM. In most systems an initialisation program and various utility routines may be stored in ROM to form what is generally called a *monitor program*.

For large amounts of data storage special memories, such as magnetic bubble types, may be used or the data may be held on a floppy disk or a magnetic cassette tape. Microcomputers generally have a small amount of scratchpad RAM for data and a medium size ROM for program storage. Most single-chip types use mask programmed ROMs, which makes them best suited to very large production levels. Some types may use programmable ROMs for the program storage and a few have erasable PROMs. These types are best suited to specials and limited production runs.

INPUT–OUTPUT

To be of any use the microcomputer must be able to communicate with the outside world. Often this may be via a keyboard or keypad for input and visual display or printer for output. Digital data in and out are transferred via data ports, which are basically latched registers connected to the data bus and selectable by the CPU for data transfers. In some cases the signals may be converted to or from analogue signals before reaching the outside world. Switches, solenoids and servos can be driven from the CPU via suitable interface circuits.

Apart from the data lines each input or output port will have a pair of control lines, often referred to as *handshake lines*. One of these lines is an output from the computer to indicate to the external device that it is ready to transfer data via the port. The second line is an input to the computer system from the external device and may be used to indicate either that the peripheral unit is ready to accept data or that it has placed data on the port lines for the computer to read. These signals may also be looked upon as a request for action in one direction and an acknowledgement signal in the other direction, or alternatively they may simply be used to indicate that the device producing an output handshake signal is busy. Handshake signals are particularly important where the microprocessor and the external device operate at different speeds.

WORD LENGTH

Microprocessors and microcomputers work with binary data, which are handled as groups of binary digits or *bits* and these groups are called data words. Typically a word may contain 4, 8, 12, 16 or 32 bits of data according to the type of system being considered.

The earlier microprocessors, such as the Intel 4004 or 4040, and many of the modern single-chip microcomputers use 4-bit data words, which are sometimes called *nibbles*. In these systems the data bus, ALU and data registers are all 4-bits wide. The numerical value of a 4-bit word can range from 0 to 15, and often a system known as *binary coded decimal* (BCD) may be used where each word is used to represent a decimal digit having a value from 0 to 9. Large binary numbers have to be processed in 4-bit segments.

Most of the popular general purpose microprocessors use an 8-bit data word, which is referred to as a *byte*. A byte may have a numerical value in the range 0 to 255 and is also convenient as a means of encoding text character information, where perhaps 96 different upper and lower case letters and various punctuation signs and numbers have to be identified. In an 8-bit system the data paths, ALU and registers are normally 8 bits wide. A data byte may be used to hold two BCD digits when that type of data is to be handled.

For large systems the word length and data path size

may be 16 bits, allowing data values from 0 to 65535. Some of the 16-bit processors may include registers 32 bits long, so that 32-bit wide data can be handled inside the CPU, but at the time of writing no 32-bit systems are available although some minicomputers can handle 32-bit wide data.

In most cases the data bus will define the word size of the processor system, but there are a few processors, such as the Intel 8088, which although having a 16-bit CPU architecture, use an 8-bit data bus and each data word is transferred as a pair of successive data bytes.

With a 4-bit processor the data word is not wide enough for use as an instruction opcode since it would allow only 15 different instructions to be used. It is normal therefore for 4-bit processors to use an 8-bit instruction word and to hold the program instructions in a separate 8-bit wide memory. A few types may use a 10-bit instruction word.

In industrial systems it is common to find 12-bit data, giving a range of values from 0 to 4095. A few microprocessor types have been produced for this word length but generally 12-bit data will be handled by an 8-bit or 16-bit CPU system.

Address systems for the 8-bit processors are usually 16 bits wide, allowing up to 65536 memory locations to be selected. For the larger 16-bit processors an address of 20 or 24 bits may be used which will allow several megabytes of memory to be directly accessed.

Sometimes in order to reduce the number of leads needed on the processor package the data and address buses may be multiplexed over a common set of lead out pins. Although this allows the use of a smaller package and may produce a less expensive CPU device, it can lead to extra complication in the external logic circuitry, which may offset the advantages gained by producing a smaller CPU.

TYPES OF DEVICE

Three basic types of device are available for use in the construction of a microcomputer system.

Firstly there are the microprocessors which contain all, or most, of the CPU section on a single silicon chip. Some types such as the 8080 do require additional external logic to provide a system clock and to control the data and address buses but the newer microprocessor types include these functions on the single chip.

For small dedicated systems it is possible to obtain a single-chip microcomputer which has the CPU, memory and input–output ports on a single chip. Such a device can provide a complete microcomputer system with just a few external discrete components for timing. Most of these devices use mask programming for the program memory where the pattern of instructions is built into the chip as it is being manufactured. A few types do have programmable read only memories for the computer program which can be set up in the field.

The third major type of processor device is the *bit slice*, where each of the CPU functions is implemented as a slice of logic typically four bits wide. Normally there will be an ALU slice and some form of program sequencer or control slice to make up the main functions of the CPU. Other slices may be used for timing, stack functions and data control. If an 8-bit wide system is needed then two 4-bit ALU slices would be operated in parallel and the program control slices may be dealt with in a similar way. These devices are generally very fast in operation and would be used for special purpose processors where high speed or some special internal organisation is desired.

FABRICATION TECHNOLOGY

Devices may be built using a wide variety of semiconductor fabrication technologies but generally these can be grouped as four major types of fabrication.

Most of the early microprocessors used pMOS, where the logic is implemented using p channel field effect transistors (FETs). These early devices normally operate from a negative voltage supply and will often have several different voltage supply rails. Their main advantage is that pMOS is an older and hence more established form of construction and generally devices using it may be cheaper to produce than other types.

The popular modern processors use nMOS technology, where the internal logic uses n channel FETs and these devices will normally be designed to operate from a single +5 V supply rail. nMOS devices are usually faster than pMOS versions, but they do require well stabilised supplies of typically ±5% tolerance. Because of high production volume their cost may not be a lot different from that of similar pMOS types.

The third major type of device is made using CMOS, where a combination of both n and p type FETs is used. Perhaps the most important feature of CMOS is its very low power consumption compared with other types of fabrication. This makes the CMOS microprocessors ideally suited to applications where battery operation and hence low power demand are needed. CMOS also has the advantage of being relatively unaffected by variations in the power supply voltage and is less sensitive to noise on its input lines. A slight disadvantage of CMOS is that it tends to be a little slower in operation than pMOS or nMOS, although some new types of CMOS device built on a sapphire substrate can achieve speeds as high as for nMOS systems.

Finally there are the processors that use bipolar devices for the logic. These may use *transistor transistor logic* (TTL), *emitter coupled logic* (ECL) or *integrated injection logic* (I^{2}L) for the actual logic circuits inside the chip. The main feature of bipolar devices is that they are very fast in operation and will normally be chosen for special functions where high speed is essential. Bipolar circuits generally use up more space on the silicon chip, so these types tend to be less complex than the types using MOS technology and bipolar devices also tend to require more power.

One factor to be considered is that all of the MOS types, pMOS, nMOS and CMOS, are susceptible to damage from static electric charges at their very high impedance inputs. Most of the devices, however, include diode protection at the inputs to reduce the risk of damage by static charges, but nevertheless some care may be required when handling this type of device.

CHOOSING A MICROPROCESSOR OR MICROCOMPUTER

Unfortunately for the system designer there is no convenient magic formula by which the optimum microprocessor or microcomputer device can be selected for a particular application. It is, of course, fairly easy to select a device which may be technically best suited for a particular project but often it will be aspects of software design or economic considerations which will dictate the type of device used.

In the following notes the general procedure involved in choosing a suitable processor for a project will be discussed and the factors which may influence the decisions at each of the stages will be considered. Although these guidelines will, it is hoped, prove useful the final decisions will usually depend very much upon the particular circumstances existing when the choice is made. In many cases the decision may well require the use of plain commonsense judgements based upon the available facts.

Basically the process of choosing a suitable processor or system can be broken down into the following stages:

(1) Define exactly what the system must do.
(2) Choose whether a microprocessor, single-chip microcomputer or bit slice system is to be used.
(3) Choose the word length.
(4) Consider the hardware factors such as speed, power requirements and availability of existing hardware.
(5) Consider software design with particular reference to available expertise and development aids.
(6) Examine the economic factors.

At each of these stages it should be possible to eliminate a number of the available types of processor until there are perhaps two or three potential devices from which the final selection can be made.

The first stage may seem very obvious and yet it is surprising how many system designers will progress to detailed design before they have defined exactly what is required. At this stage the system specification can be divided into two broad areas. First there are those requirements which are absolutely essential, and secondly there are the features which, whilst not essential, may be desirable since they may make a more versatile or attractive product. These features may be arranged in a list with some form of priority or value rating given to each. These secondary features of the system requirements may be helpful in the later stages of selection where two more or less equally attractive devices are being considered.

Once the system requirements have been defined it is important to ask the question 'Is a microprocessor needed at all?'. Consider what is involved in meeting the system specification using conventional logic, programmed arrays or off the shelf dedicated circuits. In many cases these other approaches will be impractical and a microprocessor type system is inevitable. Where the other approaches might be practical alternatives they should be considered along with the microprocessor solution. It would be ridiculous to use a microprocessor system when simple logic could provide a cheaper or simpler solution.

Choice between bit slice, microcomputer and processor will usually be dictated by the technical requirements of the system. In general the bit slice approach would be used where very high speed or some special processing function is needed. Choice between a single-chip microcomputer device and a multi-chip system based around a microprocessor is likely to prove a little more difficult.

Generally a single-chip microcomputer device would be chosen where space is limited or where a dedicated system is being produced for which the level of production is likely to be very high. Most of the single-chip microcomputers use mask programming and production runs of at least some 5000–10000 units will probably be required in order to justify the cost of designing the mask. In mass production, however, the cost per unit of a single-chip design is likely to be very much less than that of a multi-chip arrangement. An important factor here is that assembly and circuit board costs will be greatly reduced and these can contribute a large proportion of the final production cost of each unit. Another factor is that a single-chip design with fewer lead connections will be potentially more reliable than a multi-chip system.

For prototype and small batch production runs the mask programmed microcomputer becomes uneconomical, but devices such as the Intel 8748 or Motorola MC68705, with a programmable on-chip ROM, may be used. The unit cost of such devices can be fairly high and some labour will be involved in programming the on-chip ROM for each individual unit. However, a system using such devices does have many of the advantages of the single-chip approach, such as lower assembly cost, smaller size and potentially better reliability.

When the system is required to perform a variety of tasks or the production quantity is low, perhaps one off, a multi-chip system using a microprocessor with external I/O and memory devices may be used. The cost of the individual devices will generally be low since the microprocessor itself is likely to be a standard popular type, such as the 8080 or 6800, which is being mass produced. The assembly costs for such a system are likely to be relatively high and the complex interconnections on the circuit board may lead to potential unreliability.

The word length is usually fairly easy to resolve from the system technical requirements, although at this stage it may be permissible to consider alternative word lengths and leave the final elimination to a later stage.

Generally the 4-bit word length is appropriate for the smaller systems, particularly where binary coded decimal data is being handled. This is particularly true for controller type devices where the input is applied from a keypad and the output data are displayed on some form of decimal display.

Where text data are being handled and for general number processing the 8-bit word length is highly suitable. The normal set of text symbols can readily be accommodated within an 8-bit binary code. Most of the personal computer systems and small business machines use the 8-bit word length.

For large processing tasks the 16-bit word length may be desirable. In general a 16-bit machine will be faster in operation than an equivalent 8-bit type since instructions will generally be contained in a single data word and fewer memory access cycles will be required for each instruction. In a 16-bit system alphanumeric characters may be packed two to a word, again saving memory space and memory accesses. In general 16-bit types may well be used to perform the tasks that hitherto would have used a small minicomputer system.

A study of the hardware requirements, such as speed, power demand and compatibility with other systems, will often resolve the choice of fabrication technology. For battery operated and portable equipment CMOS type devices will usually be chosen, since they have very low power requirements and will tolerate wide variations in the supply voltage. For most of the other applications the *n*MOS type of device will probably be the best choice, unless the system must be interfaced with existing *p*MOS type equipment. Generally the choice of bipolar technology, such as I²L and ECL or TTL, will be reserved for applications where very high speed operation is required.

When considering the hardware aspects, especially for multi-chip systems, the availability of ready made circuit boards should be taken into account, since their use could greatly simplify hardware design and reduce design costs. In most cases these boards may contain some redundant circuits not needed for the current application, but they are usually less expensive than specially designed boards when only limited production is envisaged.

Finally we come to the software, or computer program, which can represent a major part of the cost and design effort needed for developing a microprocessor based product. Unlike conventional logic systems the microprocessor will do nothing without software.

An important factor to be considered is the availability of in house software expertise. It may well be better to use a technically less attractive processor with which the in house software team are familiar, than go to the trouble and expense of retraining the team in the software required for a newer type of processor. In some cases, however, training of the software team may be justified if the new processor is likely to be widely used in future projects. The final decision in this matter will depend upon the possible long term future benefits that might be gained by using a new processor type.

Both the software and hardware development will require some form of development aids. For small projects and as an initial training aid the simple evaluation type board is a useful development aid. However, for any serious work such a system is likely to be inadequate and a full scale system with editor, assembler and debug facilities is essential. A disk based operating system is desirable since this allows rapid operation and an efficient filing system. Some systems, such as the Motorola 6800 PDS, use a cassette filing system but it is very much slower in operation than a disk based system. Most disk systems use either standard or mini floppy disks giving perhaps 100 to 200 kbyte of storage per disk drive. It is advisable to have two disk drives since this makes copying of files much faster and simpler. One disk may be used for the operating system whilst the second is used for working files.

Debug facilities normally allow the program to be run and breakpoints to be inserted as desired. At these points the program may be stopped and data and status within the system may be examined. Also the program may be traced one instruction at a time to see exactly what is happening during its operation. These facilities allow errors in the program logic or coding to be detected and corrected.

For hardware testing an in circuit emulator may be used. Here a special probe is inserted into the processor socket on the hardware board being tested. The emulator allows the main development system to provide the processor function in the final product board and the full debug facilities may then be used to discover the cause of system failures.

In many cases the development system will be provided by the microprocessor manufacturer and will usually handle only processors made by that manufacturer. Sometimes different cards will need to be used in the system according to the actual type of processor being used.

Some development systems, such as the Futuredata AMDS produced by General Radio and the Tektronix 8000 series microprocessor lab system, are designed to handle a wide range of different manufacturers' devices. An advantage of this type of system is that the basic operating system will be the same for all processors, whereas with other systems each type has its own distinctive operating system. These multiprocessor systems generally use different processor boards for each processor type when emulation is required. These systems may also provide cross assemblers for a wide range of device types whilst using one control processor in the development system. This allows machine code programs to be produced for a range of device types without the need for board changes.

Some of the more popular processor types may have their software developed on larger computers such as the PDP11 minicomputer by using cross assembler programs.

The choice of microprocessor for a project is likely to be very much influenced by the availability of some suitable development system in house. The purchase of a development system can be a major item of expenditure and must be taken into account when choosing a processor. Here the future use of the system will be an important factor in deciding whether to use a particular processor. For a single project it may well be economical to rent a development system specifically for the project.

The cost of producing the software and the availability of a suitable development system will generally resolve the final choice of processor to be used for a project. The final decision may well be made on political or economic grounds rather than on purely technical factors. Obviously the aim should always be to choose the best technical device that can be justified.

It is hoped that these notes, used in combination with the data on microprocessor devices given later in the book, will assist readers in choosing suitable processor devices. In the final analysis, however, the decision made will often depend upon the application of common sense, past experience and perhaps a little intuitive judgement.

MICROPROCESSOR PRICES

One factor which may influence the choice of processor for a project is the unit price. No attempt will be made to give actual prices for the various types, since these are likely to vary from time to time according to the popularity of the device and the level of production. Price will also change according to the quantity purchased. However the price of one type relative to another may influence the final choice, so a guide has been provided where the prices are based upon those current in the UK at the time of preparing the book but are presented as units to a normalised scale. Although this will perhaps give some guidance to possible price relativities it is essential that the manufacturer or supplier be consulted to get realistic prices before the final choice is made if the price is likely to be a deciding factor. Generally the price will not be important until the choice has been narrowed to perhaps two or three types of device.

Relative price data

4-bit processors
Generally the 4-bit devices are microcomputer chips which are mask programmed and likely to be used in very large quantities. Final prices will depend upon negotiations with the actual chip manufacturer and the number purchased.

AMD 2900 series	8 – 20
AMI 2000 series	2 – 5
National COPS2 series	1 – 2.5
N.E.C. µCOM42 to µCOM45 series	1.5 – 3
Rockwell PPS4/1	2 – 5
Texas TMS1000	1 – 4 according to type

8-bit processors
Apart from the single-chip 8-bit microcomputers most of the 8-bit types are likely to be used in small to medium quantity and prices are based around the 100+ level.

Intel 8080A	8 – 12
Intel 8085A	9 – 14
Motorola 6800	8 – 12
Motorola 6802	10 – 15
Motorola 6809	25 – 40
MOS Tech 6502	10 – 15
RCA 1802P	10 – 15
National 8060(SCMP2)	12 – 18
Zilog Z80	8 – 12
Signetics 2650A	15 – 20
NEC µPD780C	9 – 15
Fairchild F8 CPU	10 – 15
Intel 8748	about 30

16-bit and other processors

Intel 8086	100 – 120
Motorola 68000	about 300 – 400 at present
Intersil 6100	12 – 15
Texas 9900	70 – 100
Zilog Z8000 series	150 – 200
Fairchild 9440	180 – 250
Intel 2920	200 – 250

2 4-BIT MICROPROCESSORS AND MICROCOMPUTERS

4-BIT MICROPROCESSOR TYPES

Maker	Device	ROM	RAM	I/O	Pkge	Remarks	Page
Advanced Micro Devices	Am2901				40DIL	ALU slice	16
	Am2903				40DIL	ALU slice	16
	Am2909				28DIL	bit slice	16
	Am2910				40DIL	bit slice	16
	Am2911				20DIL	bit slice	16
American Microsystems	S2000	1k	64	29	40DIL	μC	19
	S2000A	1k	64	29	40DIL	μC	19
	S2150	1.5k	80	29	40DIL	μC	19
	S2150A	1.5k	80	29	40DIL	μC	19
	S2200	2k	128	29	40DIL	μC with ADC	19
	S2200A	2k	128	29	40DIL	μC with ADC	19
	S2210	2k	128	29	40DIL	CMOS 2200	19
	S2400	4k	128	29	40DIL	μC with ADC	19
	S2400A	4k	128	29	40DIL	μC with ADC	19
Hitachi	HMCS42	512	32	22	28DIL	μC	21
	HMCS43	1k	60	32	42DIL	μC	21
	HMCS44	2k	160	32	42DIL	μC	21
	HMCS45	2k	160	44	54FP	μC	21
	HMCS42C	512	32	22	28DIL	CMOS μC	21
	HMCS43C	1k	60	32	42DIL	CMOS μC	21
	HMCS44C	2k	160	32	42DIL	CMOS μC	21
	HMCS45C	2k	160	44	54FP	CMOS μC	21
Matsushita	MN1400	1k	64		40DIL	μC	23
	MN1402	768	32		28DIL	μC	23
	MN1403	512	16		18DIL	μC	23
	MN1404	512	16		16DIL	μC	23
	MN1405	2k	128		40DIL	μC	23
	MN1430	1k	64		40DIL	pMOS 1400	23
	MN1432	768	32		28DIL	pMOS 1402	23
	MN1435	2k	128		40DIL	pMOS 1405	23
	MN1450	1k	64		40DIL	CMOS 1400	23
	MN1453	512	16		18DIL	CMOS 1403	23
	MN1454	512	16		16DIL	CMOS 1404	23
	MN1455	2k	128		40DIL	CMOS 1405	23
	MN1498		164		64DIL	ROMless 1400	23
	MN1542	2k	152	28	40DIL	μC	23
	MN1544	4k	256	28	40DIL	μC	23
	MN1562	2k	152	52	64DIL	μC	23
	MN1564	4k	256	52	64DIL	μC	23
	MN1591		256	28	64DIL	ROMless 1544	23
	MN1599		256	52	64DIL	ROMless 1564	23

Maker	Device	ROM	RAM	I/O	Pkge	Remarks	Page
Motorola	MC2901				40DIL	= Am2901	16
	MC2903				40DIL	= Am2903	16
	MC2909				28DIL	= Am2909	16
	MC2910				40DIL	= Am2910	16
	MC2911				20DIL	= Am2911	16
Motorola	MC10800				48QIL	ECL slice	24
	MC10801				48QIL	ECL slice	24
	MC10802				48QIL	ECL slice	24
Motorola	MC141000	1k	64	23	28DIL	CMOS TMS1000	36
	MC141200	1k	64	25	40DIL	CMOS TMS1200	36
	MC141099		64	23	64DIL	CMOS TMS1099	36
National	IDM2901				40DIL	= Am2901	16
	IDM2909				28DIL	= Am2909	16
	IDM2911				20DIL	= Am2911	16
National	COP402		64	23	40DIL	μP	26
	COP402L		64	23	40DIL	Low pwr 402	26
	COP402M		64	23	40DIL	μP	26
	COP410L	512	32	19	24DIL	μC	26
	COP411L	512	32	16	20DIL	μC	26
	COP420	1k	64	23	28DIL	μC	26
	COP420L	1k	64	23	28DIL	Low pwr 420	26
	COP420C	1k	64	23	28DIL	CMOS 420	26
	COP444L	2k	128	35	40DIL	μC	26
	COP440	2k	160		40DIL	μC	26
	COP2440				40DIL	dual 440	26
	COP2441				28DIL	dual 440	26
	COP2442				24DIL	dual 440	26
N.E.C.	μPD545C	1920	96	35	42DIL	pMOS μC	28
	μPD546C	2000	96	35	42DIL	pMOS μC	28
	μPD547C	1000	64	35	42DIL	pMOS μC	28
	μPD548C	1920	96	35	42DIL	HV 545	28
	μPD550C	640	32	21	28DIL	pMOS μC	28
	μPD551C	1000	64		42DIL	pMOS μC with ADC	28
	μPD552C	1000	64	35	42DIL	pMOS μC	28
	μPD553C	2000	96	35	42DIL	pMOS μC	28
	μPD554C	640	32	21	28DIL	pMOS μC	28
	μPD650C	2000	96	35	42DIL	CMOS 546	28
	μPD651C	1000	64	35	42DIL	CMOS 547	28
	μPD652C	640	32	21	28DIL	CMOS 550	28
N.E.C	μPD2901				40DIL	= Am2901	16
	μPD2909				28DIL	= Am2909	16
	μPD2911				20DIL	= Am2911	16

4-BIT MICROPROCESSORS AND MICROCOMPUTERS

Maker	Device	ROM	RAM	I/O	Pkge	Remarks	Page
OKI	MSM5840RS	2k	128	30	42DIL	CMOS μC	31
	MSM5842	768	32	21	28DIL	CMOS μC	31
	MSM5845	1280	64	30	42DIL	CMOS μC	31
	MSM58421	1536	40		60FP	LCD O/Ps	31
	MSM58423	1280	32		42DIL	CMOS μC	31
	MSM5847	1536	96			LCD O/Ps	31
Raytheon	Am2901				40DIL	= Am2901	16
	Am2903				40DIL	= Am2903	16
	Am2909				28DIL	= Am2909	16
	Am2910				40DIL	= Am2910	16
	Am2911				20DIL	= Am2911	16
Rockwell	MM75	640	48	22	28DIL	pMOS μC	34
	MM78	2k	128	31	42QIL	pMOS μC	34
	MM76	1k	48	31	40DIL	pMOS μC	34
Thomson EFCIS	SFC92901				40DIL	= Am2901	16
	SFC92903				40DIL	= Am2903	16
	SFC92909				28DIL	= Am2909	16
	SFC92910				40DIL	= Am2910	16
	SFC92911				20DIL	= Am2911	16
Texas Instruments	TMS1000	1k	64	23	28DIL	pMOS μC	36
	TMS1000C	1k	64	23	28DIL	CMOS 1000	36
	TMS1018		64	4	28DIL	pMOS μC	36
	TMS1070	1k	64		28DIL	pMOS μC	36
	TMS1098		128		64DIL	pMOS	36
	TMS1099		64		64DIL	pMOS	36
	TMS1099C		64		64DIL	CMOS 1099	36
	TMS1100	2k	128	25	28DIL	pMOS μC	36
	TMS1117	2k	128	19	28DIL	pMOS μC	36
	TMS1200	1k	64	25	40DIL	pMOS μC	36
	TMS1200C	1k	64	25	40DIL	CMOS 1200	36
	TMS1270	1k	64	25	40DIL	pMOS VF o/ps	36
	TMS1300	2k	128	23	40DIL	pMOS μC	36
	TMS1400	4k	128	22	28DIL	pMOS μC	36
	TMS1600	4k	128	33	40DIL	pMOS μC	36
	TMS1700	512	32	21	28DIL	pMOS μC	36
	TMS2000	1k	64	23	28DIL	nMOS 1000	36
	TMS2100	2k	128	25	28DIL	nMOS 1100	36
	TMS2200	1k	64	25	40DIL	nMOS 1200	36
	TMS2300	2k	128	23	40DIL	nMOS 1300	36
	TMS2098		128	25	64DIL	nMOS 1098	36
	TMS2099		64	23	64DIL	nMOS 1099	36
	TMS3000	1k	64	23	28DIL	= 1000C	36
	TMS3200	1k	64	25	40DIL	= 1200C	36
	TMS3099		64		64DIL	= 1099C	36

ADVANCED MICRO DEVICES Am2900 SERIES

The Advanced Micro Devices Am2900 series consists of 4-bit microprocessor slices which may be assembled to form a microcomputer of 4, 8, 12 or 16-bit wide data bus. The key parts in the system are a 4-bit ALU slice and a program sequence control slice which when used with appropriate memory and support chips can produce an extremely fast microcomputer.

Bit slice systems are generally designed to be used for high speed controller applications where the number of chips used is not too important but where high execution speed is essential. To achieve the required speed the 2900 series devices use bipolar technology.

Prime manufacturer

Advanced Micro Devices Inc.

Devices available

Am2901	4-bit ALU and register slice
Am2903	Enhanced version of the Am2901
Am2909	Microprogram sequencer
Am2911	Simplified version of Am2909
Am2910	Microprogram controller with 4k range

Alternative source devices

Motorola Inc.

MC2901	4-bit ALU and register slice
MC2909	Microprogram sequencer
MC2903	4-bit ALU slice
MC2910	Microprogram controller
MC2911	Microprogram sequencer

Thomson CSF

SFC92901	4-bit ALU slice
SFC92903	4-bit ALU slice
SFC92909	Microprogram sequencer
SFC92910	Microprogram controller
SFC92911	Microprogram sequencer

National Semiconductor

IDM2901	4-bit ALU slice
IDM2909	Microprogram sequencer
IDM2911	Microprogram sequencer

N.E.C.

μPB2901	4-bit ALU slice
μPB2909 and	
μPB2911	Microprogram sequencers

This series is also produced by Fairchild using prefix F in the type number and by Raytheon who use the AMD numbers.

Architecture

Unlike other microprocessors the 2900 series consist of 4-bit slices of logic which can be assembled to form a microcomputer system. The slices may be stacked side by side to produce 8, 12 or 16-bit data paths and program devices may also be set up to give 8, 12 or 16-bit memory addresses for use with a large program.

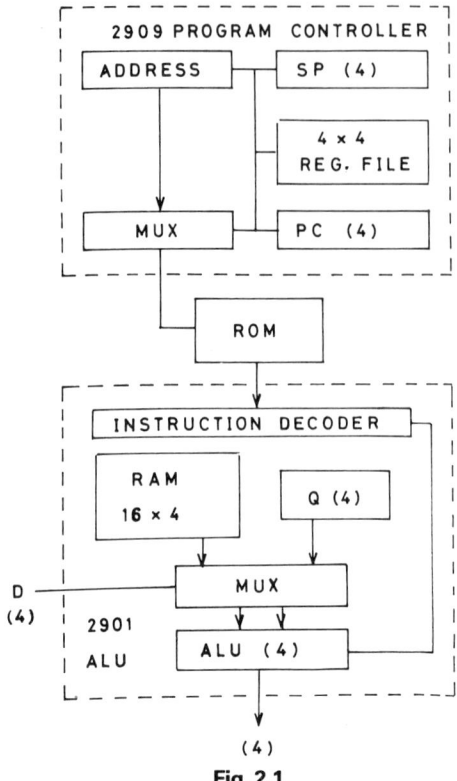

Fig. 2.1

Arithmetic and logic operations are carried out in the ALU slice which contains a 4-bit arithmetic and logic unit and a 16-word by 4-bit RAM. The RAM is a two-port type which allows two words to be accessed at a time using two separate A and B address inputs. There is also a 4-bit Q register on the chip which may be used for temporary storage and will be useful in multiplication and division routines. A 4-bit data input is available and there is also a 4-bit data output bus, both of which are connected to the internal ALU section. A multiplexer allows various combinations of RAM, input and Q register data to be applied to the ALU and the results may be fed either back to the RAM or to the data output bus. The ALU slice also provides six status flag outputs for test functions in the program.

Program control is governed by the 2909 or 2911 microprogram sequencer which generates addresses for the program memory and controls transfers of data and instructions to the ALU slice. This chip also governs conditional branches and jumps. A program counter and stack pointer are provided and there is a 4-level 4-bit stack on the chip.

The 2910 microprogram controller provides more or less similar facilities to those of the microprogram sequencers but it handles a 12-bit address bus and has a 5-level stack. The 12-bit address allows access to 4096 words of memory.

Apart from these basic chip slices a computer system will require memory for program and data, a clock and various support chips such as bus buffers, latches and so on. For faster operation a look ahead carry generator chip may be used with the ALU.

Package

Am2901, Am2910	40-pin dual in line type
Am2903	40-pin dual in line type

Am2909   28-pin dual in line type
Am2911   20-pin dual in line type

Pin connections

Am2901 ALU slice

1	A3	21	Q0
2	A2	22	D3
3	A1	23	D2
4	A0	24	D1
5	I6	25	D0
6	I8	26	I3
7	I7	27	I5
8	RAM3	28	I4
9	RAM0	29	C_n
10	V_{cc}	30	V_{ss}
11	F=0	31	F3
12	I0	32	G
13	I1	33	C_{n+4}
14	I2	34	OVR
15	CP	35	P
16	Q3	36	Y0
17	B0	37	Y1
18	B1	38	Y2
19	B2	39	Y3
20	B3	40	OE

Am2909 Microprogram sequencer

1	RE	15	ZERO
2	R3	16	S0
3	R2	17	S1
4	R1	18	Y0
5	R0	19	Y1
6	OR3	20	Y2
7	D3	21	Y3
8	OR2	22	OE
9	D2	23	C_n
10	OR1	24	C_{n+4}
11	D1	25	FE
12	OR0	26	PUP
13	D0	27	CP
14	V_{ss}	28	V_{cc}

Am2911 Microprogram sequencer

1	CP	11	S1
2	V_{cc}	12	Y0
3	RE	13	Y1
4	D3	14	Y2
5	D2	15	Y3
6	D1	16	OE
7	D0	17	C_n
8	V_{ss}	18	C_{n+4}
9	ZERO	19	FE
10	S0	20	PUP

Signal functions

A0 – A3	RAM address lines for ALU RAM
B0 – B3	RAM address lines for ALU RAM
I0 – I8	Instruction code inputs to the ALU
D0 – D3	Data inputs to the ALU
Y0 – Y3	Data output lines
OE	Output enable (active low)
OVR	Overflow flag output
P, G	Carry generate and propagate outputs used for look ahead carry with Am2902
F=0	Zero result output flag
C_n	Input carry to ALU
C_{n+4}	Output carry from ALU
CP	Clock input
RAM0, RAM3	Inputs and outputs of RAM for shifting
R0 – R3	Inputs to address register
RE	Address register enable input
FE, PUP	Control lines for stack
S0, S1	Control lines for address multiplexer
ZERO	AND gate control on address outputs
OR0 – OR4	OR inputs to address lines

On the 2909 and 2911 the Y lines are address outputs and the carry lines refer to the address incrementer register.

Signals are TTL compatible and outputs will generally drive four or five standard TTL loads.

Power requirements

V_{cc} +5 V ± 5%
V_{ss} 0 V
Supply current   2901   185 mA
                     2903   220 mA
                     2909   80 mA
                     2910   195 mA

Temperature range

0°C to +70°C   standard part
−55°C to +125°C   military part suffix M in type number

Input–output

This facility would be provided by other chips in the 2900 bit slice range.

Interrupt facilities

Interrupts would be controlled by other chips in the 2900 series but can be handled by the processor system.

Instruction set

Separate groups of instructions will affect different slices in the system but all normal computing functions are provided.

Arithmetic and logic
Arithmetic and logic functions are carried out by the ALU slice and include 4-bit addition and subtraction using either binary or BCD formats. The facilities provided also make it easy to implement multiplication and division operations. Larger numbers may be handled by merely using several slices to provide a wider data bus up to perhaps 16 bits.

Logical operations include AND, OR, EXCLUSIVE OR, NAND, NOR and EXCLUSIVE NOR, as well as complements, incrementing, decrementing and shifting or rotating of data. Individual bits of data may also be manipulated.

ADVANCED MICRO DEVICES Am2900 SERIES

Data transfer

In general data transfers can be made between any parts of the computer system merely by setting up the logic to provide the required data paths.

Branch and jump

The ALU provides a range of condition flags which may be acted upon by the program sequence unit to give conditional or unconditional branches and jumps. Sub-routines may be used and return addresses and status may be saved as required.

One major feature of this type of processor is the flexibility in programming, and since this is a mask programmed device it would even be possible to define your own instruction set.

Timing

For the 2900 series the timing will normally be generated by a 2925 clock and timing generator chip. Because these devices use bipolar logic the execution speed is very high and for a typical instruction the time might be about 125 ns. The 2903 includes facilities for multiplication and division at these speeds as well. 2901A and 2901B are faster versions of 2901.

Support chips

Since the 2900 system has a bit slice type architecture a large number of support chips are available from which a system may be assembled. Some of these are:

Am2902	High speed look ahead carry generator
Am2904	Status and shift control unit
Am2905	Bus transceiver
Am2906	Bus transceiver with parity
Am2907/8	Bus transceivers with interface logic
Am2912	Bus transceiver
Am2913	Interrupt priority encoder
Am2914	Vectored interrupt priority controller
Am2915	Bus transceiver with interface logic
Am2916	Bus transceiver with interface logic
Am2918	Quad D type register
Am2919	Quad register with tristate output
Am2920	Octal register
Am2921	One of eight decoder
Am2922/3	Eight-way multiplexer
Am2924	Demultiplexer 3-line to 8-line
Am2925	Clock generator
Am2930	Program control unit
Am2932	As 2930 but with push-pop stack
Am2940	Direct memory access address generator
Am2942	Timer counter and DMA address generator
Am2950/1	8-bit bidirectional I/O ports
Am2954/5	Octal registers
Am2956/7	Octal latches
Am2958/9	Octal line drivers and receivers
Am2960	16-bit error detection and correction unit
Am2961/2	4-bit multiple bus buffers
Am2964	DMA controller
Am2965/6	Dynamic memory drivers

Development aids

From Advanced Micro Devices there is the System 29 processor development system which provides full software development and hardware emulation facilities.

Motorola also have facilities for use with EXORCISER systems using a cross assembler, and they also have the MACE29/800 system which can handle both the 2900 and 10800 bit slice processor series.

AMERICAN MICROSYSTEMS S2000 SERIES

The AMI S2000 series is a range of 4-bit single-chip microcomputers designed primarily for dedicated applications in which input is via a keypad and output is on LED or vacuum fluorescent type displays. Most types are made in nMOS but one type, the S2210, uses CMOS for low power operation.

Typical applications will be in appliance control, such as for microwave ovens, toys and temperature control systems. This range of devices is competitive with other 4-bit types such as the TMS1000, COPS2, PPS4/1 and μCOM40 series devices. All devices use mask programmed ROM and are best suited to high volume production where minimum chip count and low cost are required.

Prime manufacturer

American Microsystems Inc.

Devices available

S2000	1024 byte ROM, 64 × 4 RAM, 29 I/O lines
S2000A	As 2000 but with high voltage outputs
S2150	1536 byte ROM, 80 × 4 RAM, 29 I/O lines
S2150A	As 2150 but high voltage outputs
S2200	2048 byte ROM, 128 × 4 RAM, A/D conv., 29 I/O
S2200A	As 2200 but high voltage outputs
S2210	CMOS version of S2200
S2400	4096 byte ROM, 128 × 4 RAM, A/D conv., 29 I/O
S2400A	As 2400 but high voltage outputs

Alternative source devices

None at present

Architecture

All devices have a 4-bit ALU and accumulator and use 4-bit data paths. Instruction codes are byte orientated and the program counter has 13 bits, allowing up to 8192 bytes of program. A 13-bit address bus may be used for ROM expansion using external memory.

The S2000 and S2150 have a 3-level stack for use with subroutines, whilst the 2200/2400 types have a 5-level stack.

All types have an on chip counter facility. On the 2000/2150 types this is a divide by 50 or 60 type primarily for use as a clock counter, but on the 2200/2400 types there is a programmable 8-bit timer/event counter. The 2200/2400 types also include either an 8-bit A/D converter or an 8-bit D/A converter on the chip.

All types have an on-chip clock generator which may be timed either by an R–C network or by a crystal for more exact timing.

Package

All types	40-pin dual in line package
Ceramic package	suffix C
Plastic package	suffix P

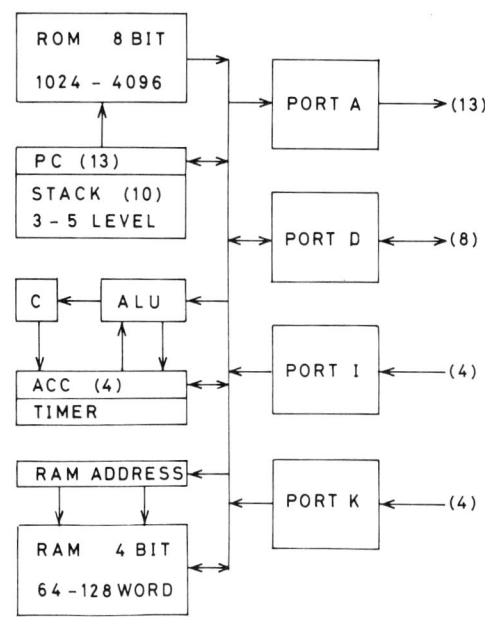

Fig. 2.2

Pin connections

S2000 and S2150 types

1	V_{ss}	21	STATUS
2	D2	22	POR
3	D1	23	CLK
4	D0	24	K_{ref}
5	ROMS	25	I1
6	EXT	26	I2
7	A12 (MSB)	27	I4
8	A11	28	I8
9	A10	29	V_{gg}
10	A9	30	K1
11	A8	31	K2
12	V_{dd}/V_{fd}	32	K4
13	A7	33	K8
14	A6	34	RUN
15	A5	35	SYNC
16	A4	36	D7
17	A3	37	D6
18	A2	38	D5
19	A1	39	D4
20	A0	40	D3

S2200, S2210 and S2400 types

1	V_{ss}	21	A5
2	SYNC	22	A4
3	CLKO	23	A3
4	CLKI	24	A2
5	V_{ref}	25	A1
6	POR/V_{ram}	26	A0
7	K5	27	A12
8	K1	28	V_{cc}
9	K7	29	D0
10	K3	30	D4
11	K6	31	D1
12	K2	32	D5
13	K4	33	D2
14	K0	34	D6
15	A11	35	D3
16	A10	36	D7

AMERICAN MICROSYSTEMS S2000 SERIES

17	A9	37	RUN
18	A8	38	ROMS
19	A7	39	EXT
20	A6	40	STATUS

Signal functions

A0 – A12	Address outputs may also be used for displays
D0 – D7	Two 4-bit I/O ports or data bus tristate
I1 – I8	Key switch inputs
K1 – K8	2000/2150 types touch switch inputs
K0 – K7	2200/2400 types programmable I/O lines for A/D or D/A converter or touch switch
POR	Power on reset input (active low)
STATUS	Status output
SYNC	Sync pulse output
EXT	External memory strobe output (active low)
CLK	Clock timing inputs. On 2000/2150 STATUS is used for one of the crystal connections and CLK for the other
K_{ref}	Reference voltage input for touch switch
V_{ref}	Reference voltage for A/D, D/A and touch switch
RUN	Run/halt input
V_{ss}, V_{gg}, V_{cc}	Power supply inputs
V_{dd}	Supply for LED output driver stages
V_{fd}	Supply for fluorescent display drivers (This applies to A versions only)

All inputs and outputs are TTL compatible and outputs are designed to drive either LED or vacuum fluorescent (VF) type displays of the seven segment type. Supply V_{dd} or V_{fd} according to type of chip is connected to +5 V or +35 V to supply the display devices.

Power requirements

V_{gg} (2000/2150 only)	+9 V
V_{ss}	0 V
V_{dd}	+5 V for LED displays
V_{fd} (suffix A types only)	+35 V for VF displays
V_{cc} (2200/2400 types)	+5 V
V_{cc} (2210 type)	+5 V

Note all 2200 types have power down facility.

Temperature range

0°C to +70°C.

Input–output

Thirteen line address bus ouput may be used either for an external ROM expansion or as display drive lines. An 8-bit bidirectional port made up of two 4-bit ports may be used as a data bus for external memory expansion or as data or lamp driver lines.

The 2000/2150 has four capacitance touch switch inputs (k1, k2, k4 and k8) and four key switch inputs (I1, I2, I4 and I8). There is also a reference voltage input (K_{ref}) for the touch switch lines.

On the 2200/2400 types an 8-bit D/A converter and 8-line multiplexer are provided. This may be configured to operate as an 8-channel A/D conversion system. A voltage reference input (V_{ref}) is provided for this analogue function. On these chips there are eight K lines (K0 to K7) which may be selected as inputs or outputs by software and used in conjunction with the A/D or D/A facility. These lines may also be used for a capacitive touch input and for timer and interrupt signals.

Interrupt facilities

The 2000 and 2150 types have no interrupt facility provided. The 2200/2400 types have an interrupt capability and have a two level stack for interrupt operations.

Instruction set

On the 2000 and 2150 types there are 51 instructions in the set and of these 49 are single-byte instructions that will execute in one instruction cycle. The 2200/2400 types have 63 instructions of which 52 are single-byte single-cycle.

Arithmetic and logic uses 4-bit data and may be either binary or decimal format. A wide range of data movement type instructions allow transfer of data within the CPU and also to the I/O lines. Immediate, implied, direct and indexed addressing modes are provided.

Branch and test instructions include a number which skip on condition after an operation, thus saving program space. Subroutines may be nested to three levels on the 2000/2150 and to five levels on the 2200/2400 types.

A useful feature not found in other 4-bit types is the ability to reconfigure the input–output lines by software as desired.

Timing

The clock generator may be timed either by an R–C network or by a quartz crystal for more accurate timing. Cycle time for all types is 4.5 μs and most instructions will be executed in one cycle.

Provision has been made for synchronisation to 50/60 Hz supply mains for timing purposes where the counter/timer is used as a real time clock.

Support chips

None required.

Development aids

Software can readily be developed on the Tektronix 8002A microprocessor development system and hardware emulation is also provided for all devices in the series.

HITACHI HMCS40 SERIES

Hitachi's HMCS40 series is a family of 4-bit single-chip microcomputers which are designed for use in dedicated applications where medium to high volume production is envisaged. There are two versions of each of the main types of the series. One of these versions is fabricated using pMOS technology and will be useful where low cost is an important consideration, whilst the alternative version is built using CMOS and is intended for applications where low power consumption is important, such as for battery operated portable equipment.

All devices contain on-chip clock generators, RAM for data storage, mask programmed ROM for instruction storage, a variety of input–output ports and individual lines, and on many of the device types there is also a counter-timer. Outputs are designed to allow LED, liquid crystal or vacuum fluorescent type displays to be driven.

Typical applications for these microcomputers would be in domestic appliance controllers, video recorder control, games, toys, automobile accessories, office equipment and for small industrial controllers. These devices have much the same type of facilities as those offered by other 4-bit computers such as the National COPS2, Rockwell PPS4/1, Texas TMS1000, OKI series 40 and perhaps NEC µCOM40 types, but it is likely that the specific features of this series may make them more attractive than other types for some applications.

Prime manufacturer

Hitachi Electronic Components.

Devices available

pMOS types

HMCS42   512 × 10 ROM, 32 × 4 RAM, 22 I/O lines
HMCS43   1k × 10 ROM, 80 × 4 RAM, 32 I/O lines, timer
HMCS44   2k × 10 ROM, 160 × 4 RAM, 32 I/O lines, timer
HMCS45   2k × 10 ROM, 160 × 4 RAM, 44 I/O lines, timer

CMOS types

HMCS42C   512 × 10 ROM, 32 × 4 RAM, 22 I/O lines
HMCS43C   1k × 10 ROM, 80 × 4 RAM, 32 I/O lines + timer
HMCS44C   2k × 10 ROM, 160 × 4 RAM, 32 I/O lines + timer
HMCS45C   2k × 10 ROM, 160 × 4 RAM, 44 I/O lines + timer

Alternative source devices

None.

Architecture

The general layout of the HMCS40 series devices is shown in fig. 2.3.

Arithmetic and logic is handled by a 4-bit accumulator

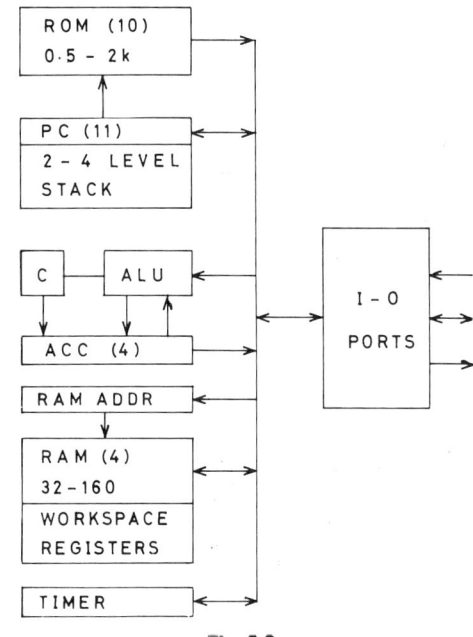

Fig. 2.3

and ALU with a carry flag flip flop for carry status. All types also contain general purpose registers, there being four in the type 42 device, six in types 43 or 45 and eight in the type 44 microcomputer.

An 11-bit program counter register allows access to the 2k ROM program memory and a two, three or four level stack is provided for return address storage for subroutine or interrupt operations.

All types except the HMCS42 contain an event counter or interval timer on chip and all of the microcomputers have a small amount of ROM available for use as a pattern memory for display decoding to produce correct output drives for seven segment or similar types of display.

Most types have facilities for battery backup functions which allow the processor to be halted or the memory to be held when the main power line is turned off.

Package

HMCS42 and HMCS42C
  28-pin dual in line plastic type
HMCS43 and HMCS43C
  42-pin dual in line plastic type
HMCS44 and HMCS44C
  42-pin dual in line plastic type
HMCS45 and HMCS45C
  54-lead flat pack

Temperature range

   −20°C to +75°C
or −40°C to +85°C by special request

Pin connections

Refer to manufacturer's data sheets.

Power requirements

pMOS types

V_{dd} −10 V
V_{ss} 0 V
Power consumption   HMCS42/43   100 mW
                    HMCS44/45   150 mW

CMOS types

V_{cc} +5 V
V_{ss} 0 V
Power consumption   HMCS42C   1.5 mW
                    Other types 2.0 mW

Input–output facilities

The HMCS42 has one 4-bit input port and two 4-bit output ports as well as six discrete output lines and four discrete lines for input or output. On the HMCS43 there are similar facilities, except that it has twelve discrete outputs and there is one 4-bit bidirectional input–output port.

On the HMCS44 types there are four 4-bit bidirectional input–output ports and sixteen discrete input–output lines. On the HMCS45 there are six 4-bit input–output ports, one 4-bit output port and sixteen discrete input–output lines.

All input–output lines can be TTL compatible on both the pMOS or CMOS versions and will drive one TTL standard load.

Interrupt facilities

On the HMCS42 type there is no interrupt facility, but on all other types there are two external interrupts and also one from the internal event counter/interval timer. The interrupt system is single level.

Instruction set

The instruction set for the HMCS40 series normally contains a total of 77 instructions, although the HMCS42 type works with a subset of only 51 instructions.

Timing

The on-chip clock generator gives a typical instruction cycle time of $10\mu s$ for all except two of the instructions in the set. Instructions normally execute in one cycle.

Support devices

None.

Development aids

For all devices in this series there is an evaluation chip to allow external RAM and ROM to be used for system emulation. For the HMCS42 and HMCS43 this chip has the type number HD38750E, but all devices in the series may be emulated by using the type HD44580E evaluation chip.

There is an evaluation kit (type H40EVKIT) which has a keyboard input and display facilities and will allow the user to program, debug and evaluate any HMCS40 series computer system configuration. This kit provides a text editor and an assembler for the HMCS40 series microcomputers and may also be used to program a PROM for evaluation of the final program before final design of the ROM mask.

MATSUSHITA MN1400/MN1500 SERIES

Matsushita (Panasonic) produce a wide range of 4-bit single-chip microcomputers which use mask programmed ROM and are intended for dedicated applications where high production volume is anticipated.

Internally the devices have a similar type of architecture to the TMS1000, COPS2 and S2000 series and will be applied to much the same projects as a small microcontroller with keypad inputs and digital display outputs. Most of the types are of nMOS construction but some CMOS and pMOS types have also been produced.

Prime manufacturer

Matsushita Electric Co.

Devices available

MN1400	nMOS, 1024 × 8 ROM, 64 × 4 RAM
MN1402	nMOS, 768 × 8 ROM, 32 × 4 RAM
MN1403	nMOS, 512 × 8 ROM, 16 × 4 RAM
MN1404	nMOS, 512 × 8 ROM, 16 × 4 RAM
MN1405	nMOS, 2048 × 8 ROM, 128 × 4 RAM
MN1430	pMOS, same as 1400
MN1432	pMOS, same as 1402
MN1435	pMOS, same as 1405
MN1450	CMOS, same as 1400
MN1453	CMOS, same as 1403
MN1454	CMOS, same as 1404
MN1455	CMOS, same as 1405
MN1498	nMOS, ROMless version of 1400
MN1542	nMOS, 2048 × 8 ROM, 152 × 4 RAM, 28 I/O lines
MN1544	nMOS, 4096 × 8 ROM, 256 × 4 RAM, 28 I/O lines
MN1562	nMOS, 2048 × 8 ROM, 152 × 4 RAM, 52 I/O lines
MN1564	nMOS, 4096 × 8 ROM, 256 × 4 RAM, 52 I/O lines
MN1591	nMOS, ROMless version of 1544
MN1599	nMOS, ROMless version of 1564

Architecture

Internal architecture follows calculator oriented style similar to that of the TMS1000 and S2000 types. Accumulator and ALU are 4-bit and the program counter has 11 bits for the 1400 series and 12 bits for the 1500 types.

The MN1400 types have a simple 2-level stack, but this is expanded to 16 levels in the 1500 series, which also has an interrupt facility.

A variety of input–output port options is provided for interface to keyboards and display devices.

Package

Types 1400, 1405, 1430, 1435, 1450, 1455, 1498, 1542 and 1544 are all in 40-pin dual in line type package
Types 1402, 1432 are in 28-pin dual in line type
Types 1403 and 1453 use 18-pin dual in line package
Types 1404 and 1454 use 16-pin dual in line package
Other types are in 64-lead dual in line package

Power requirements

nMOS and CMOS types +5 V single rail supply.
Typical current for nMOS types is 20 mA

Temperature range

0°C to +70°C

Input–output

Number of I/O lines varies according to package size; in most cases they are TTL compatible. Some types have a PLA on the chip for display drive decoding.

Interrupt facilities

None on MN1400 series, but four levels of interrupt provided on the MN1500 series.

Instruction set

The 1400 series has a basic 75 instruction set but the 1402 has a subset of only 57 instructions. The 1500 series has an enhanced instruction set of 124 instructions and can process 8-bit data as well as the normal 4-bit data.

Timing

Clock frequency of the 1400 series is from 200 to 450 kHz and gives execution times of about 10 μs, whilst the MN1500 types will execute instructions in around 2 μs.

MOTOROLA MC10800 SERIES

The Motorola MC10800 series of devices uses emitter coupled logic (ECL) for very high speed operation and is based on a 4-bit slice concept. The basic chips are a 4-bit arithmetic and logic unit slice and a microprogram controller slice, which are supported by a range of other devices to form microcomputer systems.

These processor chips are primarily designed for use in very high speed applications where *n*MOS types would be too slow. Unlike many of the other types of processor the bit slice scheme is built up from a large number of small circuits to form a custom design of processor to meet the requirements of the designer, rather than having a general purpose processor chip.

Prime manufacturer

Motorola Semiconductors.

Devices available

MC10800   4-bit ALU slice
MC10801   Microprogram controller
MC10802   Timing generator

Alternative source devices

None at present.

Architecture

The 10800 is basically a 4-bit arithmetic and logic unit with facilities for binary and BCD addition and subtraction, plus various logic functions.

Program control is governed by the 10801 sequencer chip which contains eight 4-bit registers. Of these, four are used for a subroutine or interrupt stack, one acts as the program counter, one for branch control, one for status and there is one general purpose register for data storage. This device controls the sequencing of instructions from the program memory to the ALU and controls branches and jumps.

A further chip in the series, the 10803, may be used to control access to the memory system. This device contains four 4-bit registers and a small ALU for calculating address offsets.

In constructing a system several 4-bit slices may be used to produce an 8, 12 or 16-bit wide processor, and these would be supported by a range of logic and memory chips from the Motorola MC10000 ECL device range.

Package

For the 10800 series Motorola have introduced a 48-lead quad in line package which has pins 0.05 in apart, but these are arranged in two staggered rows at each side of the package to give a pin to pin spacing of 0.1 in in each row. Actual package size is about the same as a 24-pin DIL.

Power requirements

V_{tt} −1.9 V to −2.2 V
V_{ee} −4.7 V to −5.7 V
V_{cc} 0 V
Supply current   10800   180 mA approx.
                 10801   250 mA approx.

Temperature range

−30°C to +85°C

Signal levels

These devices normally operate with ECL signal levels, but inputs and outputs can be matched to TTL compatible levels by using the MC10804 and MC10805 ECL to TTL interface chips.

Input–output

Unlike other types of processor the basic 4-bit slice units do not cater directly for input–output facilities, but these can be provided by using logic on the processor bus system and ECL to TTL translation to bring signals to the outside world.

Interrupt facilities

Interrupts can be arranged in the 10800 series and may be nested to a depth of four levels using the basic devices, or deeper if an additional stack register is used.

Instruction set

Arithmetic and logic
Facilities are provided for normal binary addition and subtraction as well as hardware implementation of BCD addition and subtraction.

Logical operations include AND, OR, NOR, NAND, EXCLUSIVE OR and EXCLUSIVE NOR as well as complements, negation and comparison of data. Incrementing, decrementing and a variety of shift operations are also provided.

Data transfer
By using the 10803 memory interface a wide range of transfer operations is possible, including associative addressing.

Branch and jump
Branch and jump operations are governed by the 10801 program controller device and include a range of conditional jumps as well as unconditional jumps and subroutine operations. It is also possible to provide multiway jump facilities roughly equivalent to computed GO TO instructions.

Timing

Timing for the 10800 series is usually provided by the 10802 Timing Function chip, which generates the basic system clock and also controls start and stop operations and single-cycle functions.

Typically the 10800 series runs with a cycle time of about 100 ns to give very fast instruction execution.

Support chips

In order to produce a working processor system using

10800 series devices a number of chips will normally be required, and these may also be combined with 10000 series ECL logic devices and memories. Some of the parts available are:

- 10800 Arithmetic and logic unit 4-bit-slice
- 10801 Microprogram controller slice
- 10802 Timing control module
- 10803 Memory interface slice
- 10804 4-bit bidirectional ECL/TTL interface
- 10805 4-bit bidirectional ECL/TTL interface
- 10806 Dual access stack RAM, 32 words by 9 bits
- 10807 5-bit bus transceiver ECL to ECL
- 10808 Programmable 16-bit shifter function

Development aids

Motorola produce a MACE 29/800 development system for use with both the 2900 and 10800 bit slice devices, allowing program development and debugging. This system may also be used as an interface to the EXORCISER development system.

NATIONAL COPS2 SERIES

The National Semiconductor COPS2 series consists of a range of single-chip 4-bit microcomputers designed primarily for use as dedicated controllers. Most of the parts use *n*MOS and have been designed for fairly low power operations, whilst some are in CMOS for very low power consumption.

This range of devices is aimed at the very large volume markets such as toys, simple appliance controllers and similar products, where low cost and low power operation are an advantage. Competitive types would be the Texas TMS1000, NEC μCOM40, AMI S2000 and other similar types. The range of types in some of the rival series is perhaps greater, but the COPS2 range is sufficient to meet most users' needs. Apart from some types, which are ROMless, the COPS2 devices have mask programmed on-chip ROMs of various sizes and also include on-chip RAM as well as a selection of input–output lines.

Prime manufacturer

National Semiconductor Corporation.

Devices available

COP402	No ROM, 64 × 4 RAM, 23 I/O lines
COP402L	Low power version of 402
COP402M	As 402 but with no interrupt facility
COP410L	512 byte ROM, 32 × 4 RAM, 19 I/O lines
COP411L	512 byte ROM, 32 × 4 RAM, 16 I/O lines
COP420	1 kbyte ROM, 64 × 4 RAM, 23 I/O lines
COP420L	Low power version of 420
COP420C	CMOS version of 420
COP444L	2 kbyte ROM, 128 × 4 RAM, 35 I/O lines
COP440	2 kbyte ROM, 160 × 4 RAM
COP2440	Dual CPU with 2 kbyte ROM, 160 × 4 RAM
COP2441	As 2440 but different number of I/O lines
COP2442	As 2440 but different amount of I/O

Alternative source devices

Western Digital have licence to make some of the range.

Architecture

The COPS2 series is typical of the 4-bit calculator style single-chip microcomputers, with separate instruction and data memory organisation. Data paths are all 4 bits wide and the instruction memory is 8 bits wide.

Arithmetic and logic are dealt with by a 4-bit ALU and accumulator and a 10-bit program counter is used to control access to the program memory. On the 444 an 11-bit program counter is used.

All types have a selection of input–output lines, which may be designed to drive LED displays or logic as required. The main difference between many of the types is the number of I/O lines and hence the package size. Most types include a serial input–output facility as well as 4-bit and 8-bit wide parallel data ports.

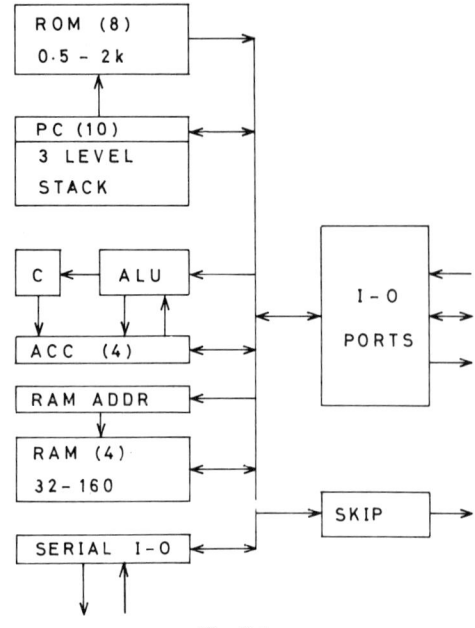

Fig. 2.4

An on-chip clock is provided which may be operated by a simple R–C timing network on some types. The 444 type has an A/D conversion facility on the chip, whilst the latest types in the 2440 series feature two CPUs sharing the same memory.

Package

COP402	40-pin dual in line type
COP410	24-pin dual in line type
COP411	20-pin dual in line type
COP420	28-pin dual in line type
COP440/444	40-pin dual in line type
COP2440	40-pin dual in line type
COP2441	28-pin dual in line type
COP2442	24-pin dual in line type

Pin connections

COP420 types

1	V_{ss}		15	L0
2	CK0		16	SI
3	CK1		17	SO
4	RESET		18	SK
5	L7		19	IN0
6	L6		20	IN3
7	L5		21	G0
8	L4		22	G1
9	IN1		23	G2
10	IN2		24	G3
11	V_{cc}		25	D3
12	L3		26	D2
13	L2		27	D1
14	L1		28	D0

Signal functions

L0 – L7	8-bit bidirectional port
D0 – D3	4-bit output port
G0 – G3	4-bit bidirectional port
CK0, CK1	Clock timing lines

SI   Serial input line
SO   Serial output line
SK   Skip flag output
IN0 – IN3   Interrupt inputs
RESET   Reset input (active low)
V_{cc}, V_{ss} Power supply inputs

Note the 402 types have an 8-bit data/address bus for use with external memory plus 2-address outputs to complete the address bus.

Signal levels for the COPS2 series are TTL compatible and outputs will in most cases drive a TTL load.

Power requirements

V_{cc} (standard parts)	+4.5 V to 6.3 V
V_{cc} (L versions)	+4.5 V to +9.5 V
V_{cc} (CMOS types)	+2.4 V to +6.3 V
V_{ss} all types	0 V
Power consumption	420 type 125 mW (25 mA)
	420L 35 mW (7 mA)
	444L 55 mW (35 mA)

Temperature range

0°C to +70°C

Input–output

A variety of input–output options is available according to the size of package used for the processor. Mask options are available for open drain outputs, pull up resistors and for full push–pull active output stages.

The serial input–output register may also be used as an on-chip event counter or timer, as well as for its serial input–output function.

Interrupt facilities

All types except the 402M have interrupt facilities and a 2 or 3-level stack is provided within the chip for program counter contents storage during interrupt servicing. Interrupts use a vector system to access the service routine.

Instruction set

The basic instruction set for this range of processors has a total of 57 instructions, but the 410 and 411 operate with a subset of 43 instructions.

Arithmetic and logic
Four-bit addition is provided, but there is no subtraction as such, so this would be done by adding a complemented number. The only logical operation is EXCLUSIVE OR and there are no shift operations provided.

Data transfer
Data are readily moved between the RAM and the accumulator and I/O ports as 4-bit nibbles. It is also possible to move data from the ROM to the L port, which makes possible the use of a conversion table for say 7-segment decoding, and this may be stored in the ROM.

Input–output instructions can address individual ports, and the serial input–output register can also be used as a counter if required.

Branch and jump
Jumps may be made both direct and indirect and there are also relative jumps within memory pages of the program memory. A subroutine jump is also provided.

Conditional operations are implemented using skip type instructions, which may also be combined with other operations making for quite compact program codes. Subroutines may be nested to three levels provided no interrupts occur.

Timing

Typical instruction time for the 420 and 440 series is 4 μs, but the 410 types and the CMOS 420 operate slower, with a typical execution time of some 16 μs.

Support chips

Normally the COPS2 series devices will operate alone, but some support chips are being produced. Among these are:

COP470   Vacuum fluorescent display driver
COP498   RAM/timer with 64 × 4 RAM

Development aids

The COP400 PDS is a development system for the COPS2 series of devices and can provide PROM programming facilities as well as software development. There is also an evaluation card with a COP402 ROMless part available.

N.E.C. µCOM40 SERIES

The µCOM40 series devices produced by Nippon Electric Co. of Japan are 4-bit single-chip microcomputers with on-chip mask programmed ROM intended for dedicated high volume applications. Most types are fabricated in pMOS but some are also produced in a CMOS version for use in low power applications.

These computers have a calculator type architecture in which the program ROM and data RAM are separately addressed, and they are aimed at applications where keypad input and a variety of display outputs are required. The simplest type is the µCOM42, intended for use in calculators and cash registers. The µCOM43, 44, 45 and 46 series devices all have similar architecture but varying sizes of on-chip ROM and RAM, plus a range of input–output ports. The µCOM46 also has an A/D converter on the chip. In general these types are intended for use in such applications as electronic toys, appliance controllers, communications systems and for industrial equipment controllers where reasonably high volume production is possible. They are competitive with other single-chip 4-bit microcomputers such as the Texas TMS1000, National COPS2, AMI S2000 and Rockwell PPS4/1 series.

Individual devices in the µCOM42, 43, 44, 45 and 46 series are given specific type numbers such as µPD546, but have the same general characteristics as others in that particular series.

Prime manufacturer

Nippon Electric Co. (N.E.C.).

Devices available

µCOM42 series

µPD545C   pMOS, 1920 × 10 ROM, 96 × 4 RAM, 35 I/O lines

µPD548C   pMOS, 1920 × 10 ROM, 96 × 4 RAM, 35 I/O lines

µCOM43 series

µPD546C   pMOS, 2000 × 8 ROM, 96 × 4 RAM, 35 I/O lines

µPD553C   pMOS, as 546 but with high voltage (35 V) outputs

µPD650C   CMOS version of 546

µCOM44 series

µPD547C   pMOS, 1000 × 8 ROM, 64 × 4 RAM, 35 I/O lines

µPD547CL   pMOS, low power version of 547

µPD552C   pMOS, as 547 but 35 V output capability

µPD651C   CMOS version of 547

µCOM45 series

µPD550C   pMOS, 640 × 8 ROM, 32 × 4 ROM, 21 I/O lines

µPD550CL   pMOS, low power version of 550

µPD554C   pMOS, high voltage (35 V) output version

µPD652C   CMOS version of 550

µCOM46 series

µPD551C   pMOS, 1000 × 8 ROM, 64 × 4 RAM, on-chip A/D conv.

Alternative source devices

None.

Architecture

Basic architecture for all N.E.C. series 40 types is as shown in fig. 2.5. All processors feature a 4-bit accumulator, 4-bit arithmetic and logic unit and 4-bit data paths to the RAM and the input–output ports.

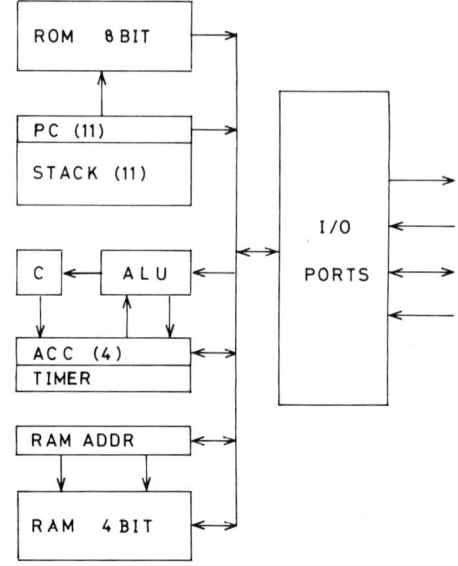

Fig. 2.5

The program counter is normally 11 bits wide, allowing access to 2048 words of program memory. In the µCOM42 type the instruction word and hence the ROM is 10 bits wide, but all other types use an 8-bit instruction word and 8-bit wide ROM.

There is a 4-level stack for storage of the program counter contents during subroutines on the µCOM42 and µCOM46. Series 43 devices have a 3-level stack, whilst types 44 and 45 have only a single-level stack.

Most types provide 35 input–output lines arranged in groups of four and some discrete lines. Some devices in the 44 and 45 series, however, have smaller packages and the number of input–output lines is reduced to 21.

µCOM43 and µCOM46 types have a 6-bit on-chip event counter or timer, whilst the latter type also has a 6-bit A/D converter on the chip.

The RAM is addressed by a 2-word data pointer and is arranged as either 2, 4 or 8 rows and sixteen columns of 4-bit words. Columns are selected by the least significant word of the data pointer and rows by the more significant word. Some types make use of six words of the RAM as general working registers.

All devices have on-chip generators and all but the µCOM44 and µCOM45 types have interrupt facilities.

Package

µPD550, µPD554, µPD652, µPD557 and µPD652

28-pin dual in line plastic package

All other types

42-pin dual in line plastic package

Pin connections

μCOM42 types

1	RESET	22	F8
2	K0	23	F9
3	K1	24	U0
4	K2	25	U1
5	K3	26	U2
6	TEST	27	U3
7	S0	28	U4
8	S1	29	U5
9	S2	30	U6
10	S3	31	U7
11	IA	32	R0
12	IB	33	R1
13	F0	34	R2
14	F1	35	R3
15	F2	36	R4
16	F3	37	R5
17	F4	38	R6
18	F5	39	R7
19	F6	40	K4
20	F7	41	V_{gg}
21	GND	42	ϕ in

μCOM43 and μCOM45 28-pin types

1	CL1	15	TEST
2	PC0	16	PF0
3	PC1	17	PF1
4	PC2	18	PF2
5	PC3	19	PF3
6	PD0	20	PG0
7	PD1	21	PA0
8	PD2	22	PA1
9	PD3	23	PA2
10	PE0	24	PA3
11	PE1	25	INT
12	PE2	26	RES
13	PE3	27	V_{gg}
14	V_{ss}	28	CL0

μCOM43 and μCOM44 42-pin versions

1	CL1	22	PG0
2	PC0	23	PG1
3	PC1	24	PG2
4	PC2	25	PG3
5	PC3	26	PH0
6	INT	27	PH1
7	RES	28	PH2
8	PD0	29	PH3
9	PD1	30	PI0
10	PD2	31	PI1
11	PD3	32	PI2
12	PE0	33	PA0
13	PE1	34	PA1
14	PE2	35	PA2
15	PE3	36	PA3
16	PF0	37	PB0
17	PF1	38	PB1
18	PF2	39	PB2
19	PF3	40	PB3
20	TEST	41	V_{gg}
21	V_{ss}	42	CL0

Signal functions

RES	Reset input
TEST	Test input
IA, IB	Interrupt inputs
K0 – K3	Port K 4-bit input
S0 – S3	Port S 4-bit input–output
R0 – R7	Port R 8-bit output port
U0 – U7	Port U 8-bit output
K4	Condition test input
F0 – F9	Discrete output lines
PA0 – PA3	Port A 4-bit input
PB0 – PB3	Port B 4-bit input
PC0 – PC3	Port C 4-bit input–output
PD0 – PD3	Port D 4-bit input–output
PE0 – PE3	Port E 4-bit output
PF0 – PF3	Port F 4-bit output
PG0 – PG3	Port G 4-bit output
PH0 – PH3	Port H 4-bit output
P10 – P12	Port I 3-bit output
CL0, CL1	Clock pins
V_{gg}, V_{ss}, GND	Power supply pins
INT	Interrupt input

Power requirements

μCOM42

V_{gg}	-10 V $\pm$ 10%
GND	0 V
Current	60 mA

μCOM 43/44/45/46, pMOS standard types

V_{gg}	-10 V $\pm$ 10%
V_{ss}	0 V
Current	25 – 35 mA

Devices with L suffix run on -8 V supply at half current.

CMOS versions of 43/44/45 series

V_{gg}	$+5$ V $\pm$ 10%
V_{ss}	0 V
Current	typically 1 mA

Temperature range

0°C to +70°C

Input–output

All inputs and outputs are compatible with TTL signals and outputs will generally drive one TTL load.

Some devices have high voltage open drain outputs to drive vacuum fluorescent type display devices. These are capable of handling 35 V signals.

Interrupt facilities

On the μCOM42 there are two interrupts, IA and IB. Of these the IA input has priority over the IB input.

Devices in the μCOM43 and μCOM46 series have an input INT for one interrupt, and a second interrupt may be provided by the on-chip counter/timer.

Instruction set

The μCOM42 has a set of 72 instructions, primarily designed for calculator type applications. There are a wide range of arithmetic operations including decimal addition and subtraction, but there are no logical type functions.

The μCOM43/44/45/46 have 80 instructions which are for controller type applications. A wide range of arithmetic and logic operations is provided, including decimal addition and subtraction and a range of useful bit manipulation type instructions.

A wide range of skip type conditional branches and the possibility of manipulating the program counter are provided. Subroutine and interrupt handling instructions are included. There are a wide variety of instructions to deal with input–output operations which will be useful in controller type applications.

Timing

The μCOM42 requires an external single-phase clock running at 100 – 200 kHz and gives an average instruction cycle time of 10 μs.

For the other types an on-chip clock generator may be used or an external clock may be applied if desired. Clock frequency may be from 150 to 440 kHz and average instruction time is about 10 μs.

Support devices

For μCOM42 the μPD5101 may be used to expand the RAM via the S0 to S4 port.

μPD555   μCOM42 evaluation chip, 64-pin DIL, external ROM

μPD556   μCOM43/44/45 evaluation chip, 64-pin DIL, external ROM

OKI SERIES 40

The OKI Semiconductor Series 40 devices are 4-bit single-chip microcomputers using CMOS technology. Each device contains some RAM for working storage and a mask programmed ROM for program instructions, plus a range of input and output lines. Some of the devices also contain a counter/timer, whilst others have provision for outputs to drive liquid crystal displays. These microcomputers are primarily intended for control applications such as for electronic toys, cash registers and appliance controllers, where sufficiently large production runs justify the use of a mask programmed unit. Their low power consumption makes them ideally suited for portable equipment.

Prime manufacturer

OKI Semiconductor.

Devices available

MSM5840	128 × 4 RAM, No ROM, 30 I/O lines
MSM5840RS	128 × 4 RAM, 2k × 8 ROM, 30 I/O
MSM5842RS	32 × 4 RAM, 768 × 8 ROM, 21 I/O
MSM5845RS	64 × 4 RAM, 1280 × 8 ROM, 30 I/O
MSM58421GS	40 × 4 RAM, 1536 × 8 ROM, LCD outputs
MSM58423RS	32 × 4 RAM, 1280 × 8 ROM
MSM5847RS	96 × 4 RAM, 1536 × 8 ROM, LCD outputs

Alternative source devices

None.

Architecture

Fig. 2.6 shows the basic architecture of the MSM5840RS unit. Others in this series have different sizes of internal ROM and RAM and different arrangements and numbers of input–output lines.

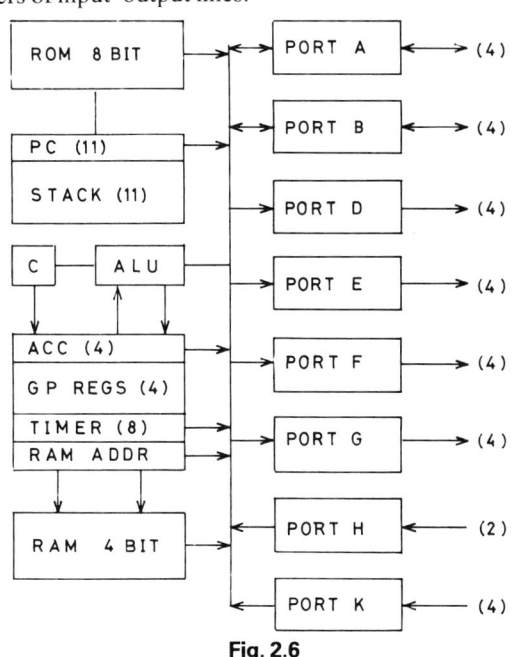

Fig. 2.6

The central processor has a 4-bit accumulator and data bus with a 4-bit ALU. Instructions from the internal ROM are handled via an 8-bit bus, whilst the program counter, which provides the ROM address, is 11 bits wide, allowing up to 2 kbytes of program to be used from the internal ROM.

To allow for system expansion the series 40 devices can use an external ROM for additional program storage. In this case the instruction data and the lower 8 bits of the program address are handled via ports A and B, whilst the upper 3 bits of the program address and a ROM enable signal are fed out via part D. Normally this allows a further 2 kbytes of external ROM to be used for program storage, but by bank switching of the external ROM expansion beyond this level is possible.

All devices have a simple 8-bit timer/counter on the chip and all have some form of stack for subroutine handling. The 5840 has a 4-level stack, 5845 has two levels and the other types usually have only a single-stack register. The 5840, 5845 and 58423 all have interrupt facilities.

Eight internal registers are provided in the 5840, four being general purpose and four for temporary storage of data. The 5845 contains only four registers and other types have a single working register. Carry and zero flag flip flops are provided on the 5840 and 5845, but other types have only the carry flag. All types have an internal clock and automatic reset facilities.

Package

The OKI series 40 microcomputers are normally supplied in the following packages:

MSM5840RS	42-pin DIL (plastic)
MSM5845RS	42-pin DIL (plastic)
MSM5842RS	28-pin DIL (plastic)
MSM58421GS	60-pin flat pack
MSM58423RS	42-pin DIL (plastic)

Devices in this series can also be supplied in 56-pin or 32-pin flat packs instead of 42 or 28-pin DIL.

Pin connections

MSM5840RS

1	PA0	22	IF
2	PA1	23	PE0
3	PA2	24	PE1
4	PA3	25	PE2
5	SYNC	26	PE3
6	INT	27	PF0
7	RESET	28	PF1
8	MODE	29	PF2
9	OSC1	30	PF3
10	OSC0	31	PG0
11	WR	32	PG1
12	RD	33	PG2
13	PK0	34	PG3
14	PK1	35	C_{IN}
15	PK2	36	PH0
16	PK3	37	PH1
17	PD0	38	PB0
18	PD1	39	PB1
19	PD2	40	PB2
20	PD3	41	PB3
21	GND	42	V_{dd}

MSM5842RS

1	PH	15	C_{IN}
2	SYNC	16	PK0
3	OSC1	17	PK1
4	OSC0	18	PK2
5	RESET	19	PK3
6	PA0	20	PD0
7	PA1	21	PD1
8	PA2	22	PD2
9	PA3	23	PD3
10	PB0	24	PE0
11	PB1	25	PE1
12	PB2	26	PE2
13	PB3	27	PE3
14	GND	28	V_{dd}

MSM5845RS

1	PK3	22	PF3
2	PK2	23	PF2
3	PK1	24	PF1
4	PK0	25	PF0
5	PB3	26	PG3
6	PB2	27	PG2
7	PB1	28	PG1
8	PB0	29	PG0
9	PA3	30	RESET
10	PA2	31	SYNC
11	PA1	32	INT
12	PA0	33	PH1
13	PD3	34	PH0
14	PD2	35	OSC2
15	PD1	36	OSC1
16	PD0	37	OSC0
17	PE3	38	HOLD
18	PE2	39	
19	PE1	40	C_{IN}
20	PE0	41	C_{OUT}
21	GND	42	V_{dd}

Signal functions

PA0 – PA3	Port A Input–output
PB0 – PB3	Port B Input–output
PD0 – PD3	Port D Output
PE0 – PE3	Port E Output
PF0 – PF3	Port F Output
PG0 – PG3	Port G Output
PH0 – PH1	Port H Latched input
PK0 – PK3	Port K Input
C_{IN} C_{OUT}	Counter/timer input–output
OSC0 – OSC2	Clock oscillator
RESET	Master reset input
WR	Write control output
RD	Read control output
SYNC	Sync output from clock
V_{dd}, GND	Power supply inputs
INT	Interrupt input
HOLD	Hold input to clock
MODE	Clock mode control input

Power requirements

V_{dd} +3 V to +6 V
GND   0 V
Typical current at +5 V   3 mA max.

Instruction set

The MSM5840RS has a comprehensive set of 98 instructions of which 93 are single-byte instructions. For the MSM5845 a subset of 49 instructions (46 single-byte) are provided and the other devices use a subset of 50 instructions.

Interrupt facilities

The MSM5840RS provides two levels of interrupt operation, but only one level of interrupt is available on the MSM5845RS and MSM58423RS. Other devices have no interrupt facilities.

Input–output

All devices provide a selection of input–output ports and in most cases these are CMOS and TTL compatible.

Ports A and B are bidirectional 4-bit ports and may be used to carry instruction data and addresses when an external ROM is used to expand the program capability.

Ports D, E, F and G are all 4-bit output ports and if an external ROM is used port D carries the most significant three bits of the address and a ROM enable signal.

Ports H and K are inputs with 4 bits on port K and one or two latched inputs on port H.

On some devices, such as the MSM58421GS, a series of segment and digit output signals for liquid crystal displays is provided.

Timing

An on-chip clock oscillator is provided on all series 40 chips and would normally be operated using an external quartz crystal. Alternatively an external clock may be used. Clock frequency may range up to 4 MHz and the clock may be stopped since the processor logic is static in operation.

The basic instruction execution time when a 4 MHz clock is used will be 8 μs.

Support devices

In most cases the series 40 microcomputers will not require external support devices, but the following types may be used:

MSM58283RS	4-digit VF driver
MSM58282RS	4-digit LED driver
MSM58292GS	5-digit LCD driver
MSM58293GS	5-digit VF driver
MSM5870RS	16-line output expander

Development aids

A development board type MPB201 can be used as a stand-alone system for software development and can also be used as an emulator, replacing the μP chip in the user's product, to test the operation of programs. A second board type MPB203 is used to interface the MPB201 to a terminal or other development system if required. In such cases the assembled program may be down loaded from the main development system for use with the MPB201.

Board type MPB202 provides an emulation system using two 2716 EPROMs to replace the normal mask programmed ROM. It uses extra logic to simulate the operation of an MSM5840RS device and its internal ROM.

Software is available for program development using the Intel ISIS system or a CP/M based development system.

Additional PC boards are available to emulate the action of VF or LCD output drivers on some types of series 40 chip.

ROCKWELL PPS4/1 SERIES

The Rockwell PPS4/1 series is a family of 4-bit *p*MOS one-chip microcomputers which are a development of the earlier PPS4 and PPS4/2 multi-chip designs. These microcomputers are designed for use in low cost high volume applications where keypad number entry is used and LED or fluorescent displays are used for the readout. Typical of such applications are domestic appliance controllers, coin operated machines, calculators, radio and television channel selector systems and simple industrial type controllers.

Various combinations of on-chip RAM and mask programmed ROM are provided, together with a selection of input–output ports and individual lines. Many devices in the series have a capability of driving LED and other types of display and have on the chip a programmable logic array (PLA) for decoding a 4-bit data signal to say 7-segment display outputs.

In capability and applications these devices are similar to other 4-bit single-chip microcomputers such as the National COPS2, NEC μCOM40, OKI series 40 and Hitachi HMCS43 types.

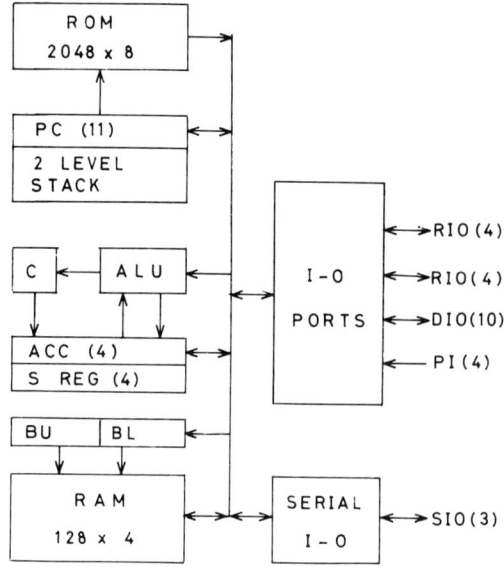

Fig. 2.7

Prime manufacturer

Rockwell International.

Devices available

MM75	640 × 8 ROM, 48 × 4 RAM, 22 I/O lines, low cost model
MM78	2048 × 8 ROM, 128 × 4 RAM, 31 I/O lines
MM76EL	1024 × 8 ROM, 48 × 4 RAM, 31 I/O lines, low power
MM78L	2048 × 8 ROM, 128 × 4 RAM, 31 I/O lines, low power
MM78LA	2048 × 8 ROM, 128 × 4 RAM, 35 I/O lines, low power

Alternative source devices

None.

Architecture

In the PPS4/1 series devices the arithmetic and logic functions are carried out in a 4-bit accumulator and ALU, together with a carry flag bit flip flop.

Instructions are 8 bits wide and are stored in the mask programmed on-chip ROM, which is accessed by an 11-bit program counter register PC. For subroutine and interrupt operations one or two 11-bit save registers are provided to store the return address. Maximum ROM size is 2048 bytes.

Data are stored as 4-bit nibbles in the on-chip RAM and are addressed by a 7-bit data address register, split for programming purposes into an upper register of 3 bits and a lower register of 4 bits. On the MM75 the data address has only 6 bits.

A single working register 4 bits wide (S) is provided for use as temporary storage. Other facilities include two interrupts and a programmable logic array which may be used as a decoder for output display drivers.

The MM78LA includes an on-chip tone generator counter and an output capable of driving a small loudspeaker for sound output.

All devices contain an on-chip clock generator and by mask options provision may be made for using an external clock if required.

Package

MM75	28-pin dual in line
MM78 and MM78LA	42-pin quad in line
MM76EL and MM78L	40-pin dual in line

Pin connections

MM75 low cost type 28-pin DIL

1	RIO 8/INT1		15	DIO 8
2	RIO 1		16	A
3	RIO 2		17	VC
4	RIO 3		18	V_{dd}
5	RIO 4		19	V_{ss}
6	DIO 0		20	PI 1
7	DIO 1		21	PI 2
8	DIO 2		22	PI 3
9	DIO 3		23	PI 4
10	DIO 4		24	PO
11	DIO 5		25	INT ϕ
12	DIO 6		26	RIO 5
13	DIO 7		27	RIO 6
14	V_{ss}		28	RIO 7

Signal functions

RIO 1 – RIO 4	Input–output channel A
RIO 5 – RIO 8	Input–output channel B
PI 1 – PI 4	Input channel 1
DIO 0 – DIO 8	Discrete input–output lines
INTϕ, INT1	Interrupt input lines
A	Clock output for sync purposes
VC	Clock control voltage input
PO	Reset input
V_{ss}, V_{dd}	Power supply inputs

When mask option for external clock is used the A terminal becomes the external clock input pin.

Power requirements

MM75 and MM78

V_{dd} -15 V $\pm 5\%$
V_{ss} 0 V
Supply power   75 mW typical

MM76EL, MM78L and MM78LA

V_{dd} -6.5 V to -11 V
V_{ss} 0 V
Typical power consumption   15 mW

Input–output

The MM75 has four parallel input lines and all other types have eight parallel input lines forming the input Port 1. If V_{ss} is set at +5 V these inputs will be TTL compatible.

All devices except the MM78LA have two bidirectional 4-bit parallel ports for input–output, which are TTL compatible. The MM78LA has a 14-line parallel output.

All devices provide discrete output lines, normally 10, but for the MM75 only 8 are provided. On the MM78, MM76EL and MM78L there are also 3 serial input–output lines provided.

For display decoding the MM75 and MM76EL have 16 × 8 bit programmable logic arrays. The MM78LA has a 32 × 14 bit PLA and also provides a 3-wire output to drive a small loudspeaker for tone output signals.

Interrupt facilities

All devices in the PPS4/1 have interrupt facilities and on all except the MM78LA there are two interrupt inputs. On the MM75 one interrupt is shared with one of the input–output data lines and operates in a multiplexed mode.

Instruction set

A total of some 70 instructions is provided in the instruction set for the PPS4/1 devices.

Arithmetic instructions include add and add with carry, complement and decimal conversion for BCD operations. There is no separate subtract instruction, this being achieved by using complement and add operations.

There are no separate logic operations available in the ALU and accumulator functions, but these could be achieved by using the range of bit manipulation and test functions provided.

Instructions are provided to allow manipulation of the RAM address register which would allow various forms of indexed addressing of data to be achieved.

A wide variety of skip and branch instructions is provided, with conditional branches on carry, bit tests and input line status tests.

Several instructions are provided to allow data to be input or output via ports A, B and I and the accumulator. Ports A and B may also have outputs fed to them via the PLA decoder matrix.

Timing

Internal clock normally runs at approximately 90 kHz and most instructions execute in one 4-phase clock cycle, giving an instruction cycle time of some 11 – 12 μs. Clock frequency is determined by external RC combination, and the maximum is about 100 kHz.

Support devices

None.

Development aids

For each microcomputer in the PPS4/1 series there is a 64-pin DIL emulation device which allows the system to be checked using external RAM and ROM. This allows testing and debugging of the final system in real time before the ROM program is committed to a mask.

An evaluation module type XPO-1 can be used for program development in conjunction with an emulator device. This unit has a hexadecimal keypad input and LED displays, and provides a cheap but relatively slow development system.

The PPS4/1 series systems can however be dealt with by the Rockwell SYSTEM 65 development system by using a personality module for the actual PPS4/1 device. This module provides a cross assembler for the PPS4/1 instruction set and also allows comprehensive debugging and simulation to be used on the SYSTEM 65.

TEXAS INSTRUMENTS TMS1000 SERIES

Designed primarily for applications where a high volume of production is envisaged, the Texas Instruments TMS1000 series are 4-bit single-chip microcomputers with on-chip RAM and mask programmed ROM. Most of the types use pMOS construction but there are also some CMOS types available.

The TMS1000 range is perhaps the most widely used of the 4-bit types and typical applications range from toys through various forms of appliance controller to small industrial controllers. Typical products including this type of device are musical door chime units and the Texas Instruments 'Speak and Spell' talking toy, which uses a TMS1000 device as the control logic.

These microcomputers compete with other 4-bit series, such as the AMI S2000, National COPS2, Rockwell PPS4/1 and the various Japanese types such as the NEC μCOM40 series. In some ways the TMS1000 types may not be quite as effective as some of the newer series, but there is a very wide range of types and options and the devices are well established and therefore both popular and relatively low in cost.

Prime manufacturer

Texas Instruments Inc.

Devices available

TMS1000	1 kbyte ROM, 64 × 4 RAM, 23 I/O lines
TMS1000C	CMOS version of TMS1000
TMS1018	No ROM, 64 × 4 RAM, 4 I/O lines
TMS1070	1 kbyte ROM, 64 × 4 RAM, VF display controller
TMS1098	No ROM, 128 × 4 RAM, prototyping device
TMS1099	No ROM, 64 × 4 RAM, prototyping device
TMS1099C	CMOS version of TMS1099
TMS1100	2 kbyte ROM, 128 × 4 RAM, 25 I/O lines
TMS1117	2 kbyte ROM, 128 × 4 RAM, 19 I/O lines
TMS1200	1 kbyte ROM, 64 × 4 RAM, 25 I/O lines
TMS1200C	CMOS version of TMS1200
TMS1270	As TMS1200 but with vacuum fluorescent display O/P
TMS1300	2 kbyte ROM, 128 × 8 RAM, 23 I/O lines
TMS1400	4 kbyte ROM, 128 × 4 RAM, 22 I/O lines
TMS1600	4 kbyte ROM, 128 × 4 RAM, 33 I/O lines
TMS1700	512 byte ROM, 32 × 4 RAM, 21 I/O lines
TMS2000	nMOS version of TMS1000
TMS2100	nMOS version of TMS1100
TMS2200	nMOS version of TMS1200
TMS2300	nMOS version of TMS1300
TMS2098	ROMless prototype device for TMS2100
TMS2099	ROMless prototype device for TMS2000
TMS3000	CMOS version of TMS1000 (same as TMS1000C)
TMS3200	CMOS version of TMS1200 (same as TMS1200C)
TMS3099	CMOS version of TMS1099

Alternative source devices

Motorola Semiconductor

MC141000	CMOS version of TMS1000
MC141200	CMOS version of TMS1200
MC141099	CMOS prototyping device for MC141000

Architecture

The internal architecture of the TMS1000 series is simple and follows the general pattern of calculator based architecture, with separate program and data memories.

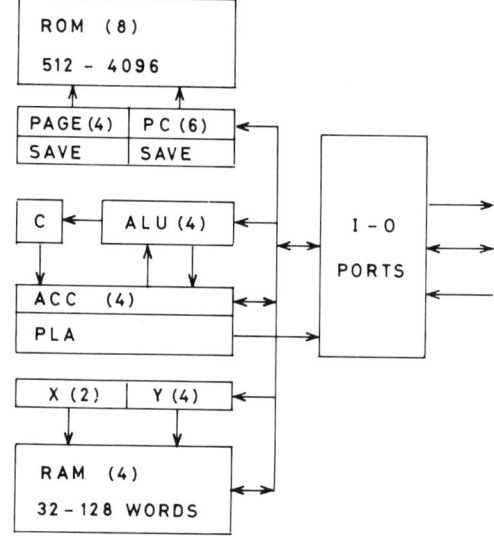

Fig. 2.8

Arithmetic and logic are handled by a 4-bit accumulator and ALU with an extra flag flip flop for carry. The data RAM is accessed by X and Y address registers with 4 bits for the Y register and either 2 or 3 bits for X to allow access to either 64 or 128 words of RAM. All data paths are 4 bits wide.

A 6-bit program counter provides access to 64 byte pages of the program memory and a page register of 4 bits allows memory to be extended to 1 kbytes. For the devices with a larger program memory one or two extra chapter flag bits are used to select banks of 1024 bytes each.

There is no stack facility as such on the TMS1000 type devices, but there is a buffer register for saving the program counter, page register and chapter flags during subroutine operations.

An on-chip clock generator is provided and there are various combinations of input and output lines provided. In some chips the outputs may be designed to drive a vacuum fluorescent type display and a programmable logic array on the chip may be used to provide segment decoding.

Package

TMS1000, TMS1100, TMS1400 and TMS1700 types

28-pin dual in line type package

TMS1200, TMS1300 and TMS1600 types

40-pin dual in line package

TMS1098 and TMS1099 prototyping devices

64-lead dual in line type package

Pin connections

TMS1200 types

1	R8	21	–
2	R9	22	–
3	R10	23	O2
4	R11	24	O1
5	R12	25	O0
6	V_{dd}	26	OSC1
7	K1	27	OSC2
8	K2	28	V_{ss}
9	K4	29	R0
10	K8	30	R1
11	INIT	31	R2
12	O7	32	–
13	–	33	–
14	–	34	–
15	–	35	–
16	O6	36	R3
17	O5	37	R4
18	O4	38	R5
19	O3	39	R6
20	–	40	R7

TMS1000 types

1	R8	15	O2
2	R9	16	O1
3	R10	17	O0
4	V_{dd}	18	OSC1
5	K1	19	OSC2
6	K2	20	V_{ss}
7	K4	21	R0
8	K8	22	R1
9	INIT	23	R2
10	O7	24	R3
11	O6	25	R4
12	O5	26	R5
13	O4	27	R6
14	O3	28	R7

Signal functions

R0 – R12	Control outputs
O0 – O7	Data outputs
K1, K2, K4, K8	Data inputs
OSC1, OSC2	Oscillator timing pins
INIT	Power on reset input
V_{dd}, V_{ss}	Power supply inputs

Signals on the TMS1000 device series are not normally TTL compatible, but are *p*MOS level signals. On the CMOS and *n*MOS types the signals may be TTL compatible.

Power requirements

*p*MOS types

V_{dd} –15 V but 1300, 1400, 1600 and 1700 will also run from a –9 V supply
V_{ss} 0 V
Current   Typically 6 – 10 mA

CMOS and *n*MOS types

V_{cc} +5 V
V_{ss} 0 V
Supply current   CMOS types 0.5 – 2 mA

Temperature range

0°C to +70°C

Input–output

Individual R output lines may be set or reset and are addressed by using the Y RAM address register. These lines are often used as strobe lines for displays for a key pad input.

The O lines are data outputs. They derive their data from the accumulator via a programmed logic array, which may be used as an encoder for say 7-segment display decoding. This PLA is made to the customer requirement as the chip is masked.

Four K inputs are provided for use with keyboards or for individual switch inputs.

Interrupt facilities

No interrupt facilities are provided in the TMS1000 series of microcomputers.

Instruction set

Most of the devices in the range have a set of 43 program instructions, although some types such as the TMS1100 and TMS1300 have sets of some 54 instructions.

Arithmetic and logic
The accumulator is used for addition and subtraction of 4-bit data and facilities are provided for decimal working. It is also possible to increment, decrement, complement and compare numbers.

Logic operations such as AND, OR, etc., are not in the instruction set and would need to be achieved by using other instructions such as bit tests and manipulation.

Data transfer
Data may readily be transferred between RAM and accumulator and the I/O ports. It is also possible to manipulate the X and Y address registers for the RAM. No stack facilities are provided.

Branch and jump
A wide selection of test, branch and skip type operations is provided. There is a CALL instruction for subroutines, but it must be remembered that in many of the devices there is only one save register for the program counter, although some types do have 2 or 3-level save stacks to allow for nesting of subroutines.

Timing

The on-chip oscillator normally runs at some 300 – 500 kHz, giving instruction execution times in the range 10 – 15 μs, although the Texas CMOS parts can operate as fast as 6 μs per instruction. All instructions normally take one machine cycle.

Support chips

No support chips are normally required since these are single-chip stand alone microcomputers.

Development aids

Two ROMless parts (TMS1098 and TMS1099) are available for prototype development and evaluation before having a mask made for the on-chip ROM.

Software and hardware development can be carried out using the Texas Instruments AMPL microprocessor development system. Motorola CMOS types can be handled by the Motorola EXORCISER microprocessor development system.

3 8-BIT MICROPROCESSORS AND MICROCOMPUTERS

8-BIT MICROPROCESSOR TYPES

Maker	Device	ROM	RAM	Max. memory	Pkge	Remarks	Page
Advanced Micro Devices	Am8035		64		40DIL	= 8035	50
	Am 8048	1k	64		40DIL	= 8048	50
	Am8080A			64k	40DIL	= 8080A	57
	Am9080			64k	40DIL	= 8080A	57
	Am8085A			64k	40DIL	= 8085A	60
American Microsystems	S6800			64k	40DIL	= 6800	66
	S6801	2k	128	64k	40DIL	= 6801	69
	S6801E	2k	128	64k	40DIL	= 6801E	69
	S6802		128	64k	40DIL	= 6802	73
	S6805	1k	64		40DIL	= 6805	77
	S6808			64k	40DIL	= 6808	73
	S6809			64k	40DIL	= 6809	79
Fairchild	F6800			64k	40DIL	= 5800	66
	F6801	2k	128	64k	40DIL	= 6801	69
	F6801E	2k	128	64k	40DIL	= 6801E	69
	F6802		64	64k	40DIL	= 6802	73
	F6803		128	64k	40DIL	= 6803	69
	F6805	1k	64		28DIL	= 6805	77
	F6808			64k	40DIL	= 6808	73
	F6809			64k	40DIL	= 6809	79
	F3850		64	64k	40DIL	F8 CPU	45
	F3870	2k	64		40DIL	= 3870	63
	F38E70	2k	64		40DIL	EPROM version	63
Fujitsu	MBL8800			64k	40DIL	= 6800	66
General Instrument	PIC1645	256			18DIL	μC	48
	PIC1650	512			40DIL	μC	48
	PIC1655	512			28DIL	μC	48
	PIC16C55	512			28DIL	CMOS 1655	48
	PIC1656	512			28DIL	μC	48
	PIC1664				64DIL	Dev. chip	48
	PIC1670	1k			40DIL	μC	48
Hitachi	HD46800			64k	40DIL	= 6800	66
	HD46801	2k	128	64k	40DIL	= 6801	69
	HD46802		64	64k	40DIL	= 6802	73
	HD46805	1k	64		28DIL	= 6805	77
	HD46809			64k	40DIL	= 6809	79
Hughes	HCMP1802			64k	40DIL	= 1802	98
	HCMP1802C			64k	40DIL	= 1802C	98

MICROPROCESSOR DATA BOOK

Maker	Device	ROM	RAM	Max. memory	Pkge	Remarks	Page
Intel	8021	1k	64		28DIL	μC	50
	8022	2k	64		40DIL	μC+ADC	50
	8035		64		40DIL	CPU	50
	8039		128		40DIL	μC	50
	8041	1k	64		40DIL	UPI	50
	8048	1k	64		40DIL	μC	50
	8049	2k	128		40DIL	μC	50
	8748	1k	64		40DIL	μC + EPROM	50
	8031		128		40DIL	μC	54
	8051	4k	128		40DIL	μC	54
	8751	4k	128		40DIL	μC + EPROM	54
	8080A			64k	40DIL	CPU	57
	8085A			64k	40DIL	CPU	60
Intersil	IM87C41	1k	64		40DIL	CMOS 8741	50
	IM87C48	1k	64		40DIL	CMOS 8748	50
Mostek	MK3850			64k	40DIL	F8 CPU	45
	MK3870	2k	64		40DIL	= 3870 CPU	63
	MK3880			64k	40DIL	= Z80 CPU	113
	MK3880A			64k	40DIL	= Z80A CPU	113
Motorola	MC3850			64k	40DIL	F8 CPU	45
	MC3870	2k	64		40DIL	3870 CPU	63
	MC6800			64k	40DIL	6800 CPU	66
	MC6801	2k	128	64k	40DIL	μC	69
	MC6801E	2k	128	64k	40DIL	Ext. clk.	69
	MC6802		64	64k	40DIL	6802 CPU	73
	MC6803		128	64k	40DIL	6803 CPU	69
	MC6805	1k	64		28DIL	6805 μC	77
	MC6808			64k	40DIL	6808 CPU	73
	MC6809			64k	40DIL	6809 CPU	79
	MC6809E			64k	40DIL	Ext. clk.	79
	MC68701	2k	128	64k	40DIL	EPROM 6801	69
	MC146805	1k	64		40DIL	CMOS 6805	82
Mullard	MAB8400		128		28DIL	CPU	85
	MAB8405	612	32		28DIL	μC	85
	MAB8410	1k	64		28DIL	μC	85
	MAB8420	2k	64		28DIL	μC	85
	MAB8440	4k	128		28DIL	μC	85
National	8060			64k	40DIL	CPU SCMP2	88
	8070		64	64k	40DIL	CPU	88
	8072	2.5k	64	64k	40DIL	μC	88
	8074	4k	64	64k	40DIL	μC	88
	8075	4k	64	64k	40DIL	μC + BASIC	88

8-BIT MICROPROCESSORS AND MICROCOMPUTERS

Maker	Device	ROM	RAM	Max. memory	Pkge	Remarks	Page
National	INS8040		64		40DIL	like 8035	50
	INS8050	1k	64		40DIL	like 8048	50
	NSC800			64k	40DIL	CPU	90
	INS8080A			64k	40DIL	= 8080A	57
	INS8085A			64k	40DIL	= 8085A	60
MOS Technology	MCS6502			64k	40DIL	CPU	93
	MCS6503			4k	28DIL	CPU	93
	MCS6504			8k	28DIL	CPU	93
	MCS6505			4k	28DIL	CPU	93
	MCS6506			4k	28DIL	CPU	93
	MCS6507			8k	28DIL	CPU	93
	MCS6512			64k	40DIL	CPU	93
	MCS6513			4k	28DIL	CPU	93
	MCS6514			8k	28DIL	CPU	93
	MCS6515			4k	28DIL	CPU	93
N.E.C.	μPD7801	4k	128	64k	64QIL	μC	96
	μPD8021	1k	64		28DIL	= 8021	50
	μPD8035		64		40DIL	= 8035	50
	μPD8039		128		40DIL	= 8039	50
	μPD8048	1k	64		40DIL	= 8048	50
	μPD8049	2k	128		40DIL	= 8049	50
	μPD8748	1k	64		40DIL	= 8748	50
	μPD8080A			64k	40DIL	= 8080A	57
	μPD8085A			64k	40DIL	= 8085A	60
OKI	MSM8080A			64k	40DIL	= 8080A	57
RCA	CDP1802			64k	40DIL	CMOS CPU	98
	CDP1802C			64k	40DIL	CMOS CPU	98
	CDP1604	2k	256	64k	40DIL	CMOS μC	98
	CDP1804C	2k	256	64k	40DIL	CMOSμC	98
Rockwell	R6500/1	2k	64		40DIL	μC	102
	R6500/1E		64	64k	64DIL	CPU	102
	R6500/1-11	3k	64		64QIL	μC	102
	R6502			64k	40DIL	= 6502	93
	R6503			4k	28DIL	= 6503	93
	R6504			8k	28DIL	= 6504	93
	R6505			4k	28DIL	= 6505	93
	R6506			4k	28DIL	= 6506	93
	R6507			8k	28DIL	= 6507	93
	R6512			64k	40DIL	= 6512	93
	R6513			4k	28DIL	= 6513	93
	R6514			8k	28DIL	= 6514	93
	R6515			4k	28DIL	= 6515	93

MICROPROCESSOR DATA BOOK

Maker	Device	ROM	RAM	Max. memory	Pkge	Remarks	Page
SGS-ATES	Z80			64k	40DIL	= Z80	113
	Z80A			64k	40DIL	= Z80A	113
Signetics	2650A			32k	40DIL	CPU	107
	8X300			8k	50DIL	CPU	105
	8035		64		40DIL	= 8035	50
	8048	1k	64		40DIL	= 8048	50
	8085A			64k	40DIL	= 8085A	60
	8060			64k	40DIL	= INS8060	88
Solid State Scientific	SCP1802			64k	40DIL	= 1802	98
	SCP1802L			64k	40DIL	= 1802C	98
Synertek	SY6500/1	2k	64		40DIL	= 6500/1	102
	SY6502			64k	40DIL	= 6502	93
	SY6503			4k	28DIL	= 6503	93
	SY6504			8k	28DIL	= 6504	93
	SY6505			4k	28DIL	= 6505	93
	SY6506			4k	28DIL	= 6506	93
Synertek	SY6507			8k	28DIL	= 6507	93
	SY6512			64k	40DIL	= 6512	93
	SY6513			4k	28DIL	= 6513	93
	SY6514			8k	28DIL	= 6514	93
	SY6515			4k	28DIL	= 6515	93
	Z8	2k	96	64k	40DIL	= Z8 μC	110
Texas Instruments	TMS8080A			64k	40DIL	= 8080A	57
Thomson EFCIS	EF6800			64k	40DIL	= 6800	66
	EF6801	2k	128		40DIL	= 6801	69
	EF6801E	2k	128		40DIL	= 6801E	69
	EF6802		64	64k	40DIL	= 6802	73
	EF6803		128	64k	40DIL	= 6803	69
	EF6805	1k	64		28DIL	= 6805	77
	EF6808			64k	40DIL	= 6808	73
	EF6809			64k	40DIL	= 6809	79
	EF6809E			64k	40DIL	= 6809E	79
	EF68701	1k	128	64k	40DIL	= 68701	69
Toshiba	TMP8048	1k	64		40DIL	= 8048	50
	TMP8080A			64k	40DIL	= 8080A	57
	TMP8085A			64k	40DIL	= 8085A	60
Zilog	Z80			64k	40DIL	CPU Z80	113
	Z80A			64k	40DIL	CPU Z80A	113
	Z8-40	2k	96	64k	40DIL	μC	110
	Z8-64		96	64k	64DIL	Dev. chip	110
Mitsubishi	M5L8080A			64k	40DIL	= 8080A	57
	M5L8085A			64k	40DIL	= 8085A	60

FAIRCHILD F8 FAMILY

When Fairchild first introduced the F8 microprocessor family they broke away from the traditional layout adopted by other processor systems, such as the Intel 8080 and Motorola 6800, to produce a two-chip microcomputer system. At that time the rival microprocessors needed some five or more chips to give a working microcomputer. Thus the F8 with its low parts count was ideal for use in small systems applications.

The central processor of the F8 family is the 3850, which is an 8-bit nMOS microprocessor, and is used in conjunction with the 3851 Programmable Storage Unit to form a complete system. The division of functions between the 3850 and 3851 is rather unusual, with some of the CPU registers, such as the program counter, being located on the memory chip and some of the input–output ports being on the processor chip. This layout however reduces the amount of interconnection between the two chips but does tend to limit the possibilities of expansion of the system.

Although the F8 system was very popular when introduced it has more recently been superseded by the Mostek 3870, which is basically a single-chip implementation of the F8 system. Consequently the F8 now tends to be used for system development and evaluation with the 3870 version built into the final product.

Prime manufacturer

Fairchild Semiconductor.

Devices available

F3850 Central processor unit
F3851 Program storage unit

Alternative source devices

Mostek

MK3850 CPU
MK3851 PSU

SGS/ATES

M3850/R CPU
M3851/R PSU

Motorola are also licensed to make 3850 and 3851, but seem to be concentrating on the single-chip MC3870 version.

Architecture

As will be seen from fig. 3.1 the internal organisation of the 3850 CPU chip is relatively simple, but it must be noted that some parts of the CPU function are contained on the 3851 memory chip.

For arithmetic an 8-bit accumulator is used together with an 8-bit arithmetic and logic unit. A 5-bit status register provides flag bits for carry, sign, overflow, zero and interrupt conditions.

It will be noted that there are no program counter and stack pointer registers included on the CPU chip. The F8 does have these registers, but they are located on the 3851 program storage chip. The program counter, designated register P0, is 16 bits wide, giving access to a 64k memory space. A 16-bit stack pointer register (P) is

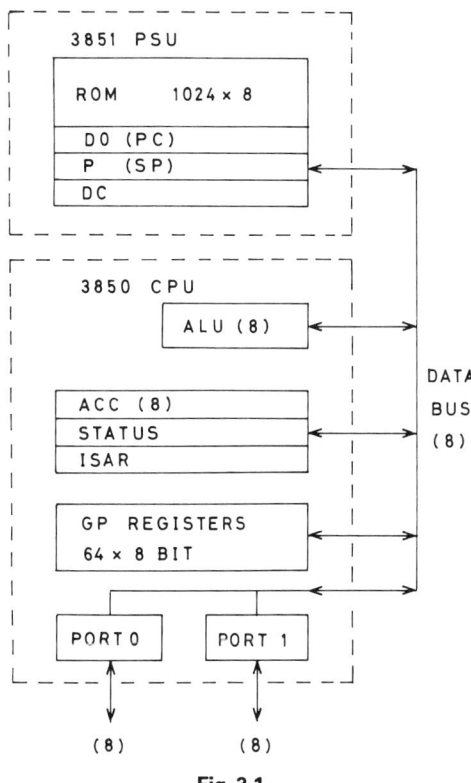

Fig. 3.1

provided for subroutine and interrupt operations. There is also a further 16-bit addressing register DC which acts as a data counter. Some support chips in the F8 series also provide a 16-bit buffer register (DC1) which may be used to save the contents of the data counter DC. By placing the addressing registers on the memory storage chip Fairchild were able to do away with an address bus and this saved interconnections between the two chips. When more memory is added by using additional 3851s each chip will contain P0, P and DC registers and will be in the same address space, but this is overcome by using a mask option to control the actual location of each 3851 within the full memory space.

On the 3850 CPU chip there is a 64-byte scratchpad RAM which can be used as a bank of working registers. Any location can be addressed indirectly via the ISAR (Indirect Scratchpad Address Register). Twelve registers at the lower end of the scratchpad memory can be addressed directly by the CPU. There are also three 2-byte registers (locations 10 – 15) which are named as the H, K and Q registers. They are used as address buffers to save the contents of the program counter, stack pointer and data pointers. Location 9 in the RAM is called the J register and may also be referred to by its mnemonic name.

In the 3851 there are an interval timer and event counter. There are also four 8-bit input–output ports available, two on the 3850 and two more on the 3851.

Package

40-pin dual in line type
Suffix P indicates a plastic package
Suffix D (Fairchild) or N (Mostek) denotes ceramic type
All SGS/ATES devices are in a ceramic package

FAIRCHILD F8 FAMILY

Pin connections

3850 CPU

1	ϕ	21	ROMC4
2	WRITE	22	ICB
3	V_{dd}	23	INT REQ
4	V_{gg}	24	V_{ss}
5	IO-03	25	IO-07
6	DB3	26	DB7
7	IO-13	27	IO-17
8	IO-12	28	IO-16
9	DB2	29	DB6
10	IO-02	30	IO-06
11	IO-01	31	IO-05
12	DB1	32	DB5
13	IO-11	33	IO-15
14	IO-10	34	IO-14
15	DB0	35	DB4
16	IO-00	36	IO-04
17	ROMC0	37	EXT RES
18	ROMC1	38	XTLY
19	ROMC2	39	XTLX
20	ROMC3	40	RC

3851 PSU

1	IO-B7	21	DB0
2	IO-A7	22	DB1
3	V_{gg}	23	IO-B1
4	V_{dd}	24	IO-A1
5	EXT INT	25	IO-A2
6	PRI OUT	26	IO-B2
7	WRITE	27	DB2
8	ϕ	28	DB3
9	INT REQ	29	IO-B3
10	PRI IN	30	IO-A3
11	DBDR	31	IO-A4
12	–	32	IO-B4
13	ROMC4	33	DB4
14	ROMC3	34	DB5
15	ROMC2	35	IO-B5
16	ROMC1	36	IO-A5
17	ROMC0	37	IO-A6
18	V_{ss}	38	IO-B6
19	IO-A0	39	DB6
20	IO-B0	40	DB7

Signal functions

IO-00 to IO-07	Port 0 I/O
IO-10 to IO-17	Port 1 I/O
IO-A0 to IO-A7	Port A I/O
IO-B0 to IO-B7	Port B I/O
DB0 – DB7	Data bus bidirectional
ROMC0 – ROMC4	Control bus CPU output PSU input
V_{dd}, V_{gg}, V_{ss}	Power supplies
RC, XTLX, XTLY	Clock lines
WRITE, ϕ	Timing pulses CPU output PSU input
EXT RES	External reset input
INT REQ	Interrupt request input CPU output PSU
PRI IN	Priority input
PRI OUT	Priority output
ICB	Interrupt control bit output
DBDR	Data bus drive output

Power requirements

V_{gg}	+12 V ± 5%
V_{dd}	+5 V ± 5%
V_{ss}	0 V
Current (3850)	I_{dd} 30 mA, I_{gg} 15 mA
Current (3851)	I_{dd} 30 mA, I_{gg} 10 mA

Temperature range

Standard part suffix C (Fairchild) /R (SGS/ATES)

0°C to +70°C

Extended part Fairchild suffix L Mostek suffix −10

−40°C to +85°C

Military part Fairchild suffix M Mostek suffix −20

−55°C to +125°C

Input–output

Input and output facilities are provided by two 8-bit ports (Port 0 and Port 1) on the 3850 processor and a further two 8-bit ports (Ports A and B) on each of the 3851 Programmable Storage Units in the system. Data may be transferred to and from the ports by special input–output instructions and the counter/timer of the 3851 chip is dealt with as a separate port in the same way.

Signals on the input and output lines are compatible with TTL. Inputs are equivalent to one TTL load and have a pull up resistor, whilst outputs will drive one TTL load.

Interrupt facilities

Interrupts may be generated either by the timer/counter on the 3851 or by external inputs. The timer and interrupt logic are interlinked and the interrupt to which the system will react is selected by software. Multilevel interrupts are possible.

Instruction set

There are a total of 76 instructions available in the F8 set. Software written for this processor will generally be capable of running on the single-chip 3870 microcomputer which has the same instruction set.

Arithmetic and logic

The accumulator can be used to add numbers together, although the carry condition has to be dealt with separately by a link instruction. There is a facility for dealing with numbers in BCD format. No direct subtraction instructions exist. This must be achieved by complementing and adding.

AND, OR and EXCLUSIVE OR logical operations are provided, and there are instructions for left and right shifting using either 1-bit or 4-bit shifts. Other operations available are complement, clear, increment, decrement and compare.

Register and memory

All locations in the scratchpad memory can be accessed via the Indirect Scratchpad Register (ISAR) and the first 12 locations in memory may be accessed directly. The H,

K and Q registers may be used to store the contents of the program counter P0, stack pointer (P) and data counter (DC) registers during subroutine or interrupt operations.

Branch and jump
Conditional branch instructions are provided for tests on the carry, sign, zero and overflow flags of the status register. There are also unconditional branch and jump instructions as well as CALL instructions for subroutines.

Input-output
All input-output ports and the timer are addressed by using IN and OUT instructions.

Addressing modes
All addressing in the program memory uses the data counter DC and implied addressing.

The scratchpad memory address is entirely independent of the program memory address, so in fact the RAM can be looked upon as a bank of general purpose working registers.

Timing

An on-chip clock generator is provided which may be controlled either by an external crystal or by an R–C timing network. An external clock may also be used and is input via pin 38 (XTLY).

Clock frequency is up to about 2 MHz, giving instruction execution times of the order $3-5$ μs.

Support chips

3851	Program storage unit, 1k mask ROM, timer, 2×8 I/O
3852	Dynamic memory interface controller
3853	Static memory interface controller
3854	Direct memory access controller
3856	As 3851 but with 2k on-chip ROM
3857	Program storage unit and static memory interface
3861	Peripheral input-output controller
3871	Peripheral input-output controller with counter

GENERAL INSTRUMENT PIC1650 SERIES

The General Instrument PIC1650 series devices were primarily designed for use as peripheral controllers and other similar applications. These are mostly *n*MOS 8-bit single-chip microcomputers with program ROM and a limited amount of RAM on the same chip as the CPU. For low power applications there is a CMOS version of the 1655 device. Devices in the range have a range of sizes of mask programmed ROM and a selection of I/O ports.

An example of a typical application for these devices is given by the GI TV1650A, which is a 1650 microcomputer used as the controller in a set of chips for teletext and viewdata decoders marketed as the GI Teleview system. Other possible uses would be in printer, plotter and VDU controllers and in a whole range of appliance controllers and similar types of application. The 1650 devices have some similarities to other 8-bit microcomputers such as the 8048 and 3870 series and can be used in similar applications. In general the facilities provided in these three series of microcomputers are similar and the choice will depend upon the particular application and how the individual facilities provided by the various types are suited to the task.

Prime manufacturer

General Instrument Microelectronics

Devices available

PIC1645	256 × 12 bit ROM and 12 I/O lines
PIC1650	512 × 12 bit ROM and 32 I/O lines
PIC1655	512 × 12 bit ROM and 20 I/O lines
PIC16C55	CMOS version of the PIC1655
PIC1656	As PIC1655 but with interrupt facility
PIC1664	ROMless part for system development
PIC1670	1024 × 12 bit ROM and 32 I/O lines

Alternative source devices

The 1650 series are also produced by:

EMM-Semi U.S.A.
Intermetall GMBH, W. Germany

Architecture

Fig. 3.2 shows the general layout of the PIC1650 series devices. Most of the available RAM on some chips is used as a register file, with the registers numbered from R0 to R47. In these devices R0 is not actually present and when this register is specified by an instruction an indirect addressing scheme via R4 is activated.

For arithmetic and logic an 8-bit accumulator (W) and arithmetic and logic unit (ALU) are used. There is a 3-bit status register (R3) with flag bits for carry, zero and half carry, the latter being used for BCD operations. Register R2 in the register file acts as the program counter and may have either 8, 9 or 10 bits according to the size of program ROM fitted to the chip. This register can be written to by the program but cannot be read. Register R4 may be used as an indirect addressing register to select one of the other registers for an operation.

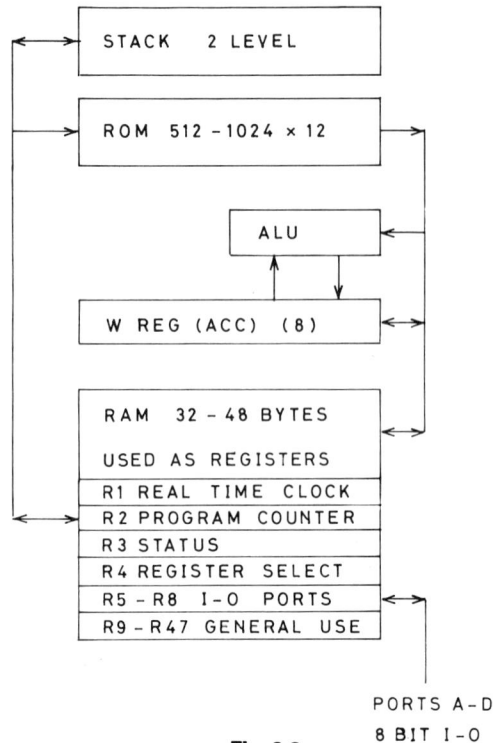

Fig. 3.2

Registers R5, R6 and R7 are used as input–output port registers, whilst R8 is used for I/O on some types and as a scratchpad register on others. Register R1 may be used as a counter or as a general register and all registers above R8 are used as scratchpad registers for data storage.

There is a stack on the chip for subroutines and this may have 2 – 4 levels depending upon the particular type. All devices in the series have on-chip clock generators.

Package

PIC1645	18-pin dual in line
PIC1650	40-pin dual in line
PIC1655	28-pin dual in line
PIC16C55	28-pin dual in line
PIC1656	28-pin dual in line
PIC1664B	64-pin dual in line
PIC1670	40-pin dual in line

Packages may be either plastic or ceramic.

Pin connections

PIC1650 type 40-pin DIL

1	V_{ss}	21	C2
2	A0	22	C3
3	A1	23	C4
4	A2	24	C5
5	TEST	25	C6
6	A3	26	C7
7	A4	27	D0
8	A5	28	D1
9	A6	29	D2
10	A7	30	D3

11	B0	31	D4
12	B1	32	D5
13	B2	33	D6
14	B3	34	D7
15	B4	35	CLK OUT
16	B5	36	OSC
17	B6	37	MCLR
18	B7	38	RTCC
19	C0	39	V_{cc}
20	C1	40	V_{xx}

Signal functions

A0 – A7	Port A 8-bit I/O
B0 – B7	Port B 8-bit I/O
C0 – C7	Port C 8-bit I/O
D0 – D7	Port D 8-bit I/O
V_{ss}, V_{cc}, V_{xx}	Power supply pins
OSC	Clock input (may be fed by RC timing network)
CLK OUT	Clock output signal
RTCC	Real time clock input to register R1
TEST	Test input not normally used
MCLR	Master reset input (active low)

Power requirements

V_{cc} +5 V ± 5%
V_{xx} +5 V or +10 V used when driving LED displays
V_{ss} 0 V
Power consumption 175 mW

CMOS version PIC16C55

V_{cc} +2.5 V to +6 V
V_{ss} 0 V
Power consumption 12 mW approx

Temperature range

0°C to +70°C

Input–output

All inputs and outputs are TTL compatible with outputs able to drive a single TTL load.

The 1650 and 1670 have four 8-bit quasi-bidirectional ports. The 1655 and 1656 have one 8-bit quasi-bidirectional port, a 4-bit input port and an 8-bit output port. On the 1645 there are three 4-bit ports, one for input, one for output, and one quasi-bidirectional.

Interrupt facilities

In general the PIC1650 devices do not have interrupt facilities, but the 1656 and 1670 can support an interrupt.

Instruction set

As one might expect the PIC1650 series has a very simple set of instructions and there are just 30 different commands in the set.

Arithmetic and logic
There are both addition and subtraction, but the carry is not included in either operation. There is no specific instruction for BCD operations so these must be carried out by software.

GENERAL INSTRUMENT PIC1650 SERIES

Logical operations provided are the normal AND, OR and EXCLUSIVE OR functions. There are also left and right rotate instructions and complement, increment and decrement functions. Individual bits of registers may be set or reset as desired.

Branch and jump
For conditional tests there are skip instructions on a zero or non-zero result and these may be combined with increment and decrement operations. There is an unconditional jump and a CALL instruction for subroutines.

Data transfer
Data may be moved between the registers and the accumulator. Note that the input and output ports are treated as registers in the main register bank. The only other data move allows the upper and lower 4 bits of either the accumulator or the selected register to be swapped.

Addressing modes

Addressing in the 1650 series is quite simple. Program memory (ROM) is addressed directly by JUMP or CALL instructions. No relative addressing mode is provided.

Registers R0 – R31 may be inherently addressed by the instruction. Alternatively, indirect addressing may be used by selecting R0 as the register address. R0 does not in fact exist, but when selected it will cause a register to be indirectly addressed via R4. The lower 5 bits of R4 will define the actual register selected when R0 is addressed. In the 1670 CPU six bits of R4 are used to allow access to up to 48 registers.

Timing

An on-chip clock generator is provided which may be controlled by either a quartz crystal or R–C network to oscillate at from 200 kHz to 1 MHz. A clock output at a quarter of this frequency is provided for use with external circuits.

Using a 1 MHz clock the instruction cycle time is 4 μs and virtually all instructions execute in one cycle. The skip instructions may take one or two cycles according to the test result.

Register R1 may be used as a real time clock and will be incremented by high to low transitions on the RTCC input. The frequency range of the RTCC input is from zero to 200 kHz.

Support devices

No support devices would normally be required since the 1650 series devices are intended to act as stand alone controllers.

Development aids

General Instrument provide an in-circuit emulator system known as PICES which is linked to a host computer system. Programs may be downloaded from the host computer and run in the PICES module for prototype development.

Cross assembler programs in FORTRAN IV are available for use on minicomputers and may also be used with the Intellec development produced by Intel.

INTEL 8048 SERIES

The 8048 series are 8-bit *n*MOS single-chip microcomputers originally introduced by Intel as their MCS48 family. These microcomputers are now second sourced by several other makers and have become an industry standard type for 8-bit single-chip microcomputers.

The basic 8048 has on-chip ROM for program storage and a small on-chip RAM for data as well as a timer counter and a selection of input–output ports. Some versions in the series are supplied with no on-chip ROM and are intended for use with external memory. Others such as the 8648 and 8748 have an EPROM on the chip for user programming. There are also versions with higher speed capability such as the 8049.

Some devices are designed for use as slave processors on an 8080/8085 type bus system, whilst others such as the 8021 and 8022 provide a simpler device or analogue input capabilities.

Among the second sources some of the devices available are not exact copies of the basic 8048 series. For example the National INS8040 and INS8050, although compatible with the 8048, have some hardware enhancements, whilst the Intersil type 87C48 is a CMOS version of the Intel part. The Mullard 8400 series also has some similarities to the 8048 types.

In general the 8048 series seems to be rather more popular than rival single-chip microcomputers such as the 3870, PIC1650 and 1804, although each type has its advantages. All of these single-chip microcomputers are intended for those high volume applications where an 8-bit capability is required.

Prime manufacturer

Intel Corporation.

Devices available

8048	1k × 8 ROM, 64 × 8 RAM, 27 I/O lines, 6 MHz
8648	As 8048 but 1k × 8 EPROM (non-eraseable)
8748	As 8048 but 1k × 8 EPROM (UV eraseable)
8035	As 8048 but no on-chip ROM
8049	2k × 8 ROM, 128 × 8 RAM, 27 I/O, 11 MHz
8039	As 8049 but no on-chip ROM
8039-6	6 MHz version of 8039
8041	1k × 8 ROM, 64 × 8 RAM, 18 I/O, 6 MHz
8741	As 8041 but with 1k × 8 UV eraseable EPROM
8021	1k × 8 ROM, 64 × 8 RAM, 21 I/O, 3.6 MHz
8022	2k × 8 ROM, 64 × 8 RAM, 28 I/O, A/D conv.

Alternative source devices

N.E.C.

µPD8021, µPD8035, µPD8039, µPD8041
µPD8048, µPD8049, µPD8741 and µPD8748

Advanced Micro Devices (AMD)

AM8041, AM8048, AM8035

Signetics

Licensed as second source.

National Semiconductor

INS8050 Enhanced version of 8048
INS8040 Similar to INS8050 but no on-chip ROM

Intersil

IM87C41 CMOS version of 8741
IM87C48 CMOS version of 8748 with UV EPROM

Architecture

Fig. 3.3 shows the basic architecture of the 8048 basic type.

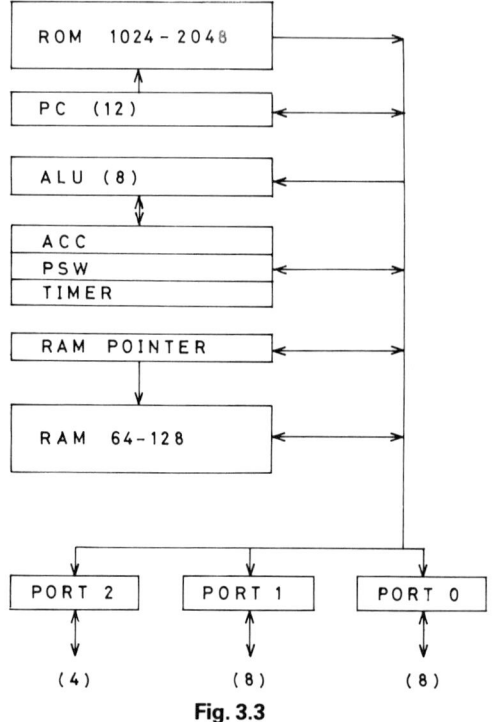

Fig. 3.3

Arithmetic and logic is dealt with by an 8-bit ALU and an 8-bit accumulator register. The carry flag bit is held in a status register with 8 bits known as the Program Status Word (PSW). This register also contains two other flag bits, a register select flag and the stack pointer address.

A 12-bit program counter register provides the address for the program ROM. The most significant bit acts as a bank select indicator and the program memory is effectively split into two banks of 2048 bytes each. Bank selection is carried out by software. The program memory is organised into pages of 256 bytes, and addressing is normally absolute within the current page. Jump instructions are needed to move from one page to another.

Program memory can be expanded by using external ROM or RAM chips. In this case the address for the external memory is fed out via the data bus (lower 8 bits of address) and the lower 4 bits of port 2. A control output is provided to select the external memory as required and instruction data are fed back into the CPU via the data bus.

The data memory is addressed separately from the CPU program memory and the memory map for the RAM is:

INTEL 8048 SERIES

```
FF  ─────
        User space
        external RAM
40  ─────
3F  ─────
        User space
20  ─────
1F  ─────  R7'
        Register
        bank RB1
18  ─────  R0'
17  ─────
        Stack
        area
08  ─────
07  ─────  R7
        Register
        bank RB0
02  ─────
01  ─────  R1
00  ─────  R0
```

Two banks of eight general purpose 8-bit registers are provided and one bank may be selected for use at a time by using register select instructions. Registers R0 and R1 (or R0' and R1') are used to address all locations in the data memory, the address of the desired location being set up in either R0 or R1. Only the registers in the selected bank may be accessed directly by program addressing.

An 8-level stack with two data bytes per level is provided between RAM locations 08 (hex) and 17 (hex) and is used for subroutine and interrupt operations to store the program status word.

An on-chip 8-bit timer or interval counter is provided, which can be used to interrupt processing if desired. An external interrupt line is also provided.

Three 8-bit I/O ports are provided, of which one is a true bidirectional bus. There are three further inputs for test signals and interrupt.

The 8021 is a cut down version of the 8048, with two 8-bit ports and one 4-pit port. It is packaged in a 28-pin unit. The 8022 has an 8-bit A/D converter on the chip and facilities for multiplexing between two analogue inputs using software.

The 8041 and 8741, although basically an 8048 type CPU, is normally specially programmed as an input–output device. It is referred to as a Universal Peripheral Interface. It has two data registers and can handle direct memory access (DMA) operations.

In the National INS8040/8050 types a Schmitt trigger is included on the interrupt inputs. There is also a circuit for charging memory back up batteries included on the chip.

All types include an on-chip clock oscillator which normally works with an external quartz crystal.

Package

8021 type uses 28-pin dual in line
All other types are 40-pin dual in line
Package may be either plastic or ceramic
Temperature range normally 0 – 70°C, but types for −55°C – +125°C also available.

Pin connections

8021 type 28-pin DIL

1	P22	15	XTAL1
2	P23	16	XTAL2
3	PROG	17	RESET
4	P00	18	P10
5	P01	19	P11
6	P02	20	P12
7	P03	21	P13
8	P04	22	P14
9	P05	23	P15
10	P06	24	P16
11	P07	25	P17
12	ALE	26	P20
13	T1	27	P21
14	V_{ss}	28	V_{cc}

Type 8022 40-pin DIL

1	P26	21	Substrate
2	P27	22	XTAL1
3	AV_{cc}	23	XTAL2
4	V_{ref}	24	RESET
5	AN1	25	P10
6	AN2	26	P11
7	AV_{ss}	27	P12
8	T0	28	P13
9	V_{th}	29	P14
10	P00	30	P15
11	P01	31	P16
12	P02	32	P17
13	P03	33	P20
14	P04	34	P21
15	P05	35	P22
16	P06	36	P23
17	P07	37	PROG
18	ALE	38	P24
19	T1	39	P25
20	V_{ss}	40	V_{cc}

Types 8035, 8039, 8048, 8049, 8648 and 8748 all 40-pin DIL

1	T0	21	P20
2	XTAL1	22	P21
3	XTAL2	23	P22
4	RESET	24	P23
5	SS	25	PROG
6	INT	26	V_{dd}
7	EA	27	P10
8	RD	28	P11
9	PSEN	29	P12
10	WR	30	P13
11	ALE	31	P14
12	DB0	32	P15
13	DB1	33	P16
14	DB2	34	P17
15	DB3	35	P24
16	DB4	36	P25
17	DB5	37	P26
18	DB6	38	P27
19	DB7	39	T1
20	V_{ss}	40	V_{cc}

INTEL 8048 SERIES

Signal functions

DB0 – DB7	8-bit bidirectional data bus
P00 – P07	8-bit I/O port (port 0)
P10 – P17	I/O port (port 1)
P20 – P27	I/O port (port 2)
XTAL1, XTAL2	Clock oscillator connections
T0, T1	Testable inputs
INT	Interrupt input (active low)
RESET	Reset input
EA	External access input used to access external program memory
SS	Single step input
ALE	Address latch enable timing output
WR	Write strobe output (active low)
RD	Read strobe output (active low)
PSEN	Program store enable output for use with external memory (active low)
AN0, AN1	Analogue inputs (8022 only)
PROG	Program pulse for EPROM (8748) input–output strobe for 8243 I/O expander
V_{ss}	0 V supply pin
V_{cc}	Main supply pin
AV_{cc}	Supply for A/D converter
V_{ref}	A/D converter reference voltage
AV_{ss}	A/D converter ground line
V_{th}	Port 0 input threshold volts (8022 only)
Substrate	Used for A/D bypassing capacitors

Power requirements

V_{cc} +5 V ± 10%
V_{ss} 0 V
V_{dd} (8748) +25 V for programming
             +5 V for normal running
Supply current   8048, 8748   135 mA
                 8039, 8049   170 mA
On 8021 and 8022 V_{cc} 5.5 V ± 1 V
                     AV_{cc} 5.5 V ± 1 V
                     Current   100 mA

Input–output

On all 8040 and 8030 series devices two 8-bit input–output ports are provided and the data bus may also be used as a bidirectional 8-bit data port. Inputs and outputs are TTL compatible with outputs driving one TTL load. On port 1 lines 0 and 1 can sink up to 7 mA current.

The T1 input can act as a zero crossing detector and may also be used as a clock input for the internal counter.

On the 8022 two analogue signal inputs are provided (AN1 and AN2) and these may be selected by software to feed the internal A/D converter.

Interrupt facilities

This series of processors has a single-level interrupt scheme with two basic interrupts, one from the external INT pin and the other from the timer/counter.

A reset causes a jump to program memory location 0, while external interrupt jumps to location 3 and timer counter interrupt goes to location 7. External and timer interrupts can be disabled by software as required. Nested interrupts are not advisable on this processor.

Instruction set

A total of 96 instructions is provided for the main 8048 series devices. The 8021 has a subset of only 64 instructions, whilst the 8022 also has a subset with 74 instructions, among which are some to deal with the analogue input signals.

Arithmetic

All arithmetic and logic is handled via the 8-bit accumulator. For arithmetic only ADD and ADD with carry are provided, but subtraction can be achieved by complementing and adding. A decimal adjust instruction is available for BCD addition. The accumulator can be incremented, decremented, complemented and cleared and there is a swap facility to swap the higher and lower 4 bit nibbles.

Logic functions include AND, OR, EXCLUSIVE OR and both right and left shifts and rotates. It is also possible to use OR and AND functions on data to and from some of the ports.

Data transfers

A wide selection of instructions allow data to be loaded immediately into the accumulator or registers and also to be transferred between the accumulator, registers and the RAM data memory. The program status word may also be moved to and from the accumulator.

Further instructions allow data to be transferred to or from the input–output ports or data bus and the accumulator.

Branch and jump

A total of 16 branch on test and unconditional jump type instructions are provided. The tests cover zero and carry states of the accumulator, as well as the states of the T0 and T1 inputs, timer and interrupt status, and also individual accumulator bits.

A subroutine CALL is provided. There are two jumps which are unconditional and allow the program to move to a new page.

Miscellaneous

A set of instructions is included to control operation of the timer/counter and to enable or disable interrupts. Memory bank and register select instructions are included to allow access to the two program memory banks and to the alternate set of working registers.

Registers may be incremented or decremented and there are instructions for controlling the flag bits in the status word.

In addition the 8022 has instructions for selecting one of the analogue inputs and for initiating A/D conversion and putting the result into the accumulator.

The 8021 and 8022 do not have register or memory bank select instructions and the 8021 has no interrupt facility.

Addressing

Program addressing is generally within the current page. Data addressing is normally via registers R0 and R1, although all registers in the selected bank can be accessed directly. Indexing is readily achieved by incrementing R0 or R1.

Timing

All instructions for the 8048 series take one or two cycles. For the 8048, 8035, 8648 and 8748 the clock is normally set at 6 MHz, giving a cycle time of 2.5 μs. The 8039 and 8049 run at a clock frequency of 11 MHz, giving a cycle time of 1.36 μs.

Slower versions of the 8039/8049 coded 8039-6, 8049-6 are available. They run at 6 MHz whilst the 8748-8 and 8035-8 run at a clock rate of 3.6 MHz.

The 8021 uses a 3.6 MHz crystal to give a cycle time of 8.4 μs, whilst the 8022 also runs at this speed. The A/D converter takes four cycle times for a conversion.

Support devices

Only one support chip is produced specifically for the 8048 series. This is the 8243 input–output expander. This permits 4 bits from port 2 on the 8048 type device to be expanded to produce four separate 4-bit I/O ports. 8243 devices can be cascaded to provide any desired number of ports.

Because the 8048 devices are compatible with the 8080/8085 type bus any of the peripheral devices designed for use with the 8080/85 may be used with the 8048 processors.

INTEL 8051 SERIES

One group of microcomputer devices recently introduced by Intel is the MCS51 family, of which the 8051 is the basic type. The family currently contains three 8-bit single-chip microcomputers, whose design concepts are similar to those used for the highly popular 8048 series. In the new family, however, a much enhanced architecture has been employed and the original 8048 instruction set has been expanded.

The 8051 contains a 4096 byte on-chip program ROM which is four times as large as that on the 8048 and twice the size of the ROM on the 8049 microcomputer. On the 8051 the RAM has also been expanded to 128 bytes. Other enhancements include twin counter timers, a full duplex serial I/O channel and a much improved interrupt system. On the software side there is a more powerful arithmetic and logic capability and efficient data handling.

Typically the single-chip microcomputers are used for dedicated controller type systems which often work in real time so that execution speed is important. The 8051 with its more efficient arithmetic is likely to be very useful for digital filters and servo systems where fairly complex data processing is required.

In terms of computing power the 8051 series compares favourably with such microcomputers as the Motorola MC6801 and Zilog Z8 types and could be competitive with them. It may have some advantages in being upward compatible with the 8048 as far as software is concerned.

The basic 8051 type comes with a mask programmed ROM for the program instruction storage and is best suited to applications where medium to high volume production is likely. For prototype development and limited production the 8751 is available with a UV eraseable PROM for program storage. The third device available is the 8031, intended for use with an external ROM.

Prime manufacturer

Intel Corporation.

Devices available

8031   Microcomputer with no ROM, 128 byte RAM, 32 I/O lines
8051   4096 byte mask ROM, 128 byte RAM, 32 I/O lines
8751   As 8051 but with UV eraseable PROM

Alternative source devices

None at present.

Architecture

Internally the arrangement of the 8051 is very complex and fig. 3.4, showing its architecture, has been very much simplified to show the general organisation of the microcomputer.

Like the 8048 devices this is a register orientated type of CPU. In the 128-byte RAM area, which has addresses from 0 to 127, one of four banks of eight 8-bit working registers may be selected for use as scratchpad or general

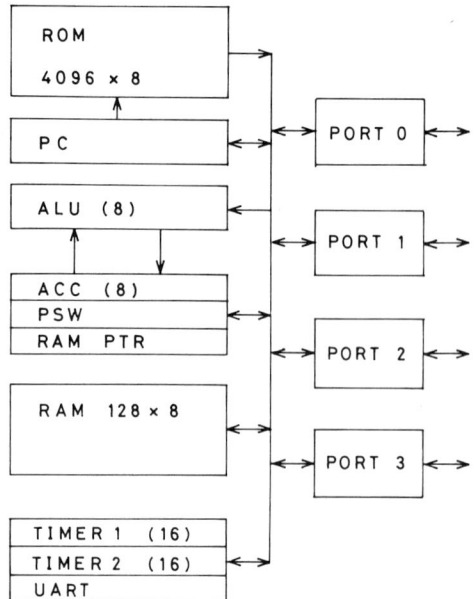

Fig. 3.4

purpose registers. In the selected register bank two registers may be used as data pointers for indirect selection of any location in the RAM or in the special function register area between locations 128 and 255.

A set of 20 special function registers is provided on the CPU chip. These include the accumulator, status register, I/O port registers, timer and serial I/O registers, interrupt control and external RAM data pointer registers.

The 8051 operates with completely separate program and data memory spaces, each of which may be up to 65 kbytes long. The on-chip ROM when fitted takes up the first 4 kbytes of the program memory space. On-chip RAM and registers are separately addressed from the external data memory. A 16-bit program counter and a 16-bit data pointer register control addressing to the external program and data memories. When external RAM and ROM are to be used the address and data are transmitted via I/O ports 0 and 2. Data and the lower 8 address bits are multiplexed via port 0, whilst the upper 8 address bits pass through port 2.

An 8-bit stack pointer register allows the generation of stacks for data storage within the RAM area. Individual stacks may be up to 128 bytes long.

There are two 16-bit timer/counters on the chip which may be configured in various ways, including two 8-bit timers with 8-bit prescaler counters.

Serial and parallel communication with peripherals may be achieved via the on-chip serial channel or via the four 8-bit parallel ports.

Package

40-pin dual in line type

Pin connections

1	P1-0	21	P2-0 (A8)
2	P1-1	22	P2-1 (A9)
3	P1-2	23	P2-2 (A10)
4	P1-3	24	P2-3 (A11)

INTEL 8051 SERIES

5	P1-4	25	P2-4 (A12)
6	P1-5	26	P2-5 (A13)
7	P1-6	27	P2-6 (A14)
8	P1-7	28	P2-7 (A15)
9	RST/VPD	29	PSEN
10	P3-0 (RXD)	30	ALE/PROG
11	P3-1 (TXD)	31	EA/V_{dd}
12	P3-2 (INT0)	32	P0-7 (AD7)
13	P3-3 (INT1)	33	P0-6 (AD6)
14	P3-4 (T0)	34	P0-5 (AD5)
15	P3-5 (T1)	35	P0-4 (AD4)
16	P3-6 (WR)	36	P0-3 (AD3)
17	P3-7 (RD)	37	P0-2 (AD2)
18	XTAL2	38	P0-1 (AD1)
19	XTAL1	39	P0-0 (AD0)
20	V_{ss}	40	V_{cc}

Signal functions

P0-0 to P0-7	Port 0 bidirectional
P1-0 to P1-7	Port 1 bidirectional
P2-0 to P2-7	Port 2 bidirectional
P3-0 to P3-7	Port 3 bidirectional
AD0 to AD7	Multiplexed address or data
A8 to A15	Address outputs for external memory
RXD	Serial data in (async) or in/out (sync)
TXD	Serial data out (async) or clock (sync)
INT0, INT1	Interrupt or counter gate inputs
T0, T1	Counter clock inputs
WR	Write strobe output
RD	Read strobe output
RST/VPD	Reset input and standby RAM power input
ALE	Address latch enable output
PROG	Programming pulse input for EPROM
PSEN	Enable output for external program memory
EA	Select input for external program memory
XTAL1, XTAL2	Oscillator timing pins
V_{dd}	21 V EPROM programming supply input
V_{cc}, V_{ss}	Power supply inputs

Power requirement

V_{cc} +5 V ± 5%
V_{ss} 0 V
Supply current 150 mA
Power down current 20 mA

Temperature range

0°C to +70°C

Input–output

All logical input and output signals on the 8051 type devices are TTL compatible and outputs will normally be capable of driving one TTL load. However the outputs from port 0 can drive up to two TTL loads.

The four input–output ports P0 – P3 may be used as 8-bit parallel ports, or alternatively each line may be selected individually as input or output to give up to 32 independent I/O lines. The ports are quasi-bidirectional and for output bits are simply set to the desired state. For input a '1' state is output to that line of the port and then on reading data it will respond to the input signal.

For expanded operation with external memory ports 0 and 2 are used as the data and address buses. Data I/O and the lower 8 bits of the address are multiplexed via port 0 and the upper 8 address bits are output via port 2.

Port 3 also has alternative functions. Two lines may be used for transmitting and receiving data on the serial data channel. Two more lines are used as interrupt inputs and two for inputs to the on-chip counter/timers, whilst the remaining two lines act as read and write strobes for the external data or program memories.

The serial channel has 4 registers which are located in the special function register group. One is used for data transmission and a second acts as the mode control register. Two registers are used for the read function to provide a fully buffered operation avoiding loss of data if the CPU is busy. All common asynchronous transmission formats can be handled. Timing for asynchronous mode is derived from counter No. 1, which may be clocked by either the CPU clock or an external clock. There is also a synchronous serial mode for use in multiprocessor systems and providing a very high speed transmission mode.

The two on-chip 16-bit counter/timers each have a pair of 8-bit registers which may be used in a variety of configurations as either counters, timers or prescalers. Each counter may be driven from an external clock applied via T0 and T1 input lines on port 3. When the CPU clock is used it is automatically divided by 12 in frequency before being applied to the selected counter.

When several processors are linked together via their serial ports it is possible to configure each processor to operate as either a master or slave. This allows distributed processing systems to be set up if desired.

Interrupt facilities

On the 8051 series of microcomputers there are five hardware interrupts available. Two are external and triggered by inputs on lines INT0 or INT1 of port 3. The two on-chip counter/timers provide individual interrupts, and there is also an interrupt available from the serial input–output channel. Each of the interrupts may be masked either individually or globally and each causes a branch to its own vector address in the program memory and thence to the appropriate service routine.

External interrupt signals are active low and may be wire-ORed from several sources. The interrupt inputs may also be programmed to respond to either level or transition type signals.

Instruction set

For the 8051 series of microcomputers the instruction set is a somewhat expanded version of that used for the 8048 series. A total of 111 different instructions is provided and these may be grouped as some 42 different types of instruction. It would be possible to run machine code programs written for an 8048 directly on the 8051.

INTEL 8051 SERIES

Arithmetic and logic

A selection of 8-bit arithmetic operations may be carried out in the accumulator. These include addition, subtraction, multiplication and division. The multiplication and division functions appear to use on-chip hardware since they are very fast in execution. For BCD arithmetic a decimal adjust type operation is provided for addition, but subtraction must be dealt with by user written software. These facilities are much more versatile than for an 8048, which has only the addition facility.

Logical operations provided in the accumulator are AND, OR and EXCLUSIVE OR. It is also possible to carry out these functions on either RAM or special function registers using immediate data as one of the inputs. Both the accumulator and any of the RAM locations or special function registers may be incremented, decremented or complemented. Shift or rotate functions are available on the accumulator only. Facilities are also provided for setting or clearing individual bits of data in the accumulator, RAM or special registers. Some logic functions may also be used on individual bits.

Data transfers

There are 30 instructions available for moving data around between the accumulator, registers, memory and stack. Most of these are MOV instructions with a range of addressing modes. Exchange instructions are available for operating on data in memory and accumulator. The stack pointer allows a data stack to be set up in the RAM and there are PUSH and POP instructions allowing directly addressed RAM data to be moved to and from the stack. Most other processors only allow data contained in the accumulator to be moved to and from the stack.

An interesting feature of the 8051 is that it provides a bit manipulation facility in which 128 individual bits in the memory may be directly addressed and operated upon.

Data transfers to the input and output ports are memory mapped, since the port registers are included in the bank of special function registers on the chip.

Branch and jump

There are 13 conditional jump operations and 4 unconditional jumps with various addressing modes. Tests include zero and carry status as well as individual bit tests on selected data. Some instructions include a decrement or compare instruction as well as the test and jump.

Two subroutine call instructions are provided with direct addressing using either 11 or 16-bit address data.

Addressing modes

Data within the internal RAM may be addressed either directly or indirectly through registers R0 and R1 of the current bank of registers in use. This also applies to data in the special function registers, which effectively occupy the upper part of the RAM address space from 128 to 255.

Jump and branch instructions are normally relative in a 256-byte page of ROM address space. Direct jumps and calls may also be made within a 2 kbyte block of program memory as with the 8048. An additional feature of the 8051 is the long jump or call to any location within a 65k address space, which is useful if an expanded program space uses external memory. These facilities avoid the requirement for program memory bank switching that is used in the 8048 series.

External data memory is accessed by using the special data pointer register to provide a 16-bit address. This may be set up by data transfers from A to the data pointer and then using an indirect move instruction to transfer data between A and the memory location pointed to by the data pointer register.

Indexed addressing is readily achieved by incrementing or decrementing registers R0 or R1 and using indirect addressing via these registers.

Timing

The on-chip clock may be controlled by an external crystal of frequency 1.2 MHz to 12 MHz. Alternatively an external clock signal may be input via the XTAL1 pin. Using a 12 MHz clock the instruction cycle time will be approximately 1 μs and most instructions will execute in either 1 or 2 μs. Multiplication and division take 4 μs each for execution.

Support chips

When the 8051 is used with external program or data memory expansion a number of 8080/8085 type support chips may be used as follows:

8212	8-bit I/O port
8282	8-bit I/O port
8283	8-bit I/O port

The above devices may be used as address latches when an external RAM or ROM is added to the system.

8255A	Programmable parallel I/O (3 × 8 bit ports)
8251A	Programmable serial I/O
8353A	Programmable interval timer
8279	Programmable keyboard and display interface
8291	IEEE488 GPIB listener/talker
8292	IEEE488 GPIB controller
8286/8287	Bidirectional bus drivers

Development aids

Full software and hardware development facilities for the 8051 series are provided on the Intel Intellec series systems. In-circuit emulation is provided by ICE51. There is also a conversion program for converting 8048 machine code to run on the 8051.

A special personality card allows the 8751 EPROM to be programmed directly in Intellec development systems.

INTEL 8080A

Intel originally developed the 8080A microprocessor as a rather enhanced version of their 8008 device, which was the first 8-bit microprocessor to be made available. At the time of its introduction the 8080 had virtually no competition and was the most powerful 8-bit microprocessor available. As a result it became very popular and today has become an industry standard type and possibly the most widely used microprocessor.

Being first in the field, however, the 8080 does have some shortcomings in comparison with its later rivals such as the Motorola 6800, MOS Technology 6502 and Zilog Z80. One problem with the 8080 is that it requires three separate power supply lines, whereas newer types normally operate from a single +5 V supply. The clock and control arrangements for the 8080 are also rather complex and usually necessitate the addition of two support chips to produce a working CPU. Intel's later 8085 microprocessor overcomes these problems and is likely to slowly replace the 8080 in all new system designs, since it is software compatible with the 8080 type.

As an 8-bit nMOS microprocessor the 8080 falls in the same class as the Motorola 6800, MOS Technology 6502, Signetics 2650 and perhaps the RCA1802 types, but is rather less powerful than the Motorola 6809 or Zilog Z80. One advantage of the 8080 is that it is available from several manufacturers and being popular is well supported by applications software. For new designs, however, the 8085 might be a better choice since it is likely to produce a simpler hardware design.

Prime manufacturer

Intel Corporation.

Devices available

8080A Basic CPU chip

There are variants for speed and temperature range as well as military specification devices.

Alternative source devices

Advanced Micro Devices

    Am9080A   Equivalent to 8080A

Nippon Electric Co. (N.E.C.)

    μPD8080A   Variant of the 8080A

Mitsubishi Electric Corp.

    MSL8080A   Equivalent to 8080A

National Semiconductor

    INS8080A   Equivalent to 8080A

Siemens A. G.

    SAB8080A   Equivalent to 8080A

Mullard-Signetics Ltd.

    MP8080A   Equivalent to 8080A

Texas Instruments Inc.

    TMS8080A   Equivalent to 8080A

OKI Semiconductor

    MSM8080AS   Equivalent to 8080A

Note that, unlike Motorola, Intel do not operate a mask interchange scheme with second source suppliers. In general the alternative devices, although equivalent, may not perform in exactly the same way as an Intel 8080A. This is particularly true for N.E.C., who have made some slight enhancements to the basic 8080A design. It is therefore wise to compare the data sheet of an equivalent device with that of the Intel type.

Architecture

It will be seen from fig. 3.5 that the 8080A is to some extent a register orientated CPU with a bank of 6 general purpose 8-bit registers which may be used for temporary data storage.

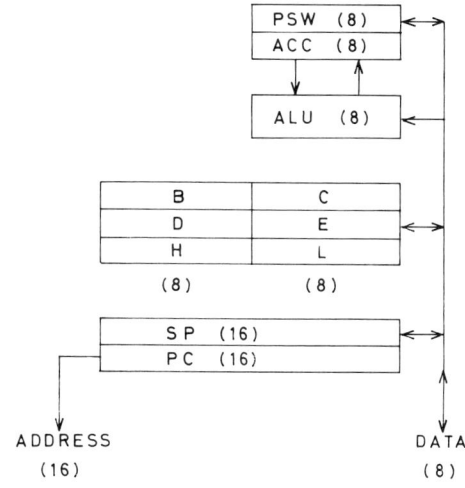

Fig. 3.5

Arithmetic and logic operations are handled by an 8-bit accumulator (A) and there is an 8-bit status word (PSW) with flags for carry, sign, zero and BCD carry as well as a parity flag bit.

A 16-bit program counter register (PC) allows the 8080A to access a full 65k of memory via a 16-bit address bus. There is also a 16-bit stack pointer register for data stacks and for saving CPU register contents during subroutine or interrupt operations. It should be noted that a separate memory may be used for the stack. The addresses may overlap those of the main data memory, since the 8080A provides control signals to differentiate between these two memory areas.

The three pairs of general purpose registers may also be used as data pointers or index registers and can be used for some 16-bit functions such as addition.

One feature of the 8080A is that its 8-bit data bus is multiplexed to allow control and timing signals to be output from the CPU. External logic is required to separate the data and control signals. An external 2-phase clock will be required and the internal timing sequence of the 8080A is fairly complex.

INTEL 8080A

Package

40-pin DIL type may be ceramic or plastic

For Intel prefix C or D is ceramic whilst P is plastic
Other makes use suffix C for ceramic or P for plastic
TI use suffix J for ceramic and N for plastic
AMD use suffix D for ceramic packages

Pin connections

1	A10	21	HLDA
2	V_{ss}	22	$\phi 1$
3	D4	23	READY
4	D5	24	WAIT
5	D6	25	A0 (LSB)
6	D7 (MSB)	26	A1
7	D3	27	A2
8	D2	28	V_{dd}
9	D1	29	A3
10	D0 (LSB)	30	A4
11	V_{bb}	31	A5
12	RESET	32	A6
13	HOLD	33	A7
14	INT	34	A8
15	$\phi 2$	35	A9
16	INTE	36	A15 (MSB)
17	DBIN	37	A12
18	WR	38	A13
19	SYNC	39	A14
20	V_{cc}	40	A11

Signal functions

A0–A15	Address bus output
D0–D7	Data bus bidirectional and control output
$\phi 1, \phi 2$	Two-phase clock inputs
INT	Interrupt input
INTE	Interrupt enable output
RESET	Reset input (active high)
HOLD	Hold input causes CPU to release address and data bus lines for external device
HOLDA	Hold acknowledge output
WAIT	Output indicating CPU in wait state
READY	Input to request CPU wait condition
WR	Read/write control output (write low)
DBIN	Output indicating data bus can accept input
SYNC	Timing pulse at start of each CPU cycle
$V_{bb}, V_{cc}, V_{dd}, V_{ss}$	Power supply inputs

Power requirements

V_{bb}	$-5\text{ V} \pm 5\%$
V_{cc}	$+5\text{ V} \pm 5\%$
V_{dd}	$+12\text{ V} \pm 5\%$
V_{ss}	0 V
I_{dd}	40 mA
I_{cc}	60 mA
I_{bb}	100 μA

Temperature range

Standard 0°C to +70°C
Suffix C (AMD) or L (TI)

Extended −25°C to +85°C
Suffix I (AMD)

Military −55°C to +125°C
Prefix M (Intel) or suffix M (AMD)

Input–output

The 8080 has special instructions for input and output of data to external devices and may address up to 256 I/O ports. External address decoding and bus control logic will be required. Alternatively, memory mapped input–output may be used with the I/O device being treated as a memory location.

All logic signals into and out of the 8080A are TTL compatible and output lines can drive one standard TTL load.

Interrupt facilities

The 8080A provides a maskable external interrupt via the INT input but has no non-maskable interrupt facility. However, the external system may be used to make the CPU execute an RST instruction to provide an operation similar to a non-maskable interrupt.

During interrupt processing the CPU expects to receive from the interrupting device an op code to start its service routine. This will normally be a CALL or RST instruction to send the CPU to a subroutine which services the interrupt. The CPU does not automatically save the register contents as an MC6800 does when an interrupt is triggered. By calling a subroutine the program counter will be stored on the stack and other CPU registers must be saved by program if desired.

There is no interrupt priority system except that a RESET will inhibit all interrupts until the reset sequence is complete. External logic can be used to deal with interrupt priority if required.

The interrupt acknowledge output is used to indicate to the interrupting device that an interrupt has been started and that an op code to the service routine must be input via the data bus. Other timing signals on the control output via the data bus will also indicate interrupt processing.

Instruction set

For the 8080A the instruction set consists of some 82 basic instructions providing a reasonably flexible set. In some cases separate instructions are provided for variations on a basic operation.

Arithmetic and logic
Addition and subtraction of 8-bit numbers either with or without a carry are catered for in the accumulator. It is also possible to carry out 16-bit additions using registers B,C or D,E or H,L as register pairs. There is a facility for BCD addition using the accumulator register.

Logical operations include AND, OR and EX-CLUSIVE OR in the accumulator only. It is also possible to shift or rotate the accumulator either left or right and to increment, decrement, complement or compare its contents. Note that unlike other processors such as the 6800 and Z80 these operations cannot be carried out on memory data.

Data transfer

A range of instructions is available for data transfers between the accumulator and the other registers and memory. Push and pull instructions allow data to be moved to and from a stack in memory.

The pairs of registers may be used as data pointers to allow indexing and indirect addressing, but indexed operation is not quite as straightforward as on later microprocessors.

The 8080A maintains a separate address space which may be used for input–output devices by using the special input and output instructions. This allows up to 256 I/O devices to be separately addressed.

Branch and jump

There are 8 conditional jump instructions covering zero, sign, carry and parity status and there is one unconditional jump instruction. A useful facility provided on the 8080A is the set of 8 conditional call instructions for subroutines as well as the normal call instruction. The 8080A also allows 8 contitional returns from subroutines. An indirect jump instruction is provided which uses the contents of the H,L register pair as a destination address. Finally, there is a Restart (RST) instruction which operates in much the same way as a subroutine call and may be used for software interrupt.

Timing

There is no internal clock for the 8080A CPU and an external 2-phase clock must be supplied. This clock has unequal $\phi 1$ and $\phi 2$ periods and is best generated by the special clock generator chip type 8224. Normally the clock has a period of 0.5 μs which requires an 18 MHz crystal for the 8224 circuit. With the standard clock an instruction cycle takes 4 clock periods on average, giving instruction execution times of from 2 to 5 μs for most instructions. The actual timing sequence is relatively complex, varying from one type of instruction to another.

There are versions of the 8080A which provide faster operation:

8080A-1	Clock period 320 ns
8080A-2	Clock period 380 ns
Am9080A-4	Clock period 250 ns (AMD only)

Support chips

There are several support chips for use with the 8080A CPU, of which the 8224 and 8228 are normally required to produce a working CPU system. Types available are:

8224	Clock generator
8228	System controller for 8080 bus system
8238	System controller for Am9080-4
INS8154	RAM and I/O chip
8202	Dynamic RAM memory controller
8212	8-bit I/O port
8214	Priority interrupt control unit
8251	Programmable serial I/O interface
8253	Triple 16-bit programmable timer
8255A	Programmable parallel I/O 24 lines
8257	Direct memory access controller
8259	Programmable interrupt controller
Am9517	High speed DMA controller
8271	Floppy disk controller
8273	Serial I/O (HDLC/SDLC) controller
8275	Programmable CRT display controller
8278	Programmable keyboard and display controller
8279	Keyboard and display controller
8291	IEEE488 GP instrument bus controller
8292	IEEE488 GPIB controller
8294	Data encryption unit
8295	Dot matrix printer controller

Development aids

From Intel several development systems in the Intellec series will support both software and hardware development. Intellec systems provide a floppy disk based operating system, editor, assemblers and loaders as well as in-circuit emulation and PROM programming facilities, allowing complete development and debugging of 8080 based projects.

N.E.C produce the TK80, which is a single-board system for evaluation of 8080 based systems and software development at the machine code level.

National Semiconductor produce a development system with the name Starplex. This like the Intel system is floppy disk based and provides full software development and debugging, as well as hardware emulation for the 8080 type processor.

Most of the general microprocessor systems such as the Futuredata AMDS2300 or Tektronix 8002 provide facilities for 8080 software development and many have hardware emulation as well. Since the 8080 is a very popular and widely used type there are many systems available which can handle it.

There are also many 8080 based microcomputer boards on the market, which will allow systems to be readily assembled from standard ready made boards.

INTEL 8085A

Following their introduction of the highly successful 8080A microprocessor Intel have developed an improved version in the 8085. This 8-bit nMOS microprocessor is software compatible with the original 8080 whilst overcoming the disadvantages of that processor and providing some degree of enhancement.

Main advantages of the 8085 over the earlier 8080 are that it uses a single +5 V supply rather than three separate supply rails. There is also an on-chip clock generator. In the 8085 the timing and control have also been simplified and the data bus is no longer multiplexed to carry status information. One enhancement of the 8085 is the provision of a serial I/O channel on the CPU chip.

The 8085 is a typical medium power 8-bit microprocessor having similar capabilities to the Motorola 6802 and the MOS Technology 6500 series, whilst being somewhat less powerful than the Motorola 6809 and Zilog Z80. In some ways the 8085 shares with the 8080 the disadvantage of being slightly less effective in some operations due to its software compatibility.

Generally the 8085 is likely to be used in applications where an 8080 might normally be chosen, since it produces a rather simpler hardware system. For designers who have used the 8080 type processor it is perhaps an obvious choice since its software is compatible. It is likely that this processor will in fact gradually replace the 8080 in new projects where an 8080 might have been used.

An 8085 system will normally be able to make use of any peripheral chips originally designed for use with the 8080.

Prime manufacturer

Intel Corporation.

Devices available

   8085A   Standard 8085 CPU chip
   8085A-2 High speed version of 8085

Alternative source devices

Advanced Micro Devices

   Am8085A   Standard 8085 CPU

Mitsubishi Electric Co.

   MSL8085A Standard 8085 CPU

Siemens A.G.

   SAB8085   Standard 8085 part

Nippon Electric Co.

   µPD8085A   Standard 8085 CPU
   µPD8085A-2 High speed version

Toshiba

   T8085A   Standard 8085 CPU

Architecture

Generally the internal architecture of the 8085 follows that of the earlier 8080, as will be seen by comparing fig. 3.6 with fig. 3.5.

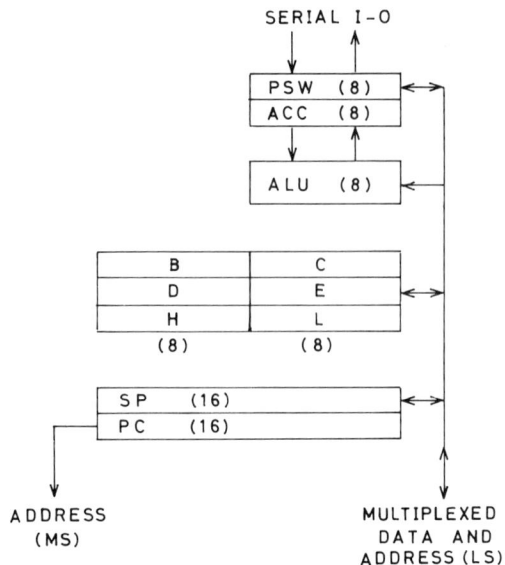

Fig. 3.6

An 8-bit accumulator is used for arithmetic and logical operations and an 8-bit status register provides condition flags for test and branch operations.

A 16-bit program counter (PC) permits access to 65 kbytes of memory, which is common to both program instructions and data. There is also a single 16-bit stack pointer which allows the use of variable length stacks anywhere within the address space for either data storage or for saving contents of CPU based registers.

Like the 8080 the 8085 has three pairs of 8-bit general purpose registers which may be used for data storage or as data pointers. In the latter role they may also function as index registers, since there is no dedicated index register in the 8085 CPU. It is possible to carry out a limited number of 16-bit operations with these registers, including addition.

One enhancement provided in the 8085 is the facility for serial input and output from the accumulator. The 8085 also has improved facilities for hardware interrupt operation.

It should be noted that on the 8085 the data bus is now multiplexed with the lower 8 bits of the address bus, and external logic is required to separate these signals. This may be seen as a disadvantage compared with other processors such as the 6800 and Z80, which do not use multiplexed buses.

An on-chip clock generator and internal control logic replace the 8224 and 8228 chips normally required by the 8080, thus simplifying the system.

Package

   40-pin dual in line type   may be ceramic or plastic

   Intel use prefix C or D for ceramic and P for plastic types

INTEL 8085A

Pin connections

1	X1	21	A8
2	X2	22	A9
3	RESET OUT	23	A10
4	SOD	24	A11
5	SID	25	A12
6	TRAP	26	A13
7	RST 7.5	27	A14
8	RST 6.5	28	A15
9	RST 5.5	29	S0
10	INTR	30	ALE
11	INTA	31	WR
12	AD0	32	RD
13	AD1	33	S1
14	AD2	34	IO/M
15	AD3	35	READY
16	AD4	36	RESET IN
17	AD5	37	CLK OUT
18	AD6	38	HLDA
19	AD7	39	HOLD
20	V_{ss}	40	V_{cc}

Signal functions

AD0 – AD7	Lower 7 bit address outputs multiplexed with data bus input–output. Tri-state
A8 – A15	Address bus output. Tri-state
S0, S1	Status outputs indicating CPU cycle
ALE	Address latch enable output
RD	Read strobe output tri-state (active low)
WR	Write strobe output tri-state (active low)
READY	Ready input requesting bus for peripheral
HOLD	Hold input request to release buses
HLDA	Hold acknowledge output
INTR	Maskable interrupt input
INTA	Interrupt acknowledge output
RST5.5, RST6.5, RST7.5	Maskable interrupts inputs
TRAP	Non-maskable interrupt input
RESET IN	Reset input (active low)
RESET OUT	Status output indicating reset cycle
X1, X2	Timing crystal pins for clock generator
CLK OUT	CPU clock output
IO/M	Output signal to select either I/O or memory
SID	Serial data input
SOD	Serial data output
V_{cc}, V_{ss}	Power supply inputs

Power requirements

V_{cc} +5 V ± 5%
V_{ss} 0 V
Supply current   170 mA maximum

Temperature range

Standard   0°C to +70°C
Military   −55°C to +125°C   Prefix M

Input–output

All signals into and out of the 8085 are TTL compatible and the outputs are capable of driving a single TTL load.

Data input and output to peripheral devices may be either memory mapped or directly addressed. In the direct addressing mode special input–output instructions are used and an 8-bit I/O device address is output via the address bus to select one of up to 256 different I/O devices. Address decoding for the peripheral devices is external to the CPU. In memory mapped I/O the peripheral device is simply treated as memory and a normal data move instruction is used for data input–output.

The SID and SOD lines allow bit-by-bit serial transfers of data to be made to and from the accumulator with access to the most significant bit of the accumulator. This is a simple serial data interface but may prove useful in many applications.

Direct memory access may be achieved with the 8085 by putting the processor into a hold state so that it releases the address and data buses. External logic will be required to control the DMA operation.

Interrupt facilities

Like the 8080 there is a maskable interrupt request line INTR for the 8085 and its associated INTA acknowledge output. There are also three further maskable interrupts, RST 5.5, RST 6.5 and RST 7.5, of which the 7.5 has the highest priority and the 5.5 lowest priority. Of these the 5.5 and 6.5 inputs are level sensitive whilst 7.5 is edge triggered.

The 8085 has a non-maskable interrupt TRAP which may be used as either a level sensitive or edge triggered input. The TRAP interrupt operates in a similar fashion to the RST type interrupts, except that it cannot be masked.

When an INTR interrupt occurs the CPU will expect to receive, via the data bus, a vector address to the start of the service routine and will then execute a subroutine call operation to that address. This operation will cause the data in the program counter to be saved on the stack. Any other CPU register contents must be saved by program instructions, since there is no automatic save sequence as in, for example, the Motorola 6800 type processors.

The RST and TRAP interrupts are vectored to addresses at the bottom of memory as follows:

TRAP 24 (hex.)
RST 5.5 2C (hex.)
RST 6.5 34 (hex.)
RST 7.5 3C (hex.)

Reset causes a branch to memory location 0000 and this must be the start of the CPU initialisation sequence.

Where a larger number of interrupts are used and a priority system is desired then external logic must be used to determine the priority of individual interrupts.

Instruction set

Basically the instruction set of the 8085 is compatible with that of the 8080, except that the 8085 has a number of extra instructions to deal with serial input–output and interrupts.

INTEL 8085A

Arithmetic and logic
The accumulator may be used for addition and subtraction of 8-bit numbers with or without a carry. There is also a BCD addition facility but no direct BCD subtraction. It is also possible to carry out 16-bit addition using some of the pairs of general purpose registers B,C, D,E or H,L.

Logical operations provided in the accumulator are AND, OR and EXCLUSIVE OR, but none are available for the other general purpose registers. It is possible to carry out left and right shift or rotate operations, incrementing, decrementing, comparison and complementing on data in the accumulator. These actions are not available on memory as they are on the Motorola 6800.

Data transfer
A useful selection of instructions is provided for transfers of data between the registers within the CPU and also to and from the memory or I/O devices. Some data transfers may use 16 bits by using pairs of registers in the CPU. It is possible to pair the accumulator with the status register for some of these operations.

Data transfers via the serial channel make use of the two new instructions RIM and SIM which operate on the accumulator and cause the MSB to be input or output via the SID or SOD lines. These instructions also allow the interrupt mask bits to be read or set up within the accumulator.

Data transfers to memory or input–output peripheral devices is differentiated by the output status signal IO/M and for input–output direct to peripherals special input and output instructions are used instead of data move instructions.

The pairs of general purpose registers may be used as 16-bit data pointer registers for indirect and indexed modes of addressing, although indexed operation is not as simple as on some later types of microprocessor.

Branch and jump
Like the 8080 this processor has 8 conditional jumps as well as 8 conditional call to subroutine instructions. Unconditional jump and call instructions are also available and there is an indirect jump to a destination address held in the H,L register pair. Returns from subroutines may also be either conditional or unconditional.

Addressing modes
For the 8085 the addressing modes available are:

Direct
Register
Register indirect
Immediate

Timing

A standard 8085 CPU operates with a CPU clock of 3 MHz, and since there is a divide by two inside the chip will require a 6 MHz timing crystal. With this clock frequency the typical instruction cycle will take about 1.5 μs and average instructions will execute in 1.5 – 6 μs.

A faster version of the 8085 which will operate with a 5 MHz CPU clock is the 8085A-2. This will require a 10 MHz timing crystal. For both types it is also possible to use an R–C timing network instead of a quartz crystal for control of clock frequency.

The status output signals S0 and S1 are provided for external devices to allow determination of the status of the CPU and the stage of operation in an instruction cycle.

Support devices

Typically the 8085 may use support devices originally designed for use with the 8080 type CPU. Some of the support chips for use with the 8085 are:

8155	RAM, I/O, timer chip 256 byte RAM, 22 I/O lines
8156	Same as 8155 but with different enable logic
8202	Dynamic RAM controller
8212	8-bit input–output port
8214	Priority interrupt controller
8251	Programmable serial I/O interface
8253	Triple 16-bit programmable timer unit
8255A	Programmable parallel I/O 24 lines
8257	Direct memory access controller
8259	Programmable interrupt controller
8271	Floppy disk controller
8273	HDLC/SDLC serial I/O controller
8275	Programmable CRT controller
8278	Keyboard and display controller
8279	Keyboard and display controller
8291	IEEE488 bus controller
8292	IEEE488 bus controller
8295	Dot matrix printer controller

Development aids

From Intel there is a single-board evaluation and software development system the SDK85, which allows machine code to be entered via a hex keyboard and has a LED display to indicate register contents or display data outputs during execution of programs.

For system development Intel provide Intellec systems with full floppy disk based operating system, editors, assembler and debug facilities, as well as in-circuit emulation and hardware debugging.

Programs for the 8085 can readily be developed and tested on the many systems that support the 8080 microprocessor, since the two types have basically the same instruction set apart from the RIM and SIM instructions.

Multipurpose development systems such as the Tektronix 8002 and Futuredata AMDS2300 will support the 8085 and many systems will provide hardware emulation facilities.

MOSTEK 3870 SERIES

The 3870 group of single-chip microcomputers manufactured by Mostek are 8-bit devices using the nMOS process. They are in fact single-chip implementations of the Fairchild 2-chip F8 series microprocessors and are totally compatible with the F8 software and hardware.

Although not quite as powerful as some of the other 8-bit single-chip microcomputers the F8 and hence the 3870 are quite effective computers, and in the single-chip 3870 form are ideal for use as communications controllers and for other control type applications.

The 3870 contains on-chip mask programmed ROM for the program instructions and a small scratchpad ROM as well as an event counter/timer and a selection of input–output ports. The instruction set is rather limited but operation is quite fast in comparison with some other 8-bit single-chip types. Some versions of the 3870 provide larger memory capacity and serial input–output facilities.

Prime manufacturer

Mostek Corporation.

Devices available

MK3870 2 kbyte ROM, 64 × 8 RAM, 32 I/O lines, timer

MK3872 4 kbyte ROM, 128 × 8 RAM, 32 I/O lines, timer

MK3873 As 3870 but with serial I/O port

MK3874 As 3872 but ROM external in piggyback socket

Alternative source devices

Fairchild

F3870 Basic 3870 part 2k ROM, 32 I/O lines and timer

Motorola

MC3870 Basic 3870 part 2k ROM, 32 I/O lines and timer

Architecture

Basically the architecture of the 3870 consists of an F8 type 8-bit processor together with its associated mask programmed ROM, input–output ports and timer/counter on a single chip, as shown in fig. 3.7.

Arithmetic and logic functions are dealt with by an 8-bit accumulator and associated ALU, together with a 5-bit status register. Status flags are provided for carry, zero, overflow, minus and interrupt conditions.

An 11-bit program counter (PD) register addresses the program instructions in the 2k ROM and a second 11-bit stack pointer register (P) is provided. Two 11-bit data pointers (DC and DC1) are provided, but of these only DC can address the ROM directly. The contents of DC and DC1 can however be exchanged. An adder/incrementer may be used with both the data pointer DC and the program counter PD to provide relative addressing.

A 64-byte scratchpad RAM is provided and each

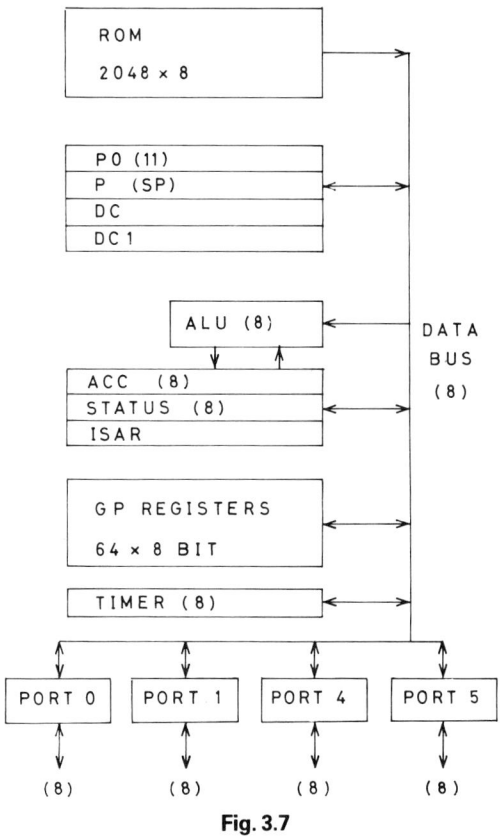

Fig. 3.7

location may be used as a working register. The first 12 registers in the RAM may be directly addressed by the CPU and registers 8 – 15 are allocated mnemonic names and are used for special operations for nested interrupts and subroutines. Register 9 is designed by the letter J, whilst locations 10 – 15 are paired off to form three 16-bit registers H, K and Q. All of the locations in the RAM may be addressed indirectly via the Indirect Scratchpad Address Register (ISAR).

An on-chip 8-bit down counter may be used as an event counter, interval timer or for pulse width measurement. This counter is used in conjunction with a prescaler which may be set for a division ratio of from 2 to 200. Control of the mode of operation of the timer and prescaler is governed by the 8-bit interrupt port register (port 6), of which only one bit (bit 7) is brought out to the EXT INT pin.

Four 8-bit input–output ports are provided for access to external devices and there is an on-chip clock generator which is controlled by external timing components.

Package

40-pin dual in line ceramic or plastic

Pin connections

1	XTL1	21	TEST
2	XTL2	22	P1-4
3	P0-0	23	P1-5
4	P0-1	24	P1-6
5	P0-2	25	P1-7
6	P0-3	26	P5-7

7	STROBE	27	P5-6
8	P4-0	28	P5-5
9	P4-1	29	P5-4
10	P4-2	30	P5-3
11	P4-3	31	P5-2
12	P4-4	32	P5-1
13	P4-5	33	P5-0
14	P4-6	34	P1-3
15	P4-7	35	P1-2
16	P0-7	36	P1-1
17	P0-6	37	P1-0
18	P0-5	38	EXT INT
19	P0-4	39	RESET
20	GND	40	V_{cc}

Signal functions

P0-0 to P0-7	Port 0 I/O 8 bits
P1-0 to P1-7	Port 1 I/O 8 bits
P4-0 to P4-7	Port 4 I/O 8 bits
P5-0 to P5-7	Port 5 I/O 8 bits
STROBE	Ready strobe output (active low)
RESET	Reset input (active low)
EXT INT	Inturrupt input (active high)
TEST	Test function input
XTL1, XTL2	Clock inputs
V_{cc} GND	Power supply inputs

Note on ports 0, 1, 4 and 5 the input–output logic signals are inverted logic.

When TEST is set high the internal data bus can be accessed via ports 4 and 5. Normally TEST is connected to GND.

Power requirements

V_{cc}	+5 V ± 10%
GND	0 V
Current	60–85 mA

Temperature range

Standard part	0°C to +70°C
F3870PL, F3870DL	−40°C to +85°C
F3870PM, F3870DM	−55°C to +125°C

Input–output

The four 8-bit input-output ports provide TTL compatible input and output capability, with outputs driving one TTL load. All signals operate with inverted logic.

When the counter is operated as an event counter it will count input pulses applied to the interrupt input. In the pulse width measurement mode the counter will count whilst a high input is applied to the interrupt input.

Interrupt facilities

Interrupts are generated either by the timer or by external signals on the INT input. Timer interrupts have priority. The interrupt vector for the timer is Hex 020, whilst for external interrupts it is Hex 0A0. Return address is automatically stored in stack register P and nested interrupts can be used by employing registers H, K and Q.

Instruction set

There are 76 instructions available. They are identical to those used by the Fairchild F8 microprocessor family, giving complete software compatibility.

Arithmetic and logic

For arithmetic a simple ADD instruction is provided and the carry is dealt with by a separate instruction. Subtraction is not provided as a discrete operation and must be achieved by using the complement and add technique. Instructions have been included to deal with BCD numbers.

Logical operations provided are AND, OR and EXCLUSIVE OR. There are also left and right shift instructions, giving either one or four bit shifts but no rotate instructions are provided. Other functions available are compare, complement, increment, decrement and clear.

Register and memory

Any of the 64 scratchpad memory locations may be accessed by loading the desired address into the ISAR. The first 12 locations may also be addressed directly and the registers designated J, H, K and Q may also be directly addressed. It is possible to manipulate the program counter P0, stack pointer P and the data counters DC and DC1 in various ways. Data transfers between P and K, P0 and Q, are possible and DC may be transferred to or from H or Q.

Branch and jump

A selection of conditional branch instructions is provided for testing the sign, carry, zero and overflow flags of the status register. There are also unconditional branches and jumps and subroutine call instructions.

Input–output

Data may be transferred to and from ports 0, 1, 4 and 5 by the use of four input–output instructions. The timer/counter can be accessed by input–output to port 7 and the control and interrupt operations are dealt with as port 6.

Timing

The internal oscillator may be used by simply grounding the XTL1 and XTL2 pins. Alternatively an external crystal, LC circuit or RC timing network may be used to determine the clock frequency. If an external clock generator is used its signal is fed in via the XTL2 pin with XTL1 left open.

Clock frequency may be from 1 MHz to 4 MHz. Instructions will execute in about 2 μs average with 4 MHz clock.

Support chips

None normally required.

Development aids

Mostek Corporation

Prototyping of hardware systems can be carried out by using the MK3874 chip, which can accept a 2716 or similar EPROM in a piggyback socket on the device package.

For software development the Z80 based MATRIX system can be used and provides text editors, assemblers and also facilities for program debugging.

Hardware systems can be evaluated using AIM70 modules, allowing in-circuit emulation and PROM programming facilities.

Fairchild

A range of FORMULATOR development systems is available for use with the 3870 and F8 type processors. These vary from simple keypad and display single-board systems up to a full floppy disk based development system. Editors, assemblers, PROM programming, emulation and debugging can be provided.

Motorola

EXORCISER and EXORTERM development systems based on the 6800 and 6809, with floppy disk operating system, can handle the 3870, providing software development, in-circuit emulation and full debugging and PROM programming facilities.

Some of the universal development systems also support the F8 and 3870 for software development and debugging.

MOTOROLA MC6800 SERIES

Originally developed at about the same time as the Intel 8080, the Motorola 6800 is an 8-bit *n*MOS microprocessor which has, like the 8080, become virtually an industry standard type.

Unlike other processors of its day the 6800 had a single power supply rail which simplified system design. A further advantage was that only 5 chips were needed to form a complete working 6800 system, whereas other types such as the 8080 needed many more chips for a working system.

As a system the 6800 is quite simple to use and its set of instructions, whilst very effective, are easy to understand. By using two accumulators the 6800 can achieve a quite high throughput and its memory mapped input–output makes system design relatively easy. These features have made the 6800 a very popular processor, perhaps second only to the 8080/8085, among 8-bit microprocessor users.

Applications of the 6800 can range from simple system controllers to small general purpose computer systems. Today the 6800 may be outclassed by some of the later designs, but being well established it is still extremely useful.

Prime manufacturer

Motorola Semiconductor Inc.

Devices available

MC6800	Basic microprocessor CPU, 1 MHz clock
MC68A00	High speed version, 1.5 MHz clock
MC68B00	High speed version, 2 MHz clock

Alternative source devices

American Microsystems Inc.

S6800	Standard part
S68A00	1.5 MHz part
S68B00	2 MHz part

Fairchild

F6800
F68A00
F68B00

Hitachi Semiconductor

HD46800D

Thomson EFCIS

EF6800
EF68A00
EF68B00

Architecture

In fig. 3.8 only the programmable registers of the 6800 have been shown.

Unlike its competitors the 6800 has two 8-bit accumulator registers ACCA and ACCB, which give it great versatility when carrying out data handling and arithmetic operations. Double length (16 bit) arithmetic

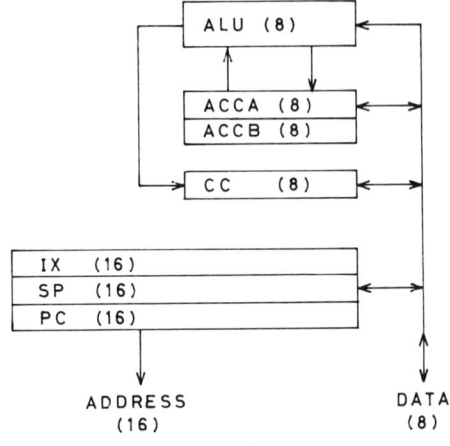

Fig. 3.8

is relatively easy with the 6800. There is an 8-bit condition code (CC) or status register with flag bits for carry, sign, zero, overflow and interrupt mask.

A 16-bit program counter register (PC) allows address access to 64 kbytes of memory, whilst a 16-bit index register (IX) allows indexing through the full 64 kbyte range.

There is a 16-bit stack pointer (SP) for subroutine or interrupt operations and for creating data stacks within the memory. Stacks may be of any length up to 64k and multiple stacks may be set up by storing the stack pointer contents to memory for those stacks not currently in use.

Unlike other processors, such as the 8080, the 6800 has no general purpose registers in the CPU, but it can use any memory location as a general purpose register. There are also many instructions for operating directly on memory data without working through the accumulators.

Input and output are memory mapped so that the 6800 will treat all input–output devices as memory locations. This can make for very flexible input–output operation, but external logic is needed at the input–output peripherals for decoding the memory address signals.

Package

40-pin dual in line package
MC6800P   Plastic
MC6800L   Ceramic
Fairchild use suffix D for ceramic
EFCIS use suffix C for ceramic package
AMI use C for ceramic and P for plastic

Pin connections

1	V_{ss}	21	V_{ss}
2	HALT	22	A12
3	$\phi 1$	23	A13
4	IRQ	24	A14
5	VMA	25	A15
6	NMI	26	D7
7	BA	27	D6
8	V_{cc}	28	D5
9	A0	29	D4
10	A1	30	D3
11	A2	31	D2
12	A3	32	D1
13	A4	33	D0

14	A5	34	R/W
15	A6	35	–
16	A7	36	DBE
17	A8	37	$\phi 2$
18	A9	38	–
19	A10	39	TSC
20	A11	40	RESET

Signal functions

A0 – A15	Address bus outputs tri-state
D0 – D7	Data bus bidirectional tri-state
$\phi 1$ and $\phi 2$	Two-phase clock inputs
RESET	Reset input (active low)
IRQ	Maskable interrupt input (active low)
NMI	Non-maskable interrupt input (active low)
VMA	Valid memory address output
BA	Bus available output
HALT	Halt input (active low)
DBE	Data bus enable input
TSC	Tri-state control input
R/W	Read – write output (write low)
V_{cc}, V_{ss}	Power supply input

Power requirements

V_{cc} +5 V ± 5%
V_{ss} 0 V
Supply current 100 mA

Temperature

Standard part	0°C to +70°C
Extended temp. range	−40°C to +85°C
Motorola suffix C	Fairchild suffix L
Military temperature range	−55°C to +125°C
Motorola suffix QCS	Fairchild suffix M

Input–output

As mentioned in the architecture notes the 6800 has no special I/O system but uses memory mapping for input–output.

Interrupt facilities

There are two interrupts available on the 6800, one being non-maskable (NMI) and the other maskable (IRQ). When an interrupt is accepted the contents of the program counter, index register, both accumulators and the status register are automatically pushed on to the stack. The processor then jumps to a vector address which is stored at the top of memory. Separate vectors are available for NMI, IRQ, software interrupt and reset and are stored at the locations FFF8 to FFFF (hex) as shown:

FFFF	
FFFE	Reset vector
FFFD	
FFFC	NMI vector
FFFB	
FFFA	SWI vector
FFF9	
FFF8	IRQ vector

Multiple interrupts can be nested with the 6800, but interrupt priority must be resolved by external hardware. In the CPU NMI has priority over IRQ.

Instruction set

The 6800 provides 72 basic instruction types, most of which can have several addressing modes.

Arithmetic and logic
The A and B accumulators can carry out addition or subtraction, and facilities are provided for BCD addition, but there is no direct BCD subtraction capability. Arithmetic operations may be made either with or without the carry.

Logical operations provided are AND, OR and EXCLUSIVE OR and may be used with both A and B accumulators, Shift and rotate operations as well as increment, decrement, complement and clear functions can be carried out on either accumulators or memory locations.

Data transfers
A wide range of addressing modes may be used for transfers of data between the accumulators, index or stack registers and memory. The stack and index contents can readily be exchanged and the status register can be manipulated. One shortcoming of the 6800 is that the index and stack pointer contents cannot readily be transferred to the accumulators unless they are first stored in memory. It would also have been a great advantage to have had another index register, since the index addressing technique used in the 6800 tends to be inconvenient for some operations.

Branch and jump
The 6800 is very well endowed with contitional branch type operations which use relative addressing to ± 128 bytes. A subroutine branch or jump is available and there are also unconditional branch and jump instructions.

Timing

A 2-phase non-overlapping clock is required for the 6800 and the timing sequence is very simple. Memory access occurs during phase $\phi 2$ of the clock and execution during phase $\phi 1$. Most instructions will execute in 2, 3 or 4-clock cycles to give a high execution rate with a relatively low frequency clock.

The standard 6800 uses a 1 MHz clock to give execution times of 2 – 4 µs for most instructions. For higher speed the 68A00 part may be used with a 1.5 MHz clock or the 68B00 may run with a 2 MHz clock. There are also plans to produce a 68H00 device with a clock frequency of 2.5 MHz.

Support chips

A wide range of support chips is available for use with the 6800 series of microprocessors. Some of these are:

6810 1k × 8 bit static RAM

6820 Peripheral interface adapter 16 I/O lines
6821 Improved version of 6820
6828 Interrupt priority controller
6840 Programmable timer (three 16-bit timers)
6843 Floppy disk controller
6844 Direct memory access controller
6845 CRT controller
6847 Video display controller
6848 IEEE488 interface bus controller
6849 Floppy disk controller
6850 Async. communications interface adapter (ACIA)
6852 Sync. serial data adapter
6854 Advanced data link controller
6860 0–600 b.p.s. digital modem
6862 2400 b.p.s. digital modem
6871 Two-phase clock generators
6875 Clock generator
6880 Quad tri-state bus transceiver
6881 Triple bidirectional bus switch
6882 Octal tri-state buffer latch
6885/86/87/88 Hex. bus buffers
6889 Non-inverting 6880

Development aids

Motorola

Simple evaluation board kit MEK6800D2 and 6800D5 provides keypad entry and LED displays to allow program development and system testing for simple applications.

Motorola also have their EXORCISER, EXOR-TERM type development systems with full floppy disk operating systems. These systems provide editors, assemblers, linker/loaders and full debugging and emulation capabilities.

Thomson EFCIS

This firm provides copies of the Motorola development system under a licensing agreement and also has its own version with similar facilities.

Most of the general purpose microprocessor development systems such as Futuredata AMDS, Tektronix and Hewlett Packard support the 6800 series for both software development and hardware debugging and in-circuit emulation.

MOTOROLA MC6801 and MC6803

The Motorola MC6801 is an 8-bit nMOS single-chip microcomputer which has been developed from the highly successful MC6800 microprocessor. In order to achieve the high component packing density the Motorola HMOS fabrication technique has been used.

A 2048-byte mask programmed ROM is included on the 6801 chip for program storage and there is also a 128-byte RAM. The 6803 version of this microcomputer has no on-chip ROM. Also on this chip there are a 16-bit counter/timer and a serial input–output facility.

The 6801 provides enhanced facilities compared with the original 6800 microprocessor, but is basically compatible with other 6800 series processors and support chips. The program coding is also compatible at the machine code level.

Among 8-bit single-chip microcomputers the 6801 ranks as one of the more powerful types and is comparable with the Z8 and 9940 types. This microcomputer would typically be used for high level applications where a fairly high volume of production is anticipated. For prototype development and for small quantity production there is a version of the 6801 with a UV eraseable PROM on the chip.

Unlike some other single-chip microcomputers the 6801 can be expanded to handle up to 65 kbytes of memory and will also work with most of the support chips designed for use with 6800 based systems.

Prime manufacturer

Motorola Semiconductor Inc.

Devices available

MC6801	Standard version with 2 kbyte mask ROM
MC6801E	Modified version for use with external clock
MC68701	Version of 6801 with 2 kbyte UV EPROM
MC68701E	As 68701 but with external clock option
MC6803	Version of 6801 with no on-chip ROM
MC6803E	External clock version of 6803

Alternative source devices

As with all 6800 series devices Motorola provide all second source licensed manufacturers with original masks.

American Microsystems Inc.

S6801	Standard mask programmed 6801
S6801E	External clock version of 6801

Fairchild Semiconductor

F6801	Standard mask programmed 6801
F6801E	External clock version of 6801

Hitachi Electronic Components

HD6801S0	Standard mask programmed 6801

Thompson EFCIS

EF6801	Standard mask programmed 6801
EF6801E	External clock version of 6801
EF6803	ROMless version of 6801
EF6803E	External clock version of 6803

Architecture

Fig. 3.9 shows only those registers and other sections of the microcomputer which can be accessed by the programmer. It will be seen that the CPU arrangement is the same as that of a 6800 type microprocessor.

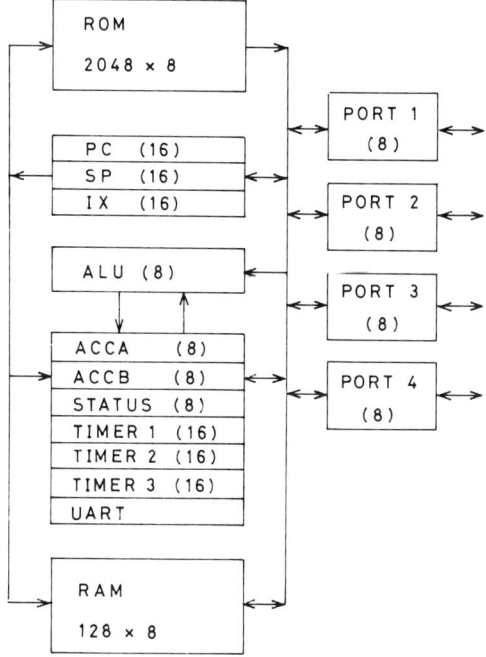

Fig. 3.9

Two 8-bit accumulators ACCA and ACCB are used for all arithmetic and logic operations, together with an 8-bit status register ST. Unlike the 6800 the 6801 and 6803 have provision for treating the two accumulators as a single 16-bit double length accumulator for handling 16-bit numbers.

A 16-bit program counter is provided which can address up to 65 kbytes of memory. Facilities are provided on the 6801 to allow it to work with external memory up to 65 kbytes. An on-chip mask programmed ROM or EPROM is normally used for program storage and is located at the top of the memory map.

There is a 16-bit programmable counter/timer within the 6801 which has a variety of operating modes. This timer uses three 16-bit registers and an 8-bit control and status register.

For serial communication there is a sophisticated serial input–output channel which can handle both NRZ and bi-phase data formats at various data rates.

A 128-byte internal RAM is provided which may be used for data storage or as a bank of general purpose registers, since the 6800 system allows considerable manipulation of data within its memory locations. The RAM has a standby low power mode which allows data to be retained in the first 64 bytes of RAM whilst the microcomputer itself is switched off.

MOTOROLA MC6801 AND MC6803

There are 4 major input–output ports which may in some modes of operation of the 6801 be used as data and address buses to access external memory and peripheral devices.

The memory map of the 6801 is as follows:

```
FFFF ─────
           Internal ROM
           or EPROM
F800 ─────
F7FF
           External RAM,
           ROM or I/O devices
0200 ─────
01FF
           External RAM,
           non-multiplexed
           mode
0100 ─────
00FF
           Internal RAM
0080 ─────
007F
           External RAM
0020 ─────
001F
           Control and data
           registers for the
           I/O ports, counter
           and serial I/O
0000 ─────
```

The data and control registers for the 4 I/O ports occupy locations 00 to 07 of memory. The counter/timer system uses locations 08 to 0F and the serial communications channel uses locations 10 to 14 for its data and control registers. At present locations 15 to 1F are reserved for possible future use.

In the 6803 the lower 8 bits of the memory address are multiplexed with the data bus to provide signals for an external memory. The upper 8 bits of the address are brought out directly. This reduces the available input–output lines but the timer and serial channel are provided on the chip.

Package

40-pin dual in line type may be ceramic or plastic
Suffix P denotes plastic type
Motorola use suffix L for the ceramic package
Fairchild use suffix D for ceramic

Pin connections

MC6801   Standard version

1	V_{ss}	21	$V_{cc}(S)$
2	XTAL1	22	P47
3	EXTAL2	23	P46
4	NMI	24	P45
5	IRQ	25	P44
6	RESET	26	P43
7	V_{cc}	27	P42
8	P20	28	P41
9	P21	29	P40
10	P22	30	P37
11	P23	31	P36
12	P24	32	P35
13	P10	33	P34
14	P11	34	P33
15	P12	35	P32
16	P13	36	P31
17	P14	37	P30
18	P15	38	SC2
19	P16	39	SC1
20	P17	40	E

Signal functions

P10 – P17	Port 1 I/O
P20 – P24	Port 2 I/O and mode control
P30 – P37	Port 3 I/O or address or data
P40 – P47	Port 4 I/O or address
XTAL1, EXTAL2	Timing crystal inputs
NMI	Non-maskable interrupt input (active low)
IRQ	Maskable interrupt input (active low)
RESET	Reset input (active low)
E	Enable clock output
SC1	Input strobe or address output strobe
SC2	Output strobe for read–write (write low)
V_{cc}, V_{ss}	Power supply inputs
$V_{cc}(S)$	Standby power supply input

On the 6803 some signal functions are changed. Port 4 becomes the upper 8 address bits and port 3 is multiplexed between the 8-bit data bus and the lower 8 address bits. This also applies to the 6801 in some modes of operation.

Power requirements

V_{cc}	+5 V ± 5%
$V_{cc}(S)$	+5 V ± 5%
V_{ss}	0 V
Power dissipation	1.2 W

Temperature range

0°C to +70°C

Input–output

All inputs and outputs of the 6801 and 6803 microcomputers are TTL compatible and outputs can normally drive one standard TTL load. Some outputs have no pull up resistors and therefore if used to drive CMOS logic will require an external resistor.

For the MC6801 there are 3 modes of operation and the signal functions of the input–output lines will depend on the particular mode being used. Modes are selected according to the state of the P20, P21 and P22 input lines during the reset sequence. The three modes are:

(1) Single-chip mode
(2) Expanded mode
(3) Expanded multiplexed mode

In the single-chip mode ports 1, 3 and 4 act as 8-bit input or output ports, whilst port 2 is a 5-bit port. On each port a data direction register can be set up to select each line of the port for either input or output. Each port has a data register and a data direction register and these are located in the first 8 bytes of the memory map from 0000 to 0007 hex. Port 3 also has a status and control register located at 000F. The SC1 and SC2 lines may be used to provide a handshake system for port 3 if desired.

In the expanded mode of operation the 6801 can access an extra 256 bytes of memory located at 0100 in the address map. Data is transmitted via port 3 which acts as the data bus, whilst port 4 provides a 7-bit address for the external memory.

When the expanded multiplexed mode is selected port 4 carries the upper 8 bits of the address whilst the lower 8 bits are output via port 3. Since port 3 is also used for the data bus the address and data signals are multiplexed over the 8 lines of port 3. Under these conditions strobe output SC1 acts as an address strobe whilst SC2 provides the read–write select output to control the data bus. When this mode is selected the 6801 can access up to 65 kbytes of memory.

The MC6803 does not have mode selection but effectively operates in the same way as an MC6801 with the extended and multiplexed mode selected.

A 16-bit programmable timer on the chip uses three 16-bit registers, one as a clock pulse counter, one as a data capture register which samples and holds a value from the free running counter on command. The third register is used to compare the counter value with some preset number and an output pulse may be produced and fed out via port 21. There is also a control and status register of 8 bits which sets and controls the timer mode of operation. The registers for the timer are located between 0008 and 000E in the memory map.

Full duplex serial communication can be provided by a serial communication interface on both the 6801 and 6803. Various modes of operation are possible and the transmission rate may also be selected by program. Either non-return to zero (NRZ) or biphase format signals may be produced. There are six 8-bit registers within the serial interface, of which three are accessible by the programmer.

Inputs and outputs for the serial channel are through port 2, with bit 3 as data input, bit 4 as data output and bit 2 as a clock output for asynchronous transmission if desired. The programmable registers for the serial channel are located at 0010 to 0013 in the memory map. Two status and control registers govern the bit rate and mode of operation.

Interrupt facilities

Apart from the reset function both the MC6801 and MC6803 have 5 hardware interrupts, of which four are maskable whilst the fifth is non-maskable. There is also a software interrupt which may be invoked by the SWI instruction.

As with other 6800 based microprocessors the interrupts use a vectoring system to access the interrupt service routines. The starting addresses of the various routines are stored as vectors at the top of the memory map in the on-chip ROM as shown:

	Hex. address	
	FFFF	Reset vector
	FFFE	
	FFFD	NMI vector
	FFFC	
	FFFB	SWI vector
	FFFA	
Hex. memory address	FFF9	IRQ1 vector (port 3)
	FFF8	
	FFF7	IRQ2 (timer input capture)
	FFF6	
	FFF5	IRQ2 (timer compare)
	FFF4	
	FFF3	IRQ2 (timer overflow)
	FFF2	
	FFF1	IRQ2 (serial I/O)
	FFF0	

Each of these vector addresses is stored with its upper 8 bits in the lower of the two memory addresses, as is common in all 6800 systems. When an interrupt or reset occurs the CPU will complete execution of the current instruction and if the interrupt is accepted the contents of the program counter, index and status registers as well as those of the two accumulators will automatically be pushed to the stack before the program branches to the address contained in the appropriate interrupt vector location. At the end of the interrupt service routine the contents of the CPU registers are restored by pulling them from the stack. This automatic saving of registers tends to slow down interrupt processing a little but does save program instructions.

A priority system operates for the interrupt facilities, with the reset having highest priority and the other types of interrupts being arranged in descending priority as shown:

Top priority	Reset
	Non-maskable interrupt (NMI)
	Software interrupt (SWI)
	IRQ1 Port 3 interrupt
	IRQ2 Timer input capture
	IRQ2 Timer output compare
	IRQ2 Timer overflow
Lowest priority	IRQ2 Serial input–output

If several devices are connected to port 3 an external logic system must be used to determine their interrupt priority relative to one another.

Instruction set

Both the 6801 and 6803 microcomputers can execute all of the instructions in the 6800 microprocessor instruction set. They have in addition a number of new instructions which permit a limited amount of 16-bit data processing.

Arithmetic and logic
As with the 6800 it is possible to carry out 8-bit addition

and subtraction in either the A or B accumulators, and there is a facility for addition of BCD format numbers. Note that there is no direct facility for BCD subtraction, which requires a small software routine. A new feature of the 6801 and 6803 is the ability to treat the two accumulators as a double length register, allowing direct 16-bit addition and subtraction. There is also an eight by eight hardware multiplier function provided, by which the product of the contents of A and B are returned as a 16-bit number in the double length register.

Logical operations provided are AND, OR and EXCLUSIVE OR as well as a range of shift and rotate instructions. The shift and rotate operations may also be applied directly to memory, thus allowing memory locations to be used as general purpose registers. Other operations common to accumulators and memory are increment, decrement, complement and negate.

Data transfer

Eight-bit data transfers between memory and either of the two accumulators are provided and there are instructions for the transfer of 16-bit data to and from the double length accumulator. Data may also be transferred between the memory and either the index register (IX) or the stack pointer register (SP) as 16-bit data.

The stack pointer allows the creation of variable length stacks at any point in memory and 8-bit data may be pushed to or pulled from the stack via either the A or B accumulators. The index register allows data table handling using indexed addressing. A new feature of the 6801/3 is that the contents of the A accumulator may be added to the IX register to give more flexible indexing.

As with other 6800 type systems all input-output uses a memory mapping technique. The on-chip ports have addresses at the bottom of the memory map. When the 6801 is used in expanded modes or a 6803 is in use the external devices are treated as memory locations and appropriate address decoding must be provided externally.

Branch and jump

There are 14 conditional branches and two unconditional. All conditional branches use relative addressing in the range ± 128 bytes, but an unconditional jump is provided which may use either direct or indexed addressing. Both relative and direct branches to subroutines are provided.

Addressing modes

Motorola specify 7 addressing modes for the 6801/6803 type microcomputers:

Accumulator addressing (A or B)
Immediate addressing
Direct addressing
Extended addressing
Indexed addressing
Implied addressing
Relative addressing

The direct addressing mode is effectively zero page addressing, since it allows access to the first 256 bytes of memory. In the indexed mode an 8-bit offset in the instruction is added to the contents of the index register to obtain the address. This produces slightly different results from indexing in other processor types but allows indexing throughout the entire 65 kbyte memory space. There is no auto incrementing in the indexed mode.

Timing

For both the 6801 and 6803 a 1 MHz 2-phase CPU clock is used. When the on-chip generator is employed a 4 MHz crystal will be needed since there is a divide by four circuit on the chip. At 1 MHz clock rate the average instruction execution time will be some 2 – 4 μs.

As with other 6800 systems memory access occurs during phase 2 of the CPU clock cycle and the output pulse E may be used to synchronise external memory and I/O devices.

Support devices

When the 6801 or 6803 are used as stand alone microcomputers they will not normally require any support chips, apart from logic buffers if the loads applied to the ports are greater than one TTL load. In the multiplexed mode of the 6801 or if external memory or I/O is used with the 6803 then any of the support chips designed for use with the 6800 microprocessor may be used with these microcomputers.

Development aids

From Motorola the EXORCISER and EXORTERM development systems may be used to develop software and test the hardware for 6801 and 6803 based systems. These provide a floppy disk based operating system with editor, assembler and loader facilities. Hardware emulation and debugging facilities will also become available on the EXORCISER system.

Thomson EFCIS and other authorised second sources are also expected to provide similar development facilities.

Microprocessor development systems such as the Tektronix 8001 and 8002 or the Futuredata AMDS2300 systems may also be used for software development, since the 6801 and 6803 are software compatible with the 6800 microprocessor. However, such systems will not support the new instructions included in the 6801 and 6803, so these would need to be manually coded during the software writing stage and might need macro routines for software debugging.

MOTOROLA MC6802 SERIES

The Motorola MC6802 is a development of the very popular 6800 type microprocessor also produced by Motorola. The 6802 is an 8-bit nMOS type microprocessor designed to work in conjunction with the MC6846 combination chip to form a 2-chip microcomputer system for small dedicated applications. Alternatively the MC6802 can be used as a replacement for the 6800 in larger systems, since it is both hardware and software compatible with that processor, although not pin compatible.

There are 128 bytes of RAM on the 6802 chip and of these 32 bytes have a memory retention feature using a separate +5 V standby power supply so that the main chip supply can be shut down to conserve power. Unlike the 6800 the 6802 has its own on-chip 2-phase clock oscillator.

The companion MC6846 chip provides 2048 bytes of mask programmed ROM and an 8-bit input–output port with two handshake lines. There is also a 16-bit counter/timer on the chip.

Typical applications for the 6802 would generally be similar to those for the 6800, but the 6802 has an advantage in smaller systems where only 2 chips would be needed, as compared with a minimum of 5 chips for a 6800 processor. A 6802 system can compete favourably with most single-chip 8-bit microcomputers, since it will generally provide greater processing power than such systems.

For low power applications Mitel have developed a CMOS equivalent to the 6802 which has total hardware and software compatibility. Another variant of the 6802 is the MC6808, in which there is no on-chip RAM.

Prime manufacturer

Motorola Semiconductor Inc.

Devices available

MC6802   Basic CPU chip with 128 bytes of RAM
MC6808   Same as 6802 but with no on-chip RAM
MC6846   ROM, I/O and timer combo chip for 6802

Alternative source devices

It should be noted that unlike many other manufacturers Motorola operate a full mask exchange agreement with second sources so that alternative nMOS devices will use identical masks to the original Motorola version.

American Microsystems Inc.

S6802   Standard 6802 microprocessor
S6808   6802 without RAM
S6846   Combo chip

Hitachi Electronic Components

HD46802   Basic 6802 processor
HD46846   Combo chip

Fairchild Semiconductor

F6802   Basic 6802 chip
F6808   RAMless version
F6846   Combo chip

Thomson EFCIS

EF6802   Basic 6802 microprocessor
EF6808   RAMless version of 6802
EF6846   Combo chip

Mitel Semiconductor

MD46802   CMOS version of the 6802 processor
MD46846   CMOS version of 6846 combo chip

Plessey Semiconductors

MV68SC02   CMOS version of 6802 (Mitel mask)
MV68SC46   CMOS version of 6846

Architecture

As will be seen from fig. 3.10 the internal architecture is basically identical to that of the 6800, except for the on-chip RAM.

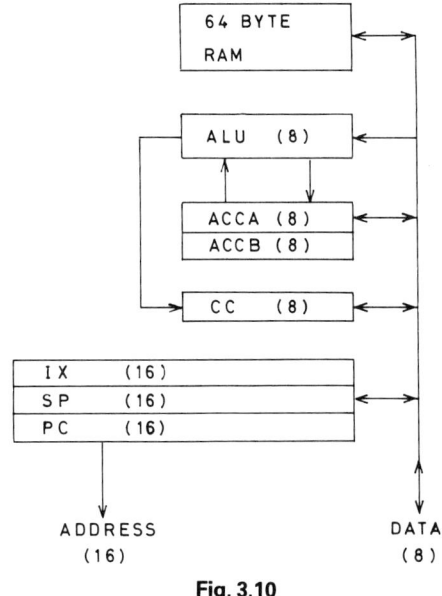

Fig. 3.10

Two 8-bit accumulators ACCA and ACCB are used for logic and arithmetic operations, using 8-bit binary data. An 8-bit status register provides flag bits for zero, sign, carry and overflow as well as a half carry flag for BCD operation and an interrupt mask flag.

A 16-bit program counter (PC) allows access to 65k of program memory. In the 6802 as with all other 6800 type CPUs a single common memory space is used for program, data and input–output. There is a 16-bit stack pointer register (SP) which permits location of the stack at any point in the 65k memory map. Stacks can be of any length and expand downwards through the memory. Multiple stacks may be set up within the memory as required.

A single 16-bit index register (IX) is provided in the 6802 and will permit indexing throughout the whole memory map. There are no general purpose registers in the CPU but as with other 6800 type processors the 6802 uses memory locations as registers and therefore the on-chip RAM could be used for this purpose.

The on-chip RAM of the 6802 is located from 0000 to 007F (hex) within the processor memory map. Care

MOTOROLA MC6802 SERIES

must be taken to ensure that there is no conflict with external memory if it is used.

An 8-bit bidirectional bus is provided for data and a 16-bit address bus allows access to 65 kbyte of memory. In this processor all memory reference operations occur during phase 2 of the processor clock.

Package

40-pin dual in line type may be ceramic or plastic
Suffix L (Motorola), D (Fairchild) or C signifies ceramic
Suffix P signifies a plastic package

Pin connections

MC6802   Microprocessor

1	V_{ss}	21	V_{ss}
2	HALT	22	A12
3	MR	23	A13
4	IRQ	24	A14
5	VMA	25	A15
6	NMI	26	D7 (MSB)
7	BA	27	D6
8	V_{cc}	28	D5
9	A0 (LSB)	29	D4
10	A1	30	D3
11	A2	31	D2
12	A3	32	D1
13	A4	33	D0 (LSB)
14	A5	34	R/W
15	A6	35	$V_{cc}(S)$
16	A7	36	RE
17	A8	37	E
18	A9	38	XTAL
19	A10	39	EXTAL
20	A11	40	RESET

MC6846   ROM, I/O, timer chip

1	V_{ss}	21	P0
2	A7	22	P1
3	A6	23	P2
4	A5	24	P3
5	A4	25	P4
6	CS0	26	P5
7	R/W	27	P6
8	D0 (LSB)	28	P7
9	D1	29	V_{cc}
10	D2	30	A3
11	D3	31	A2
12	D4	32	A1
13	D5	33	A0 (LSB)
14	D6	34	CP1
15	D7 (MSB)	35	CP2
16	CS1	36	IRQ
17	CTG	37	RES
18	CTC	38	A10
19	CTO	39	A9
20	E	40	A8

Signal functions

D0 – D7	Data bus bidirectional tri-state
A0 – A15	Address bus (6802 O/P 6846 I/P) tri-state
R/W	Read–write (write low) 6802 out 6846 in
VMA	Valid memory address output
NMI	Non-maskable interrupt input (active low)
HALT	Halt input to CPU (active low)
BA	Bus available output from CPU
RESET	System reset input (active low)
IRQ	Interrupt request (active low 6802 I/P 6846 O/P)
EXTAL, XTAL	Timing crystal for CPU clock
E	Enable X (Phase 2 of CPU clock)
MR	Memory ready input for slow memory use
RE	RAM enable input for on-chip 6802 RAM
P0 – P7	Peripheral data programmable I/O lines
CP1	Control input for interrupt use
CP2	Control line may be either input or output
CS1, CS0	Chip select inputs for ROM and I/O timer
CTO	Counter/timer output
CTC	Counter/timer clock input (active low)
CTG	Counter/timer gate input (active low)
$V_{cc}(S)$	Standby supply for RAM retention
V_{cc}, V_{ss}	Power supply inputs

Note that MC6808 has same pin connections and functions as 6802.

Power requirements

V_{cc} +5 V ± 5%
$V_{cc}(S)$ +5 V ± 5%
V_{ss} 0 V
Supply current MC6802   120 mA typical
In power down mode memory current is 8 mA typical
Supply current MC6846   120 mA

Temperature range

0°C to +70°C

Input–output

As with all 6800 series microprocessors and microcomputers the 6802 uses memory mapped input–output in which the processor treats all input–output devices as memory locations.

All signals to and from the 6802 and 6846 are TTL compatible and the output lines can normally drive a single TTL load.

On the 6846 the individual lines of the 8-bit I/O port can be programmed to act as either inputs or outputs, using a control register on the chip and appropriate software. The timer can also be programmed to act as either a timer or an event counter. When used as a timer it uses the CPU clock fed in via signal E. Alternatively the timer may be programmed to use an external clock signal. Two handshake lines CP1 and CP2 are provided for the parallel I/O port.

When the 6846 is not used the 6802 can be used in the same way as the 6800 to access external memory and I/O devices by decoding the address bus output and using the VMA and E signals for timing.

Interrupt facilities

There is a maskable interrupt line IRQ and two non-maskable interrupts NMI and RESET. A software interrupt using the op code SWI may also be used.

Interrupt service routine vectors are located at the top of the memory map as shown:

	FFFF	
		Reset vector
	FFFE	
	FFFD	
		NMI vector
Hex. address	FFFC	
	FFFB	
		SWI vector
	FFFA	
	FFF9	
		IRQ vector
	FFF8	

Note that in the 6802 system the lower of the two address bytes is the most significant part of the 16-bit address. On receiving an interrupt the processor will push the contents of the program counter, index register, both accumulators and the status register on to the stack. This is an automatic action. At the end of the interrupt routine an RTI instruction causes the stored register contents to be restored to the CPU registers.

There is no built in priority for maskable interrupts and an external priority system must be used. NMI and SWI type interrupts will have priority over IRQ, with NMI at the highest priority level. Nested interrupts may readily be catered for with the 6802 system.

Instruction set

For the 6802 and 6808 microprocessors the instruction set is identical to that of the 6800. Thus these processors are fully compatible with software for the 6800 type. A total of 72 different instruction types is provided.

Arithmetic and logic
Both accumulators can be used for 8-bit arithmetic operations including add, add with carry, subtract and subtract with carry. The two accumulators are readily chained together to handle 16-bit arithmetic or larger formats by storing partial results. There is a facility for BCD addition but no direct operation for BCD subtraction, although this can be achieved by software.

Logical operations provided are AND, OR and EXCLUSIVE OR, as well as a range of shift and rotate operations. In the 6802 there are no general purpose CPU registers but memory may be used for this purpose since data within the memory may be shifted, rotated, complemented, negated, incremented, decremented and tested. These operations may also be carried out on the two accumulators.

Data transfer
Data are readily transferred between the two accumulators and memory. Input-output is dealt with as a memory transfer since a memory mapping system is used.

Data in the accumulators may be pushed to stack or pulled from the stack at will. The stack pointer itself may also be transferred to and from memory to allow the setting up of a number of separate stacks within memory.

Indexed data transfers may be carried out between the accumulators and memory using the index register to modify the addressing. In the 6800 system the offset specified in the instruction is added to the contents of the index register to produce the effective address. This arrangement can have some disadvantages but does allow very large data tables to be used. The contents of the index register may be transferred to and from memory and also exchanged with the stack pointer contents. There is however no facility for transfers directly between the accumulators and index register without going via the memory.

Branch and jump
There are 14 conditional branch instructions, probably the most comprehensive set in any microprocessor, allowing a wide range of tests to be carried out. All branches are relative with an address range of ± 128 bytes from the current program address. Two unconditional operations are available, one a relative branch and the other a direct jump which may also be indexed.

Branch relative and direct jump to subroutine are provided. When branching to a subroutine the CPU automatically saves the program counter contents on the stack. Since the stack can be up to 65 kbyte long very deeply nested subroutines are possible.

Individual bits in the accumulators may be tested by the contitional instructions.

Timing

The normal frequency of operation of the crystal oscillator is 4 Mhz, giving a processor 2-phase clock of 1 MHz. For typical instructions the execution time will be 2 – 4 μs.

The CMOS version produced by Mitel and Plessey will run with a 5 MHz clock frequency to give slightly faster operation. It should be noted that the *n*MOS version uses dynamic logic on the chip and must have a minimum 2-phase clock frequency of 100 kHz. An external clock oscillator may be used by injecting the signal on pin 39 (EXTAL).

Memory and I/O access occurs during phase 2 of the 2-phase CPU clock and external circuits may be synchronised by using the E output from the 6802. The VMA output indicates that a valid memory address is present on the address bus. The instruction execution normally occurs during phase 1 of the CPU clock.

Support chips

Since the 6802 and 6808 are basically similar to the 6800 it is possible to use any of the support chips designed for use with the 6800. Some of these are:

6820/21	Peripheral interface adapter 16-bit parallel I/O
6828	Interrupt priority encoder

6840	Programmable timers (three 16-bit timers)
6843	Floppy disk controller
6845	CRT display controller
6847	Video display controller (graphics and text)
6849	Floppy disk controller dual density
6850	Asynchronous serial interface
6852	Synchronous serial interface
6854	Advanced data link controller
6860	0 – 600 b.p.s. digital modem
6862	2400 b.p.s. digital modem
6880	Quad bus transceiver inverting type
6881	Triple bidirectional bus switch
6882	Octal tri-state buffer latch
6885/86/ 87/88	Hex. bus buffers
6889	Quad bus transceiver non-inverting
6894	Data encryption chip
68488	IEEE488 GP instrument bus interface
S68047	Enhanced version of 6847
6844	Direct memory access controller

Development aids

For low level development and debugging the Motorola single-board MEK6802D5 evaluation board may be used. This provides keypad entry and an LED display system for monitoring or may be used with a VDU terminal. Alternatively the MEK6800D2 evaluation board for the 6800 may also be used for 6802 systems.

The Motorola EXORCISER system provides a complete floppy disk based system for software development, debugging and in-circuit hardware emulation for the 6802. This system provides EPROM programming facilities for popular EPROM types.

A variant of the EXORCISER is the EXORTERM system, which has a built in VDU and may use a floppy disk operating system. Facilities provided are similar to those of the EXORCISER.

Thomson EFCIS have an agreement by which they can supply direct equivalents to the Motorola EXORCISER and EXORTERM.

MOTOROLA MC6805 SERIES

The Motorola MC6805 is an 8-bit *n*MOS single-chip microcomputer designed for economical dedicated systems where the computing power of a 6800 type processor is required. The CPU is effectively an MC6800 and this is combined with some RAM, a timer and a mask programmed ROM on a single chip. A slightly simplified instruction set is used for the 6805.

Typical applications are for dedicated systems where minimum chip count is required and where volume is sufficiently high to justify the use of a mask programmed ROM. This device would be competitive with the 8048, 8051 and 6500/1 types. For prototype work and limited production the MC68705 has a UV erasable ROM which is field programmable.

Prime manufacturer

Motorola Semiconductor Inc.

Devices available

MC6805 1100-byte mask ROM, 64-byte RAM, 20 I/O lines
MC68705 1100-byte UV EPROM, 64-byte RAM, 20 I/O lines

Alternative source devices

Hitachi

HD6805SO   Mask ROM version

American Microsystems Inc.

S6805   Mask ROM type

Thomson EFCIS

EF6805   Mask ROM type

Architecture

Fig. 3.11 shows the internal layout of the 6805 in simplified form. It will be seen that the CPU section is a simplified version of the normal 6800 type CPU.

For arithmetic and logic an 8-bit ALU is combined with one 8-bit accumulator (A) and an 8-bit status register (CC). The index register has been reduced in length from 16 bits, for a normal 6800, to just 8 bits and the stack pointer has just 8 bits, of which only 5 can be accessed by program.

Whereas the program counter for a standard 6800 has 16 bits the 6805 has an 11-bit program counter register (PC) to allow access to 2048 bytes of memory.

There are 1088 bytes of read only memory on the chip, of which 116 bytes may be used for test purposes and 8 bytes are used for interrupt vectors. A 64-byte scratch-pad RAM is provided and there is also an 8-bit timer/counter with a 7-bit prescaler counter. The chip also includes a clock generator.

Three input–output ports are provided, giving a total of 20 parallel input–output lines.

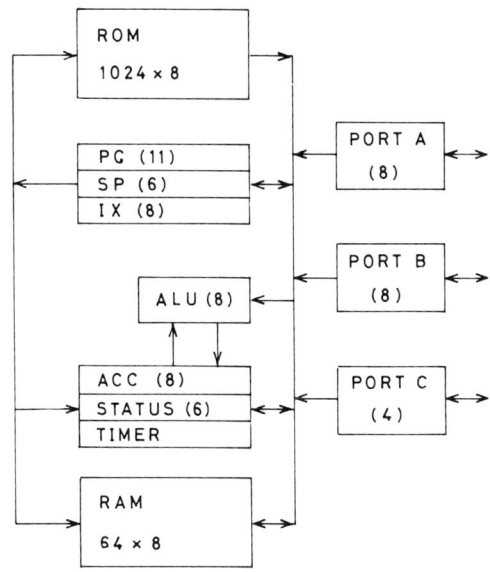

Fig. 3.11

The memory map for the 6805 is:

```
              7FF  _____
                         ROM
Hex.          3C0  _____
address       3BF
                         Unused
              100  _____
              0FF
                         ROM
              080  _____
              07F
                         RAM
              040  _____
              03F
                         I/O and timer
              000  _____
```

Package

28-pin dual in line type
Suffix L indicates ceramic type
Suffix P indicates plastic type
68705 has quartz window in lid for UV erasure of ROM

Pin connections

1	V_{ss}	15	B3
2	INT	16	B4
3	V_{cc}	17	B5
4	XTL	18	B6
5	EXTL	19	B7
6	TEST	20	A0
7	TIMER	21	A1
8	C0	22	A2
9	C1	23	A3
10	C2	24	A4
11	C3	25	A5
12	B0	26	A6
13	B1	27	A7
14	B2	28	RESET

MOTOROLA MC6805 SERIES

Signal functions

A0 – A7	Port A 8-bit bidirectional bit programmed
B0 – B7	Port B 8-bit bidirectional bit programmed
C0 – C3	Port C 4-bit bidirectional bit programmed
RESET	Reset input (active low)
XTL, EXTL	Timing crystal inputs
INT	Interrupt input edge triggered by falling edge
TIMER	Timer input mask option. This may be timer clock input or enable input
TEST	Test input for checking on-chip ROM
V_{cc}, V_{ss}	Power supply inputs

Power requirements

V_{cc} +5 V ± 5%
V_{ss} 0 V

Temperature range

0°C to +70°C

Input–output

The individual lines of the 3 I/O ports may be programmed as either input or output by setting bits in associated data direction registers. Port A, B and C data registers are at locations 0, 1 and 2 in memory, whilst their data direction registers are at locations 4, 5 and 6. After reset all I/O lines are programmed as inputs.

Inputs and outputs are TTL compatible and outputs can drive one TTL load. Mask options permit CMOS or LED drive outputs to be provided.

The timer/counter data register is at location 8 and its associated control register is at location 9 in memory.

Interrupt facilities

Interrupts are vectored in the same way as for the 6800 type, with the interrupt vectors stored at the top of the memory. Eight bytes are used for the vectors, with 2 bytes for each. The four vectors are for reset, external interrupt, timer interrupt and software interrupt using instruction SWI. The external and timer interrupts are maskable by setting a bit in the status register.

When an interrupt occurs the program counter and status are pushed on to the stack automatically.

Note that the interrupt input INT can be used as a sine wave zero crossing detector as well as a conventional edge triggered input.

Instruction set

A set of 61 instructions is provided which is a simplified version of the 6800 set. A number of extra branch operations are provided.

Arithmetic and logic

Eight-bit arithmetic is carried out in the accumulator and includes addition and subtraction either with or without carry. As with the 6800 it is possible to increment, decrement, clear, negate and complement either the accumulator or memory data.

Logical operations include AND, OR and EX-CLUSIVE OR, as well as shift and rotate and compare operations. There are also several bit manipulation instructions.

Data transfers

Data may be transferred between the accumulator or the index register and memory. Since the I/O ports are memory mapped they are simply treated as memory locations, as is the timer.

After reset the stack pointer is initialised at memory location 7F (hex.), which is the top of the on-chip scratchpad RAM. Stacks may have any length within the available space and multiple stacks may be set up if desired. Data can be pushed to or pulled from the current stack as required. The stack pointer may be reset to 7F by an RSP instruction.

A useful feature not provided on the standard 6800 is the ability to transfer data between the accumulator and the index register. Indexed addressing operates in the same way as for the standard 6800.

Branch and jump

There are 16 conditional branch instructions which all use relative addressing with a range of ± 128 bytes. An unconditional branch and unconditional jump are also provided as well as branch and jump to subroutine.

There are also bit test branch instructions which allow branching on tests of individual bits in memory data.

Addressing modes

The 6805 supports the 12 addressing modes available for the standard 6800 microprocessor.

Timing

Maximum crystal oscillator frequency is 4 MHz, giving a CPU clock of 1 MHz and typical instruction execution times of 2–4 μs.

Support chips

None.

Development aids

Full software and hardware support is provided on the Motorola EXORCISER and EXORTERM type systems, giving a floppy disk type operating system, assembler, editor, loader and full debug facilities.

MOTOROLA MC6809 SERIES

The Motorola MC6809 is an 8-bit *n*MOS microprocessor, which is a somewhat enhanced development of the highly popular 6800 type microprocessor.

Other processors developed by Motorola from the 6800 have generally been hardware and software compatible with the original processor. For the MC6809 Motorola have broken away from this pattern to develop a new instruction set, optimised to take advantage of the hardware features of the 6809. Although similar to the 6800 instruction set it is not directly compatible with programs written for the 6800.

The general design philosophy of the 6809, however, follows that of the original 6800, except that a number of new features have been incorporated to overcome the shortcomings of the original 6800 microprocessor design.

With the possible exception of the Zilog Z80, and the National CMOS version of the Z80, it would seem that the 6809 is the most powerful and flexible 8-bit microprocessor currently available. It can provide fast and efficient processing which makes it ideally suited to the more demanding applications, yet at the same time it would make an ideal substitute for the 6800 or 6802 microprocessor and similar types in less demanding applications. The 6809 has quite a useful capability for handling 16-bit data and arithmetic which could give it an advantage in many applications where the older or simpler 16-bit microprocessors might normally be employed. It seems likely that the 6809 will, like the 6800 and 8085, become an industry standard microprocessor.

Prime manufacturer

Motorola Semiconductor Inc.

Devices available

MC6809	Standard 1 MHz clock processor
MC6809E	As 6809 but external clock required
MC68A09, MC68A09E	1.5 MHz clock versions
MC68B09, MC68B09E	2 MHz clock versions

Alternative source devices

As with the 6800 design, Motorola have a direct mask exchange agreement with licensed second sources and all manufacturers produce identical devices.

American Microsystems Inc.

S6809	Standard microprocessor device
S6809E	External clock version
S68A09, A68A09E	1.5 MHz versions
S68B09, S68B09E	2 MHz versions

Fairchild Semiconductor

F6809	Standard 6809 microprocessor
F6809E	External clock version

Hitachi Electronic Components

HD6809	Standard 6809 microprocessor

Thompson EFCIS

EF6809	Standard 6809 microprocessor
EF6809E	External clock version of 6809

Architecture

As will be seen from fig. 3.12, which shows only those CPU registers accessible to the programmer, the general arrangement of the 6809 is similar to that of the 6800, but with some additional registers.

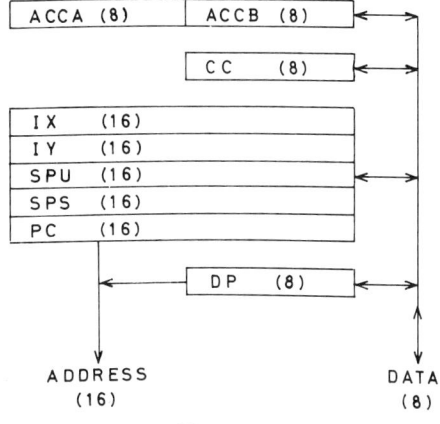

Fig. 3.12

Arithmetic and logic are dealt with by two accumulators ACCA and ACCB, which may also be used as general purpose data registers. In the 6809 the two accumulators can be treated as a single 16-bit double length accumulator which permits the handling of 16-bit data during arithmetic operations. An 8-bit status register CC is used for conditional flags, and the 6809 uses all 8 bits for this purpose whereas the original 6800 used only 6 of the status register bits.

The program counter is a 16-bit register allowing a full 65 kbyte memory space to be addressed. In the 6809 there are 2 stack pointer registers compared with only one in the 6800. One of these 16-bit registers is used as the system stack pointer, whilst the second is intended for user data stacks. In practice both stack pointers may be used for data stacks if desired. As with the 6800 the stacks created in memory may be of variable length and may be located anywhere within the 65 kbyte address space. Multiple stacks may be handled by saving the stack pointer contents to memory when a new stack is to be selected.

In the 6800 direct page addressing using a single-byte address always accesses the first 256 bytes of the memory map. The 6809 contains a direct page register which allows the page selected for direct page addressing to be placed anywhere in the memory map. Here the direct page register will supply the upper 8 bits of the memory address. Direct page addressing has the advantage of giving faster execution than the extended 2-byte addressing mode normally required for memory access.

One limitation of the 6800 was that it had only one index register. This deficiency has been remedied in the 6809 by the provision of two 16-bit index registers IX and IY. At the same time a much wider range of indexed addressing modes has been incorporated into the 6809.

Like all other 6800 based processors the 6809 employs a common memory space for program, data and input–output. All input–output is memory mapped

MOTOROLA MC6809 SERIES

so that peripheral devices are simply treated as memory locations.

An 8-bit bidirectional data bus is used for data transfer to and from memory and I/O devices and there is a separate 16-bit address bus. A relatively simple set of control lines is used to govern the operation of the CPU and the data/address buses. Direct memory access operations can be achieved but an external controller is normally required. It is also possible to use the 6809 in multiprocessor systems.

Package

40-pin dual in line type plastic or ceramic
Suffix P indicates plastic type
Motorola use suffix L and Fairchild suffix D for ceramic type

Pin connections

1	V_{ss}	21	A13
2	NMI	22	A14
3	IRQ	23	A15 (MSB)
4	FIRQ	24	D7 (MSB)
5	BS	25	D6
6	BA	26	D5
7	V_{cc}	27	D4
8	A0 (LSB)	28	D3
9	A1	29	D2
10	A2	30	D1
11	A3	31	D0 (LSB)
12	A4	32	R/W
13	A5	33	BREQ
14	A6	34	E
15	A7	35	Q
16	A8	36	MR
17	A9	37	RESET
18	A10	38	EXTAL
19	A11	39	XTAL
20	A12	40	HALT

Signal functions

A0 – A15	Address bus output tri-state
D0 – D7	Data bus bidirectional tri-state
NMI	Non-maskable interrupt input (active low)
IRQ	Maskable interrupt input (active low)
FIRQ	Fast interrupt input (active low)
EXTAL, XTAL	Timing clock crystal lines
Q	Quadrature clock output
E	Enable output (phase 2 of the CPU clock)
R/W	Read–write control output (write low)
HALT	CPU halt control input (active low)
RESET	Reset input (active low)
MRDY	Memory ready input for slow memories
BREQ	Bus request input for DMA etc. (active low)
BA	Bus available output
BS	Bus status output
V_{cc}, V_{ss}	Power supply inputs

The 6809E external clock version of E and Q signals become inputs whilst the EXTAL, XTAL, MRDY and BREQ are replaced by other signals. The new signals on the 6809E are:

TSC	Tri-state control for address and R/W replaces BREQ
LIC	Last instruction cycle output
BUSY	Busy status output for multiprocessor operation

Power requirements

V_{cc}	+5 V ± 5%
V_{ss}	0 V
Power dissipation	1 W

Temperature range

0°C to +70°C

Input–output

All signals into and out of the 6809 are TTL compatible and outputs are capable of driving a single TTL load. Address and data buses are tri-state.

Input and output to peripheral devices makes use of the memory mapping technique, where the peripherals are treated as memory locations. External address decoding will be required to select the desired peripheral and data must be transferred during phase 2 of the CPU clock indicated by the E output, possible using the Q output as a strobe signal.

Interrupt facilities

The 6809 has two maskable hardware interrupts, one non-maskable interrupt, a reset interrupt and three software interrupts. Of the hardware interrupts NMI has the highest priority, followed by FIRQ, with IRQ at the lowest level. Reset takes precedence over all interrupts.

Each type of interrupt is vectored to its service routine by an address vector stored in the top locations of the memory. The layout of these interrupt vectors is:

FFFF	
	RESET
FFFE	
FFFD	
	NMI
FFFC	
FFFB	
	SWI
FFFA	
FFF9	
	IRQ
FFF8	
FFF7	
	FIRQ
FFF6	
FFF5	
	SWI2
FFF4	
FFF3	
	SWI3
FFF2	

Multiple interrupt sources at the IRQ or FIRQ levels can be handled, but external logic is required to deal with the priority of individual interrupts on each of these lines. For NMI, IRQ and the 3 SWI interrupts the CPU automatically saves the contents of all CPU registers except the system stack pointer. In the FIRQ interrupt operation the CPU saves only the program counter and status registers. The register contents are in each case pushed to the system stack and on an RTI instruction they are pulled from the stack and replaced into the appropriate CPU registers.

Instruction set

Unlike the other 6800 derived microprocessors the 6809 is not software compatible with the original 6800, although many of the instructions may look similar to those of the 6800. There are 71 basic instructions, each with many different addressing modes, giving over 1000 variations.

Arithmetic and logic

Normal 8-bit arithmetic performed in either the A or B accumulators includes addition and subtraction either with or without carry, as well as an 8 × 8 multiply function taking A × B and placing the result in the double length A+B register. It is also possible to use the A and B registers as a double length 16-bit D register for 16-bit addition and subtraction. For BCD arithmetic there is a decimal adjust function which operates only on the A accumulator and only for BCD addition. BCD subtraction must be corrected by user written software.

Logical operations available in both the accumulators are AND, OR and EXCLUSIVE OR. It is also possible to use an OR function on the status register. Shift and rotate operations are available for both the accumulators and memory locations. It is also possible to increment, decrement, complement, clear and negate both memory and accumulators. Compare functions are available for accumulators, stack and index registers.

Data transfers

Data may readily be transferred between the memory and both accumulators, stack pointers and index registers. Both stacks have push and pull instructions allowing the stacking of data. Transfer instructions are available for moving data between the accumulators and various other registers within the CPU.

For table handling a variety of indexing modes may be used.

Branch and jump

There are 16 conditional branch instructions all using relative addressing. Two versions of each instruction may be used, one giving an address range of ± 128 bytes whilst the other covers the whole memory address space. Three branches are unconditional, using either relative or other types of addressing. There are also 3 subroutine branches.

Individual bits of the two accumulators may be tested and it is also possible to test any memory location for use with conditional branches.

Addressing modes

There are 11 basic addressing modes: immediate, inherent, accumulator, direct, extended, indexed, relative, indexed indirect, relative indirect, extended indirect and absolute indirect. The indexed mode, however, contains five sub modes giving a wide variety of indexed addressing options.

Instructions for the 6809 may consist of either one, two, three or four successive bytes.

Timing

Standard 6809 microprocessors have an on-chip oscillator which is divided by four internally to produce the 2-phase clock for the CPU system. The standard 6809 uses a 4 MHz crystal to give a 2 MHz CPU cycle frequency. Average instructions will have execution times of about 2 – 6 µs.

For faster operation the 68A09 may be used with a 1.5 MHz CPU clock and the 68B09 will operate with a 2 MHz CPU clock.

The 6809E uses an external clock drive and corresponding A and B versions of this processor will run at 1.5 MHz and 2 MHz.

As with the 6800 the memory access occurs during phase 2 of the CPU clock and instruction execution during phase 1.

Support chips

Generally the support chips are those designed for use with the 6800 type microprocessor and include the following:

6821	Parallel interface with two 8-bit I/O ports
6828	Interrupt priority controller
6840	Programmable timer with three 16-bit timers
6843	Floppy disk controller
6844	Direct memory access controller
6845	CRT display controller
6847	Video display controller
68488	IEEE488 GPIB controller
6849	Floppy disk controller dual density
6850	Asynchronous serial I/O controller
6852	Synchronous serial I/O controller
6854	Serial data link controller for SDLP/HDLP
6860	Digital modem 0 – 600 b.p.s.
6862	Digital modem 2400 b.p.s.

Development aids

For software development Motorola produce the EXORSET system which provides editor, assembler, loader and debug facilities. This is a single stand alone unit with mini floppy disks for file storage and the operating system.

Full software and hardware development for the MC6809 is provided by the EXORCISER and EXORTERM systems. This includes in-circuit emulation for hardware debugging and also a logic analyser function. It is also possible to use some high level languages such as FORTRAN, BASIC and PASCAL with these two systems.

Thomson EFCIS provide similar facilities for hardware and software development and the 6809 can be handled by most of the Universal systems such as the Futuredata AMDS 2300 series and Tektronix 8001/8002 series.

MOTOROLA MC146805 SERIES

The Motorola MC146805 series devices are 8-bit CMOS types based upon the design of the MC6805 microcomputer. They are single-chip microcomputers with on-chip mask programmed ROM.

Typical applications will be those where low power is an advantage, such as for battery operated and portable equipment, and where fairly complex processing power is required. They would compete with types such as the RCA 1800 series, although the 146805 can offer more computing power and higher speed. Because of the CMOS construction the 146805 is relatively tolerant of supply voltage variations and is ideal for use in battery operated equipment. Versions will be made available for operation at 3 V and also for operation on much higher voltages, although the standard type is designed for a +5 V supply.

Use of a masked ROM version implies high production volume, but the 146805E version is available for use with an external ROM and will be useful for prototype work and for small quantity custom designs.

Prime manufacturer

Motorola Semiconductor Inc.

Devices available

MC146805E2   No ROM, 112-byte RAM
MC146805F   1.1 kbyte mask ROM, 64-byte RAM
MC146805G   2 kbyte mask ROM, 112-byte RAM

Alternative source devices

None at present.

Architecture

The MC146805 has basically the same architecture as the *n*MOS MC6805 microcomputer and follows the general philosophy of the Motorola 6800 series.

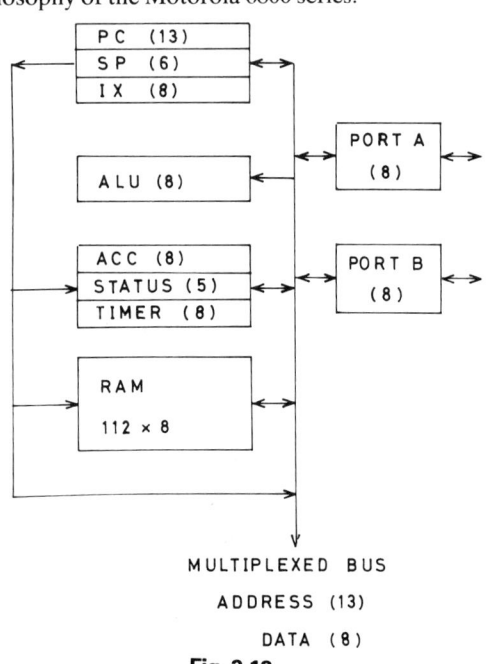

Fig. 3.13

Arithmetic and logic are governed by an 8-bit accumulator and ALU, together with a 5-bit condition code or status register. There are no general purpose registers since, as with other 6800 types, the 146805 can use memory locations as general purpose registers.

A 13-bit program counter register is used, divided into an 8-bit lower byte and a 5-bit upper section. This allows access to 8 kbyte of memory which will be common for program, data and input–output.

The 146805 has a 6-bit stack pointer which is combined with a fixed bit pattern to place the stack in RAM at the addresses from hex. 40 to hex. 7F. The stack will be automatically initialised at the top of the RAM when the CPU is reset and stacks build downwards through memory. An 8-bit index register IX is used to provide indexed addressing.

The 146805 has an on-chip clock generator and also an 8-bit timer/counter and 7-bit prescaler counter. On-chip RAM of 117 bytes is provided for use as a scratchpad memory and as general purpose registers. There are two programmable bidirectional input–output ports. Access to external memory is provided by a 13-bit address bus, the lower 8 bits of which are multiplexed with the data bus.

Package

MC146805F   28-pin dual in line type
Other types 40-pin dual in line type

Pin connections

MC146805E2

1	RESET	21	B7
2	IRQ	22	B6
3	LI	23	B5
4	DS	24	B4
5	R/W	25	B3
6	AS	26	B2
7	PA7	27	B1
8	PA6	28	B0
9	PA5	29	PB7
10	PA4	30	PB6
11	PA3	31	PB5
12	PA2	32	PB4
13	PA1	33	PB3
14	PA0	34	PB2
15	A12	35	PB1
16	A11	36	PB0
17	A10	37	TIMER
18	A9	38	OSC2
19	A8	39	OSC1
20	V_{ss}	40	V_{dd}

Signal functions

PA0 – PA7	Port A 8-bit programmable I/O lines
PB0 – PB7	Port B 8-bit programmable I/O lines
B0 – B7	Multiplexed data/address bus tri-state
A8 – A12	Address bus outputs tri-state
RESET	Reset input (active low)
OSC1, OSC2	Timing crystal pins
TIMER	Timer input clock line
DS	Data strobe output
AS	Address strobe output
IRQ	Interrupt request input (active low)

MOTOROLA MC146805 SERIES

R/W   Read–write control output (write low)
LI   Instruction fetch status output
V_{dd}, V_{ss} Power supply inputs

All signals are TTL compatible and outputs will probably drive one TTL load when a +5 V supply is used. Inputs have protection diodes for static protection.

Power requirements

V_{dd} +4.5 V to +6 V
V_{ss} 0 V
Supply current   4 mA typical
Versions will be available for 3 V operation and for higher voltages than 6 V

Temperature range

0°C to +70°C

Input–output

The MC146805 like other members of the 6800 family uses a memory mapped I/O system where input–output devices are simply treated as memory locations.

In the 146805 two programmable 8-bit ports are provided, each port with a data register and a data direction register. Lines are programmed as outputs by placing a '1' into the corresponding bit position of the data direction register. The port A data register is at memory address 0 and the port B data register at address 1, whilst the data direction registers are located at addresses 4 and 5. Data are read from or written to port registers by normal memory load and store instructions.

The on-chip timer has two registers associated with it. One register provides timer control whilst the other is the timer/counter data register. The control register allows a prescaler count from 1 to 128 in binary steps to be selected. Four modes of timer operation can be selected. In mode 1 the timer operates from the internal prescaler clock, whilst mode 2 allows the TIMER input signal to be ANDed with the internal clock to allow pulse width measurement. In mode 3 the timer is dialled and in mode 4 the timer is clocked by a signal from the timer input pin. The timer data register is located at address 8 in the memory map and the control register is at address 9.

In the memory map the on-chip RAM normally resides from location 16 (hex. 10) to 127 (hex. 7F) and the upper 64 bytes may be used for the stack. Other memory addresses in this area up to location 127 may be used by external memory.

Interrupt facilities

The 146805 provides one external maskable interrupt as well as two timer interrupts and a software interrupt. All interrupts are vectored, with the vectors located at the top of the memory map:

Address	Vector
1FFF	Reset vector
1FFE	
1FFD	SWI vector
1FFC	
1FFB	External interrupt
1FFA	
1FF9	Timer interrupt
1FF8	
1FF7	Timer (WAIT) interrupt
1FF6	

External interrupts may be activated by an input to the IRQ line, which may be either edge or level sensitive and requires a signal falling to the zero state. These interrupts may be masked as required.

The timer has two forms of interrupt operation, but both are triggered when the timer decrements to zero. In one case if the CPU is in a wait condition the timer interrupt will go to the vector at location 1FF6/7 instead of to the normal vector at 1FF8/9. Timer interrupts may be masked in the same way as external interrupts.

A software interrupt may be generated by using the SWI instruction and its basic action will be the same as for a hardware interrupt except that it cannot be masked. Reset acts like an interrupt and uses the vector at 1FFE/F.

When an interrupt occurs the contents of the accumulator, status register, index register and program counter are saved automatically on the stack and will be returned during an RTI instruction execution at the end of the interrupt routine.

Instruction set

There are 65 instructions in the available set, which is the same as for the *n*MOS 6805 processor. General instruction format is similar to that of the 6800 with 1, 2 or 3-byte operation codes.

Arithmetic and logic
Eight-bit addition and subtraction, either with or without a carry, are provided and facilities are available for decimal arithmetic.

Logical functions provided are AND, OR and EX-CLUSIVE OR, as well as a range of shift and rotate operations. The shift and rotate functions also work on memory, as do the increment, decrement, negate and complement instructions. Comparisons can be made in the accumulator and there are some operations allowing individual bits to be manipulated.

Data transfer
Data are readily transferred between the accumulator, memory, index and status registers as well as via the input–output ports.

There is no facility for a data stack on this processor and hence no push or pull instructions. The stack is used only for saving machine contents during subroutines and interrupts.

Branch and jump

There are 18 conditional branch operations, including some bit tests, and there are two unconditional branches plus a single unconditional jump. Branch and jump to subroutine are provided as well as appropriate return instructions for both subroutine and interrupt operations.

Addressing modes

The processor supports 10 addressing modes, including direct, implied, immediate, extended direct, relative, 3 modes of indexing and 2 forms of bit addressing.

Timing

Instruction cycle time is typically 1 μs, giving instruction execution times of from 2 to 6 μs. The on-chip oscillator has a typical frequency of 4 MHz.

Support chips

Not normally required, but this device can use any of the support chips designed for use with the 6800 series of microprocessors.

Development aids

Facilities are provided on the Motorola EXORCISER system for handling software development and hardware testing of this range of processors.

MULLARD MAB8400 SERIES

The 8400 series is a family of *n*MOS 8-bit single-chip microcomputers developed by Mullard for use in controller type applications and fabricated using the Philips 700 *n*MOS process.

The design of the 8400 devices has been developed from that of the popular industry standard 8048 series and their basic architecture and instruction sets are similar. The pin layout and packaging of the 8400 series are similar to those of the Intel 8021.

The 8400 series offers a range of sizes for internal RAM and mask programmed ROM, whilst all devices have 20 I/O lines available. An interesting feature is the provision of a serial input–output facility by which several 8400 devices can be made to communicate with one another.

Prime manufacturer

Mullard Ltd.

Devices available

MAB8400	128-byte RAM, external ROM
MAB8405	32-byte RAM, 512-byte ROM
MAB8410	64-byte RAM, 1 kbyte ROM
MAB8420	64-byte RAM, 2 kbyte ROM
MAB8440	128-byte RAM, 4 kbyte ROM

Note that the MAB8400 has a socket for mounting a 4k or 8k ROM or EPROM on the package.

Alternative source devices

None at present.

Architecture

The basic processing power is provided by an 8-bit accumulator and ALU which permit both binary and BCD arithmetic as well as logical operations. Carry, accumulator zero and individual bit tests are provided for the control of branch operations.

The 13-bit program counter register allows addressing of up to 8 kbyte of program ROM, which is divided up into banks of 2 kbyte each and further subdivided into pages of 256 bytes. Bank switching is governed by memory bank select instructions, whilst jump and call instructions are used for crossing page boundaries within the program memory. The first 8 bytes of the program memory space are reserved for reset and interrupt service routine vectors.

A separate data address register is used to access the RAM, which may consist of up to 128 bytes. The first 16 bytes of RAM are normally used to provide a bank of 8 registers and an 8-level stack. The first two registers are used as indirect pointers to the rest of the RAM. A second bank of 8 registers may be set up in locations 24 – 31 and used during interrupt operations or subroutines if desired. The stack uses 2 bytes per level to store the program address and 3 processor status bits. The RAM locations above 32 are used for general purpose storage.

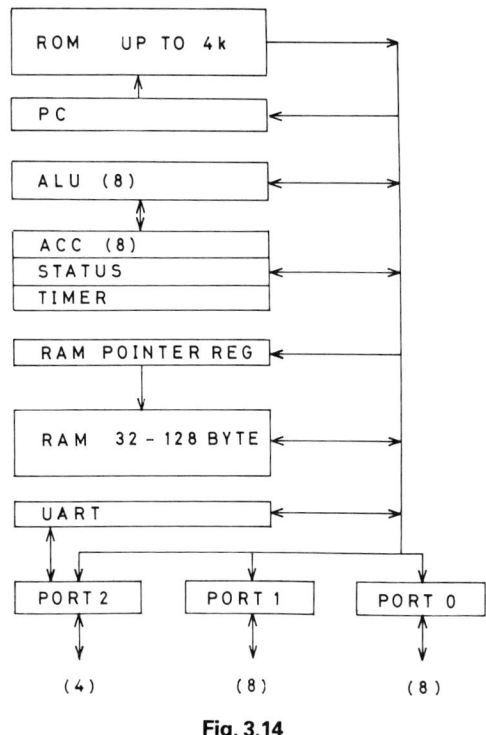

Fig. 3.14

The memory map for the on-chip RAM is:

```
127  _____
            User RAM
 32  _____
 31
            Register
            Bank2
 25  _____ R1'
 24  _____ R0'
 23
            Stack
  8  _____
  7
            Register
            Bank 1
  2  _____
  1  _____ R1
  0  _____ R0
```

An on-chip 8-bit counter/timer is provided and there are a total of 20 quasi bidirectional input–output lines arranged as two ports of 8 lines each and one port of 4 lines. One line can also be used for serial data transfer and a separate serial clock output line is also provided. Two trigger inputs are provided, one being used as a zero crossing detector and the other for interrupt operation.

An on-chip generator may be used with an external crystal or alternatively an external clock may be applied.

Package

28-pin dual in line

MULLARD MAB8400 SERIES

Pin connections

1	P22	15	XTAL1
2	P23	16	XTAL2
3	SCLK	17	RESET
4	P00	18	P10
5	P01	19	P11
6	P02	20	P12
7	P03	21	P13
8	P04	22	P14
9	P05	23	P15
10	P06	24	P16
11	P07	25	P17
12	INT/T0	26	P20
13	T1	27	P21
14	V_{ss}	28	V_{cc}

Signal functions

P00 – P07	Port 0 8-bit I/O
P10 – P17	Port 1 8-bit I/O
P20 – P23	Port 2 4-bit I/O
SCLK	Serial clock I/O
XTAL1, XTAL2	Timing crystal
RESET	Reset input (active high)
INT/T0	Interrupt input (active low)
T1	Test input (zero crossing)
V_{cc}	Power supply +5 V
V_{ss}	Power ground
P23	Used for serial I/O
XTAL1	Used for external clock input

Power requirements

V_{cc} +5 V ± 10%
V_{ss} 0 V

Input–output

Input lines to the 8400 device are TTL compatible but not latched. Input T1 can be used as a zero crossing detector by a.c. coupling the input via 1 μF, and will detect within ± 100 mV up to 1000 Hz. Maximum input level is 3 V p–p. This input may also be used to drive the internal counter.

Output lines are normally push pull and will drive one TTL load. Alternative mask options for the output lines are open drain either with or without pull up resistors. Output signals are internally latched.

The serial input–output facility contains its own data and status registers and can operate independently of the CPU, thus reducing program load for handling serial I/O. It also contains an address register which allows several 8400 devices to communicate with one another selectively by using a different address code for each device. The address code is sent as part of the serial data stream. The serial I/O clock can also be programmed over a wide range by a clock control register.

Four outputs (P10, P11, P23 and SCLK) are designed to sink high currents of about 7 mA.

A positive going pulse on the reset input causes the CPU system to be reset and all input–output lines to be set to the input mode. Following reset the I/O lines must be programmed to their desired mode.

Instruction set

The basic instruction set is the same as for the 8048 but with 15 instructions omitted and 10 new instructions added to deal with the serial I/O, larger ROM size and to provide extra facilities. There are a total of 87 instructions in the set, mostly single-byte but with some 2-byte instructions.

Accumulator

ADD	Add to accumulator
ADDC	Add with carry
ANL	AND accumulator
ORL	OR accumulator
XRL	EXCLUSIVE OR accumulator
RL, RR	Rotate left or right
RLC, RRC	Rotate l. or r. through carry
DAA	Decimal adjust for BCD work
Increment, Decrement, Clear and Complement accumulator	
SWAP	Swap upper and lower nibbles of accumulator

Data moves

MOV A,n	Move data to accumulator
MOV n,A	Move data from accumulator
MOV n,data	Move data to register or RAM
XCH A,n	Exchange data between A and n
MOV A,PSW	Move status word to acc.
MOV PSW,A	Stores bit 3 of acc. in bit 3 of PSW

Branch operations

Only JMP (unconditional) allows a branch outside a page but within a 2k bank of program memory.

Conditional jumps within a page can be made on the states of carry, T0 input, T1 input, timer flag and not zero result of decrementing a register or RAM location. Jumps are also available for bit tests on accumulator and on zero/non-zero contents of accumulator.

Subroutines are accessed by a CALL and returned from by RET instruction. The instruction RETR is used for interrupt service routine returns.

Control

SEL MBn	Selects program memory bank (must precede JMP)
SEL RBn	Selects register banks RB0 or RB1
ENI, DISI	Enable or disable interrupt
CLRC, CPLC	Clear or complement carry flag

Input–output and timer

Instructions are provided for transfer of data between the accumulator and the I/O ports or the timer/counter and for control of the serial I/O interface. These include start and stop instructions for the counter and interrupt control for both counter and serial I/O. To use a line as input a '1' state is written to the corresponding output latch.

Register operations

Registers may be directly incremented or decremented.

Addressing modes

For most of the arithmetic, logic, move and exchange instructions three basic addressing modes are used, as illustrated for an ADD instruction.

ADD A,Rx   Add contents of register Rx to acc.
ADD A,@Rx   Add RAM data addressed by Rx to acc. (x=0 or 1)
ADD A,data Add data in following byte to acc.

Note that only registers R0 to R7 or R0' to R7' can be addressed directly, according to which register bank has been selected. All other RAM locations are addressed indirectly by using the contents of R0 or R1 and the @ form of addressing.

Indexed addressing is readily achieved by incrementing or decrementing the pointer register R0 or R1 as required.

Timing

The 8400 devices are generally intended to be run using a 4.43 MHz crystal for the clock oscillator, under which conditions the instruction cycle time is 6.77 μs. All instructions will be executed in either one or two cycles. This is somewhat slower than the 2.5 μs cycle time of the 8048, but faster than the 10 μs time of the 8021.

Because the 8400 family uses dynamic logic on the chip the clock frequency, when an external clock is used, must be higher than 600 Hz.

Support devices

No support devices are normally used with this microcomputer.

Development aids

The most comprehensive development aid for the 8400 family is the Philips PM4421 microcomputer development system. This has editor, assembler, cross assembler and linker software for the 8400 series and can provide debugging and emulation facilities.

For evaluation or simple prototype design the PM4300 design aid is available. This allows programs to be written and debugged.

Software for the 8400 can readily be developed on any system which supports the 8048 series computers and has a macro assembler, since the new instructions of the 8400 can be handled by macros. The resultant program might then be down loaded to a PM4300 to allow emulation of the prototype design.

The MAB8400 chip can be used for prototyping since it has a piggyback socket for an external ROM and the prototype design can be tested before production of the ROM mask.

NATIONAL 8060/8070 SERIES

The National Semiconductor INS8060 is an 8-bit medium power *n*MOS microprocessor, originally introduced as the SC/MP2. It was a replacement for the earlier SC/MP 8-bit *p*MOS microprocessor. National have also introduced the 8070 series of devices, with a slightly enhanced architecture and including on-chip RAM and ROM facilities.

In terms of computing power the 8060/8070 types fall into much the same group as the 8048, MC6805 and F8 types. The design aim was to produce an effective but low cost microprocessor system, and typical applications would be in controllers and small microcomputer systems. The 8060 has been popular in Europe for use in hobbyist computer systems because of the relative simplicity and low cost of construction. The 8070 series devices provide single or 2-chip systems which are ideal for small dedicated controller applications.

Prime manufacturer

National Semiconductor Corp.

Devices available

INS8060	Basic SC/MP2 CPU chip
INS8070	CPU with 64-byte RAM
INS8072	CPU with 2.5 kbyte ROM and 64-byte RAM
INS8074	CPU with 4 kbyte ROM and 64-byte RAM
INS8075	As 8074 but with on-chip BASIC interpreter

Alternative source devices

Signetics

8060 Basic CPU chip

Architecture

The CPU has 8-bit data paths and uses an 8-bit ALU and accumulator for arithmetic and logic. There is also an 8-bit extension register for use with the accumulator.

The program counter has 16 bits, allowing access to 65 kbyte of memory. The address bus, however, is only 12 bits wide and the 4 upper bits of the address are output on the 4 lower bits of the data bus. A strobe output is provided to allow these bits of the address to be latched externally.

Four 16-bit pointer registers are provided, of which PTR0 is the program counter. All four registers may be used as index or stack pointers.

An 8-bit status register is provided for condition flags. An interesting feature is that two flag bits may be controlled by hardware inputs and three other flags may be used to provide input signals.

Four status and control signals are multiplexed on the upper four bits of the data bus to indicate the state of the CPU and the type of instruction cycle being executed.

The 8070 series devices have a variety of options of on-chip ROM and RAM and have a 16-bit address bus which is completely independent of the data bus. These chips also have hardware multiplication and division logic for higher speed arithmetic operation.

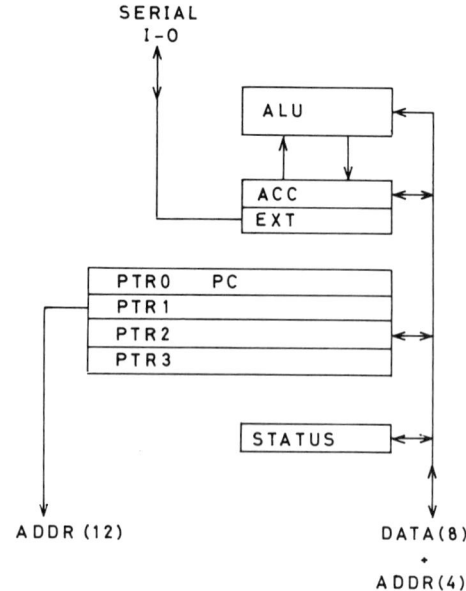

Fig. 3.15

The 8060 has a serial input–output channel provided on the chip but this is not available on the 8070 versions.

Package

40-pin dual in line type plastic or ceramic

Pin connections (8060 type)

1	NWDS	21	FLG1
2	NRDS	22	FLG2
3	NEN_{IN}	23	S_{OUT}
4	NEN_{OUT}	24	S_{IN}
5	NBREQ	25	A0
6	NHOLD	26	A1
7	NRST	27	A2
8	CONT	28	A3
9	DB7	29	A4
10	DB6	30	A5
11	DB5	31	A6
12	DB4	32	A7
13	DB3	33	A8
14	DB2	34	A9
15	DB1	35	A10
16	DB0	36	A11
17	SENSA	37	X_{IN}
18	SENSB	38	X_{OUT}
19	FLG0	39	NADS
20	V_{ss}	40	V_{cc}

Signal functions

A0 – A11	Address bus outputs tri-state
DB0 – DB7	Data bus bidirectional tri-state
X_{IN}, X_{OUT}	Timing crystal connections
SENSA, SENSB	External status inputs
FLG0, FLG1, FLG2	Flag output lines
NRST	Reset input (active low)
NADS	Address strobe output (active low)
NRDS	Data read strobe output (active low tri-state)

NWDS	Data write strobe output (active low tri-state)
NBREQ	Bus request/busy bidirectional
NEN$_{IN}$	Data bus enable input (active low)
NEN$_{OUT}$	Bus status output (active low)
NHOLD	Hold input for slow memories (active low)
S$_{IN}$, S$_{OUT}$	Serial input and output lines
CONT	Halt/continue input
V$_{cc}$, V$_{ss}$	Power supply inputs

Power requirements

V$_{cc}$ +5 V ± 5%
V$_{ss}$ 0 V
Supply current   8060 type 45 mA max.
  8070 series 100 mA max.

Temperature range

0°C to +70°C

Input–output

All logical input and output signals are TTL compatible and outputs will generally drive one TTL load.

For parallel output a memory mapped technique may be used where the I/O device is treated as a memory location and the normal load and store type instructions are used.

On the 8060 (SC/MP2) a serial input–output facility is provided via the S$_{IN}$ and S$_{OUT}$ lines. Data are transferred to and from the extension register with bit 0 being output to the S$_{OUT}$ line and bit 7 being loaded from the S$_{IN}$ line. A single SIO instruction is used for this purpose.

Data may also be input via the SENSA and SENSB lines, when they will be transferred directly to the status register whilst the flag bits of the status register may be used to output data to the FLG output lines of the CPU.

Interrupt facilities

The 8060 has a rather elementary masked interrupt facility which is activated by an input to the SENSA line. A mask bit in the status register may be used to enable and diable the interrupt.

Unlike other processors the 8060 does not automatically save any register contents. This must be done by program instructions. On the arrival of an accepted interrupt the contents of the program counter are exchanged with those of pointer register PTR3, which must contain the start address of the interrupt service routine. No specific return from interrupt is provided, and this must be achieved by exchanging PTR3 with the program counter at the end of the service routine.

Instruction set

There are 46 different single and double-byte instructions for the 8060 type processor, and the 8070 series includes an enhanced instruction set.

Arithmetic and logic

Standard 8-bit addition and subtraction in either binary or decimal format are provided. In the 8070 versions hardware multiply and divide are also implemented.

Logical functions provided in the accumulator are AND, OR and EXCLUSIVE OR, as well as shifts, rotates, complement and increment or decrement. The accumulator is the only register on which these functions are provided.

Data transfer

Data transfers between accumulator and memory or pointer and status registers are provided. The CPU does not support data stack operations directly, but these can be achieved by program operations. In the 8070 series push and pop instructions are provided for use with a data stack.

Branch and jump

There are 3 conditional jumps and one unconditional one. In the 8060 there is no jump to subroutine instruction, and this is achieved by exchanging the contents of the program counter with those of a pointer register to branch to the subroutine and restoring them from the pointer register at the end of the subroutine.

Timing

The 8060 and 8070 processors have on-chip clock logic which may be timed by an external crystal. Operating frequency is 1 MHz and typical instruction execution time is 10 μs.

Support chips

No specific support chips are produced for this series, but types intended for other processors such as the 2650 and 8080 may readily be used with the 8060 and 8070 type devices.

Development aids

An evaluation kit and keyboard unit are available for the 8060 SC/MP2 type device and software development may be carried out on the 8080 based National Semiconductor STARPLEX type microprocessor development system.

The INS8075 has a BASIC interpreter programmed into its on-chip ROM to enable it to execute directly BASIC language programs. This is, however, a somewhat limited version of the BASIC language.

NATIONAL NSC800

Using their new double polysilicon CMOS (P²CMOS) fabrication process National Semiconductor have developed a new and very powerful microprocessor called the NSC800.

This processor appears to combine a number of features from both the Intel 8085 and the Zilog Z80 processors, whilst providing very low power consumption and a wide tolerance of power supply voltage variations. Internally the arrangement of working registers is similar to that of the Z80. There is also a serial input–output facility similar to that provided by the 8085.

In terms of processing power the NSC800 ranks at the same level as the Z80 and Motorola 6809, and might be used in similar applications to those processors. With its low power demand and tolerance of supply variation the NSC800 is highly suited to portable equipment and battery operated systems in which complex processing ability is required.

The NSC800 acts as the central processor unit for use with a series of support devices also fabricated in CMOS and designed to work together to form a powerful microcomputer system. It seems likely that this particular family of parts could become very popular in the future.

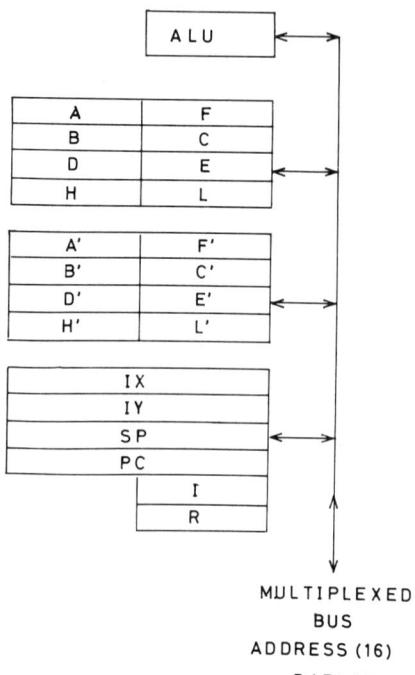

Fig. 3.16

Prime manufacturer

National Semiconductor Corp.

Devices available

NSC800 Central processor unit

Alternative source devices

None at present.

Architecture

As will be seen from fig. 3.16 the internal architecture is similar to that of the Zilog Z80, with some features of the 8085.

At the centre of the CPU is a large bank of general purpose 8-bit working registers. This in fact divides into two groups, with eight 8-bit registers in each group. An 8-bit accumulator A is used as the primary accumulator register and there is an associated 8-bit flag register F. These registers may, for some operations, be paired together to form a 16-bit register. The other 6 registers may also be paired as BC, DE and HL to form 16-bit registers or may operate separately as 8-bit registers with some arithmetic capability. The other set of 8 registers A'F', B'C', D'E' and H'L' may be used as an alternative working register bank when a subroutine or interrupt is being processed.

The program counter has 16 bits and allows access to a total of 65 kbytes of address space for program instructions. There is a 16-bit stack pointer register which allows stacks of varying length to be set up anywhere in memory. Two 16-bit index registers IX and IY permit very efficient forms of index addressing.

Two registers also found in the Z80 are the I register, which provides the upper 8 bits of the interrupt vector address, and the R register, which controls dynamic memory refresh operation.

Unlike the Z80 the National NSC800 uses multiplexing on the lower eight bits of the address bus which share the same package pins with the data bus lines. This arrangement allows the NSC800 to have many more control inputs and outputs and is similar to that used for the Intel 8085. The pin layout, however, is not compatible with either the 8085 or Z80 types.

Package

40-pin dual in line package plastic or ceramic
Suffix N signifies a plastic package (NSC800N)
Suffix J signifies a ceramic package

Pin connections

1	A8	21	NMI
2	A9	22	RSTA
3	A10	23	RSTB
4	A11	24	RSTC
5	A12	25	INTR
6	A13	26	INTA
7	A14	27	SI
8	A15	28	RFSH
9	CLK	29	SO
10	X_{OUT}	30	ALE
11	X_{IN}	31	WR
12	AD0	32	RD
13	AD1	33	RESET IN
14	AD2	34	IO/M
15	AD3	35	BACK
16	AD4	36	BREQ
17	AD5	37	RESET OUT
18	AD6	38	WAIT
19	AD7	39	PS
20	V_{ss}	40	V_{cc}

Signal functions

AD0 – AD7	Multiplexed address/data bus. Lower 8 bits of address output when ALE goes low. Bus is tri-state
A8 – A15	Upper 8 bits address bus, output tri-state
RESET IN	Reset input (active low)
RESET OUT	Reset status output (active high)
CLK	Clock output
X_{IN}, X_{OUT}	Timing crystal pins (external clock to X_{IN})
RD	Read strobe output (active low)
WR	Write strobe output (active low)
PS	Power save input selects low power hold mode when set low
WAIT	Wait request input (active low)
NMI	Non-maskable interrupt input (active low)
BREQ	Bus request (active low) input
BACK	Bus acknowledge status output (active low)
ALE	Address latch enable output high to low change indicates valid address output on AD lines
INTR	Interrupt request input (active low)
INTA	Interrupt acknowledge output (active low)
RSTA, RSTB, RSTC	Restart interrupt inputs (active low)
S0, S1	Bus status outputs
RFSH	Dynamic RAM refresh status output (active low)
V_{cc}, V_{ss}	Power supply inputs

Power requirements

V_{cc}	+3 V to +12 V
V_{ss}	0 V
Supply current at V_{cc}	+5 V 10 mA

Temperature range

Standard commercial part 0°C to +70°C

Industrial temperature range −40°C to +85°C
Indicated by suffix I in the type number

Military temperature range −55°C to +125°C
Indicated by suffix M in the type number

Input–output

The NSC800, like the Z80 and 8085, can directly address up to 256 input–output devices. When an input–output instruction is being executed the IO/M output control line goes high and the lower 8 bits of the address refer to an input–output device rather than external memory. Data are transferred via the data bus and external logic may be needed to control the bus access by memory and I/O devices.

All logical input and output signals are CMOS compatible and when the supply voltage is +5 V they will also match with TTL devices. Output lines are capable of driving a single TTL load. Inputs have diode protection against static voltages, but the device should be treated in the same way as other CMOS types.

Like the Z80 this processor is capable of carrying out block transfers of data to or from input–output devices. It is also possible to handle input–output in the memory mapped mode by treating the external device as one or more memory locations and using conventional data transfer instructions.

Interrupt facilities

On the NSC800 the interrupt system is organised in much the same way as that of the 8085. Five hardware interrupts are provided, one being non-maskable (NMI) and the remaining four maskable.

The hardware interrupts of the NSC800 have been given built in priority, with NMI having the highest level, followed by RSTA, RSTB and RSTC. The INTR interrupt has the lowest of the priority levels. Reset takes priority over all interrupts.

When an NMI interrupt occurs the CPU will save the contents of the program counter on the stack and then jump to location 66 (hex.), which contains the start of the service routine.

Restart interrupts RSTA, RSTB and RSTC operate in a similar way to NMI, except that they can be disabled. In this case the restart vector addresses are 3C, 34 and 2C (hex.) respectively.

The INTR interrupt can operate in three different modes which may be selected by software. In mode 0 it operates in much the same way as the interrupt on an 8080 processor. On acceptance of the interrupt the CPU puts a signal out on the INTA line and expects to receive an instruction code via the data bus from the interrupting device. This instruction will normally be a branch to the interrupt service routine.

Mode 1 operation is similar to that of the NMI interrupt and vectors the CPU to an interrupt service routine starting at location 38 (hex.) in the memory.

In mode 2 the programmer may set up a table of interrupt vector addresses for different interrupt service routines and on receipt of the interrupt the CPU will expect an 8-bit address byte from the peripheral device. This byte is used as the lower 8 bits of the interrupt vector, whilst the upper 8 bits are supplied by the I register which would have been loaded before the interrupt. This arrangement allows jumps to any part of program memory for the interrupt routine.

The NSC800 also permits software interrupts which use the restart (RST) instruction and may be vectored to addresses in the first page of the memory map.

Instruction set

For the NSC800 the instruction set is basically the same as that of the Zilog Z80, and programs written for that device should run on the NSC800. There are 121 instructions in the set.

Arithmetic and logic

All 8-bit arithmetic is carried out in the currently selected accumulator register A or A'. Functions provided are addition, subtraction and decimal mode addition. All operations may be either with or without the carry bit.

It is possible to carry out 16-bit additions using the register pairs AF, BC, DE and HL, with the result being placed in one of the register pairs. In the case of the HL register pair it is also possible to carry out 16-bit subtraction with carry.

Logical operations provided in the accumulator are AND, OR and EXCLUSIVE OR. It is also possible to increment, clear, decrement, complement and compare the contents of registers in the currently selected bank. Shift and rotate operations to either left or right are provided for all registers.

It is possible to set, reset and test individual bits of data in either the memory or the working registers of the NSC800.

Data transfers

There are 41 instructions for moving data around within the NSC800 system. These include a range of 8-bit and 16-bit load and store instructions for memory to register transfers and a range of load, store and exchange instructions for register to register data transfers.

Data stacks may be created within memory and may have variable length. Data may be pushed and popped on the stack from the working registers as 16-bit 2-byte words.

One useful feature of the NSC800 is the ability to make block transfers of data to and from the memory using only one instruction. These operations use the contents of register pair BC as a byte counter. During block transfers the address may be either incremented or decremented after the transfer of each data byte. It is also possible to carry out a search function through a block of memory in which the contents of successive memory bytes are compared with accumulator data.

As mentioned earlier input–output instructions may be used to access up to 256 separately addressed peripherals. It is also possible to carry out block transfers of data using register pair BC as a byte counter and registers HL as the data pointer.

Data within the memory may be shifted and rotated in the same way as data in the current register bank.

Branch and jump

There are two unconditional jump instructions, one being direct and the other indirect in addressing. One conditional jump is provided. This may seem limited, but in fact the conditional jump may specify a wide range of conditions according to the operand used in the instruction, and is equivalent to the whole range of conditional branches used in other processors such as the 8080 or 6800.

There are two subroutine calls, one being unconditional and the other responding to the same range of conditions as the conditional jump. Returns from the subroutine may also be made either conditional or unconditional. For subroutines only the program counter contents are saved on the stack.

System control

A number of instructions are provided for system control. These instructions include selection of interrupt mode, setting of interrupt enable mask, CPU halt and selection of current bank of working registers.

Addressing modes

The addressing modes provided include immediate, direct, register direct, register indirect, indirect, indexed and relative.

Timing

The internal clock generator is designed to operate with a 5 MHz timing crystal, to produce a 2.5 MHz CPU clock which is output via the clock CLK output line for system timing use. Instruction cycle time at this frequency is 1.6 μs and typical execution times will be from 2 to 5 μs.

A faster version of the NSC800 will also be available, giving a 4 MHz CPU clock, 1 μs instruction cycle time and typical execution times of 1 – 3 μs.

An external clock generator may be used by feeding the single-phase clock signal into the X_{IN} input line.

Support chips

At the present time few specially designed support chips are available for use with the NSC800:

NSC810 RAM—I/O—timer device
  This CMOS chip provides 128 bytes of static RAM, two 16-bit programmable counter/timers and 3 programmable 8-bit input–output ports in a 40-pin DIL package.

NSC830 ROM—I/O device
  This CMOS chip provides 2 kbyte of mask programmed ROM and three 8-bit programmable input–output ports in a 40-pin DIL package.

NSC831 I/O device
  This chip is basically the same as the NSC830 except that it has no on-chip ROM.

It should also be possible to use with the NSC800 any chips designed for use with the Z80 and possibly the 8085. CMOS support devices designed for the CDP1802 type CPU may also be useful in NSC800 based systems.

Development aids

Full hardware and software development facilities will be available on the National STARPLEX development system, which uses a floppy disk based operating system and will provide emulation and debugging facilities.

MOS TECHNOLOGY MCS6502 SERIES

The MOS Technology 6502 series microprocessors are *n*MOS 8-bit types, of which the 6502 is probably the most commonly found. Other processors in this series are mainly simplified variants designed to fit into smaller packages.

In many respects the basic design philosophy of the 6502 follows the same lines as that of the Motorola 6800 series. The 6502 is a slightly less complex processor in terms of its architecture, but it can in some respects be considered as an enhanced version of the 6800, particularly in its comprehensive range of addressing modes.

Because of the similar hardware design, the bus systems for the 6502 and 6800 appear to be the same, but in fact they are not directly compatible. Generally the support chips for the 6800 can readily be used with a 6502 CPU and the reverse is also true, although in some cases additional external logic may be required. The instruction sets may also appear to be similar, but are totally incompatible as far as machine code is concerned.

Some of the wide popularity of the 6502 series can be attributed to their use in such popular personal computer systems as the CBM PET and the Apple II.

Prime manufacturer

MOS Technology Inc., which is a subsidiary of Commodore Business Machines (CBM).

Devices available

MCS6502	Basic type 65k address on-chip clock
MCS6512	As 6502 but external clock
MCS6503	4k address range on-chip clock
MCS6504	8k address range on-chip clock, no NMI
MCS6505	4k address range on-chip clock, no NMI
MCS6506	4k address range on-chip clock, no NMI
MCS6507	8k address range on-chip clock, no interrupts
MCS6513	As 6503 but external clock
MCS6514	As 6504 but external clock
MCS6515	As 6505 but external clock

Alternative source devices

Rockwell

R6502, R6503, R6504, R6505, R6506, R6507
R6512, R6513, R6514, R6515

Synertek

SY6502, SY6503, SY6504, SY6505, SY6506, SY6507
SY6512, SY6513, SY6514, SY6515

EMM-Semi

6502, 6503, 6504, 6505, 6506, 6507
6512, 6513, 6514, 6515

Note that all of the 6502 series types are available with various clock speed options, with versions for 1 MHz, 2 MHz and 3 MHz maximum clock frequency.

Architecture

If the architecture diagram for the 6502 (fig. 3.17) is compared with that of the 6800 it will be seen that the 6502 is similar in design to the 6800, though rather less complex.

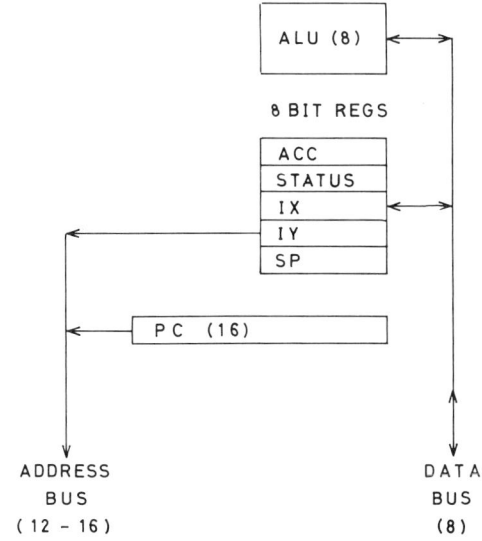

Fig. 3.17

Only one 8-bit accumulator is provided, compared with the two accumulators of the 6800, and this handles all arithmetic and logic operations via the ALU. Although slightly less flexible when dealing with 16-bit numbers, the single 8-bit accumulator is perfectly adequate for all normal computing requirements.

An 8-bit status register provides flags for zero, minus, carry and overflow results of operations, and for the interrupt, break and decimal modes.

Unlike the 6800 the 6502 has two 8-bit index registers rather than a single 16-bit index register. This limits the index range to 256 but provides much greater flexibility in dealing with data tables.

The stack pointer of the 6502 has only 8 bits and the stack is always located within page 1 of the memory map. It is possible to have any stack length up to 256 bytes and a number of separate stacks may be set up within page 1. This is slightly less flexible than the 6800, where the stacks may be set up anywhere in memory, but is perfectly adequate.

As with the 6800 there are no general purpose registers provided in the 6502, since it uses general memory locations for this purpose. Similarly all input–output devices will be treated simply as memory locations by the processor.

In the 6502 and 6512 the program counter register is 16 bits wide, allowing up to 65k of memory to be addressed. In other devices of the series the program counter length is cut to 12 or 13 bits, allowing either 4k or 8k of address space.

Like the 6800 the bus system of the 6502 comprises an 8-bit bidirectional data bus, a 16-bit address bus and some control signals. All operations are controlled by a 2-phase clock, and memory access is made on phase 2 of each cycle of the clock. Internal operations occur during phase 1.

The basic memory map for the 6502 is:

MOS TECHNOLOGY MCS6502 SERIES

```
FFFF  ─────  Vectors for int.
FFFA         and reset
FFF9  ─────
             Main user
             space
0200  ─────
01FF
             Stack area
0100  ─────
00FF
             Zero page
0000  ─────
```

Package

The 6502 and 6512 are supplied in 40-pin dual in line
All other types use a 28-pin dual in line package
All types use a plastic encapsulation

Pin connections

6502 and 6512

1	V_{ss}	21	V_{ss}
2	RDY	22	AB12
3	$\phi 1$	23	AB13
4	IRQ	24	AB14
5	No conn. (6502)	25	AB15
	V_{ss} (6512)		
6	NMI	26	DB7
7	SYNC	27	DB6
8	V_{cc}	28	DB5
9	AB0	29	DB4
10	AB1	30	DB3
11	AB2	31	DB2
12	AB3	32	DB1
13	AB4	33	DB0
14	AB5	34	R/W
15	AB6	35	No conn.
16	AB7	36	No conn. (6502)
			DBE (6512)
17	AB8	37	$\phi 0$ (6502)
			$\phi 2$ (6512)
18	AB9	38	S.O.
19	AB10	39	$\phi 2$ OUT
20	AB11	40	RESET

6503 28 pin

1	RESET	15	AB9
2	V_{ss}	16	AB10
3	IRQ	17	AB11
4	NMI	18	DB7
5	V_{cc}	19	DB6
6	AB0	20	DB5
7	AB1	21	DB4
8	AB2	22	DB3
9	AB3	23	DB2
10	AB4	24	DB1
11	AB5	25	DB0
12	AB6	26	R/W
13	AB7	27	$\phi 0$ IN
14	AB8	28	$\phi 2$ OUT

6504/6507 28 pin

1	RESET	15	AB10
2	V_{ss}	16	AB11
3	IRQ (6504)	17	AB12
	RDY (6507)		
4	V_{cc}	18	DB7
5	AB0	19	DB6
6	AB1	20	DB5
7	AB2	21	DB4
8	AB3	22	DB3
9	AB4	23	DB2
10	AB5	24	DB1
11	AB6	25	DB0
12	AB7	26	R/W
13	AB8	27	$\phi 0$ IN
14	AB9	28	$\phi 2$ OUT

Other 28-pin types have same AB and DB connections as above, according to whether they have 12 or 13-bit address. Other pins are different and manufacturer's data sheets should be consulted.

Signal functions

DB0–DB7	Bidirectional data bus
AB0–AB15	Address bus (output)
V_{ss}, V_{cc}	Power supplies
R/W	Read–write (low = write)
IRQ, NMI	Interrupt req. inputs active low
RDY	Ready input used to halt CPU
SYNC	Output (1 during instruction fetch)
RESET	Reset input (active low)
S.O.	Set overflow input
$\phi 0$, $\phi 1$, $\phi 2$	Clock signals
DBE	Data bus enable (active high)

Power requirements

V_{ss} = 0 V
V_{cc} = +5 V ± 5%
Power dissipation 700 – 800 mW

Signal levels

Inputs are TTL compatible 300 μA loading
Outputs will drive one TTL load
Data bus is tri-state

Input–output

The 6502 series treat all input–output as memory locations, data being presented or accepted via the data bus.

Interrupt facilities

The 6502 provides both maskable (IRQ) and non-maskable (NMI) interrupts. There is also a software interrupt facility using the BRK instruction. On an interrupt execution the program counter and status register are pushed to the stack. These are restored by the RTI instruction at the end of the interrupt routine. BRK is the same as IRQ, but not maskable and sets a flag bit in the status register. Interrupt vector addresses are stored at the top of memory as shown:

FFFF	IRQ vector	(MSB)
FFFE	IRQ vector	(LSB)
FFFD	Reset vector	(MSB)
FFFC	Reset vector	(LSB)
FFFB	NMI vector	(MSB)
FFFA	NMI vector	(LSB)

Reset causes a reset sequence within the CPU and the instruction address is obtained from FFFC/FFFD.

Multilevel interrupt operation is readily achieved and priorities may be dealt with either by polling software or by external hardware.

Instruction set

The 6502 instruction set contains 52 different instructions, and at first sight may appear to be very similar to that for the 6800 series microprocessors. Instructions may have one, two or three bytes.

Arithmetic and logic
Addition and subtraction with carry or borrow are provided using the 8-bit accumulator. A decimal mode also allows addition and subtraction of BCD format numbers. There are no complement or negate instructions and the accumulator cannot be directly incremented or decremented, although memory locations can.

AND, OR and EXCLUSIVE OR operations can be carried out between accumulator and memory. There are also shift and rotate left and right instructions for both memory and accumulator.

Branch and jump
A useful series of conditional branch instructions is provided, although this is not as extensive as those on the 6800. Status register bits may be set and reset by program. Tests for zero, negative, carry and overflow are provided.

Only unconditional jump and jump to subroutine are available. A subroutine jump automatically stores the return address on the stack.

Register and transfer operations
Data can readily be transferred between the A accumulator, the X and Y index registers and the stack pointer, or memory. Push and pull instructions allow data from the accumulator or status register to be transferred to the stack. Both index registers may be incremented or decremented.

Memory or accumulator words may be tested bit by bit if desired.

Timing

Like the 6800, the 6502 series uses a 2-phase processor clock, and all memory access is carried out during $\phi 2$ clock cycles. Most instructions take 2, 3 or 4 clock cycles and may use 1, 2 or 3 bytes of machine code.

The standard parts operate with a 1 MHz clock, giving instruction execution times of some 2 – 4 μs. Special high speed parts are available with clock frequencies of 2 or 3 MHz. These are coded with suffix A (6502A) for 2 MHz operation or suffix B (6502B) for 3 MHz operation.

Types 6502 to 6507 have on-chip clock phase generators but need an external crystal oscillator to provide the $\phi 0$ input, whilst types 6512 to 6515 require an external 2-phase non-overlapping clock signal applied to the $\phi 1$ and $\phi 2$ clock inputs.

Support devices

A wide range of support devices is available for the 6502 series microprocessors. Some of these are:

6520 PIA	Two 8-bit bidirectional programmable ports (identical to 6820)
6522	Versatile interface adapter (VIA) 2 × 8-bit ports as in 6520, plus 2 × 16-bit interval timers and a serial I/O facility
6530	1k ROM, 64-byte RAM, 2 × 8-bit parallel ports plus an 8-bit interval timer.
6531	2k ROM, 128 byte RAM, 2 × 8-bit parallel I/O, serial I/O and a 16-bit timer/counter
6532	128-byte RAM, 2 × 8-bit parallel I/O ports, 8-bit timer
6541	Keyboard/display controller
6545	Raster scan CRT controller
6551	Asynchronous serial I/O
6591	Floppy disk controller

The 6502 series may also be used with most of the 6800 series support devices. Some care may be needed with address decoding, however, since the 6500 has its lower address byte in the lower memory location whilst the 6800 stores its addresses in memory with the high address byte first.

Development aids

MOS Technology

KIM1	Stand alone board with keypad and LED displays

N.E.C. µPD7801 MICROCOMPUTER

The N.E.C. µPD7801 is an *n*MOS 8-bit single-chip microcomputer which appears to be an enhanced version of the 8080 CPU with some ROM, RAM and timer facilities on a single chip.

Designed for dedicated systems where minimum numbers of chips are desirable, this microcomputer is comparable to the Rockwell 6500/1, Motorola 6801 and Zilog Z8 types and has many of the features of the Z80 microprocessor.

Prime manufacturer

Nippon Electric Co. (N.E.C.)

Devices available

µPD7801   Single-chip 8-bit microcomputer

Alternative source devices

None.

Architecture

The basic architecture of the CPU is almost identical to that of the Zilog Z80 microprocessor.

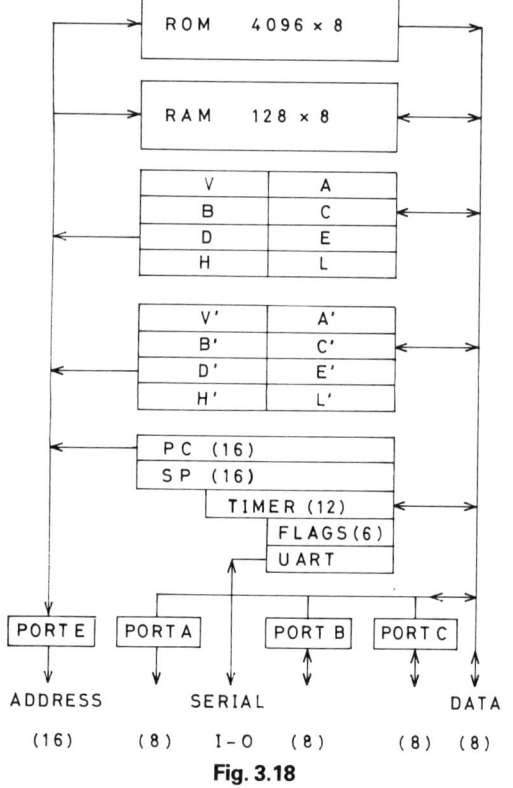

Fig. 3.18

Two general purpose register banks, each containing eight 8-bit registers, are used for arithmetic and logic operations. Only one group of eight registers is used at a time. An 8-bit ALU provides the arithmetic and logic processing.

A 16-bit program counter allows access to 65 kbyte of memory which is common for both program and data. There is a 16-bit stack pointer register allowing data stacks to be set up anywhere in the memory, also being used for subroutine and interrupt processing.

Five 8-bit input–output ports are provided on the chip and three of these may also be used to provide an 8-bit data bus and 16-bit address bus for use with external memory if required. Also provided on the chip is a 12-bit counter/timer and the clock generator for the CPU system.

A 4096 byte mask programmed ROM is used for the program memory and there is also a 128-byte on-chip RAM for use as a scratchpad memory and for the stack.

Package

64-pin quad in line type plastic package

Pin connections

1	PE15	33	PA0
2	CLK	34	PA1
3	DB7	35	PA2
4	DB6	36	PA3
5	DB5	37	PA4
6	DB4	38	PA5
7	DB3	39	PA6
8	DB2	40	PA7
9	DB1	41	PB0
10	DB0	42	PB1
11	INT2	43	PB2
12	INT1	44	PB3
13	INT0	45	PB4
14	WAIT	46	PB5
15	M1	47	PB6
16	WR	48	PB7
17	RD	49	PE0
18	PC7	50	PE1
19	PC6	51	PE2
20	PC5	52	PE3
21	PC4	53	PE4
22	PC3	54	PE5
23	PC2	55	PE6
24	PC1	56	PE7
25	PC0	57	PE8
26	SCK	58	PE9
27	SI	59	PE10
28	SO	60	PE11
29	RESET	61	PE12
30	X2	62	PE13
31	X1	63	PE14
32	V_{ss}	64	V_{cc}

Signal functions

PA0 – PA7	Port A 8-bit output
PB0 – PB7	Port B 8-bit bidirectional
PC0 – PC7	Port C 8-bit bidirectional
DB0 – DB7	Data bus bidirectional
PE0 – PE15	Port E and address bus output
INT0 – INT2	Interrupt request inputs
X1, X2	Timing crystal connections
SI, SO, SCK	Serial port input, output and clock
WR	Write strobe output
RD	Read strobe output
RESET	Reset input

WAIT	Wait state request input
M1	CPU cycle timing output
CLK	CPU clock output
V_{cc}, V_{ss}	Power supply inputs

All inputs and outputs have TTL compatible signals

Power requirements

V_{cc} +5 V ± 5%
V_{ss} 0 V

Temperature range

0°C to +70°C

Input–output

The 7801 provides five 8-bit data ports, although two of these are shared by the address bus outputs and port C is also used for various control inputs and outputs. Port A provides an output facility only, but others are bidirectional, except the address port which is also output only.

A serial port facility is provided with a separate clock line, which may be programmed for either input or output as required.

The on-chip timer is a 12-bit down counter, which can be programmed and includes a prescaler facility.

Interrupt facilities

There are 5 hardware interrupts, three from external lines INT0, INT1 and INT2, and two internal interrupts from the timer and the serial input–output port. Interrupts are vectored to their service routines by a series of vectors in the low end of memory from location 0 to location 64. Note that the ROM on the chip occupies the first 4 kbyte of the memory map and the on-chip RAM is located at the top of the memory space.

Instruction set

The instruction set of the µPD7801 is similar to that of the Zilog Z80 and contains 125 instructions.

Timing

The on-chip clock generator allows a cycle time of some 2 µs to be achieved by the CPU, giving execution speeds of the same order as those of the Z80 microprocessor. An external clock may also be used if desired by feeding it to the X1 input. The CLK output signal may be used for system timing and is half the frequency of the crystal clock.

Support chips

Normally the µPD7801 would be used as a stand alone computer or controller, but it can be used with external memory and is completely compatible with support chips designed for use with the 8080 and 8085 type microprocessors.

Development aids

There is an evaluation chip type µPD7800 which has no ROM on the chip and may be used for simple system development and testing.

There is a cross assembler available for use on the Intel Intellec type development system, and it is expected that further development aids will be available from N.E.C. in the future.

RCA 1800 SERIES

The 1802 is a CMOS 8-bit microprocessor developed by RCA and generally referred to by them as the COSMAC microprocessor. Although designed as a general purpose microprocessor it is not perhaps in the same class as the Z80, 6800 or 8080. Like the F8 and 3870 it is generally more suited to those simpler applications where its internal register arrangement can be used to advantage.

Being of CMOS construction the 1800 has very low power requirements and can operate over a wide range of supply line voltage. This makes it ideal for applications in portable battery operated equipment. Since the CPU logic is static the clock can be run at any speed or even stopped with no ill effects.

Unlike most other 8-bit microprocessors the 1802 offers a basic form of direct memory access and control of input–output devices without the need for support chips. This can also be an advantage in small systems.

Whilst the 1802 device is a microprocessor the 1804 with its on-chip RAM and mask programmed ROM operates as a single-chip 8-bit microcomputer which is pin and software compatible with the 1802 and can support external memory if desired.

One possible disadvantage of the 1802/1804 is that its internal architecture and software organisation are different from most other types of processor and may be found slightly more difficult to program.

Prime manufacturer

Radio Corporation of America (RCA).

Devices available

1802 microprocessor

CDP1802D	4 – 10.5 V
CDP1802E	4 – 10.5 V
CDP1802CD	4 – 6.5 V
CDP1802CE	4 – 6.5 V

1804 microcomputer
64-byte RAM, 2 kbyte ROM and 8-bit timer/counter on chip

CDP1804D	4 – 10.5 V
CDP1804E	4 – 10.5 V
CDP1804CD	4 – 6.5 V
CDP1804CE	4 – 6.5 V

Note RCA also plan to introduce silicon on sapphire versions of 1802 and 1804 which will operate at higher speed.

Alternative source devices

Hughes Microelectronics

HCMP1802 equivalent to 1802
HCMP1802C equivalent to 1802C
D suffix indicates ceramic package
P suffix indicates plastic package

Note Hughes plan to introduce an advanced 1800 type processor under the type number HCMP1806.

Solid State Scientific
SCP1802
SCP1802L

Architecture

A central feature of the 1800 architecture is an array of 16 general purpose 16-bit registers, each organised as two bytes. Memory addressing is by a 16-bit word, multiplexed as two successive bytes on the 8 address lines. Addresses are generated by selected registers in the array. Unlike other 8-bit processors which usually have dedicated registers for the program counter, stack pointer and data pointers, the 1800 is unique in that any of the 16 registers may be allocated to these functions at any time as required by the program.

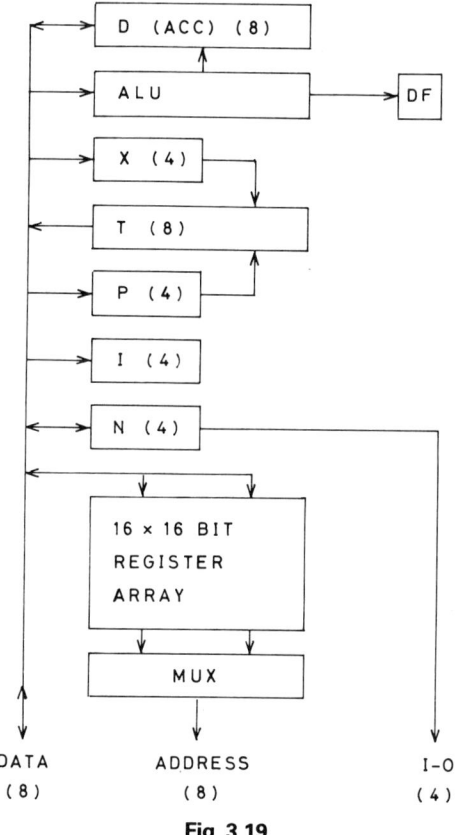

Fig. 3.19

Three 4-bit registers designated P, X and N are used to select the registers in the array. The P register selects one of the array registers as a program counter to generate instruction addresses for the memory, whilst the X register selects one of the array registers as a data pointer to give a data access address for the memory. The N register contains the lower 4 bits of the instruction code and may be used to select registers for data transfers to and from the accumulator and for some other register operations.

Arithmetic and logic operations are carried out in the 8-bit accumulator or D register which also handles all data transfers between registers, memory and input–output. A flag flip flop DF provides a carry flag for the accumulator. A further flag flip flop Q can be set or reset by program and used for branch control and for output control.

There are facilities for programmed data transfers to input–output peripherals which may be selected by the contents of the N register. Under these conditions data may be directly transferred between the memory and the peripheral device. As an extension of this facility it is also possible to have a basic direct memory access (DMA) facility. These facilities seem to be unique to the 1800 series and eliminate the need for external hardware for DMA and peripheral control in small systems.

A further 8-bit register, designated the T register, is used to store the contents of the P and X registers during interrupt servicing and possibly for subroutine operations. Memory addresses are normally latched in a 16-bit A register.

An on-chip clock generator is provided and because the internal logic of the processor is static the clock rate may be reduced to zero if desired. Various timing signals are output to control memory address demultiplexing and to indicate the operating state of the processor.

In the 1804 type device the basic processor is an 1802, but there are 64 bytes of RAM, 2 kbyte of mask programmed ROM and an 8-bit counter/timer included on the chip to provide a complete microcomputer system.

Package

1802D and 1804D types   Ceramic 40-pin DIL
1802E and 1804E types   Plastic 40-pin DIL
Hughes devices use the suffix P for plastic package types

Pin connections

1	CLOCK	21	EF4
2	WAIT	22	EF3
3	CLEAR	23	EF2
4	Q	24	EF1
5	SC1	25	MA0
6	SC0	26	MA1
7	MRD	27	MA2
8	DB7	28	MA3
9	DB6	29	MA4
10	DB5	30	MA5
11	DB4	31	MA6
12	DB3	32	MA7
13	DB2	33	TPB
14	DB1	34	TPA
15	DB0	35	MWR
16	V_{cc}	36	INT
17	N2	37	DMA OUT
18	N1	38	DMA IN
19	N0	39	XTAL
20	V_{ss}	40	V_{dd}

Signal descriptions

DB0–DB7	Bidirectional data bus
MA0–MA7	Memory address outputs
TPA	Timing pulse indicating high byte address on MA0–MA7
TPB	Timing pulse for I/O control
MRD, MWR	Memory read and write control outputs
SC0, SC1	State code outputs; these indicate the type of operation cycle being performed by the CPU
N0, N1, N2	Input–output peripheral select outputs
INT	Interrupt request input (active low)
DMA IN, DMA OUT	DMA request inputs (active low)
Q	Output showing state of Q flip flop
EF1–EF4	Testable inputs (active low)
WAIT, CLEAR	Inputs to control the operating mode of the CPU. Modes available are LOAD, RESET, RUN and PAUSE. Inputs are active low
CLOCK	External clock input
XTAL	Used with CLOCK for on-chip clock timing
V_{cc}, V_{dd}, V_{ss}	Power supply inputs

Note that on 1804 microcomputer the V_{cc} pin is designated EMS and is used for memory expansion when external memory is used.

Power requirements

1802 and 1804

$V_{ss} = 0$ V $V_{dd} = +4$ V to $+10.5$ V
(normally +5 V or +10 V)

1802C and 1804C

$V_{ss} = 0$ V $V_{dd} = +4$ V to $+6.5$ V
(normally +5 V)

V_{cc} is the I/O interface supply and is isolated from V_{dd} but must be less than or equal to V_{dd}. Normally this would be set at +5 V to allow interfacing to TTL type signal levels. The output signals from the 1802/1804 swing between V_{ss} and V_{cc}.

Typical quiescent supply current is less than 200 μA.

Temperature range

RCA types
  Suffix D $-55°$C to $+125°$C
  Suffix E $-40°$C to $+85°$C

Input–output

There are no specifically dedicated input–output ports on the 1800 series devices, but direct transfers of data between the memory and peripheral devices over the data bus can be made by using input–output instructions.

The three output lines N0, N1 and N2 may be used to identify a particular peripheral device, and the state of the MRD line will indicate whether transfer of data is into or out of the memory.

The 4 flag inputs may be used by peripheral devices to indicate their status and may be tested and used to control branch operations in the CPU.

In general the arrangements for input–output are very flexible and can be organised by the user to suit his own requirements.

Direct memory access may readily be achieved by using the DMA IN and DMA OUT input control lines. Here again the data transfer may be made to or from memory via the data bus to external devices or memory.

The data bus and input–output control signals are all TTL/CMOS compatible, provided that V_{cc} is set at +5 V. Outputs will generally drive one low power TTL load, whilst inputs are typically high impedance CMOS type.

Interrupt facilities

Interrupts are triggered by a low input on the INT line and may be masked by program control. When an interrupt occurs the contents of the P and X registers are stored in register T and registers P and X are set to 1 and 2 respectively. Thus in the register array register 1 points to the interrupt routine and register 2 becomes the stack pointer. At the end of interrupt servicing the values of P and X are restored from T. Normally only one level of interrupt would be handled at a time, but by careful programming it would be possible to have multilevel nested interrupts.

Instruction set

The instruction set of the 1800 series may appear to be rather unusual when compared with that of other types. There are no specific registers for stack pointer, index, program counter or status, but all of these functions are readily achieved by using the register array and the various testable flags. It will also be noted that all data transfers are made via the D register or accumulator except for input–output and DMA operations. Thus quite a few instructions may be needed to load the register array but for some types of operation once this has been done the machine can be very efficient, as for example in handling data arrays.

Arithmetic
    ADD either with or without carry
    SUB either with or without carry
    Note, subtract can be either $D = D-M$ or $D = M-D$
    There appears to be no direct BCD facility
    All arithmetic is 8 bit

Logic
    AND   accumulator with memory or immediate data
    OR   accumulator with memory or immediate data
    XOR   Exclusive OR with memory or immediate data
    Shift or rotate D register either right or left using the DF flag bit as carry

Data move and register
Registers may be incremented or decremented using either X or N to select the register acted upon.

Data bytes (high or low) may be transferred between selected registers and the accumulator.

Data may be transferred between memory and accumulator, the memory being pointed to by registers designated by either X or N.

Branches and jumps
There are 33 branch instructions, allowing tests on the DF, Q and EF flag bits and on the state of the D register.

No direct individual bit test is provided for the accumulator (D register), but this can be achieved by shifting and testing the DF flag bit.

Other operations
Instructions are provided to allow the contents of P and X to be set up and for saving them on the stack. Also Q flag may be set or reset and interrupts may be enabled or disabled.

Addressing modes

Because of the register oriented arrangement no direct address mode to the memory is available, but immediate, register direct, indexed and indirect addressing are readily achieved. Jump and branch instructions either obtain the new address from one of the registers or operate as a simple skip type operation.

Timing

For the 1802 the maximum clock frequency is 5.0 MHz and the average instruction execution time is 3.2 μs when the supply voltage V_{dd} is +10 V.

For the 1802C and 1802 operating with a +5 V supply the maximum clock frequency is 2.5 MHz, giving an average instruction time of 6.4 μs.

Timings for the 1804 are the same as for the 1802.

Average instruction takes two cycles, except for long branch instructions which take three cycles. Each machine cycle is 8 clock cycles in duration.

DMA transfer rates are 312 kbyte/s at +5 V and 625 kbyte/s at +10 V supply, assuming maximum clock frequency. Clock frequency may be varied between zero and maximum since internal logic of CPU is static.

Compared with most nMOS processors this machine is relatively slow, but its unique architecture can make it faster than a comparable nMOS type for some types of operation.

The internal oscillator timing is controlled by a crystal connected between the XTAL and CLOCK inputs.

Support devices

There are a number of support devices designed for use with the 1802 and 1804 processors and some of these are:

1851	I/O interface providing 20 lines
1852	I/O 8-bit data port
1853	Decoder for the N0–N2 I/O control lines
1854A	UART for serial I/O
1855	8-bit hardware multiply/divide unit
1856/1857	4-bit bus buffers
1858/1859	4-bit memory latch/decoder
1861	Video display controller (NTSC)
1862	Colour generator (NTSC)
1863	Programmable frequency generator
1864	PAL compatible TV interface
1869	Video/sound generator (NTSC/PAL)
1870	Colour video generator (NTSC/PAL)
1871	Keyboard encoder

There are also available a range of RAM and ROM devices in CMOS designed to work with the 1800 series processors.

Development aids

RCA produce the COSMAC development system with dual floppy disk operating system to provide software development, hardware emulation and debugging for the 1800 series. It has both low level macro assembler and linker facilities as well as high level language software.

From Hughes the H900 development system supports a wide range of processor types, including the 1800 series. It has a floppy disk operating system and can operate under CP/M to provide both software and hardware development for the 1800.

Solid State Scientific also produce a disk based system for the 1800 series which can support the FORTH language.

Several universal development systems such as the AMDS from Futuredata and 8000 series from Tektronix can provide software and hardware development facilities for the 1800.

Lower level evaluation and development can be carried out using RCA's evaluation kit or the ELF2 personal computer.

ROCKWELL R6500/1 SERIES

Rockwell's R6500/1 series of devices are designed as 8-bit single-chip nMOS microcomputers for dedicated applications where a fast and relatively powerful 8-bit microcomputer is required. The basic CPU used on the chip is a 6502, combined with RAM for data storage, mask programmed ROM, an event counter/timer and a range of input–output ports. Effectively this device is a 6502 and a variant of the 6531 combination chip packaged onto a single silicon chip.

These devices are suitable for applications where a faster or more powerful processor than say an 8048 is required. There is of course a wide range of software already available for the popular 6502 processor and this could be used to advantage in any application where a 6502 type of processor might have been used. The 6500 will under these conditions give the cost and space saving advantages of a single-chip microcomputer system.

Prime manufacturer

Rockwell International.

Devices available

R6500/1	Standard 1 MHz part
R6500/1A	2 MHz version
R6500/1-11	Enhanced version with 3k ROM
R6500/1-11Q	Enhanced version with 3k ROM
R6500/1E	1 MHz part for use with external ROM
R6500/1AE	2 MHz part (external ROM)
R6500/1EB-1	Version for piggyback 2716 EPROM
R6500/1EB-2	Version for piggyback 2532 EPROM
R6500/1EB-3	Version for piggyback 2732 EPROM
R6500/1EB-4	Version for piggyback 2758 EPROM
R6500/2-11	ROMless emulator for 6500/1-11 types

Alternative source devices

MOS Technology, Synertek and EMM-SEMI are all licensed under a mask exchange scheme to manufacture this series of parts.

Architecture

The basic internal arrangement of the 6500/1 type of device is shown in fig. 3.20.

At the centre of the system is a standard 6502 type CPU which has an 8-bit accumulator for arithmetic and logic type operations. Two 8-bit registers act as index pointers and a single 8-bit stack pointer is provided. An 8-bit status register provides flags for carry, overflow, zero, negative, decimal arithmetic mode and interrupt conditions. A 16-bit program counter register governs the operation of the program instruction sequence.

Apart from the central processing unit there are on the chip a 2 kbyte ROM, a 64-byte RAM and four 8-bit input–output ports. The chip also contains a 16-bit programmable counter/timer or event counter. The on-chip RAM has a standby power facility for use with memory battery back-up.

In the 6502 the stack is normally located within page 1 (locations 100–1FF hex.), but on the 6500/1 it will be located within page 0 and must be initialised to the top location of the RAM (03F hex.) after a reset operation.

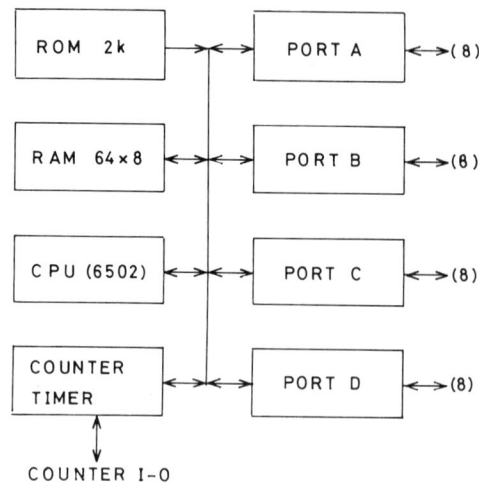

Fig. 3.20

As with the 6502 the stack may have any length within the limits of available RAM (64 bytes). Input–output ports and the counter/timer are treated as memory locations and are located between 80 hex. and 8F hex. within the memory map. On-chip ROM is located in pages 8 – 15 of the memory map, with the reset and interrupt vector addresses at the top of the ROM space. The memory map for a typical 6500/1 system is:

Address		Description
FFF	————	
		IRQ vector
FFE	————	
FFD	————	
		Reset vector
FFC	————	
FFB	————	
		NMI vector
FFA	————	
FF9	————	
		User program ROM
800	————	
7FF		
		Extra ROM space on R6500/1E or R6500/1EB
400	————	
3FF		
		Not used
090	————	
08F	————	Control reg.
08E		
		Not used
08B	————	
08A	————	Clear PA1 flag
089	————	Clear PA0 flag
088	————	Write counter latch
087		
		Read counter
086	————	
085		
		Write counter
084	————	
083	————	Port D
082	————	Port C

```
081  ─────  Port B
080  ─────  Port A
07F
              Not used
040  ─────
03F
              RAM
000  ─────
```

The R6500/1-11 features an enhanced version of the 6502 processor, 192 bytes of RAM and 3 kbyte of ROM, as well as the normal 4 I/O ports, and there are two timer/counters. There is also a serial I/O port on this device. In the R6500/1-11Q the input–output is further increased by the addition of three more 8-bit I/O ports to the basic 6500/1-11 configuration.

Package

R6500/1, R6500/1-11 and R6500/1EB
40-pin dual in line plastic package
R6500/1E   64-pin dual in line plastic package
R6500/1-11Q   64-pin quad in line package

Pin connections

R6500/1

1	V_{rr}	21	CNTR
2	PD7	22	PB7
3	PD6	23	PB6
4	PD5	24	PB5
5	PD4	25	PB4
6	PD3	26	PB3
7	PD2	27	PB2
8	PD1	28	PB1
9	PD0	29	PB0
10	XTL1	30	V_{cc}
11	XTL0	31	PA7
12	V_{ss}	32	PA6
13	PC7	33	PA5
14	PC6	34	PA4
15	PC5	35	PA3
16	PC4	36	PA2
17	PC3	37	PA1
18	PC2	38	PA0
19	PC1	39	RES
20	PC0	40	NMI

Signal functions

PA0–PA7	Port A I/O quasi-bidirectional
PB0–PB7	Port B I/O quasi-bidirectional
PC0–PC7	Port C I/O quasi-bidirectional
PD0–PD7	Port D I/O quasi-bidirectional
V_{cc}, V_{ss}	Main power supply
V_{rr}	Battery back-up supply for RAM
RES	Reset input (active low)
NMI	Non-mistakable interrupt input (active low)
XTL0, XTL1	Timing crystal pins for clock generator
CNTR	Counter/timer input–output line

On the 6500/1E emulator device an 8-bit data bus and 12-bit address bus are brought out to control the external ROM and RAM. This device allows an additional 1024 bytes of RAM to be used if desired.

Power requirements

V_{cc}	+5 V ± 10% (± 5% for R6500/1A)
V_{ss}	0 V
V_{rr}	+3.5 V to +5 V
Power requirement	500 mW
Standby RAM current	10 mA

Temperature range

0°C to +70°C
Extended temperature versions available, −40°C to +85°C

Input–output

The input–output ports of the 6500/1 series devices are quasi-bidirectional in operation. To select a line for input a '1' is written to the corresponding bit position in the output register for the port by writing to the port address location. On reading the port location the states of those lines with an output bit set at '1' will be read into the accumulator. For output the desired bit pattern is simply written to those bits corresponding to the required output lines.

All input–output lines are TTL level compatible and the outputs will drive one TTL logic load.

Two inputs (PA0 and PA1) on port A may be used as edge detectors and will set flag bits in the control register at 08F hex. in memory when a falling edge is detected in the PA0 or PA1 input signals.

Interrupt facilities

On the 6500/1 a non-maskable interrupt can be generated by an input pulse on the NMI pin and a software interrupt is given by using the BRK instruction. There are three maskable interrupts which are triggered by the counter/timer or by the edge triggered inputs of port A.

Interrupt and reset vectors are located at the top of the program ROM address space, as shown in the memory map. It is relatively easy to deal with nested interrupts with this microcomputer as with the 6502. An interrupt or BRK causes the program counter and status register to be saved on the stack.

Instruction set

There are 56 basic instruction types available for the 6500/1, and it is software compatible with the 6502 series devices. An extra four instructions are available with the 6500/1-11 type microcomputers.

Arithmetic and logic
Addition and subtraction are available for binary integers, either signed or unsigned, and there is a decimal mode which allows addition and subtraction of BCD format numbers. All arithmetic operations include the carry bit.

Logical operations include AND, OR and EX-CLUSIVE OR as well as a range of shift and rotate operations both right and left. Increment, decrement, complement and clear, as well as the shift operations will operate on either the accumulator or directly on memory.

Data transfers
Data can readily be transferred between the accumulator and other registers within the CPU and also with memory using a variety of addressing modes. Two index registers may be used for indexed data transfers for table handling.

Input–output uses memory mapping and the input–output ports of the 6500/1 are located in the lowest (zero) page of the memory map. The counter/timer is also treated as memory as far as the program is concerned.

Branch and jump
There are 8 conditional branch instructions for testing the zero, sign, overflow and carry bits of the status flag register. These branches all use relative addressing. An unconditional jump and a subroutine jump complete the list. There is also a break instruction which causes a software interrupt.

Instructions have been included which allow bit tests and comparisons to be carried out between the accumulator and memory locations. In the 6500/1-11 types the extra instructions are used for setting and resetting individual bits in the memory or branching on the result of a bit test on memory.

Timing

All 6500/1 microcomputers have on-chip clock generation circuits which may be controlled by an external crystal. For the standard 6500/1 type the clock frequency is 1 MHz, whilst the 6500/1A will operate at 2 MHz.

With 1 MHz typical instructions will execute in 2 – 4 μs, and on the 2 MHz part execution time will be halved.

Internally the processor uses a 2-phase clock and all memory accesses are made during phase $\phi 2$, whilst execution of instructions occurs during phase $\phi 1$.

Support chips

No support chips would normally be required, but if the 6500/1E type devices are used they would be compatible with any 6502 series support chips.

Development aids

For prototype development the R6500/1E and R6500/1EB devices may be used.

Rockwell provide a complete development system called the SYSTEM 65 which can handle software development for the 6500 series microcomputers. This system provides text editor, assembler, debugging and in-circuit emulation facilities and uses a floppy disk based operating system.

Software development could be carried out using the AIM65. This is an interactive microcomputer system based on the 6502 microprocessor and is software compatible with the 6500/1. This unit features a standard keyboard for data entry and a small matrix printer unit on the processor board provides a printout of data or program. The system can also be used with a teletype or a VDU terminal.

Many other development systems, such as the Futuredata AMDS, Tektronix universal system and Hewlett Packard system can handle 6500 based software. In some systems emulation may also be provided, although this may use a different type of microprocessor such as the Z80.

SIGNETICS 8X300

The Signetics 8X300 is an 8-bit Shottky TTL microprocessor, primarily intended for use in high speed controller applications.

This microprocessor has a relatively simple internal architecture and small instruction set, but is ideally suited to applications such as floppy or hard disk controllers, where high speed is essential and the operations follow a fairly simple control logic format. At present there is little in the way of competitive devices apart from perhaps the bit slice products such as the AMD2900 series and Motorola MC10800 types which both require a larger number of chips.

Prime manufacturer

Signetics Corporation.

Devices available

8X300 Microcontroller

Alternative source devices

None.

Architecture

The 8X300 has a fairly simple architecture, with an 8-bit ALU handling the arithmetic and logic plus a stack of eight 8-bit registers for data storage.

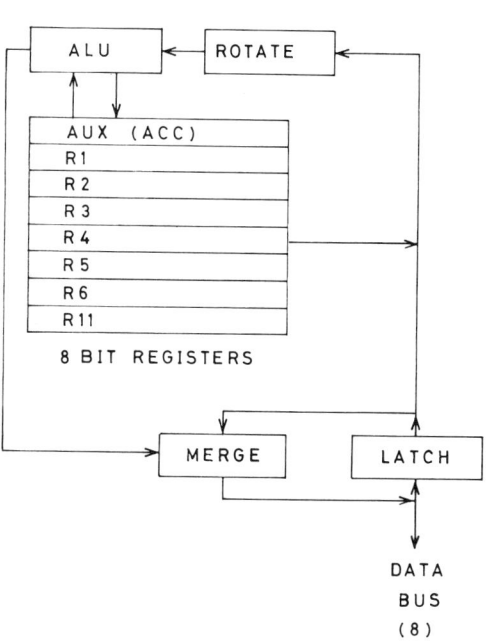

Fig. 3.21

A 13-bit program counter register allows access to 8192 bytes of program memory. There is no stack pointer and no facilities for saving data for subroutines, but this CPU is not designed to handle subroutines anyway.

Only one status flag is provided, which is effectively a carry bit although it is labelled overflow in the literature.

Package

50-pin dual in line ceramic type

Pin connections

1	V_{cr}	26	I13
2	A7	27	I14
3	A6	28	I15
4	A5	29	SC
5	A4	30	WC
6	A3	31	LB
7	A2	32	RB
8	A1	33	IVB7
9	A0	34	IVB6
10	X1	35	IVB5
11	X2	36	IVB4
12	GND	37	V_{cc}
13	I0	38	IVB3
14	I1	39	IVB2
15	I2	40	IVB1
16	I3	41	IVB0
17	I4	42	MCLK
18	I5	43	RESET
19	I6	44	HALT
20	I7	45	A12
21	I8	46	A11
22	I9	47	A10
23	I10	48	A9
24	I11	49	A8
25	I12	50	V_r

Signal functions

A0 – A12	Instruction address output bus
I0 – I15	Instruction data input bus
IVB0 – IVB7	Bidirectional data bus (inverted signals)
X1, X2	Timing crystal for clock oscillator
MCLK	Master clock output for I/O devices
WC	Write control output
SC	Indicates address output on IV bus
LB, RB	I/O device enable ouputs (active low)
HALT	Halt input (active low)
RESET	Reset input (active low)
V_r, V_{cr}	Voltage regulator signals
V_{cc}, GND	Power supply inputs

All inputs and outputs are TTL compatible.

Power requirements

V_{cc} +5 V ± 5%
GND   0 V

Temperature range

Standard part   0°C to +70°C
Military version S8X300   −55°C to +125°C

SIGNETICS 8X300

Input–output

Input and output data are passed via the IVB bus lines, and the I/O devices may also be addressed by outputting an address via the IVB bus. External logic is used to deal with input–output data as required.

Interrupt facilities

None.

Instruction set

The instruction set of the 8X300 consists of 8 operation codes, MOVE, ADD, AND, EXCLUSIVE OR, XMIT, NZT, XEC and JUMP. The XMIT is effectively an immediate address load instruction, NZT is a conditional branch on a zero result, XEC is a relative branch and JUMP is a direct jump operation.

All instructions use a 16-bit format, which allows the source and destination addresses to be specified where they are required. All instructions will execute in one cycle. Data can be moved from register to register, register to and from I/O and directly between I/O devices if required.

Timing

The timing oscillator runs with a crystal frequency of 8 MHz, giving instruction execution times of the order 250 ns. For slower speed operation a capacitor across X1, X2 may be used for timing. It is also possible to make use of an external clock.

Support devices

The following support devices may be used with the 8X300:

8T32	I/O port
8X350	256 × 8 bit random access memory
82S215	512 × 8 bit ROM
8T33	I/O port
8T35	I/O port
8T36	I/O port
8T39	Bus expander
8T58	Bus expander

Development aids

Signetics produce a design kit 8X300KT100SK which allows evaluation and simple program and hardware development. There is also a cross assembler program for the 8X300 which will run on some popular minicomputers.

SIGNETICS 2650A

The 2650A, developed by Signetics, is an 8-bit microprocessor using *n*MOS technology. It provides a minicomputer like system architecture and has a very flexible addressing system.

In terms of computing power the 2650A is comparable with other early designs of 8-bit microprocessor such as the 8080, 6800 and 6502. Unfortunately the 2650A has not been able to gain the same popularity as some of the other types although it is a very flexible device. At present the 2650A is made only by Signetics, which perhaps makes it less attractive than other devices which are available from several manufacturers.

Applications for the 2650A will be similar to those for other comparable 8-bit processors and will include small general purpose computer systems, dedicated controllers and communications equipment. Philips and Atari use the 2650A as the central processor element for their programmable video games units, whilst Mullard use it together with some special integrated circuits for their Viewdata decoders.

Prime manufacturer

Signetics Corporation.

Devices available

2650A   Standard CPU with 1.25 MHz clock
2650A-1   High speed version with 2 MHz clock

Alternative source devices

National Semiconductor are licensed to manufacture the 2650A but do not appear to be in production at present.

Architecture

From fig. 3.22 it will be seen that the 2650A has a fairly straightforward internal architecture for the CPU chip.

Arithmetic and logic are dealt with by an 8-bit ALU and 8-bit accumulator register. The accumulator of the 2650A is designated as R0. Apart from the accumulator there are six general purpose 8-bit registers, grouped into two banks of three registers each. One bank contains registers R1A, R2A and R3A, whilst the other comprises R1B, R2B and R3B. One bank of registers may be selected for use at any time. A control bit in the status register is used to select the operational register bank.

Unlike most other 8-bit microprocessors the 2650A has two 8-bit registers for status information, including the normal flag bits, interrupt control, stack addressing and the register bank selection.

A 15-bit program counter register (PC) allows access to 32 kbytes of memory, as compared with the 65 kbyte normally accessed by competitive 8-bit processors. The memory of the 2650A is common to both program instructions and data. In the 2650A system memory is divided into four 8192-byte pages which are selected by the most significant 2 bits of the program counter register. These bits are not incremented during program execution and the new page is entered by using a jump instruction.

There is an 8-level stack in the 2650A, for storage of return addresses for subroutines and interrupts. Other

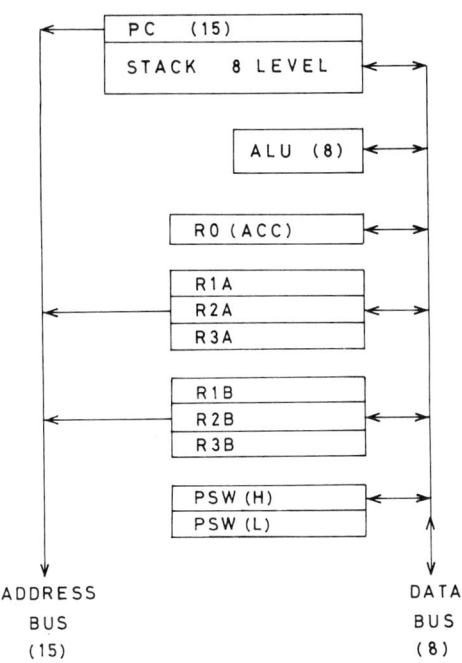

Fig. 3.22

processors such as the 8080 and 6800 can support data stacks within memory, but this facility is not provided with the 2650A. This is not really a difficult problem since data can readily be saved by other techniques.

Indexed addressing is provided on the 2650A by using an 8-bit index register, the contents of which are used as an offset to the specified address when in the indexed mode.

Input–output devices on the 2650A can be addressed separately from memory with up to 256 directly accessible devices. There is also a facility for direct memory access. An 8-bit data bus and 16-bit address bus are provided for the external memory, but it should be noted that the two most significant bits of the address must be latched externally since these lines are multiplexed with control signals. The 2650A provides a variety of control signals, both input and output, which make it a very flexible CPU.

Package

40-pin dual in line package

Pin connections

1	SENSE	21	V_{ss}
2	ADR12	22	WRP
3	ADR11	23	R/W
4	ADR10	24	OPREQ
5	ADR9	25	DBUSEN
6	ADR8	26	DBUS7
7	ADR7	27	DBUS6
8	ADR6	28	DBUS5
9	ADR5	29	DBUS4
10	ADR4	30	DBUS3
11	ADR3	31	DBUS2
12	ADR2	32	DBUS1
13	ADR1	33	DBUS0
14	ADR0	34	INTACK
15	ADREN	35	RUN/WAIT

SIGNETICS 2650A

16	RESET	36	OPACK
17	INTREQ	37	PAUSE
18	ADR14 D/C	38	CLOCK
19	ADR15 E/NE	39	V_{cc}
20	M/IO	40	FLAG

Signal functions

ADR0 – ADR15	Address bus outputs
DBUS0 – DBUS7	Data bus bidirectional
ADREN	Address bus enable input (active low)
DBUSEN	Data bus enable input (active low)
R/W	Read–write control output (read low)
RESET	Reset input (active high)
INTREQ	Interrupt request input (active low)
INTACK	Interrupt acknowledge output
WRP	Write strobe pulse output
M/IO	Memory or I/O reference output (I/O low)
D/C	Data or control output (control low)
E/NE	I/O instruction length (NE low)
SENSE	Control input
FLAG	Control output
RUN/WAIT	Run status output (wait low)
OPREQ	Request output to external device
OPACK	Acknowledge input from ext. device (active low)
PAUSE	Wait request input (active low)
CLOCK	Clock input single phase
V_{cc}, V_{ss}	Power supply inputs

Power requirements

V_{cc}	+5 V ± 5%
V_{ss}	0 V
Supply current	150 mA

Temperature range

All types 0°C to +70°C

Input–output

All logical signals into and out of the 2650A are compatible with TTL levels and outputs will drive one TTL load.

The 2650A treats input–output devices as separate from the external memory and may address up to 256 external units. When an I/O instruction is being executed the M/IO output line goes low and data are then transferred via the data bus. Two modes of I/O addressing are available, governed by the state of the E/NE output control line. When this line is low only one I/O device is assumed and data are transferred via the bus. If the E/NE output is high an I/O device address is output on ADR0 to ADR7 and this must be decoded by logic outside the CPU to select the appropriate external device. During operations requiring an external device data transfer the CPU will output a request signal on the OPREQ line and may monitor an acknowledge signal on the OPACK input line.

Serial input and output may be achieved by using the SENSE input and FLAG output lines to transfer data one bit at a time.

Memory mapped input–output could be used with the 2650A by using conventional data move instructions and treating the I/O device as a memory location.

Direct memory access is possible with the 2650A if the CPU is placed in the WAIT state by using the PAUSE input line. This will cause the address and data buses to be released by the CPU for use by another device or processor.

Interrupt facilities

There is one external hardware interrupt input line (INTREQ) available on the 2650A and any interrupt priority system must be resolved by external logic. Interrupts use a vectoring scheme which allows each external I/O device to send the program to its own unique service routine.

When an interrupt request is accepted by the CPU it will save the contents of the program counter on the stack and then reset the program counter to zero. At this point a branch type instruction is set up and the CPU expects to receive one byte of data from the external device. This byte of data is used as an address offset for the branch instruction, causing a branch to some address within the first 256 bytes of memory. At this address a further branch or call instruction will direct the program to the appropriate interrupt service routine. During processing of an interrupt all other interrupts are masked.

Instruction set

There are 75 different instructions in the 2650A set. They may have lengths of one, two or three bytes of machine code.

Arithmetic and logic
Addition and subtraction of 8-bit data may be carried out between registers and accumulator or between registers and the memory. These operations may include or exclude the carry bit, according to the state of control bits in the status register. BCD operations are catered for by a decimal adjust instruction which can be used with any register. As with most other 8-bit processors, multiplication and division must be achieved by software.

Logical operations may be carried out on any of the currently selected registers. Operations include AND, OR and EXCLUSIVE OR, as well as rotate and shift instructions, compare, increment, decrement and complement. It is also possible to operate on individual data bits within a register.

Data transfers
The 2650A provides a wide selection of instructions for moving data between registers and to or from the memory. It is also possible to transfer data between the accumulator and the status register.

There are no instructions for pushing data to a stack or pulling it out, since the stack is used purely for return address storage.

Input–output devices may be accessed by read and write instructions, which may also specify any one of 256 different input—output devices.

Serial data transfers to the SENSE and FLAG lines are achieved by manipulating bits within the status register.

Branch and jump

There are 20 branch and jump instructions for the 2650A, of which 16 are conditional operations. Some of these operations allow incrementing and decrementing of register contents before or after the branch. There are also several conditional calls to subroutines and a conditional return from subroutines.

During subroutine and interrupt operations the contents of the current register bank can readily be saved by simply selecting the alternative register bank for use during the subroutine or service routine.

Addressing modes

Eight modes of addressing are provided on the 2650A, including immediate, register, direct, indirect, indexed direct, indexed indirect, relative direct and relative indirect. Indexing may operate with auto-incrementing or auto-decrementing of the address. This range of addressing options is probably more flexible than that provided by most of the other competitive 8-bit microprocessors.

Timing

For the standard 2650A CPU chip the clock frequency is 1.25 MHz, giving a processor cycle time of 2.4 μs. Typical instructions take about 2 or 3 CPU cycles, giving execution times of 4.8 – 7.2 μs, which makes this quite a fast processor. For higher speed operation the 2650A-1 operates with a clock of 2 MHz to give execution times of 3 – 4.5 μs.

An important point to note is that, unlike the 8080 and 6800 types, the 2650 has static logic on the chip. This allows the clock to operate at any frequency down to zero without loss of internal register contents.

Support chips

A number of support chips have been designed for use with the 2650A type processor, and these are:

2621	Universal sync. generator for 2636 (PAL system)
2622	Universal sync. generator for 2636 (NTSC system)
2636	Programmable video interface providing text and graphics video display in colour plus sound effects
2641	Asynchronous serial I/O interface, including baud rate generator and programmable data format
2651	Programmable communications interface for serial I/O with sync./async. formats and baud rate generator
2652	Multiprotocol communications controller for sync. serial I/O using SDLC, HDLC, etc., protocols
2653	Polynomial generator and checker for parity checks and encryption systems
2655	Programmable parallel interface (3 × 8 bit ports)
2661	Enhanced communications interface is an enhanced version of the 2651 serial interface
2670	Character and graphics generator ROM

The 2650A may also be used with many of the interface chips designed for other processors such as the 8080 and 6800.

Development aids

For prototype development of systems using the 2650A CPU the Signetics ABC1500 Adaptable Board Computer may be used. This provides a 2650A CPU with 512 byte of RAM and 1024 byte of ROM. There is a serial input–output facility for use with a computer terminal or VDU. The on-board memory may be expanded to 24 kbyte and there is a resident monitor program provided in the on-board ROM. Facilities are provided for single step and interrupt operations to permit program debugging.

A desk top development system called the Instructor 50 is available and provides a keypad input system and LED type displays for monitoring CPU status and stored data. Monitor program facilities provided include breakpoints and single step operations for debugging purposes. This computer has 512 byte of RAM available and uses an audio cassette system for program and data storage.

For more serious development a larger floppy disk based system call TWIN may be used. This provides comprehensive program development facilities, including text editing, an assembler, debug facilities and an in-circuit emulator.

Cross assembler programs for the 2650A written in FORTRAN IV are available for several of the popular minicomputers.

ZILOG Z8

The Z8, developed by Zilog, is perhaps the most sophisticated of the 8-bit single-chip microcomputers currently available. It is fabricated using the nMOS process. Although most of the other manufacturers have based the design of their single-chip microcomputers on that of one of the other microprocessors in their product range, Zilog chose a completely new design for both internal architecture and instruction set for their Z8. Thus the Z8 is different from both the Z80 and the larger 16-bit Z8000. However, it tends to adopt a similar basic design philosophy to the Z8000, with a large bank of general purpose registers in the CPU section and a simple, yet very flexible, instruction set.

As with other 8-bit microcomputer devices the Z8 has a mask programmed ROM and a small amount of RAM on the chip, as well as a counter/timer and various input–output ports. Since the ROM is mask programmed the Z8 is ideally suited to those dedicated applications where complex processing is required, with a medium to high volume production. There is, however, a version of the Z8 which carries a piggyback socket for use with a 2716 type UV eraseable PROM. It is useful for system development or for small production runs.

When compared with other types of 8-bit microcomputer the Z8 has some similarities to the 1804 with its register file, but does provide much more flexibility. The possibility of selecting many different banks of registers within the on-chip RAM is similar to the scheme adopted by the Texas 9980, although the latter is basically a 16-bit microprocessor. A feature of the Z8 not found in some other single-chip microcomputers is that it can readily be expanded to use large external memories for both program and data storage.

Prime manufacturer

Zilog Incorporated.

Devices available

Z8-01   Basic device with 2k mask ROM and 128-byte RAM
Z8-02   ROMless version of the Z8 with all addressing lines brought out for use with external ROM
Z8-03   Version of the Z8 with a piggyback socket for a 2 kbyte 2716 type UV EPROM

Alternative source devices

Synertek Inc.

Z8-01 MCC   Basic mask ROM Z8
Z8-02 MPD   Version of Z8 for external ROM
Z8-03 MPE   Z8 with piggyback 2716 EPROM socket

Architecture

As will be seen from fig. 3.23 a central feature of the Z8 is a bank of 124 general purpose registers which may be used in groups of 16 at a time as the CPU registers. A workspace pointer register (WP) is used to select a particular bank of 16 registers from the 124 for use by the

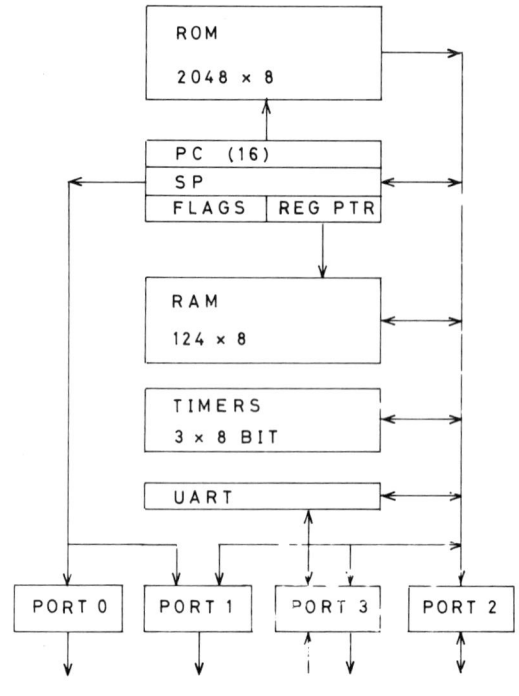

Fig. 3.23

CPU. This scheme is similar to that used in the Texas 9980, although the Z8 does use a separate stack pointer register in the CPU itself. Any of the 16 selected working registers may be used as an accumulator or index register as well as for general data storage. The 124-register bank may include a stack area. Registers within the selected group of 16 may be addressed directly, whereas others are simply treated as RAM.

A 16-bit program counter register (PC) permits access to up to 65 kbyte of memory, of which 2k is on-chip ROM and 63k may be external ROM. When external memory is used the ROM address is fed out via ports 0 and 1, whilst the data come out on port 1 multiplexed with part of the address signal. The Z8 uses separate program and data memory spaces which may use the same address code but are identified by output control lines. Thus the Z8 can also address up to 65 kbyte of data memory as well as 65 kbyte of program space.

There are 128 bytes of RAM on the Z8 chip. Of these the first four bytes are used for input–output port registers, and the remainder are general purpose registers or data storage locations. External RAM is addressed via ports 0 and 1, with data multiplexed via port 1.

Two fully programmable 8-bit counter/timers are provided on the Z8 chip. Each of them has a fully programmable 6-bit prescaler counter.

Four input–output ports are provided and these may be programmed in various ways to give byte, nibble and single-bit outputs or inputs. A full duplex asynchronous serial channel is also provided for input–output.

The Z8 chip has an on-chip clock generator and also has internally generated timing circuits for the serial I/O channel.

Package

Z8-01   40-pin dual in line
Z8-02   64-pin quad in line

ZILOG Z8

Z8-03 40-pin dual in line
The Z8-01 MCC is available in either plastic or ceramic types from Synertek, with suffix P for plastic or C for ceramic

Pin connections

Z8-01 Basic MCU

1	V_{cc}	21	P1-0
2	XTAL2	22	P1-1
3	XTAL1	23	P1-2
4	P3-7	24	P1-3
5	P3-0	25	P1-4
6	RESET	26	P1-5
7	R/W	27	P1-6
8	DS	28	P1-7
9	AS	29	P3-4
10	P3-5	30	P3-3
11	V_{ss}	31	P2-0
12	P3-2	32	P2-1
13	P0-0	33	P2-2
14	P0-1	34	P2-3
15	P0-2	35	P2-4
16	P0-3	36	P2-5
17	P0-4	37	P2-6
18	P0-5	38	P2-7
19	P0-6	39	P3-1
20	P0-7	40	P3-6

Z8-02 ROMless development chip

1	P3-6	33	A8
2	P3-1	34	A9
3	P2-7	35	A10
4	P2-6	36	A11
5	P2-5	37	D3
6	P2-4	38	D2
7	P2-3	39	D1
8	P2-2	40	D0
9	P2-1	41	MDS
10	P2-0	42	SCLK
11	P3-3	43	SYNC
12	P3-4	44	IACK
13	P1-7	45	P0-7
14	P1-6	46	P0-6
15	P1-5	47	P0-5
16	P1-4	48	V_{ss}
17	P1-3	49	P0-4
18	P1-2	50	P0-3
19	P1-1	51	P0-2
20	P1-0	52	P0-1
21	D7	53	P0-0
22	D6	54	P3-2
23	D5	55	P3-5
24	D4	56	AS
25	A0	57	DS
26	A1	58	R/W
27	A2	59	RESET
28	A3	60	P3-0
29	A4	61	P3-7
30	A5	62	XTAL1
31	A6	63	XTAL2
32	A7	64	V_{cc}

Pin functions

A0–A11	Address outputs to external ROM
D0–D7	Data inputs from external ROM
P0-0 to P0-7	Port 0 I/O
P1-0 to P1-7	Port 1 I/O
P2-0 to P2-7	Port 2 I/O
P3-0 to P3-7	Port 3 I/O
XTAL1, XTAL2	Clock timing pins for external crystal
RESET	Reset input (active low)
R/W	Read–write output (write low)
DS	Data strobe output (active low)
AS	Address strobe output (active low)
V_{cc}, V_{ss}	Power supply inputs
IACK	Interrupt acknowledge output
SYNC	Sync. output (active low)
SCLK	Serial I/O clock output

Power requirements

V_{cc} +5 V ± 5%
V_{ss} 0 V

Temperature range

0°C to +70°C

Input–output

The Z8 provides a total of 32 input–output lines grouped into 4 ports. All signals to and from the Z8 chip are compatible with TTL, and outputs will generally drive one TTL load. Each of the ports is programmable and three of them may be used in different modes to carry address or control information when not being used as an input–output data channel.

Port 0 is an 8-bit bidirectional port which may be set up as two 4-bit ports or as a single 8-bit port. When the AS output is active this port carries 8 bits of address for selection of external ROM expansion or for external data RAM.

Port 1 is an 8-bit bidirectional port which can be set up for either input or output of data in bytes. This port is also used to carry 8 bits of the address output when the AS strobe output is active. When the DS strobe is active the port becomes a data bus for input or output of data to the external ROM or RAM.

Port 2 consists of 8 separate individually programmed lines which may be set up for either input or output as desired. This port may be set up for nibble or byte wide data or as separate signal lines. It has no other functions.

Port 3 consists of a 4-line input port and a 4-line output port and is not programmable. It carries the full duplex serial input–output data and its associated handshake signals. The 4 input lines may alternatively be used for interrupt inputs. There is also provision for using the output lines to carry status information. The Z8 maintains separate address spaces for program and data (ROM and RAM) and one of the output lines of port 3 may be used to indicate to the external expansion memory whether the address being output is a program address or a data memory address. The timer input–output signals also pass through port 3.

ZILOG Z8

Although the input–output port functions are flexible not all of these functions can be used simultaneously.

Interrupt facilities

Four external interrupt lines are provided through port 3, and there are also interrupts for both the counter/timer and the asynchronous serial input–output channel. All interrupts are vectored to their individual service routines and a priority system is built into the Z8.

Instruction set

At first glance the instruction set of the Z8 seems deceptively simple, since there are only some 40 basic instructions. However, each of these is very flexible, giving a wide range of operations. In practice the instructions are similar to those provided on the more modern 16-bit microprocessors which also have relatively simple looking instruction sets.

Arithmetic and logic

The Z8 provides both addition and subtraction, either with or without a carry. A decimal adjust facility is included for use with binary coded numbers.

Logical operations provided in the Z8 are AND, OR and EXCLUSIVE-OR. There are also instructions for left and right shift or rotate operations. Data in the registers may also be incremented, decremented, complemented and compared.

All arithmetic and logic operations may be carried out on any of the 16 general purpose registers selected by the workspace register pointer.

Data transfers

A very wide range of data manipulation instructions may be used with the workspace registers and with other registers in the on-chip RAM area. Data transfers to external memory are not so versatile, since data have to be transferred through the use of the input–output ports acting as address and data buses.

Data can be manipulated as bytes, nibbles or individual bits as desired. Nibbles within registers may be swapped and there are facilities for moving blocks of data. Stacks can be set up within the 124-register array on the chip, and may be used for either data or address and status storage for subroutines and interrupts.

Any of the on-chip registers may be used for indexing and there are facilities for auto-incremented indexing.

Branch and jump

There are several conditional branch operations available in the Z8, as well as unconditional jumps. There is also a call instruction for subroutines.

Addressing modes

The Z8 provides immediate, direct, indexed, relative, register direct and register indirect modes of addressing.

Timing

The Z8 contains an on-chip clock generator which may use a crystal, RC network or LC network for timing. Alternatively an external clock signal may be used. The maximum frequency for the clock is 8 MHz, but the internal clock rate for the CPU is 4 MHz.

Using an 8 MHz crystal the typical execution time for instructions is some $1.5-2.5$ μs.

The serial input–output channel can operate at up to 62500 b.p.s. and timing is derived internally.

Support chips

Normally the Z8 will operate as a stand alone computer, but various types of peripheral chip such as those for the Z80 may be employed if desired. In fact some of the peripheral devices for use with the Z80 are versions of the Z8.

Development aids

For low level development the Z8-02 ROMless version of the Z8 may be used with external RAM, and ROM. This chip may also be used to evaluate the Z8 system before its program is committed to a ROM mask. For small production runs the Z8-03 with its plug-in piggyback EPROM provides a convenient alternative to a mask programmed Z8 microcomputer.

From both Zilog and Synertek a single-board development module called the Z8-DM is available. This contains two Z8-02 microcomputers, one acting as the system controller and the second acting as an emulator for the target system. The unit contains 2 kbyte of RAM and a ROM based monitor system which allows testing and debugging of programs. An on board 2716 type EPROM may also be used to test the final program.

Zilog provide development facilities for the Z8 type microcomputer on their ZLAB80 development system, providing assembler, debug facilities and hardware emulation.

Synertek also provide facilities for Z8 microcomputer system development on their MDT2000 microprocessor system, which provides a PASCAL based disk operating system.

ZILOG Z80

Designed originally as an enhanced version of the Intel 8080, the Zilog Z80 is an 8-bit *n*MOS microprocessor. The Z80 has a much larger and more versatile instruction set than the 8080, but does include the 8080 instructions as a subset. Hence it will run 8080 machine code programs directly. This and its similarity to the 8080 have made it a very popular processor.

From the hardware point of view the Z80 is quite a bit different from the 8080 and has a simple single-line power supply instead of the three lines needed by the 8080. The bus structure and timing system of the Z80 are simpler than those of the 8080 and whereas the 8080 needs two support chips to produce a working CPU the Z80 provides the whole CPU system on a single chip.

Internally the Z80 follows the same basic philosophy as the 8080, but has some additional registers which make it much more flexible. When compared with the Motorola 6800 the Z80 is somewhat more powerful, giving similar facilities to the later Motorola 6809 type processor. Although like the Motorola types the Z80 has two accumulator registers, it only uses them one at a time, though it can use its other registers as accumulators as well. With perhaps the exception of the 6809 and the NSC800, which is basically a CMOS version of the Z80, the Zilog Z80 is probably the most powerful of the available 8-bit processors.

Applications of the Z80 will generally be in medium to large size microcomputer systems where its computing power can be used to advantage. Currently the Z80 is used as the CPU in several personal and small business computers and in some of the universal microprocessor development systems. Competitive processors are likely to be the Intel 8085, Motorola 6800 and Motorola 6809.

Although the Z80 can use some of the support chips for the 8080 it may need some extra logic to provide the correct signals. There are several support chips specifically designed for the Z80 which will meet most application needs.

Prime manufacturer

Zilog.

Devices available

Z80 CPU	Basic CPU chip for Z80 system
Z80A CPU	4 MHz version

Alternative source devices

Mostek

MK3880	Basic CPU
MK3880A	4 MHz version
MK3880-4	4 MHz version

Nippon Electric Co. (N.E.C.)

µPD780C	Basic version
µPD780C-1	4 MHz version

SGS-ATES

Z80 CPU	Basic version
Z80A CPU	4 MHz version

Fairchild Semiconductor

F3880	Basic Z80 CPU
F3880A	4 MHz version

Architecture

Fig. 3.24 shows the programmable registers of the Z80. It will be seen that the general arrangement is similar to that of the Intel 8080 and 8085 type processors.

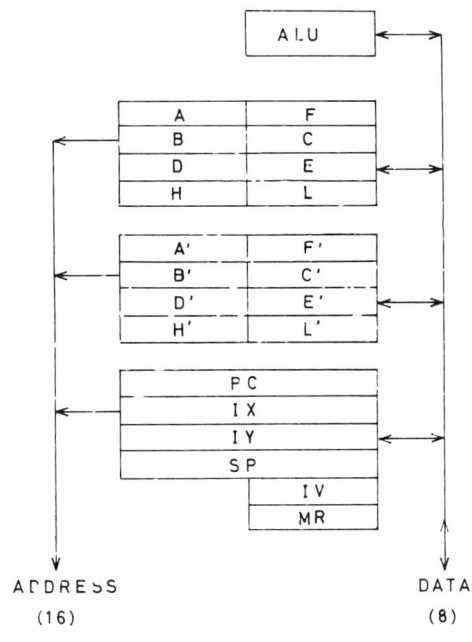

Fig. 3.24

For arithmetic and logic the Z80 has an accumulator A which provides 8-bit operations. A status register PSW has flags for carry, sign, zero and overflow. There are also flags for subtraction and an auxiliary carry.

The Z80 also has a second accumulator A' and status word PSW', but unlike the Motorola 6800 it can only use one of these at a time.

There are 6 general purpose registers B, C, D, E, H and L, each of 8 bits, which may also be used as secondary accumulators for some arithmetic operations. These registers may also be paired to act as 16-bit data pointers BC, DE and HL, or as general 16-bit storage registers. As with the status and accumulator there is a second set of general purpose registers B', C', D', E', H' and L', which may be selected for use by a register bank swap command. This arrangement makes the Z80 a very flexible and powerful processor.

The program counter PC is a 16-bit register allowing access to the full 64 kbyte memory space for program use. A 16-bit stack pointer SP and two 16-bit index registers IX and IY are also provided. To complete the register set there are an 8-bit interrupt vector register and an 8-bit counter for the automatic control of dynamic memory refresh cycles.

The Z80 has an 8-bit data bus and a 16-bit address bus for communication with the external memory and peripherals. Timing and control signals on the Z80 are different from those for the 8080, but by using some external logic the support chips designed for the 8080 system may be used with the Z80. Provision has been made for direct memory access, although this will normally be controlled by an external support chip.

Package

40-pin dual in line   Ceramic or plastic
Zilog uses suffix C for ceramic types and P for plastic
Mostek use suffix P for ceramic and N for plastic
SGS-ATES use suffix /Z for ceramic and /R for plastic
N.E.C. makes only the plastic package version
Fairchild use suffix C for ceramic and P for plastic

Pin connections

1	A11	21	RD
2	A12	22	WR
3	A13	23	BUSAK
4	A14	24	WAIT
5	A15	25	BUSRQ
6	φ	26	RESET
7	D4	27	M1
8	D3	28	RFSH
9	D5	29	GND
10	D6	30	A0
11	V_{cc}	31	A1
12	D2	32	A2
13	D7	33	A3
14	D0	34	A4
15	D1	35	A5
16	INT	36	A6
17	NMI	37	A7
18	HALT	38	A8
19	MREQ	39	A9
20	IORQ	40	A10

Signal functions

A0 – A15	Address bus output tri-state
D0 – D7	Data bus bidirectional tri-state
φ	CPU clock input
RFSH	Dynamic memory refresh output (active low)
HALT	CPU halt status output (active low)
RESET	Reset input (active low)
INT	Interrupt request input (active low)
NMI	Non-maskable interrupt input (active low)
BUSRQ	Bus request input (active low)
BUSAK	Bus acknowledge output (active low)
WAIT	Wait request input (active low)
RD, WR	Read–write control outputs tri-state (active low)
IORQ	I/O operation status output tri-state (active low)
MREQ	Memory operation status output tri-state (active low)
M1	Output pulse on instruction fetch cycle (active low)
V_{cc}, GND	Power supply inputs

Power requirements

V_{cc}	+5 V ± 5%
GND	0 V
Supply current	200 mA max.

Temperature range

Standard part 0°C to +70°C
   Zilog suffix S
   Fairchild suffix C

Extended range −40°C to +85°C
   Zilog suffix E
   Mostek suffix −10
   Fairchild suffix L

Military temperature range −55°C to +125°C
   Zilog suffix M
   Mostek suffix −20
   Fairchild suffix M

SGS-ATES and N.E.C. devices are 0°C to 70°C range only

Input–output

All logic inputs and outputs of the Z80 are TTL compatible as far as signal levels are concerned. Output lines will drive a single TTL load.

For data input–output to peripheral devices the Z80 can address up to 255 ports by using the least significant 8 bits of the address but (A0 – A7). An identification signal IORQ output from the Z80 goes low when an input–output operation is in progress, and this may be used to activate the peripheral device and to disable the memory. Data are transferred to or from the I/O device via the data bus. It is also possible to operate I/O devices in the memory mapped mode, in which case data would be written to a memory address occupied by the I/O device.

Addressing of I/O devices may be either direct or via an 8-bit address set up in the C register. Arrangements can also be made for block transfers of data from the memory via the Z80 to or from the peripheral device.

Interrupt facilities

Normally maskable interrupts can be generated by applying an external signal to the INT input. An interrupt input to the NMI pin is not maskable and will have priority over the INT input interrupt. There is also a reset input which may be used to initialise the Z80 when it is initially powered up.

There are three modes in which the Z80 can operate for interrupt processing. These may be selected by the program instructions. In mode 0 the processor having acknowledged the interrupt request will expect to receive an 8-bit interrupt vector address from the peripheral device via the data bus. This address will point to the first of a pair of locations in page 0 of the memory, which will contain the address of the first instruction of the interrupt service routine. When it acknowledges the interrupt the Z80 will automatically push the contents of the program counter to the stack. This mode of operation is similar to that used by the 8080 and 8085.

In mode 1 the Z80 will pick up the address of the start of the interrupt routine from locations 56 and 57 (hex.) in memory.

Mode 2 makes use of the interrupt vector register to provide the most significant 8 bits of the interrupt vector address whilst the peripheral device provides the lower 8 bits. In this case the interrupt vector location can be at any point in memory. Since the address of the interrupt routine takes two bytes the least significant bit of the interrupt vector address is always set at 0 so that it will always point to an even location. The Z80 will now go to the location indicated by the interrupt vector address and then branch to the address contained in those two successive locations to reach the service routine.

An NMI type interrupt picks up the address of the interrupt service routine from location 66 (hex.) in memory and the reset operation goes to location 0 in memory for its service routine.

Multiple interrupts can be handled by appropriate software, but priority must be dealt with by external logic. The RST instruction can be used for software interrupt operation.

Instruction set

The Z80 has the largest and, perhaps, most flexible instruction set of all the 8-bit microprocessors. There are 156 different instructions available in the basic set and several addressing modes are available.

Arithmetic and logic

The basic accumulator can be used for addition and subtraction in both binary and BCD formats, either with or without carry. It is also possible to carry out 16-bit additions or subtractions using the HL register pair, and 16-bit additions only on the IX and IY index registers.

Logical AND, OR and EXLUSIVE OR operations can be made using the accumulator with data which are either immediate in the instruction, from a register or from memory. Accumulator or other register contents may be shifted left or right and rotated in either direction.

Other operations available include incrementing, decrementing, complementing and comparing of data. Individual bits in accumulator, register or memory data may also be set or reset as desired.

Data transfer

The Z80 probably has the most flexible set of instructions for data transfer between accumulator, registers and memory of all the 8-bit processors.

Included among the data transfer operations are some in which the data transfer may be repeated to allow movement of a complete block of data with just one program instruction. In such operations the source and destination addresses for the data are automatically incremented or decremented as required. These operations can be useful in moving data to and from the external peripheral via input–output instructions.

Branch and jump

There are some 14 jump instructions, most of which operate on the condition flags in the status register. There is a call instruction for subroutines which may also be conditional. There is also a return from subroutine which is conditional.

Other

An instruction is included which selects the mode of operation of the interrupt system and there are separate instructions for data input and output to peripherals.

An instruction is available to allow either the status word only or all of the registers in the two alternative banks of registers to be selected for use.

Addressing modes are direct, implied and indexed via the IX and IY registers. Jump instructions may be either relative or direct.

Timing

The timing logic for the CPU is included on the Z80 chip and the only external signal required is a single-phase clock. An instruction may take from about 4 to 20 clock periods for its execution. The standard Z80 runs with a 2.5 MHz clock and will execute most instructions in about $2-5$ μs. There is also a faster 4 MHz version available and Zilog have a 6 MHz version.

Type number for the standard version is either Z80 or for the Mostek and Fairchild types MK3880 or F3880. The N.E.C. version has the number μPD780.

The faster 4 MHz version is called Z80A, 3880A, 3880-4 or μPD780-1 according to the manufacturer.

Support devices

Support chips available for use specifically with the Z80 are:

Z80-PIO (MK3881) parallel I/O controller
This provides two 8-bit input–output ports which are fully programmable with interrupt facilities.

Z80-CTC (MK3882) counter timer circuit
This provides 4 counters, each with prescalers.

Z80-DMA (MK3883) direct memory access controller
This provides the external control logic needed for direct memory access operations with the Z80 processor.

Z80-SIO (MK3884/5/7) serial I/O controller
This device provides both synchronous and asynchronous modes of serial input–output.

Z80-DART dual asynchronous receiver transmitter
This chip provides two channels of asynchronous serial input–output for the Z80 bus system.

There are also a number of new devices available which have been adapted from the Zilog Z8000 series support chips:

Z8530   Serial communications controller
Z8536   Counter/timer and parallel input–output
Z8538   FIFO input–output buffer unit
Z8560   Expansion for the Z8538
Z8590   Universal peripheral controller

Mostek produce a combination chip for the Z80 which provides a static RAM, two counter/timers and some interrupt logic.

Development aids

Zilog
The ZDS-1 system provides development facilities for Z80 based systems and includes in-circuit emulation.

The Z80 MCS microcomputer system provides up to 65k of RAM, floppy disk operating system, relocatable assembler and linker, BASIC interpreter and PROM programmer.

4 16-BIT MICROPROCESSORS AND MICROCOMPUTERS

16-BIT MICROPROCESSOR TYPES

Maker	Device	Address bits	Data bits	Pkge	Remarks	Page
Advanced	Am8001	24	16	48DIL	= Zilog Z8001	154
Micro	Am8002	16	16	40DIL	= Zilog Z8002	154
Devices	Am29116	–	16	52DIL	TTL slice ALU	121
	Am29112	16	16	40DIL	Prog. seq.	121
American	S9900	16	16	64DIL	μP = 9900	141
Microsystems	S9940	16	16	40DIL	μC = TMS9940	144
	S9980	16	8	40DIL	μP = TMS9980	147
Data General	Micronova	15	16	40DIL	μP	123
Fairchild	F68000	24	16	64DIL	= MC68000	136
Fairchild	9440		16	40DIL	Similar to	123
	9445	16	16	40DIL	Micro Nova	123
Ferranti	F100L	15	16	40DIL	Bipolar μP	125
General Instrument	CP1600	16	16	40DIL	nMOS μP	127
Hitachi	HD68000	24	16	64DIL	= MC68000	136
Intel	8086	20	16	40DIL	nMOS μP	129
	8087		16	40DIL	Arith. proc.	129
	8088	20	8	40DIL	nMOS μP	132
Mostek	MK68000	24	16	64DIL	= MC68000	136
Motorola	MC68000	24	16	64DIL	nMOS μP	136
National	NS16008	16	8	40DIL	μP	139
	NS16016	16	16	40DIL	μP	139
	NS16032	16	16	48DIL	32-bit internal	139
Philips	68000	24	16	64DIL	= MC68000	136
Rockwell	R68000	24	16	64DIL	= MC68000	136
SGS-ATES	Z8001	24	16	48DIL	= Zilog Z8001	154
	Z8002	16	16	40DIL	= Zilog Z8002	154
Signetics	68000	24	16	64DIL	= MC68000	136
S.M.C.	9980	16	8	40DIL	= TMS9980	147

MICROPROCESSOR DATA BOOK

Maker	Device	Address bits	Data bits	Pkge	Remarks	Page
Texas Instruments	TMS9900	16	16	64DIL	nMOS μP	141
	TMS9980	16	8	40DIL	nMOS μP	147
	TMS9940	16	16	40DIL	μC 2k ROM	144
	TMS9940E	16	16	40DIL	μC 2k EPROM	144
	TMS9985	16	8	40DIL	μC no ROM	144
	TMS9995	16	16	40DIL	μP	150
	SBP9900	16	16	64DIL	I^2L type 9900	141
Thomson EFCIS	EF68000	24	16	64DIL	= MC68000	136
Western Digital	CP1611	16	16	40DIL	CPU	152
	CP1612	16	16	40DIL	Control chip	152
Zilog	Z8001	24	16	48DIL	nMOS CPU	154
	Z8002	16	16	40DIL	Non. seg. memory	154
	Z8003	24	16	48DIL	Virtual mem.	154
	Z8004	16	16	40DIL	Virtual mem.	154

ADVANCED MICRO DEVICES Am29116

The Advanced Micro Devices Am29116 is a very fast TTL 16-bit microprocessor, designed using a similar philosophy to that of the 2900 4-bit slice devices. In fact the 29116 would normally be used with the 29112 microprogram sequencer and a selection of 2900 bit slice chips to form a complete system.

This microprocessor is intended for very fast controller type applications, but can also be used as a fast general purpose computer system. Compared with nMOS types such as the 8085 or Z8000 the Am29116 can give speed improvements of the order of thousands of times faster.

In a typical system the 29116 will carry out the basic arithmetic and logic operations and instruction decoding, but the program control will be performed by the 29112. Some other functions such as interrupt, input–output and memory control would be performed by other chips of the 2900 series.

Prime manufacturer

Advanced Micro Devices Inc.

Devices available

Am29116   Arithmetic and instruction decode chip
Am29112   Microprogram sequencer

Alternative source devices

None at present.

Architecture

The 29116 chip contains a 16-bit accumulator and ALU for its arithmetic and logic functions. Unlike other processors the ALU can handle three 16-bit inputs and has full look ahead carry. Another unusual feature is that one input to the ALU is a barrel shifter, allowing data at that input to be rotated up to 16 bits.

A 32-word by 16-bit wide RAM on the chip acts as a register file for storage of data being used by the ALU. An 8-bit status register is used for condition flags. The ALU also has a priority encoder facility which may be used for interrupt priority control and for other applications which need a priority facility.

Two 16-bit buses are used on the 29116, one to handle data whilst the other handles the instruction codes from the microprogram sequencer. Both buses have data latches.

The 29112 microprogram sequencer controls the memory access for program instructions. It also has a 31-level stack for use in subroutines and interrupt operations. It handles an 8-bit data bus and normally two 29112 chips would be used with the 29116 system, allowing access to 65 kbyte of external memory.

Package

Am29116   52-pin dual in line ceramic type
Am29112   40-pin dual in line ceramic type

Power requirements

V_{cc} +5 V ± 5%
V_{ss} 0 V

Temperature range

0° to +70°C

Input–output

Although the internal logic uses ECL for high speed operation the input and output signals are TTL compatible.

Inputs and outputs from a system using the 29116 would be handled by separate chips such as the Am2950 and Am2951 8-bit input–output ports.

Interrupt facilities

The Am29116 itself does not deal with interrupt operations. These are handled by other chips such as the 29112 and 2914.

Instruction set

The instruction set of the 29116 contains a total of 167 instructions, covering all of the operations of the ALU and status sections of the CPU.

Arithmetic and logic
Sixteen-bit arithmetic operations include addition and subtraction, either with or without carry. These operations can also be combined with shifts and rotates on one input. This allows fairly simple implementation of multiplication and division operations.

Logical operations include AND, OR, EXCLUSIVE OR, NAND, NOR and EXCLUSIVE NOR, as well as shifts and the rotation of data by the barrel shifter. Data may also be incremented, compared, complemented and negated. There are also several instructions for bit manipulation.

A wide range of conditional tests may be carried out by the 29116. These affect the status register and may pass flag conditions to the microprogram sequencer.

Data transfer
The 29116 itself does not control data transfer, since this is a function of other chips in the system such as the 29112.

Branch and jump
Control of the program sequence is governed by the 29112 and it will cause jumps and branches to be performed according to the status flags presented by the 29116. This chip also has the stack control and provides part of the interrupt system.

Timing

The 29116 is designed to be very fast in operation, with a typical microcycle time of only 100 ns and an execution time of 100 ns for a 16-bit addition.

Support devices

Unlike other microprocessors, some of which can operate alone, the 29116 will need several chips just to implement the basic CPU function as well as others for input–output and interrupt control.

Among the support chips designed for use with the 29116 are:

Am2904	Status controller
Am2910	Microprogram controller
Am2914	Interrupt controller
Am2925	Clock generator
Am2940	DMA address generator
Am2942	As 2940 but with timer/counter
Am2950	8-bit parallel I/O port
Am2951	8-bit parallel I/O port
Am29112	Microprogram sequencer with interrupt

Development aids

The System 29 from Advanced Micro Devices is a development system for the complete 2900 series of devices. It has a floppy disk based operating system, with assembly language compiler for the 29116 and some debug and emulation facility.

A cross assembler is also available for use on the Intel Intellec development systems.

FAIRCHILD MICROFLAME 9440/45

The Fairchild Microflame series are 16-bit microprocessors whose architecture and software emulate those of the Data General Nova series of minicomputers. By using integrated injection logic (I^2L) bipolar technology these devices can achieve a high execution speed.

In comparison with other 16-bit types the Microflame I or 9440 device has a very simple internal architecture but makes up for this by high speed. The later Microflame II or 9445 is a slightly enhanced version of the 9440, and is claimed to be faster than any other 16-bit processor currently available, and can probably outperform some of the newer types such as the MC68000 and Z8000 series. These microprocessors are designed for applications where a medium to large size minicomputer might normally be used and could readily replace computers of the Nova series since they are software compatible with those types.

Prime manufacturer

Fairchild Semiconductor.

Devices available

9440/8	Basic CPU chip with 8 MHz clock (Microflame I)
9440/10	10 MHz version of 9440
9440/12	12 MHz version of 9440
9445	Enhanced version (Microflame II)

Alternative source devices

None.

Architecture

As will be seen from fig. 4.1 the internal architecture of the 9440 is extremely simple and is basically similar to that of the Data General Nova minicomputers and Micronova series microcomputers.

Four 16-bit accumulators are used as the working registers for arithmetic and logic functions. The ALU however is only 4 bits wide on the 9440, so data are processed in 4-bit slices. The later 9445 processor has a full 16-bit ALU and operates in a similar fashion to other 16-bit microprocessors. AC2 and AC3 may be used as index registers.

In the 9440 there is no stack pointer register, but the 9445 does have a 15-bit stack pointer and also a 15-bit frame pointer register which may be used to hold the addresses of important data within the stack, but cannot actually be used to access the memory.

A 16-bit multiplexed data and address bus is provided by both the 9440 and 9445 devices.

The 9440 CPU does not have a status register as such, but includes some flag and test lines from the ALU which allow the same functions to be achieved. In the 9445 a status register is included.

Package

40-pin dual in line type   ceramic package

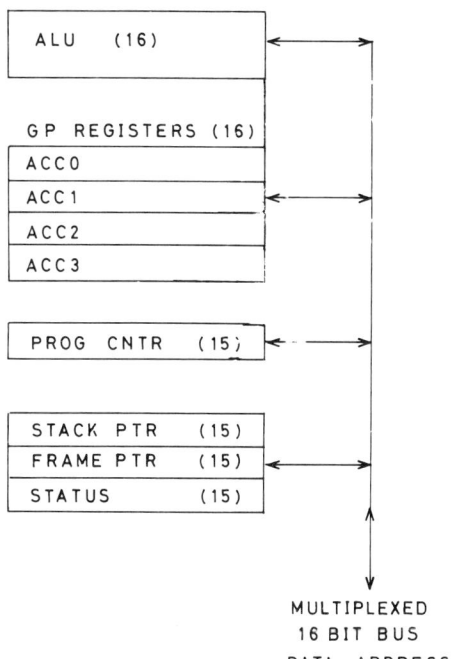

Fig. 4.1

Pin connections

9440 Microflame I

1	C3	21	AD7
2	C2	22	AD8
3	C1	23	AD9
4	C0	24	AD10
5	DMAR	25	AD11
6	O1	26	AD12
7	INTR	27	AD13
8	O0	28	AD14
9	INTE	29	AD15
10	GND	30	GND
11	RUN	31	V_{cc}
12	IINJ	32	MBUSY
13	CRY	33	SYN
14	AD0	34	RESET
15	AD1	35	XTL
16	AD2	36	CP
17	AD3	37	CKO
18	AD4	38	M2
19	AD5	39	M1
20	AD6	40	M0

Signal functions

AD0 – AD15	Address/data bus multiplexed bidirectional
M0 – M2	Memory control outputs
C0 – C3	Console panel control signal outputs
O0, O1	Input–output control signal outputs
XTL, CP	Clock inputs for timing crystal
CKO	System clock output
DMAR	Direct memory access request input (active low)
INTR	Interrupt request input (active low)
INTE	Interrupt enable output (active low)
RUN	CPU run status output

CRY	Carry bit status output
RESET	Reset input (active low)
SYN	Synchronising signal output (active low)
MBUSY	Memory busy input (active low)
IINJ, V_{cc}, GND	Power supply inputs

Note that the data/address bus signals have inverted logic levels. All signals are basically TTL compatible.

Power requirements

V_{cc}	+5 V ± 5%
GND	0 V
Power consumption	approximately 1 W

Temperature range

0°C to +70°C

Input–output

The Microflame series devices use a separate addressing scheme in which the six low order bits of the instruction code will identify the I/O device, thus allowing up to 64 I/O channels. External logic must be used to extract these addresses during an instruction fetch cycle and to control the actual I/O data transfer via the multiplexed data bus. The O0 and O1 signals are used to indicate instruction fetch, DMA and I/O cycles of operation and must be used by external logic.

Coding of the O0 and O1 outputs is:

O0	O1	Function
0	0	Instruction fetch
0	1	DMA operation
1	0	I/O operation
1	1	No data transfer

The four signals C0 to C3 may be used to control the operation of a console front panel and provide facilities for displaying the contents of the accumulators or memory data on the console and for loading data into the accumulators, memory or program counter from the console panel switches.

Interrupt facilities

Interrupts may be activated by inputting a signal on the INTR line. When an interrupt is accepted the processor will save the contents of the program counter at location 0 in memory and then jump to location 1. This should contain the start address for the interrupt service routine.

Interrupts can be masked and an output signal INTE will indicate to the interrupting device if interrupts are enabled or not. Multilevel interrupts can be handled by appropriate software design.

Instruction set

The instruction set of the Microflame series is the same as that of the Data General Nova 1200 for the Microflame I and like that of the Nova 3 and Nova 4 for the Microflame II.

There are 42 instructions. This may seem a rather small set but their power lies in the use of multiple fields in the instruction word and the ability to perform several operations with just one instruction.

Arithmetic and logic

Addition, subtraction, multiplication and division operations are provided. In the 9445 type the multiplication and division use on-chip hardware for increased execution speed.

Only the AND operation is provided for logic but the other functions such as OR and EXCLUSIVE OR may be achieved by combining AND with complement operations and tests. Data may be shifted, incremented and negated as required. Many of the operations may be combined, since shifts are controlled by a field within the instruction word rather than by using separate instructions.

Data transfers

Operations provided include data transfers between internal registers, memory and I/O devices. Indexed operations make use of the AC2 and AC3 registers as data pointers. In the 9440 there are no stack operations, but the 9445 does have facilities for transferring data to and from a stack in the memory.

Branch and jump

There is an unconditional jump instruction and also a jump to subroutine function. Conditional operations use the skip type operation and may also be combined with other instructions.

Timing

The 9440 and 9445 both have on-chip clock generators, controlled by an external crystal. For the 8 MHz version (9440/8) average instructions will execute in about 1 μs and for the faster 12 MHz version the execution is 50% faster. The 9445 is designed to work with a 20 MHz clock and will give instruction execution times of the order 400 ns for many instructions. Multiplication and division are much faster on the 9445 because of the on-chip hardware.

Support chips

Some support chips have been designed specifically for the Microflame series for handling memory and I/O bus control. These are:

9441	Memory controller chip
9442	Input–output bus controller chip

Development aids

For low level development and evaluation of Microflame systems the SPARK16 is a single-board module with 2k ROM and 4k RAM, including the FIREBUG monitor program and facilities for DMA and a serial I/O port. This may be used as a stand alone computer with a suitable terminal for control.

For hardware and software development there is the Microflame development system, which can handle both the 9440 and 9445 devices. It also includes the FIRE-LINK hardware in-circuit emulation system for hardware testing.

FERRANTI F100L

The Ferranti F100L is a 16-bit bipolar microprocessor which uses the Ferranti CDI process for fabrication. It is the only microprocessor to have been developed in Europe and is one of the few processors with full military specifications, although some other types do meet the military temperature range.

The general design of the F100L follows that of the Ferranti minicomputers and tends to be somewhat simpler than that of the newer 16-bit nMOS microprocessors such as the MC68000 and Z8000.

In terms of computing power the F100L is very flexible, but possibly not as powerful as the 68000 or Z8000 types. Compared with these processors, which can access megabytes of memory, the F100L allows only 32k words, which is however perfectly adequate for virtually all small to medium size applications. The F100L also has a rather less comprehensive instruction set compared with other processors, and requires an external chip for hardware multiply and divide functions. Speed of operation is comparable with that of other types of 16-bit microprocessor.

Prime manufacturer

Ferranti Ltd.

Devices available

F100L   Basic 16-bit microprocessor chip

Alternative source devices

None at present.

Architecture

As will be seen from fig. 4.2 the internal architecture of the F100L is extremely simple with virtually no working registers.

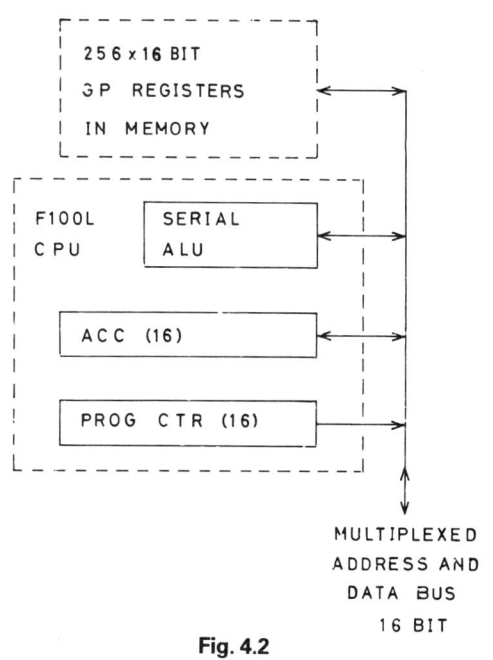

Fig. 4.2

A 16-bit accumulator and arithmetic and logic unit (ALU) deals with the main processing functions. An interesting feature is that the ALU operates in bit serial mode rather than parallel as in other microprocessors. There is also a status register for condition flags and processor status.

The program counter has 15 bits, to provide addressing of up to 32k words of external memory.

No index registers or stack pointers are provided on the CPU itself, since these are implemented within the first 256 words of the external memory. Thus the processor can have up to 256 directly accessible working registers in external memory. These may also be used as data pointers for indirect and indexed addressing.

A 16-bit multiplexed data and address bus is used to communicate with memory and input–output devices.

Package

40-pin dual in line type   ceramic

Power requirements

V_{cc} $+5\ V \pm 5\%$
V_{ss} $0\ V$
Supply current   270 mA

Temperature range

Commercial type   0°C to +70°C
Industrial type   −40°C to +85°C
Military type   −55°C to +125°C

Input–output

The F100L uses a common address space for memory and input–output devices. When a data transfer is to occur the F100L outputs the address of the source or destination device and indicates the direction of data flow. The device must then produce a handshake signal, following which data transfer occurs over the common multiplexed 16-bit bus.

Facilities are provided for direct memory access when the F100L is not using the bus. A DMA request is input to the CPU and when acknowledged by the F100L the bus is released for use by external devices.

External devices are interfaced to the bus via a set of three interface chips. They provide control, data and memory interfaces to the processor bus system.

Interrupt facilities

A single maskable interrupt line is provided on the F100L. On receipt of an interrupt request the CPU saves the contents of the program counter and status register on a stack located within the memory system. The stack pointer is location 0 of the main memory. The CPU then issues an interrupt acknowledge output and expects to receive from the interrupting device a 16-bit vector address, from which the CPU will pick up the start address of the interrupt service routine. These vector addresses are located either from location 2048 or location 16384 in memory, forming a table of up to 64 vectors. Vector 0 is shared with the reset/start vector and some care must be exercised if this is used for interrupt routines.

There is no interrupt priority system and therefore any priority scheme must be handled by external hardware.

Instruction set

There are 153 different instructions in the F100L set, which may be grouped as 28 types of operation.

Arithmetic and logic

For 16-bit arithmetic operations both addition and subtraction are provided and may be executed either with or without carry. Double length (32 bit) arithmetic operations may also be used on the F100L. An interesting feature is that in subtraction the accumulator contents are subtracted from memory contents and the result may be placed either in memory or accumulator as required.

There are no direct instructions for dealing with BCD numbers or for multiplication and division, so these functions must be programmed by software.

Logical operations provided are AND and EXCLUSIVE OR as well as a selection of shift and rotate operations, some of which operate on double length words. There is no logical OR function provided. Other operations include compare, increment and decrement.

Data transfers

All data transfers are effectively between the accumulator and either memory or input–output devices, since the registers are located in the lower 256 words of memory.

The stack is not used for data in the F100L. Its use is reserved for subroutine and interrupt operations, where the program counter and status register contents are saved.

Branch and jump

There are 23 branch and jump operations, of which 12 are conditional. Four subroutine call instructions are included with different addressing modes, and all are unconditional. During subroutine calls the program counter and status register are pushed to the stack.

Addressing modes

The F100L supports four basic addressing modes, which are direct, immediate, immediate indirect and pointer indirect. The last mode may be used for indexing with autoincrement or with autodecrement.

Timing

The F100L requires an external clock generator and normally runs with a 20 MHz clock, to give instruction execution times of the order 3–4 μs.

Support chips

Several support chips have been specially designed for use with the F100L type CPU:

F111-L	Control interface chip
F112L	Data interface chip
F113L	Memory interface chip, high speed type
F114L	Memory interface chip, low speed type and low power
F101L	Hardware multiplier and divider
F115L	Timer and interrupt controller
F116L	Timer chip
F117	Interrupt controller
ZN1001	Clock generator for F100L

Development aids

Ferranti produce a comprehensive development system for the F100L, which uses a floppy disk based operating system and can provide full hardware and software development and debugging facilities. This is the FDS10 development system, which can also support the real time language CORAL66. F100 resident software includes a text editor, assembler and link editor.

GENERAL INSTRUMENT CP1600

The General Instrument CP1600 microprocessor was one of the earliest of the 16-bit microprocessors to appear, in 1975. Fabricated using *n*MOS technology, its basic design philosophy appears to be very similar to that of the popular Digital Equipment PDP11 minicomputer. This makes the CP1600 a relatively powerful and effective processor.

In some ways the CP1600 arrived before the market was ready for it, and for some time it did not seem to be particularly popular. Recently, however, it has been used in video games and now enjoys healthy production levels. When compared with some of the more modern 16-bit processors such as the Z8000 or 68000 the CP1600 may appear to be a relatively simple microcomputer and it is undoubtedly less flexible than some of these more modern devices. Nevertheless the CP1600 is still a very effective processor, and with its long established design and production it could well show some cost advantage over its more sophisticated modern rivals.

Prime manufacturer

General Instrument Corporation.

Devices available

CP1600	Standard part, 3.3 MHz clock
CP1600A	High speed version, 5 MHz clock
CP1610	Economy version, 2 MHz clock

Alternative source devices

None.

Architecture

The general architecture of the CP1600 is relatively simple, as will be seen from fig. 4.3.

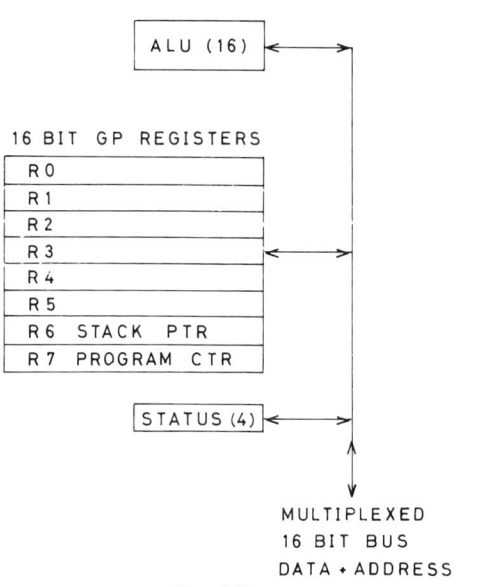

Fig. 4.3

The central feature of the processor is a bank of eight general purpose 16-bit registers. There is no specific accumulator register as in other processors, since any of the eight registers may be used for arithmetic or logic operations. In practice one might consider register R0 as being the normal accumulator, since all of the other registers also perform other functions.

Register R7 provides a 16-bit program counter allowing access to 64k of memory space. This processor is unusual in allowing the program counter to be used as a general purpose register, and this provides some useful programming facilities.

Register R6 is used as a 16-bit stack pointer and builds a stack upwards through the memory. Registers R1 – R5 may be used as data pointers and registers R4 and R5 provide an autoincrementing facility for indexing.

A 4-bit status register provides flags for negative, zero, carry and overflow conditions. There are also facilities for testing up to 16 external flag conditions.

The data and address signals are multiplexed over a 16-bit common bus and will need external logic to separate them. Timing control signals are encoded onto 3 lines and will require external decoding to separate the 8 timing pulses. Further external logic is required to deal with the external status lines. Here a 4-bit code output by the CP1600 must be decoded and used to select one of 16 status signals for input to the processor chip.

Input and output devices are all treated as data memory locations. The CP1600 has provision for direct memory access (DMA), allowing rapid data transfer between the peripheral devices and memory without passing through the CPU.

There is no on-chip clock generator in the CP1600, and an external 2-phase clock signal must be provided.

Package

40-pin dual in line package   Ceramic or plastic

Pin connections

CP1600 and CP1610

1	EBCI	21	D2
2	MSYNC	22	EBCA3
3	BC1	23	EBCA2
4	BC2	24	EBCA1
5	BDIR	25	EBCA0
6	D15	26	TCI
7	D14	27	INTRM
8	D13	28	INTR
9	D12	29	BUSAK
10	D11	30	HALT
11	D10	31	BUSRQ
12	D9	32	STPST
13	D8	33	BDRDY
14	D0	34	V_{cc}
15	D1	35	V_{bb}
16	D7	36	V_{dd}
17	D6	37	$\phi 2$
18	D5	38	$\phi 1$
19	D4	39	GND
20	D3	40	PCIT

Signal functions

D0 – D15   Data bus bidirectional (address or data)

GENERAL INSTRUMENT CP1600

STPST	Stop/start control input (active low)
HALT	Halt status output
MSYNC	Master sync. input (active low)
EBCA0 – EBCA3	External status select outputs
EBCI	External status input
BDIR, BC1, BC2	Bus control outputs
BUSRQ	Bus request input (active low)
BUSAK	Bus released acknowledge output
INTR, INTRM	Interrupt inputs (active low)
PCIT	Program counter inhibit/trap control input–output
TCI	Terminate current interrupt output
BDRDY	Bus data ready input
$\phi1, \phi2$	Two-phase clock inputs
V_{cc}, V_{bb}, V_{dd}, GND	Power supply pins

Power requirements

V_{dd}	$+12\ V \pm 5\%$
V_{cc}	$+5\ V \pm 5\%$
V_{bb}	$-3\ V \pm 10\%$
Supply current	110 mA

Temperature range

0°C to +70°C

Input–output

Logic signal inputs are TTL compatible and outputs will drive one TTL type load.

No specific input–output ports are provided, since all input–output devices are treated as memory and external latch and address decoding logic must be provided.

Status signals from external devices may be selected by using the 4-line EBCA0 – EBCA3 binary coded outputs and feeding the selected status signal to the EBCI input.

Interrupt facilities

Two external interrupts are provided. The INTR signal is not maskable and takes priority over the INTRM input. The INTRM interrupt can be masked by software.

Multiple interrupts and nested interrupts can be dealt with, but external priority logic will be required. When an interrupt occurs the interrupt service routine address must be placed on the bus. A software interrupt is also provided.

Instruction set

Addition and subtraction of 16-bit numbers can be carried out using any of the 8 general purpose registers. The data may be either immediate from the instruction, from another register or from memory. There is no direct facility for BCD arithmetic, which must be achieved by software.

Logical operations provided are AND and EX-CLUSIVE OR. There is no OR instruction. Left and right shift and rotate operations are provided, either direct or via the carry bit. Data may also be compared, complemented and negated.

Data transfer

A comprehensive range of instructions is provided for moving data between the general purpose registers and memory. Data may also be pushed to or pulled from the stack pointed to by register R6.

For indexing any of the registers R1 – R7 may be used as a data pointer, whilst registers R4 and R5 provide an autoincrementing facility.

Branch and jump

Conditional branch instructions are provided for tests on the carry, zero, negative and overflow flags in the status register, and also on the status of a selected external status line.

Unconditional and subroutine jumps are provided, and in some cases a jump may be combined with enabling or disabling the masked interrupt.

Addressing modes

Addressing modes provided on the CP1600 are immediate, direct, indirect, implied and relative. Branch instructions use the relative addressing mode, whilst indirect addressing may be used with jump instructions.

Timing

The standard CP1600 uses an external 2-phase clock at 3.3 MHz, whilst the faster CP1600A can operate at clock rates up to 5 MHz, and with the economy CP1610 a clock of 2 MHz is used. Instruction cycles use 4-clock cycles, and the average time for instructions is 8 instruction cycles, giving average instruction times of about 10 μs for the standard part.

Support chips

IOB1680	16-bit programmable input–output buffer
RO-3-9500	2k × 10 bit mask ROM with address latch
RO-3-9501	2k × 10 bit mask ROM and 1k ext. RAM latch
RO-3-9502	2k × 10 bit mask ROM and 64k ext. RAM latch

Development aids

For low level development and evaluation of CP1600 systems there is a kit called the GIMINI 8950 which provides the 1600 processor, ROM, RAM and TV interface.

INTEL iAPX86 SERIES

The Intel iAPX86 series of microprocessor systems is based upon the 8086 nMOS 16-bit processor chip. The 8086 itself, also known as the iAPX86/10, was the first 16-bit microprocessor to be developed by Intel and has some unique features.

One unusual feature is that some of the signal lines may have their functions reallocated according to the mode of operation selected. These are control signals which in one mode are selected to be suitable for use in a single-processor system, whereas in the alternative mode they are changed to a new set of signals more suited for use in a multi-processor configuration. A second feature designed to speed processing is the provision of separate bus interface and execution sections in the CPU, which provide a pipelined instruction system.

In terms of computing power the 8086 comes into the same class as the Texas 9900 series and the GI CP1600, but is possibly faster in operation. Typical applications would be those normally suited to a medium sized minicomputer. For the larger tasks it seems likely that processors such as the new Motorola 68000 and Zilog Z8000 series are more attractive, but Intel are themselves introducing more powerful types, such as the iAPX432, to handle this type of application.

The iAPX86/20 system is a 2-chip microprocessor with an 8086 as the CPU and an 8087 co-processor connected together in parallel to produce a very high speed numerical processor, typically 100 times better than the 8086 alone.

One useful aspect of the 8086 is that it is designed to be upward compatible with software designed for the 8-bit 8080 and 8085 processors, although it will not execute object code written for these processors.

Prime manufacturer

Intel Corporation.

Devices available

8086 (iAPX86/10)	Basic 16-bit CPU
8086-1 (iAPX86/11)	10 MHz version of 8086
iAPX86/20	8086/8087 combination 2-chip system

Alternative source devices

Siemens A.G.
8086
Mostek are licensed for 8086 but appear to have chosen to produce the 68000 16-bit CPU instead

Architecture

Internally the 8086 is divided into two major sections which work asynchronously relative to one another. The execution unit carries out arithmetic, logic, etc., in response to the instructions acquired from memory by a bus interface section. This section contains a first in, first out memory which allows it to stack up a queue of 6 bytes of instruction code ready for the execution unit. The scheme is effectively an instruction pipeline which allows for faster and more efficient execution of programs.

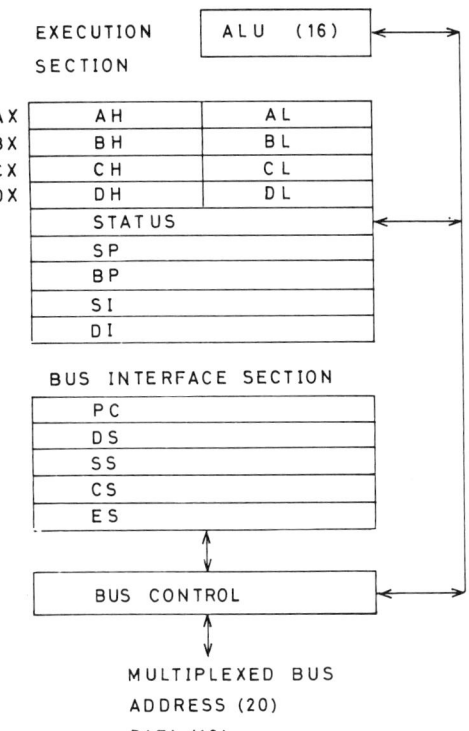

Fig. 4.4

Fig. 4.4 shows the registers which are accessible to the programmer. Arithmetic and logic are performed in a 16-bit ALU working in conjunction with a bank of four 16-bit general purpose registers AX, BX, CX and DX. All of these registers may be used as accumulators, but in general register AX is used as the primary accumulator register, register BX may be used as a base address register for data addressing, whilst register CX is generally used as a loop counter register and DX provides the addresses of input–output devices during I/O operations.

These four 16-bit registers may also be treated as a set of eight 8-bit registers, when the architecture takes on the familiar form of the 8080 register set with the exception of the flag register. Here the lower half of the AX register is equivalent to the 8080 accumulator. Register BX replaces the 8080 HL register pair, whilst CX represents the BC pair and DX the DE pair.

A 16-bit status register (ST) provides condition flags and the interrupt mask. There are also four 16-bit pointer registers provided. The stack pointer is SP whilst BP acts as a base address pointer, with SI and DI acting as the source and destination index pointers.

Up to 65 kbyte of program memory may be accessed by the 16-bit program counter (PC), but by using segment registers the total memory space is extended to 1 megabyte. The four segment registers define different segments of memory for data (DS), stack (SS), program code (CS) and an extra segment (ES). The contents of these registers are left shifted 4 bits and then added to the appropriate address to produce a complete 20-bit effective address. Segments may start anywhere in memory and different types of segment may overlap one another in the physical memory.

Data and address buses for the 8086 are multiplexed on the same lines and the upper 4 address bits are multiplexed with status signals. External logic will be needed to deal with these signals. There is no on-chip clock generator and for this an 8284 clock generator chip is normally used. Bus control is usually governed by an 8288 bus controller chip.

Package

40-pin dual in line package   ceramic

Pin connections

1	V_{ss}	21	RESET
2	AD14	22	READY
3	AD13	23	TEST
4	AD12	24	INTA (QS1)
5	AD11	25	ALE (QS0)
6	AD10	26	DEN (S0)
7	AD9	27	DT/R (S1)
8	AD8	28	M/IO (S2)
9	AD7	29	WR (LOCK)
10	AD6	30	HLDA (RQ/GT1)
11	AD5	31	HOLD (RQ/GT0)
12	AD4	32	RD
13	AD3	33	MN/MX
14	AD2	34	BHE/S7
15	AD1	35	A19/S6
16	AD0	36	A18/S5
17	MNI	37	A17/S4
18	INTR	38	A16/S3
19	CLK	39	AD15
20	V_{ss}	40	V_{cc}

Note that pins 24 – 31 take up the function shown in the parenthesis when MN/MX is set at 0 V, and their normal function when MN/MX is set at +5 V.

Signal functions

AD0 – AD15	Multiplexed address/data I/O tri-state
A16 – A19	Address/status outputs tri-state
S3, S4	Segment identifier outputs
S5	Interrupt enable status output
S6, S7	Status outputs
RD	Read control output tri-state (active low)
INTR	Maskable interrupt input
NMI	Non-maskable interrupt input
RESET	Reset input
READY	Wait state request input
TEST	Wait for test input (active low)
CLK	Single-phase clock input
BHE	High order byte strobe output (active low)
MN/MX	Minimum/maximum mode select input (MX low)

The following signals appear on pins 24 – 31 when MN/MX is set high to give a minimum system configuration:

ALE	Address latch enable output
DEN	Data bus enable output tri-state (active low)
DT/R	Data transmit/receive output tri-state (R low)
HLDA	Hold acknowledge output
HOLD	Hold request input
INTA	Interrupt acknowledge output (active low)
M/IO	Memory/IO strobe output tri-state (IO low)
WR	Write control output tri-state (active low)

The following signals occur in the maximum system configuration mode, when MN/MX is set low:

S0, S1, S2	Machine cycle status outputs tri-state
QS0, QS1	Instruction queue status outputs
LOCK	Bus hold control output tri-state (active low)
RQ/GT0, RQ/GT1	Bus priority controls bidirectional
V_{cc}, V_{ss}	Power supply inputs

All signals, except the clock input, are TTL compatible. Outputs will generally drive one TTL standard load. Suitable clock drive signals may be supplied by the 8284 clock chip.

Power requirements

V_{cc}	+5 V ± 5%
V_{ss}	0 V
Supply current	275 mA max.

Temperature range

0°C to +70°C
Military types for −55°C to +125°C may be available with the type number prefix M

Input–output

Input and output of data for an 8086 system allows up to 65536 separate 8-bit input–output ports to be addressed. It is possible to address the port either directly or through an address held in the DX register. Data may be transferred as either 8-bit bytes or as 16-bit words. An alternative is to use memory mapped input–output in which the I/O device is treated as memory and ordinary data move instructions would be used to transfer data to and from the peripheral device.

In the 8086 system input–output operations are indicated by the state of the M/IO output control line. This will be used to select the memory or I/O device for connection to the data and address bus system.

Block transfers of data to or from an input–output unit may readily be carried out with the 8086 when the CX register will be used to keep track of the byte or word count as the data are transferred.

Interrupt facilities

The 8086 provides both maskable and non-maskable hardware interrupts and also software interrupt facilities. Reset acts in a similar fashion to the NMI type of interrupt. When either type of interrupt occurs the program counter and status flags will be saved on the stack and then the program will go to a vector table located in the first 1024 bytes of memory. The interrupting device upon receipt of an interrupt acknowledge signal must present a byte of data on to the bus to point to the required vector in the table. Four bytes are used for each vector, one pair giving the CS segment register data whilst the second pair gives the program counter data. This vector will produce an effective address pointing to the start of the appropriate interrupt service routine. To access the table the data from the I/O device are multiplied by four to give the memory address in the vector table.

In the vector table vector 0 is used for a divide by zero error routine, and vector 1 is used for a single step routine. Non-maskable interrupt uses vector 2 whilst the two software interrupts INT and INT0 make use of vectors 3 and 4. User vectors for maskable interrupts normally start at vector 32 and may extend up to vector 255.

The single step mode is effectively a software interrupt process initiated by setting a flag bit in the status register.

Instruction set

The 8086 has a very large set of instructions. They may be grouped into 108 basic types of instruction, many of which have a wide range of addressing and other options. Programs written for the 8080 and 8085 types are upward compatible to the 8086 at the assembly language level but not at object code level. This may be useful when upgrading an 8080 or 8085 based system to use an 8086 CPU.

Arithmetic and logic
Both 8-bit and 16-bit unsigned or signed arithmetic is readily carried out, giving addition, subtraction, multiplication and division functions. Decimal numbers may be dealt with as two BCD digits when addition and subtraction are available. If one BCD digit is used at a time then all four arithmetic functions can be used for decimal numbers. Addition and subtraction may be carried out in the BX, CX and DX registers if desired.

Logical functions provided are AND, OR, EXCLUSIVE OR and NOT. There are also the usual range of shift, rotate, clear, increment, decrement, negate, complement and compare functions available, some of which may be applied directly to data in the memory.

Data transfer
A wide range of data transfer instructions handling bits, bytes, words and BCD digits may be used. Block data moves may be made with a data count being kept in the CX register. This type of operation is useful in handling data strings.

Data may be transferred to and from the stack, which has a separate address space from the normal data memory. A number of separate stacks may be set up in memory if required, but the contents of the stack pointer will need to be saved when any particular stack is not in use. Stacks build downwards in the memory.

Branch and jump
There are 26 conditional jump instructions. Of these 12 are duplicated with different names, leaving only 14 actual jump on condition operations. Unconditional jump and call to subroutine instructions are also provided. Some of these allow a jump or call into a new segment of program code memory.

Timing

The standard 8086 (iAPX86/10) device operates with a 5 MHz CPU clock. This will normally be provided by an 8284 clock driver chip. Actual instruction execution time will vary according to the prevailing conditions in the CPU and whether the FIFO instruction queue in the bus interface is full or not. The execution unit will deal with any instructions in the queue independently of the CPU clock which mainly governs the operation of the bus interface. At times, however, the execution unit will stop whilst it waits for the bus selection to set up new instructions in the queue. In general with a 5 MHz clock instructions will execute in some 600 ns to 4 μs, depending upon whether memory access is required or not.

Various speed options are available for the 8086 CPU:

8086-1 (iAPX86/11)   10 MHz clock
8086-2   8 MHz clock
8086-4   4 MHz clock

Support devices

Some support chips have been designed for the 8086 type CPU:

8284   Clock generator chip
8288   Bus controller chip
8289   Bus arbiter chip for multi-processor systems
8087   Numerical co-processor
       (used in iAPX86/20 set)
8089   Input–output processor including DMA facility

The 8086 may also be used with many of the support chips for the 8080 and 8085 series of processors, such as:

8251   Serial communications interface
8253   Triple programmable timer
8255   Programmable peripheral interface 24 parallel lines
8271   Floppy disk controller
8272   Floppy disk controller dual density
8273   Serial controller for SDLC/HDLC protocols
8275   CRT display controller
8291   IEEE488 GPIB bus interface
9292   IEEE488 GPIB master controller
8294   Data encryption unit
8295   Dot matrix printer controller

Development aids

There is a single board SDK86 development module for use in evaluation and software development. It provides debugging facilities and machine code level programming.

For software and hardware development the Intel Intellec series II development systems may be used. This has a floppy disk based operating system providing text editor, assembler, relocatable macroassembly and linker loader facilities and can also operate with high level languages such as PL/M and FORTRAN. The system also provides facilities for debugging of software and the ICE86 module may be used for in-circuit hardware emulation and testing.

Some of the universal microprocessor development systems have facilities for software development using either a cross assembler system or an emulation scheme.

INTEL iAPX88 SERIES

The Intel iAPX88 series of microprocessor systems are based around the 8088 nMOS 16-bit microprocessor chip. The 8088, also known as the iAPX88/10, is a modified version of the 8086 and uses an 8-bit data bus in place of the 16-bit bus used on the 8086 type. Like the 8086 it has some unique features.

One feature is that, like the 8086, some of its signal lines can have their functions reallocated for two different modes of operation. One mode is used where the 8088 is working alone, whilst the alternative mode provides control signals suitable for working in a multiprocessor environment. To speed up program execution the 8088 device is divided into two major sections, one being the execution unit which controls instruction execution, whilst the other is a bus interface controlling access to the system bus and allowing several instruction bytes to be stacked to give pipeline operation.

The 8088 is similar to the Texas 9980 in terms of computing power, and like the 9980 it uses an 8-bit data bus system. This processor would be suitable for applications which might normally use a small to medium size minicomputer and where fairly complex programs are to be executed.

The iAPX88/20 is a 2-chip microcomputer system, where the 8088 is paired with an 8087 co-processor and is designed to provide very high speed mathematical operations, particularly using floating point and trigonometric operations. The iAPX88/20 is claimed to be about one hundred times more effective than a normal iAPX88 system.

Like the 8086 the iAPX88 system is upward compatible for software written for the 8-bit 8080 and 8085 type processors.

Prime manufacturer

Intel Corporation.

Devices available

iAPX88/100 (8088)	Basic CPU chip	5 MHz clock
iAPX88/20	Two-chip set comprising 8088 and 8087	

Alternative source devices

Siemens A.G. are licensed to manufacture the 8088.

Architecture

The two sections of the 8088 chip, the execution unit and the bus interface unit, work asynchronously. The bus unit stacks up to 4 bytes of machine code in a first in, first out (FIFO) buffer and is controlled by the system clock. The execution unit processes instructions from this stack which acts as an instruction queue, and if there are no instructions in the queue the execution unit will simply wait until new ones are fetched from memory. This arrangement tends to make for faster code execution.

In fig. 4.5 only those registers which are accessible to the programmer are shown. For arithmetic and logic there is a bank of four 16-bit general purpose registers AX, BX, CX and DX, which may also be treated as a set of eight 8-bit registers. These registers may be used to

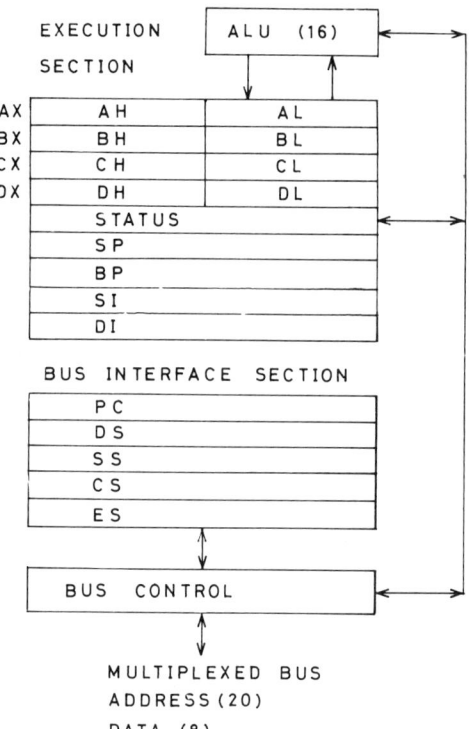

Fig. 4.5

emulate those in an 8080 or 8085 processor, in which case the lower byte of the AX register acts as the accumulator, BX replaces the HL register pair, CX acts as the BC register pair and DX replaces the DE register pair. In the 8088 the AX register is used as the accumulator, whilst BX acts as a base address register for data addresses, CX acts as a counter and DX is used to address I/O devices.

Status flags and interrupt control are provided by a 16-bit status register (ST) and there are four 16-bit address pointer registers. Register BP acts as a program base address pointer, SP is the stack pointer, and SI and DI act as index pointers giving source and destination addresses.

The 16-bit program counter (PC) allows access to 65k byte of memory, but by using segmented addressing the total memory may be expanded to 1 megabyte. Four 16-bit registers provide segment addresses and in each case the contents of the segment register are shifted 4 bits to the left and then added to the effective address to give a complete address of 20 bits. Segments may exist anywhere in memory and may even be overlapped. Four types of segment are supported. They are data (DS), stack (SS), program code (CS) and finally there is an extra segment (ES) available.

In the 8088 the data are multiplexed with the 8 lower bits of the address bus and the upper 4 bits of address are multiplexed with processor cycle status signals. Because of multiplexing the lower and upper address lines will need to be latched externally, but bits 8 – 15 of the address bus are latched outputs. Bus control is usually provided by using an 8288 chip.

There is no on-chip clock generator on the 8088 and an external chip such as the 8284 will be required as a clock generator.

Package

40-pin dual in line type   ceramic

Pin connections

1	V_{ss}	21	RESET
2	A14	22	READY
3	A13	23	TEST
4	A12	24	INTA (QS1)
5	A11	25	ALE (QS0)
6	A10	26	DEN (S0)
7	A9	27	DT/R (S1)
8	A8	28	M/IO (S2)
9	AD7	29	WR (LOCK)
10	AD6	30	HLDA (RQ/GT1)
11	AD5	31	HOLD (RQ/GT0)
12	AD4	32	RD
13	AD3	33	MN/MX
14	AD2	34	BHE/S7
15	AD1	35	A19/S6
16	AD0	36	A18/S5
17	NMI	37	A17/S4
18	INTR	38	A16/S3
19	CLK	39	A15
20	V_{ss}	40	V_{cc}

Note that pins 24 – 31 take up the function shown in the parenthesis when input MN/MX is set at V_{ss} (0 V) and have their normal function when MN/MX is set at V_{cc} (+5 V).

Signal functions

AD0 – AD7	Multiplexed address/data I/O tri-state
A8 – A19	Address outputs tri-state
S3, S4	Segment identifier outputs
S5	Interrupt enable status output
S6, S7	Status outputs
RD	Read control output tri-state (active low)
INTR	Maskable interrupt request input
NMI	Non-maskable interrupt request input
RESET	Reset input
READY	Wait state request input
TEST	Wait for test condition input (active low)
CLK	Single-phase CPU clock input
BHE	High order byte strobe output (active low)
MN/MX	Minimum/maximum mode select input (MX low)

When MN/MX is high the minimum system configuration is set and signals on pins 24 – 31 are:

ALE	Address latch enable output
DEN	Data bus enable output tri-state (active low)
DT/R	Data transmit/receive output tri-state (R low)
HLDA	Hold acknowledge output
HOLD	Hold request input
INTA	Interrupt acknowledge output (active low)
M/IO	Memory/IO strobe output tri-state (IO low)
WR	Write strobe output tri-state (active low)

In the maximum configuration with MN/MX set low the signals become:

S0, S1, S2	Machine cycle status outputs tri-state
QS0, QS1	Instruction queue status outputs
LOCK	Bus hold control output tri-state (active low)
RQ/GT0, RQ/GT1	Bus priority controls bi-directional
V_{cc}, V_{ss}	Power supply inputs

All logical signals, except the CPU clock, are TTL compatible and in general outputs will drive one standard TTL load. The clock drive signals may be generated by using the 8284 clock generator chip designed for use with the 8088.

Power requirements

V_{cc}	+5 V ± 5%
V_{ss}	0 V
Supply current	275 mA max.

Temperature range

0°C to +70°C

Input–output

For input and output to peripheral devices the 8088 treats the I/O devices as being separate from memory and is able to address external devices individually. During the input–output operation the contents of the DX register are output via the address bus and act as an I/O device address. Since this is a 16-bit address the 8088 can select up to 65536 individual I/O ports. Data are transferred as 8-bit bytes via the data bus. Since the data and address are multiplexed it will be necessary to provide external address latches and decoding logic. An I/O port address is identified by the state of the M/IO output status line. This will go to a low state when an input–output operation is in progress and indicates that the address and data buses are being used for input–output.

Blocks of data may be transferred to or from an input–output device, in which case the CX register is normally used to keep track of the number of bytes of data transferred.

Input–output, although normally directly addressed, may also be operated as memory mapped I/O. In this case the I/O devices are simply treated as if they were memory and the normal memory data transfer operations are used to transfer data to the peripheral devices.

Interrupt facilities

On the 8088 there are available both maskable and non-maskable interrupts for hardware operation as well as some software interrupt facilities.

When an interrupt occurs the contents of the program and status registers will be saved on the stack and then the program will be vectored to the service routine via a vector table located in the lower 1 kbyte of memory. On receipt of an interrupt acknowledge output from the processor the device causing the interrupt will be required to input via the data bus an address to point to the required vector in the table. Four data bytes are used for each vector table entry. Two bytes give the data to be placed in the CS segment register whilst the second pair of bytes give the program counter contents. The vector data are then used to form an address within the memory at which the start of the interrupt service routine is stored.

In the vector table there are 256 vectors and the data byte input by the external device is multiplied by 4 to produce the required memory address. Vector 0 is used for the reset operation. Vector 1 is for a single-step mode which is effectively a software interrupt. The non-maskable interrupt (NMI) uses vector 2, whilst vectors 3 and 4 are used for two further software interrupts produced by the INT and INT0 instructions. Vectors 5 – 31 are reserved and vectors 32 – 255 may be used by the programmer for maskable interrupts.

Interrupt priority will need to be resolved by either using a polling technique or by using external hardware logic to select the priority.

Instruction set

The basic instruction set of the iAPX88 series is identical to that of the 8086 processor. The large set of instructions provided can be grouped into some 108 basic types, many of which have a wide range of addressing modes and options.

Programs written for the 8-bit 8080 and 8085 type microprocessors are upward compatible with the 8088, although the machine code for these machines is not compatible. Programs written in assembler language, however, can be used with the 8088 assembler, with the exception of the RIM and SIM instructions of the 8085 which are not implemented on the 8088.

Arithmetic and logic
Although the 8088 data bus is only 8 bits wide the internal system provides normal 8 or 16-bit arithmetic functions, including addition, subtraction, multiplication and division of both signed and unsigned binary numbers. All four functions are also available in the decimal mode for unpacked BCD data where each byte contains one BCD digit. For data packed with 2 digits per byte only the addition and subtraction facilities are provided.

Logical operations include AND, OR, EXCLUSIVE OR and a NOT function which is effectively a complement. Rotate and shift operations are provided as well as increment, decrement, compare, negate and clear.

Most functions can be carried out on any of the four general purpose registers and some are available for directly manipulating the memory contents.

Data transfer
The 8088 has a wide selection of data transfer operations to allow data to be moved between all of the registers and the memory and I/O system. Blocks of data may be moved using one single instruction, in which case the CX register will be used as a data counter. This type of operation may be useful for handling data strings.

The stack pointer allows the creation of data stacks in the memory, and data may be pushed to or popped from the stack as required. Multiple stacks may be set up provided the stack pointer contents of those stacks not currently in use are held in the memory. Stacks build downwards in memory. Note that since there is only one stack pointer the stack will also be used by subroutines and interrupts for data storage.

Input and output data transfers to external devices are dealt with by special input–output instructions and the I/O ports are separately addressed.

Branch and jump
Although there are 26 different mnemonics for conditional branch and jump instructions, 12 of these are duplicated with different names, leaving only 14 actual operations. In these duplicated instructions one of the mnemonics used is that for the 8080/8085 instruction set.

The 8088 also has unconditional jump instructions and various call to subroutine instructions. Some jump and call instructions allow access to a new segment of program memory by altering the contents of the CS register.

Timing

Normally the 8088 will operate with a 5 MHz CPU clock. It is difficult to define the execution time since this depends on the way in which instructions stack up in the bus interface unit and are then executed by the execution unit. In some cases where the queue is full the execution may be very fast, but at other times the execution unit may be kept waiting by the bus system. In general instructions will execute in about 1 μs with a 5 MHz clock.

Because of the 8-bit data bus the execution time for an 8088 will be about 30% longer than that for an 8086, since for many operations two bus accesses must be made for data instead of one.

Support devices

Devices specifically designed for use with the 8088 processor are:

8284   Clock generator
8288   Bus controller
8289   Bus arbiter for multi-processor systems
8087   Numerical co-processor (used for iAPX88/20)
8089   Input–output processor including DMA facility

The 8088 may also be used with most of the 8080/8085 based interface devices, such as:

8251   Serial communications interface
8253   Programmable timer with 3 timers
8255   Programmable parallel interface 24 lines
8271   Floppy disk controller
8272   Floppy disk controller
8273   HDLC/SDLC serial data controller
8275   CRT display controller
8279   Keyboard and display interface
8291   GPIB (IEEE488) interface
8282   GPIB (IEEE488) bus controller
8294   Data encryption unit
8295   Dot matrix printer controller

Development aids

A single board evaluation kit SDK86, although primarily for use with the 8086 processor, can also be used for the 8088 for software development.

Full software and hardware development facilities are provided by the Intel Intellec series II systems, and these include in-circuit emulation for hardware debugging. The system uses a floppy disk based operating system and can be used with high level languages such as PL/M and FORTRAN. For software development there are editor, macroassembler and fully relocatable linker loader facilities provided.

Some of the universal microprocessor development systems also provide software development facilities for the 8086 and 8088 type microprocessors.

MOTOROLA MC68000 SERIES

By using VLSI techniques and their high density HMOS process, Motorola have produced the 68000. It is a 16-bit *n*MOS microprocessor, and at the present time probably the most powerful 16-bit processor in production.

Internally the 68000 has a largely 32-bit wide data organisation and a very flexible array of working registers which give it a very high processing throughput. Included on the chip are hardware multiplication and division logic to increase further the processing speed in complex calculations. The system is able to handle 32-bit operations with ease.

Unlike many other 16-bit microprocessors the 68000 has separate data and address buses which make for much simpler external logic and also increase the execution speed. Other types usually multiplex data or address or both in order to reduce the munber of pins on the package. The address of the 68000 uses 23 bits to provide over 16 megabyte of directly addressable memory space. In fact all 32 bits are available for addressing within the chip and the address is basically limited by the number of pins available for the bus output.

The 68000 has the effective processing power of a minicomputer of medium size and is primarily suited to tasks in which a large amount of complex processing is required and where a minicomputer might normally be used. Applications such as speech analysers, complex control systems and real time simulator systems would be ideal for this type of microprocessor, but of course it is also effective in smaller type applications where its high execution speed may be useful.

Prime manufacturer

Motorola Semiconductor Inc.

Devices available

MC68000   Microprocessor chip available with various clock speeds up to 8 MHz

Alternative source devices

Rockwell

  R68000C4   4 MHz part
  R68000C6   6 MHz part
  R68000C8   8 MHz part

Thomson EFCIS

  EF68000

Fairchild

  F68000

Mostek Corporation

  MK68000

Hitachi Semiconductors

  HD68000

Philips/Signetics

  68000

Architecture

The internal architecture, as with many of the modern 16-bit microprocessors, is arranged on the same lines as that of a mini or mainframe computer such as the PDP11 or some of the larger IBM machines. Only the programmable registers have been shown in fig. 4.6.

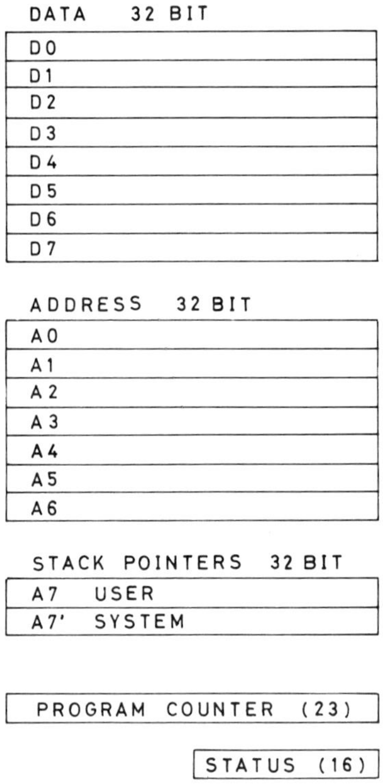

```
DATA    32 BIT
┌─────────────────┐
│ D0              │
│ D1              │
│ D2              │
│ D3              │
│ D4              │
│ D5              │
│ D6              │
│ D7              │
└─────────────────┘

ADDRESS 32 BIT
┌─────────────────┐
│ A0              │
│ A1              │
│ A2              │
│ A3              │
│ A4              │
│ A5              │
│ A6              │
└─────────────────┘

STACK POINTERS 32 BIT
┌─────────────────┐
│ A7   USER       │
│ A7'  SYSTEM     │
└─────────────────┘

┌─────────────────┐
│ PROGRAM COUNTER (23) │
└─────────────────┘
        ┌──────────────┐
        │ STATUS (16)  │
        └──────────────┘
```

Fig. 4.6

Unlike the smaller microprocessors the 68000 has no dedicated accumulator register. Instead it uses a bank of eight 32-bit general purpose registers D0 – D7, of which any can be used as an accumulator as required. These registers normally handle data which may be in the form of either 4-bit BCD digits packed 8 to a register, bytes with 4 bytes per register, pairs of 16-bit words or double length 32-bit words. These various types of data may then be manipulated as desired within the register array.

There are also a further eight 32-bit address registers which can be addressed by the program. Of these register 7 is in fact two separate 32-bit registers which act as stack pointers, although only one will be in program operation at any given time. One operates as the system stack pointer and the other is the user stack pointer. Each of these stack pointers generates a stack which moves downwards through the memory.

A further 32-bit register acts as the program counter. At present only the lower 23 bits of this register are used, although there are 32 bits on the chip and it is possible that the address space might be further expanded in future developments of the 68000 series processors to make it a full 32-bit machine.

There is a 16-bit status register which provides a wide selection of conditional flags.

To increase the speed of execution the arithmetic and logic unit incorporates hardware for integer multiplication and division which may be called directly by program.

As with the 6800 and 6809 8-bit processors the 68000 addresses all input–output devices as memory locations and most of the 6800 series support chips can therefore be used directly with the 68000 processor.

Package

64-pin dual in line ceramic

Pin connections

1	D4	33	A5
2	D3	34	A6
3	D2	35	A7
4	D1	36	A8
5	D0	37	A9
6	AS	38	A10
7	UDS	39	A11
8	LDS	40	A12
9	R/W	41	A13
10	DTACK	42	A14
11	BG	43	A15
12	BGACK	44	A16
13	BR	45	A17
14	V_{cc}	46	A18
15	CLK	47	A19
16	GND	48	A20
17	HALT	49	V_{cc}
18	RESET	50	A21
19	VMA	51	A22
20	E	52	A23
21	VPA	53	GND
22	BERR	54	D15
23	IPL2	55	D14
24	IPL1	56	D13
25	IPL0	57	D12
26	FC2	58	D11
27	FC1	59	D10
28	FC0	60	D9
29	A1	61	D8
30	A2	62	D7
31	A3	63	D6
32	A4	64	D5

Pin functions

A1 – A23	Address bus output tri-state
D0 – D15	Data bus bidirectional tri-state
R/W	Read–write output (write low)
AS	Address strobe output (active low)
UDS, LDS	Data strobe output (active low)
DTACK	Data transfer acknowledge input (active low)
BR	Bus request input (active low, wired OR)
BG	Bus grant (active low)
BGACK	Bus grant acknowledge input (active low)
IPL0 – IPL2	Interrupt priority level inputs (active low)
BERR	Bus error input (active low)
RESET	Processor reset input (active low)
HALT	Halt input (active low)
E	Enable output for 6800 devices
VMA	Valid memory address output (active low)
VPA	Valid peripheral address (active low)
PC0, PC1, PC2	Processor status outputs
CLK	Single-phase clock input
V_{cc}, GND	Power supply inputs

Power requirements

V_{cc}	+5 V ± 5%
GND	0 V
Power consumption	1 W

Temperature range

0°C to +70°C

Input–output

All input and output peripheral devices on the 68000 system are treated as memory locations.

Interrupt facilities

Seven levels of interrupt priority are provided by using the interrupt priority inputs.

Interrupt vectors are located in the supervisor data memory space. It should be noted that the 68000 can allocate address areas to either user program, user data, supervisor program or supervisor data, and these are indicated by the output code on the FC0, FC1 and FC2 status lines. During an accepted interrupt the processor goes into supervisor state and the system stack pointer is brought into play. There are a wide range of possible conditions in the 68000 interrupt processing system.

Interrupts are handled by an exception processing scheme which also takes into account reset, program trace, traps and various bus conditions.

Instruction set

There are 56 basic instruction types in the 68000 set. This may seem rather small compared with the large number of instructions in some 8-bit processors sets, but it must be remembered that 68000 instructions are 16-bits long and may have up to two further 16-bit words to define addresses. The first word is an instruction word which defines the type of operation, mode and registers involved, whilst other words define the source and destination address.

Arithmetic and logic
Arithmetic operations provided are addition, subtraction, multiplication and division. There are also BCD versions for addition and subtraction. Addition and subtraction may also be carried out on double length words (32 bits) and on individual bytes.

Logical operations include AND, OR and EXCLUSIVE OR, as well as the usual range of shift and rotate operations, either left or right, and comparison operations.

Data transfer
A selection of move and exchange type instructions allow data to be manipulated at will between registers and memory in a range of data formats including bytes, 16-bit words and 32-bit double length words.

MOTOROLA MC68000 SERIES

Branch and jump

A wide selection of possible combinations of conditional branch instructions is possible and there are also various unconditional branch and jump operations as well as the usual subroutine jumps. Some conditional branches also allow bit manipulation to be carried out conditionally as well.

Addressing modes

There are 14 different basic addressing modes provided on the 68000:

- Data register direct
- Address register direct
- Address register indirect
- Indirect post incremented
- Indirect predecremented
- Indirect with displacement
- Indirect with index
- Absolute short address
- Absolute long address
- Program counter with displacement
- Program counter with index
- Immediate
- Condition code or status
- Implied reference

Timing

The 68000 requires an external single-phase clock normally operating at 4 MHz, but high speed parts are available to operate with clock rates of 6 MHz and 8 MHz.

Using a 4 MHz clock register instructions execute in about 0.5 μs and average instruction execution might be 1 – 2 μs.

Support chips

MC68120		Intelligent peripheral controller
MC68230		Parallel interface and timer unit
MC68450		Direct memory access controller
MC68451		Memory management unit
MC68340		Dual port RAM
MC68560		Serial DMA interface
MC68341		Floating point mathematics ROM
MC68454		Disk controller

The 68000 will also work with the following support devices designed for the 6800/6809 type processors:

MC6822	PIA	Two 8-bit programmable I/O ports
MC6840	PTM	Three programmable 16-bit counter/timers
MC6843	FDC	Floppy disk controller logic
MC6847	VDG	Video display generator (NTSC)
MC6849	DDFDC	Floppy disk controller dual density
MC6850	ACIA	Asynchronous serial I/O interface
MC6852	SSDA	Synchronous serial I/O controller
MC6854	ADLC	Advanced data link I/O controller
MC68488	GPIA	IEEE488 GPIB instrument bus controller

Development aids

Motorola

MEX68KDM. This is a single board evaluation and development module. It contains an MC68000 CPU, 32 kbyte of RAM, two RS232 serial I/O ports, two 16-bit parallel ports, a triple timer/counter and sockets for 4k of ROM (2716 or similar). There is a 4 kbyte ROM based monitor called MACSBUG on the board which allows machine code program development and a debugging facility.

A cross assembler is available for use in the EXORCISER development system. The 68KDM board can be connected into an EXORCISER system and the assembled program down loaded into the on-board RAM for execution. There is also a PASCAL type compiler available for use with the EXORCISER system.

For a full development system Motorola have introduced the EXORMACS system, which provides full software development, debugging and in-circuit emulation facilities for the 68000. This uses a floppy disk based operating system and also has PASCAL and MPL facilities. Multi-user systems are also planned.

Thomson EFCIS, Rockwell and Hitachi will also be able to supply similar development systems under a full licensing arrangement with Motorola.

The Futuredata AMDS2300 development system provides a cross assembler for the 68000 microprocessor and it seems likely that an emulator will become available in the future.

Cross assemblers for the 68000 are also available to run on computers such as the IBM370 and DEC PDP11. There is also an emulator package which will run on the IBM370.

NATIONAL NS16000 SERIES

National Semiconductor are currently introducing a complete new family of 16-bit *n*MOS microprocessors and support chips known as the NS16000 series.

The three processors that have been announced cover a range of computing power and applications, from the higher end of the 8-bit processors to virtually 32-bit capability. The largest member of the family is the NS16032. It seems to be similar in power to the 68000 from Motorola but has a higher execution speed. For smaller applications the NS16008 and NS16016 have been announced. The first of these has an 8-bit data bus and conventional 16-bit address and internal registers, whilst the second is effectively a 16-bit machine.

Applications for these microprocessors will be similar to those for which the MC6800 and Z8000 might be chosen and which might currently be executed by a minicomputer such as the PDP11. A useful feature of the NS16032 is the vast size of memory that it can access and the possibility of using a form of virtual memory operation with this processor.

Prime manufacturer

National Semiconductor Corporation.

Devices available

NS16008	CPU with 8-bit data bus and 16-bit architecture
NS16016	Full 16-bit CPU
NS16032	16-bit CPU with 32-bit internal architecture

Alternative source devices

None at present.

Architecture

Fig. 4.7 shows the layout of the programmable registers of the NS16032 type CPU. The other types have a similar type of architecture, but use 16-bit internal registers and in the case of the NS16008 an 8-bit data bus.

A bank of eight 32-bit general purpose working registers R0 – R7 are used for data handling, arithmetic and logic. It is possible to handle data as bytes, 16-bit words, 32-bit double length words or strings of up to 8 BCD digits.

A group of dedicated 24-bit registers is used for the program counter and various other pointer registers. A processor status register (PSR) provides normal condition code flags as well as various status bits for the processor system control.

Two stack pointer registers are provided, one for the user stack (US) and the other for the system or interrupt stack (IS). Only one of these pointers will be selected for use at any time.

A further pointer is the frame pointer (FP), which points to a stack containing the parameters for a currently active subroutine. The static base register (SB) points to an area in data memory and the module register (MOD) points to the currently executing segment of program. These registers allow easy relocation of the program modules within the memory.

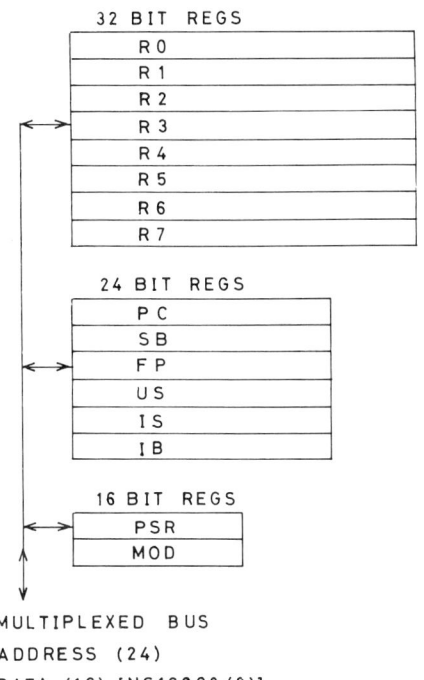

Fig. 4.7

Finally there is an interrupt base register (INTBASE) which points to a table of interrupt vectors in the memory.

On the 16032 a 24-bit wide address bus is used to allow direct access to 16 megabytes of external memory. The other types use a 16-bit address bus. In the 16000 system the 16-bit data bus shares the same pins as the address bus and will be multiplexed with it to reduce the package size.

Package

NS16032	48-pin dual in line type
NS16016	40-pin dual in line type
NS16008	40-pin dual in line type

Pin connections

Not available.

Instruction set

The instruction set for the NS16000 series devices includes over 100 types of instruction and is claimed to be extremely flexible and powerful.

The two lower members of the family (NS16008 and 16016) have an interesting software feature which allows them to be switched into an operating mode where they can emulate an 8080 type processor and execute its machine code instructions directly. This is designed to allow easy conversion of existing programs written for the 8080 to run on the 16000 system.

The normal machine code of the 16008 and 16016 will be upward compatible on the 16032 type processor, thus allowing a system to be upgraded to the 16032 without major software revision.

NATIONAL NS16000 SERIES

Arithmetic and logic

Integer arithmetic using bytes, words or 32-bit numbers is provided for all general purpose registers. Functions are addition, subtraction, multiplication and division. There is also a decimal capability which can handle strings of up to 8 BCD digits.

Logic operations include the usual AND, OR and EXCLUSIVE OR functions, as well as a logical NOT function. Numbers may also be complemented, compared, incremented and decremented.

A good selection of bit testing and manipulation type instructions is provided.

Data transfer

The NS16000 supports a very wide range of data transfer type operations, including byte, word and double word movements. There are facilities for handling block transfers and for dealing with string arrays. The 16000 series also supports direct memory to memory type operations.

Branch and jump

Branches and jumps may be either conditional or unconditional, and are addressed relative to the program counter using 8, 16 or 32-bit displacements to allow access to the full memory space.

Instructions have been included to allow external subroutines to be called without the need to specify an address in the instruction. This would be effective when handling procedures in high level languages. Internal housekeeping is automatically handled by these instructions.

Addressing modes

Apart from the normal addressing modes such as immediate, direct, indexed, relative and indirect the 16000 series has some unique addressing modes. A total of 9 addressing modes is available.

One useful mode provided is the ability to use relative addressing with a memory location as the reference rather than the program counter.

An external addressing mode allows program modules to be relocated in the memory without the need for a linking editor. A scaled indexing system allows easy access to multibyte data by automatically adding a 1, 2, 4 or 8-byte offset to the effective address.

Slave processor operations

The 16000 software set includes a number of instructions which allow operations to be carried out in slave special function processors connected to the system. Typically these include a floating point arithmetic processor and a memory management unit. The software is able to access registers directly in these processors and to pass instructions to them.

The floating point processor permits 32-bit and 64-bit format floating point arithmetic operations, whilst the memory management unit permits the implementation of a virtual memory system as used on the larger minicomputers.

Timing

The NS16000 series devices require an external clock which may conveniently be generated by the NS16201 clock generator chip.

Instruction execution is claimed to be very fast, with typical execution times of from 0.3 to 2.5 μs. This is faster than any other currently available processor type.

Support chips

A number of support chips have been specially designed for use with the NS16000 series of processors, and some of these are:

NS16201   Clock generator
NS16202   Interrupt controller
NS16203   Direct memory access controller
NS16204   Bus arbitration chip for multiprocessing
NS16081   Floating point arithmetic processor
NS16082   Memory management unit

Development aids

National Semiconductor will be providing full hardware and software development systems for the NS16000 family, including full debugging facilities. These systems will also support high level languages such as PASCAL, BASIC and FORTRAN.

TEXAS INSTRUMENTS TMS9900

From Texas Instruments one of the early 16-bit microprocessors to appear was the 9900. This is a 16-bit nMOS microprocessor with the CPU on a single chip.

Internally the organisation of the 9900 is unique since its working registers have been sited in the external read–write memory rather than on the CPU chip itself. This makes for some unusual features, such as direct memory to memory data transfers and multiple banks of working registers. As a result the 9900 produces a versatile 16-bit system.

In terms of processing power the 9900 compares well with many minicomputers and other early 16-bit microprocessors, but it is perhaps rather limited when compared with modern types such as the 68000 and Z8000. This processor has perhaps not achieved the popularity that it deserves.

For signal processing applications the 9900 is a very effective processor and its flexible architecture and use of memory make it useful for many other applications. It seems likely that the 9900 will remain useful for quite a few more years, but will eventually be rendered obsolete by the newer and even more flexible devices now being introduced.

For low power applications a bipolar version of the 9900 using I^2L technology has been developed. This is the SBP 9900, which provides the same operating speed as the 9900.

Prime manufacturer

Texas Instruments Inc.

Devices available

TMS9900   Standard nMOS part
SBP9900 I^2L bipolar version

Alternative source devices

American Microsystems Inc.

  S9900

Standard Microsystems Corporation

  9900

Architecture

From fig. 4.8 it is seen that the internal architecture of the CPU is very simple, with only four programmable 16-bit registers and an ALU.

Unlike other processors the 9900 places its working registers, including the accumulator and stack pointer, out in the external memory. The workspace register within the CPU points to the first of a set of 16 consecutive 16-bit words in memory which may then be used as a bank of 16 general purpose working registers. Any of these memory locations may be used as an accumulator or index register as required. It is usual to reserve the last three words in the group for storage of program counter, workspace register and status register contents when the bank of registers in use changes. This might happen in a subroutine operation. At the end of the routine the contents of the last three words are restored

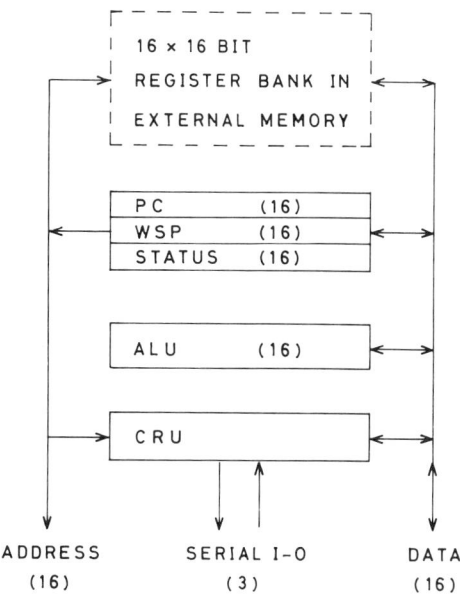

Fig. 4.8

and operation is switched back to the original set of registers in the memory space.

A 16-bit program counter (PC) is provided which allows 32k words of memory to be addressed. In the 9900 the memory is actually addressed in bytes and the address bus is moved two bytes at a time to pick up the correct 16-bit data words for the data bus.

The status register contains 16 bits and provides a selection of condition flags and interrupt priority status. There is also a memory address register to drive the address bus.

Data and address buses are separate in the 9900. A serial input–output facility is provided via a so called communications register unit (CRU). A 4-phase external clock is required to drive the 9900 but the SBP9900 uses a single-phase clock.

Package

64-pin dual in line ceramic

Pin connections

TMS9900

1	V_{bb}	33	IC3
2	V_{cc}	34	IC2
3	WAIT	35	IC1
4	LOAD	36	IC0
5	HOLDA	37	–
6	RESET	38	–
7	IAQ	39	–
8	$\phi1$	40	V_{ss}
9	$\phi2$	41	D0
10	A14	42	D1
11	A13	43	D2
12	A12	44	D3
13	A11	45	D4
14	A10	46	D5
15	A9	47	D6
16	A8	48	D7

TEXAS INSTRUMENTS TMS9900

17	A7	49	D8
18	A6	50	D9
19	A5	51	D10
20	A4	52	D11
21	A3	53	D12
22	A2	54	D13
23	A1	55	D14
24	A0	56	D15
25	$\phi 4$	57	–
26	V_{ss}	58	–
27	V_{dd}	59	V_{cc}
28	$\phi 3$	60	CRUCLK
29	DB_{IN}	61	WE
30	CRU_{OUT}	62	READY
31	CRU_{IN}	63	MEMEN
32	INTREQ	64	HOLD

Signal functions

D0 – D15	Data bus bidirectional tri-state
A0 – A14	Address bus output tri-state
CRU_{IN}, CRU_{OUT}, CRUCLK	Communication register control
$\phi 1 - \phi 4$	Four-phase clock inputs
INTREQ	Interrupt input (active low)
IC0 – IC3	Priority inputs for interrupt (IC0=MS)
DB_{IN}	Data bus status output
MEMEN	Memory enable output (active low)
WE	Write enable output (active low)
HOLD	Hold input (active low)
HOLDA	Hold acknowledge output
READY	Memory ready input
WAIT	Wait status output
IAO	Output indicating instruction fetch cycle
LOAD	Non-maskable interrupt input (active low)
RESET	Reset input active low
V_{dd}, V_{bb}, V_{cc}, V_{ss}	Power inputs

Power requirements

TMS9900

V_{bb}	-5 V $\pm 5\%$
V_{cc}	$+5$ V $\pm 5\%$
V_{dd}	$+12$ V $\pm 5\%$
Supply current from V_{cc}	50 mA

SBP9900

Single supply voltage of $+1.5 - +30$ V
Maximum supply current 450 mA depending on speed of operation

Temperature range

TMS9900	0°C to +70°C
SBP9900	−55°C to +125°C
SBP9900A	0°C to +70°C
SBP9900E	−40°C to +85°C
SBP9900M	−55°C to +125°C

Input–output

All input and output logic signals to this processor are TTL compatible except the 4-phase clock inputs which require 12 V signals. Outputs will drive one TTL standard load.

Data input and output to peripherals use direct memory addressing, treating peripheral devices as memory locations. There is also an unusual form of serial input–output via the communications register unit which allows bit by bit output or input. Direct memory access uses the HOLD control signals.

Interrupt facilities

Hardware interrupts are maskable and activated by applying an interrupt request on the INT REQ line and simultaneously placing a 4-bit priority code on lines IC0 – IC3. The interrupt when accepted will cause a switch in the working register set and the interrupt vector address will be called from a set of locations in the lowest 128 bytes of memory. An input on LOAD causes a non-maskable interrupt and there is also a range of software interrupts for trap operation.

Instruction set

The instruction set of the 9900 is quite versatile, though perhaps not as good as those of some of the newer processors. There are 64 basic types of instruction in the set.

Arithmetic and logic

For addition, subtraction, multiplication and division of 16-bit integer numbers the 9900 can make use of any of the registers in the currently selected working area of memory. Addition and subtraction may also be carried out on bytes within the registers if desired. No direct instructions are included for dealing with BCD format data.

The absolute value of data can be taken and register contents can be incremented, decremented, complemented and cleared to zero.

Logical operations available are AND, OR and EXCLUSIVE OR. There are left and right shift operations, but rotate only operates to the right. Individual bits may also be manipulated within the register array.

Data transfer

Data can readily be moved around between the registers and other areas of the memory. Here it must be remembered that these are effectively direct memory to memory moves, since the registers are all located in the external memory.

Input and output are achieved by moving data to memory locations occupied by peripheral devices and a series of instructions are available for bit by bit serial input or output via the communications register port.

Branch and jump

A good selection of conditional jump instructions has been provided, allowing tests for zero, sign carry and overflow. There is also a test for odd parity which is useful for dealing with serial data transmission. Unconditional jump and branch operations are also provided.

There is a subroutine jump operation and also some

instructions for context switching. In this operation the bank of memory used for the general purpose registers is changed. During this process the previous contents of the program counter, workspace address register and status register are stored in registers 13, 14 and 15 of the new set of working registers. If a return is made to the first set of working registers the program counter, workspace and status registers are restored to their original values by reloading them from the workspace being vacated. A similar operation occurs for subroutines and interrupt operations.

Addressing modes

Memory addressing is normally either direct or implied and may be indexed in either mode. There is also an instruction which causes execution of the instruction stored in a specified register.

Timing

The standard 9900 CPU requires a 4-phase non-overlapping clock. The clock frequency is typically 3 MHz with a minimum of 2 MHz, since the 9900 has dynamic internal logic.

A single-phase clock generator may be used with the I^2L SEP9900 type CPU, and the frequency may range from zero to about 3 MHz.

With a 3 MHz clock frequency typical instructions will execute in about 12 clock cycles or roughly 4 μs. Multiplication and division operations are carried out much more slowly, taking some 16 or 32 μs respectively.

Support devices

A range of support chips have been developed for use with the 9900 series microprocessors. All are available from Texas, but newer types may not be available from alternative sources.

TMS9901	Programmable interrupt and I/O interface
TMS9902	Asynchronous serial communication controller
TMS9903	Binary synchronous interface
TMS9904	Four-phase clock driver
TMS9905	Data selector and multiplexer (= 74LS251)
TMS9906	Eight bit addressable latch (= 74LS259)
TIM9907	Eight to three line priority encoder (= 74LS148)
TIM9908	Tri-state version of 9907 (= 74LS348)

Development aids

Texas Instruments provide a series of single-board computers based on the TMS9900, which may be used for prototype design and development. These provide 1 – 4 kbyte of RAM and up to 8 kbyte of EPROM or ROM which may incorporate a monitor and debug system.

For more serious development work a series of systems based on the Texas 990 minicomputer and called AMPL990 may be used. These systems are based around a floppy disk type operating system. They provide full software development with editors, assembler and debug facilities as well as hardware emulation. High level languages such as BASIC, FORTRAN and PASCAL may be used and in some of the newer systems two users may operate on a time-shared basis.

TEXAS INSTRUMENTS TMS9940 AND 9985

Although several of the newer 8-bit microcomputers can perform some 16-bit operations, the Texas Instruments TMS9940 is the only true 16-bit single-chip microcomputer currently available. This device is fabricated using silicon gate nMOS.

Basically the 9940 contains a 9900 type CPU combined with 2048 bytes of read only memory and 128 bytes of RAM. The standard version uses a mask programmed ROM and is best suited for dedicated applications where medium to high production volume can be achieved. An alternative version of the 9940 has a UV eraseable type EPROM and can conveniently be used for system development and for limited production runs.

The Texas Instruments 9985 is a microprocessor which has the same basic chip design as the 9940, but in place of the ROM it has an extra 128 bytes of RAM. This chip has only an 8-bit data bus to the outside world, although internally it is a 16-bit processor. A 16-bit address bus allows external ROM to be used with the 9985.

In general the 9940 microcomputer is likely to be very useful for industrial applications where data are commonly in 12-bit binary format. In such applications it has the advantage of higher speed and a more compact set of instructions when compared with competitive 8-bit microcomputers. The 9900 type architecture with its large bank of working registers may also be of advantage in some applications.

Prime manufacturer

Texas Instruments Inc.

Devices available

TMS9940M	2 kbyte mask ROM, 128-byte RAM, 32 I/O lines
TMS9940E	2 kbyte UV EPROM, 128-byte RAM, 32 I/O lines
TMS9985	256-byte RAM, external ROM

Alternative source devices

American Microsystems Inc.

S9940N	2k mask ROM, 128-byte RAM, 32 I/O lines
S9940E	2k UV EPROM version

Architecture

Basically the architecture of the 9940 is derived from that of the 9900, as shown in fig. 4.9. Like the 9900 the CPU uses three 16-bit control registers for the program counter (PC), workspace pointer register (WP) and status register (ST).

As with the 9900 a bank of sixteen 16-bit general purpose registers is set up in the RAM for use as accumulators, index registers or for general data storage. The location of the 16 registers currently in use is indicated by the workspace pointer register, and in the 9940 four separate register banks can be selected within the 128-byte RAM.

The 32 general purpose input–output lines may either

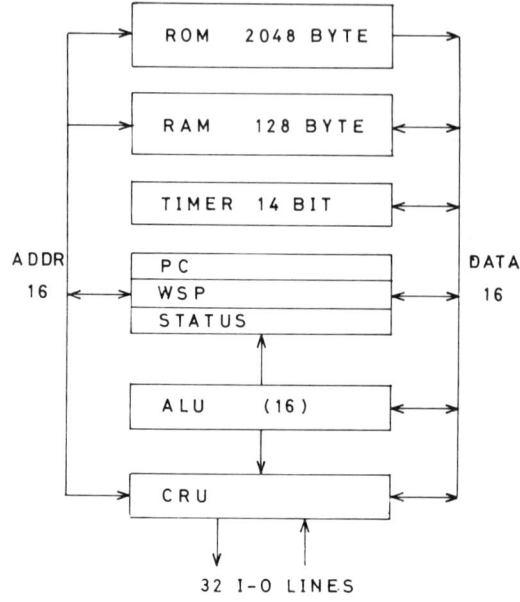

Fig. 4.9

be used individually or in groups of up to 16 lines. Some of these lines perform a dual function to provide I/O expansion. In the 9985 the input–output lines may be configured to act as a 16-bit address bus and an 8-bit multiplexed data bus.

It should be noted that there is no arrangement on the 9940 for memory expansion, although there is a facility which allows multiple processor operation.

There is a 14-bit event counter/interval timer provided on the 9940, linked to the communications register unit (CRU), which may be used for serial output and is used to control data transfer to the output lines.

Package

40-pin dual in line type   ceramic or plastic
On TI types suffix J is used to denote the ceramic package and suffix N plastic

Pin connections

TMS9940M and TMS9940E

1	P23	21	XTAL1
2	P22	22	XTAL2
3	P21	23	P0/A1
4	P20	24	P1/A2
5	P19	25	P2/A3
6	P18	26	P3/A4
7	P17/EC	27	P4/A5
8	P16/IDLE	28	P5/A6
9	P15/HLDA	29	P6/A7
10	P14/HLD	30	P7/A8
11	P12/TD	31	P24
12	V_{cc1}	32	P25
13	V_{cc2}	33	P26
14	P11/TC	34	P27
15	P13/ϕ	35	P28
16	P10/CRUCLK	36	P29
17	P9/CRU$_{OUT}$	37	INT2/PROG
18	P8/CRU$_{IN}$	38	P30
19	INT1/TST	39	P31
20	RST/PE	40	V_{ss}

Signal functions

P0 – P31	General purpose I/O lines

Note many I/O pins have multifunctions and may not be used as I/O under some conditions.

A1 – A8	May be configured as address output for I/O expansion
XTAL1, XTAL2	Oscillator crystal connections
ϕ (pin 15)	Can be used as clock output line
RST	Reset input (active low)
INT1, INT2	Interrupt inputs (active low)
CRU_{IN}, CRU_{OUT}, CRUCLK	Communication register signals used for I/O expansion
PROG, PE	Program pulse and program enable signals for programming the internal EPROM
HLD	Hold input to stop CPU (active low)
HLDA	Hold acknowledge output (active low)
EC	Event counter input
IDLE	Output signal indicating power down state (active low)
TC, TD	Transfer clock and data strobe lines for use in a multiprocessor configuration
TST	Test mode select input
V_{ss}, V_{cc2}	Main power supplies
V_{cc1}	Standby supply for memory and interrupt logic

Power requirements

V_{cc1}	+5 V ± 5%
V_{cc2}	+5 V ± 5%
V_{ss}	0 V
I_{cc1}	10 mA
I_{cc2}	160 mA

Temperature range

0°C to +70°C

Input–output

All inputs and outputs to the 9940 and 9985 are TTL compatible and outputs will generally drive a single TTL load.

Input and output lines can be individually set or reset via the internal CRU system and may also be configured as either input or output lines. They may also be grouped into sets of from 2 to 16 bits for input–output as required. It is possible to expand the number of input–output lines to 256 by using external expansion logic.

Interrupt facilities

The 9940 provides 4 levels of interrupt priority, with reset at the highest priority (level 0). The external interrupt INT1 operates at priority level 1 and the internal counter/timer at level 2, whilst the second external interrupt INT2 operates at the lowest priority level.

Interrupt vectors are stored at the bottom of the ROM with reset at address 0000 hex. Note that in the 9940 the ROM is at the bottom of the memory map, occupying the space from 0000 to 07FF (hex.) whilst the internal RAM is located from 8300 to 837F (hex.).

Instruction set

The instruction set for the 9940 is virtually the same as that of the TMS9900, and software developed for the latter type can run on a 9940 with some restrictions on memory space.

Arithmetic and logic

A full complement of 16-bit addition, subtraction, multiplication and division instructions is available and any of the current group of working registers can be used for arithmetic.

Logical operations provided are AND, OR and EX-CLUSIVE OR, as well as the usual range of shift and rotate operations. There are also instructions for incrementing, decrementing, complementing and comparing data in registers.

Data transfer

A wide range of instructions are included for data transfers between register in the current group and also to other parts of the available RAM space. Data can also be manipulated bit by bit and can be transferred to the input–output lines as required.

Branch and jump

The 9940 provides 12 conditional jump instructions, covering a wide selection of tests. There are also two unconditional branch instructions. Two subroutine branch instructions are provided, one of which causes a new bank of working registers to be selected. Instructions are provided for changing the working register group, and the current values of program counter, status and workspace registers are saved in three of the registers within the new group.

Addressing modes

Addressing is basically via the registers in the working bank and may be direct or indexed. Direct, indirect and relative addressing are used for program instructions.

Timing

The 9940 and 9985 have on-chip clock generators which are timed by an external crystal. The standard TMS9940 uses a 5 MHz clock, but there are variants for other rates as follows:

TMS9940-10	1 MHz clock
TMS9940-20	2 MHz clock
TMS9940-30	3 MHz clock
TMS9940-40	4 MHz clock

Support chips

The 9940 and 9985 can use any of the support chips designed for use with the 9900 series microprocessors. Some of these are:

TMS9901	Programmable interrupt and I/O interface
TMS9902	Serial asynchronous I/O controller
TMS9912	Single-chip modem
TMS9914	GPIB IEEE488 bus controller

TMS9918   Colour graphics video controller
TMS9927   Video timer and controller
TMS9903   Synchronous serial I/O controller

Development aids

Texas Instruments provide a small development system for the 9940 which is called the TM990/40DS. This uses a 9900 microprocessor as the controller and provides facilities for programming the 9940 EPROM and for in-circuit emulation.

The AMPL 990 development system provides a floppy disk controlled operating system and full development facilities for both hardware and software for the 9940.

Several of the general purpose development systems such as the Tektronix 8001 and 8002 development laboratory systems provide software development and debugging for the 9900 and can also be used to produce programs for the 9940 and 9985.

TEXAS INSTRUMENTS TMS9980

The Texas Instruments TMS9980 series of devices are 16-bit *n*MOS microprocessors, and are basically cut down versions of the TMS9900 type. To produce a processor more suitable for the smaller 16-bit applications Texas Instruments reduced some of the facilities provided on the 9900 and managed to pack the 9980 into a 40-pin package rather than the 64-pin version used for the original 9900 series.

To reduce the number of pins required the data bus was cut from 16 to 8 lines and the address bus was also reduced in size. The original 4-phase clock of the 9900 has been cut to a single phase on the 9980 by building the 4-phase logic into the CPU chip.

In terms of its general internal architecture and the software a 9980 is basically the same as a 9900. In most cases programs written for one processor will run in systems using the other type.

Typical applications for the 9980 series are those in which a small minicomputer might normally be employed. The 9980 is effective where relatively complex processing and an interrupt driven system are required.

The 9980 is relatively unsophisticated in comparison with more modern 16-bit processors such as the 68000 and Z8000, but nevertheless it is still useful for some applications.

Prime manufacturer

Texas Instruments Inc.

Devices available

TMS9980   Basic CPU chip using external clock
TMS9981   Same as 9980 but with on-chip clock generator

Alternative source devices

American Microsystems Inc.

S9980   Standard 9980 CPU

Standard Microsystems Corporation

SMC9980   Standard 9980 CPU

Architecture

From fig. 4.10 it will be seen that the 9980 CPU has the same basic architecture as the TMS9900 processor, except that the data bus is only 8 bits wide instead of 16 and a smaller address bus is used.

On the CPU chip there are three 16-bit registers which can be accessed by the programmer. These are the program counter register (PC), the status register (ST) and the workspace pointer register (W).

Like the 9900 this processor has no dedicated accumulator or index registers, but instead uses a bank of 16 working registers in the external memory. These 16-bit registers can be set up anywhere in the memory and the first register in the bank is pointed to by the workspace register W. At any time during execution of a program the bank of registers in use may be changed. In this case the workspace register will be changed to point to a new part of memory to select a new set of 16 registers.

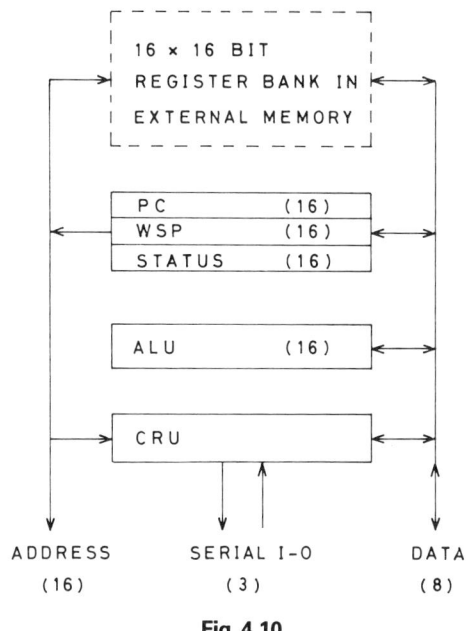

Fig. 4.10

Normally the contents of the program counter, status register and workspace register will be saved in the last three registers of the new set.

Any of the working registers in use may be employed as an accumulator and registers R1 – R15 may be used as index registers. Since the working registers are located in memory it is easy to perform direct memory to memory transfers, a feature not found in most other microprocessors.

Unlike the 9900 with its 16-bit bus the 9980 has a limited memory range of only 16 kbyte, or 8k 16-bit words using the 14-bit address bus. Although the data bus has also been reduced to 8 bits the 9980 still operates on 16-bit words but transfers them over the bus as two 8-bit bytes. Internally the 9980 uses 16-bit data paths and operations.

Parallel input–output uses memory mapping and treats I/O devices as memory. For serial input–output there is a special communications register unit (CRU) to enable a serial bit by bit data transfer to be made on a special I/O line.

A 16-bit status register (ST) provides condition flags and masking for the interrupt system.

Package

40-pin dual in line   ceramic or plastic
On TI devices a J suffix denotes a ceramic type package and an N suffix indicates a plastic package part.

Pin connections

1	HOLD	21	V_{bb}
2	HOLDA	22	$\phi 3$
3	IAQ	23	INT2
4	A13/CRU$_{OUT}$	24	INT1
5	A12	25	INT0
6	A11	26	D0
7	A10	27	D1
8	A9	28	D2

9	A8	29	D3
10	A7	30	D4
11	A6	31	D5
12	A5	32	D6
13	A4	33	D7
14	A3	34	C_{IN}
15	A2	35	V_{ss}
16	A1	36	V_{dd}
17	A0	37	CRUCLK
18	DB_{IN}	38	WE
19	CRU_{IN}	39	READY
20	V_{cc}	40	MEMEN

Signal functions

A0 – A13	Address bus outputs tri-state
D0 – D7	Data bus bidirectional tri-state
CLN	Clock input
$\phi 3$	Phase $\phi 3$ clock signal output (active low)
INT0 – INT2	Interrupt priority input
DB_{IN}	Control output indicates data bus ready for input
IAQ	Output indicating instruction fetch cycle
READY	Input indicating memory is ready for read–write
HOLD	Bus request input (active low) used for DMA
HOLDA	Bus acknowledge output (active high)
CRU_{IN}	Data input to CRU for serial I/O
CRU_{OUT}	Data output from CRU for serial I/O
CRUCLK	CRU clock (strobe) output
WE	Write enable output (active low)
MEMEN	Memory enable output (active low)
V_{bb}, V_{cc}, V_{dd}, V_{ss}	Power supply inputs

Power requirements

V_{bb}	-5 V $\pm 5\%$
V_{cc}	$+5$ V $\pm 5\%$
V_{dd}	$+12$ V $\pm 5\%$
Supply current from V_{cc} and V_{dd}	50 mA
Bias current from V_{bb}	1 mA

Note that the 8851 does not require the V_{bb} (-5 V) rail.

Temperature range

0°C to +70°C

Input–output

For normal parallel input–output over the data bus the 9980 uses memory mapped I/O in which the I/O device is treated as one or more memory locations. Address decoding logic external to the CPU must be used to select the appropriate I/O device to be connected to the data bus.

For serial input–output via the CRU channel up to 2048 bits of data in memory can be selected bit by bit for input or output.

Direct memory access can readily be set up on the 9980 by using the HOLD and HOLDA bus control signals and external DMA logic to multiplex the data as required.

Interrupt facilities

The 9980 provides 5 levels of interrupt priority, these being selected by the inputs INT0 – INT2. Level 0 has the highest priority and is reserved for the reset function. External interrupts occupy levels 1 – 4 and may be masked at each of the levels.

There is a LOAD function which provides a non-maskable interrupt and uses the code 010 on the INT0 to INT2 lines. The reset function is triggered by code 000 or 001 on these lines.

Interrupts may be masked by a combination of the least significant 4 bits of the status register. Priority will be allocated, with level 1 at the highest priority and level 4 at the lowest. Normally an external interrupt logic system will be used to provide the correct input codes to INT0, INT1 and INT2.

The interrupt vectors are stored in the first 64 words of memory, each vector containing two words, one for program counter and the second for workspace pointer. Words 32 – 63 are reserved for software trap vectors.

The reset vector is stored in words 0 and 1 of memory and the vector for the load operation is stored in the last two words of memory (bytes 3FFC (hex.) to 3FFF (hex.)).

Instruction set

The instruction set of the 9980 and 9981 is basically the same as that of the larger 9900 microprocessor. Although perhaps not as versatile as some of the more modern 16-bit designs the 9980 has a quite effective instruction set for most purposes. There are 64 basic types of instruction in the set.

Arithmetic and logic
Addition, subtraction, multiplication and division of 16-bit integer numbers are provided. The multiplication and division operations use internal software and are relatively slow in operation when compared with some modern types which use a hardware multiplier unit. Any of the currently selected bank of registers may be used as the accumulator for these types of operation, which makes for some flexibility in comparison with 8-bit types where a dedicated accumulator is used. There are no special instructions for dealing with BCD format numbers.

Absolute values of register contents may be taken and it is possible to increment, decrement, complement and compare the contents of registers.

Logical functions provided are AND, OR and EX-CLUSIVE OR, as well as right and left data shift operations on all working registers. There is a rotate operation, but only to the right. Individual bits may be manipulated within the registers and between them.

Data transfer
Data may be transferred between registers and memory. Since the registers themselves are in memory, this amounts to direct memory to memory transfers. For input–output the data will be transferred to a memory location occupied by the external I/O device.

Special instructions are included to control bit by bit data transfers via the CRU channel for serial input–output.

Branch and jump

There are 12 conditional branch instructions covering a wide range of status conditions. There are also a pair of unconditional branches, one with relative addressing and the second using indirect addressing via a register.

Two branch to subroutine instructions are provided. In one of these the register bank in use is changed to another which controls the subroutine operations.

Addressing modes

In the 9980 the addressing of memory is normally either direct or implied via a register. Indexing is possible in either mode. There is also a form of instruction which allows the contents of a specified memory location to be executed as an instruction.

Relative addressing is used for conditional branches and one unconditional branch.

Timing

Although internally the 9980 uses a 4-phase clock system, like that of the 9900 processor the clock generator logic is built into the chip so that only a single-phase clock signal is needed to drive the processor. Phase $\phi 3$ of the internal 4-phase clock is brought out for synchronisation of any external devices that may be required.

The 9981 contains an on-chip oscillator which is brought into play by simply connecting the C_{IN} pin to V_{dd}. If an external clock is to be used with the 9981 a TTL level clock signal is simply applied to C_{IN}.

Maximum clock frequency is 8 MHz, which produces a 2 MHz cycle frequency for the internal 4-phase system. With this clock frequency instruction execution times will be around $10-20$ μs for most operations, but rather slower for the multiplication and division functions.

Support devices

The 9980 and 9981 being members of the general 9900 family can use suppor devices designed for the 9900 and SBP9900. Some of these are:

TMS9901	Programmable interrupt and I/O interface
TMS9902	Asynchronous communication controller for serial I/O
TMS9909	High speed serial I/O controller
TMS9911	Direct memory access (DMA) controller
TMS9912	Single-chip modem for serial I/O systems
TMS9913	A/D converter controller
TMS9914	General purpose interface bus (GPIB) controller for use with IEEE488 type instrument bus
TMS9915	Dynamic RAM refresh controller
TMS9916	Bubble memory controller for TI memories
TMS9918	Colour graphics video display controller
TMS9903	Synchronous serial I/O controller
TMS9927	Video timer and controller

Development aids

From Texas Instruments the main microprocessor development system covering the 9980 and 9981 processors is the AMPL system, based on the Texas 990 minicomputer. This provides a floppy disk based operating system with editor, assembler and linker loader as well as high level languages such as BASIC, FORTRAN, CORAL and PASCAL.

Facilities are available for full software debugging and for hardware emulation. There is also a logic analyser facility for use in hardware testing. The system comes in the form of a desk unit with the computer system in a rack under the desk and with a desktop VDU.

For lower level development and for evaluation of the hardware system Texas provide a range of single-board microcomputers based on the TMS9900, together with a range of other cards for support systems, input–output and memory. There is also a range of sizes of bubble memory boards for use with this system.

Other systems which support development of 9980 type microprocessors are the Tektronix 8001 and 8002 microprocessor laboratory development systems.

There are also software development packages available which will allow 9980 programs to be developed and debugged on various popular minicomputer systems.

TEXAS INSTRUMENTS TMS9995

One of the latest microprocessors to come from Texas Instruments is the 9995, based on the TMS9900 series of 16-bit processors. The TMS9995 uses *n*MOS technology and provides a 16-bit microprocessor with an 8-bit data bus system.

Typically this processor will compete with types such as the Intel 8088 and some of the more advanced 8-bit types such as perhaps the MC6809 and Z80. It is specifically designed for minimum chip count, thus making it ideal for the smaller applications where a 16-bit machine and where complex and fast numerical processing are required. In comparison with the 8088 the TMS9995 seems to be about 50% faster in instruction execution, and apart from memories it needs few support chips.

The TMS9995 has some similarities to the TMS9985 but with some enhancements in the CRU hardware and new features in software aimed at speeding up numerical operations.

Prime manufacturer

Texas Instruments Inc.

Devices available

TMS9995   Basic microcomputer CPU chip

Alternative source devices

None at present.

Architecture

Internally the architecture of the TMS9995 follows the same basic pattern as that of other processors in the Texas 9900 series, as will be seen from fig. 4.11.

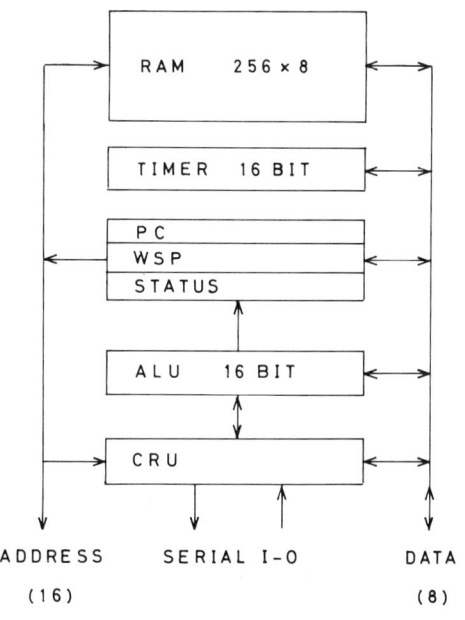

Fig. 4.11

The CPU has two basic registers, one being the 16-bit program counter and the other a 16-bit workspace pointer register which points to a group of 16 general purpose 16-bit registers located in the on-chip RAM. Any one of 8 separate groups of registers may be selected for use at a time. Each register file group occupies a total of 32 bytes of the on-chip RAM. Note that register to register operations use 16-bit data paths and are therefore much faster than data operations involving external memory. The registers may all be used for arithmetic and logic, or as data pointers, or just as data storage as required. In a subroutine operation it is simple merely to select a new bank of working registers for the subroutine program to use and to revert to the original set of registers on returning to the main program.

One feature of the TMS9995 is that like other types in the 9900 series it can readily carry out direct memory to memory data transfers.

A 16-bit address bus allows access to 65 kbyte of external memory, and data are transferred over a separate 8-bit data bus to avoid the time penalties involved in using a multiplexed data and address bus system. The use of two separate buses also simplifies external logic, since there is no need for address latches and demultiplexer logic.

Like other 9900 processors the 9995 has a communications register unit (CRU) which allows individual bits of memory to be addressed and permits serial input and output operations. Whereas other members of the 9900 processor family allow up to 4096 bits of data to be addressed by the CRU, the TMS9995 will permit up to 32768 bits to be accessed in this way.

A 16-bit flag and status register has been provided in the TMS9995. There are also facilities for a 16-bit timer or event counter on the chip. Another useful feature of the 9995 is the provision of internal wait state control logic for use with slow memories, which may be programmed out if fast memory is to be used. The TMS9995 has its own on-chip generator for the CPU clock, thus saving the need for an external clock.

Package

40-pin dual in line

Power requirements

V_{cc} +5 V ± 5%
V_{ss} 0 V

Temperature range

0°C to +70°C

Signal levels

All input and output logic signals are TTL compatible. In general outputs will drive one standard TTL load.

Input–output

For parallel data transfers via the 8-bit data bus the 9995 uses a simple memory mapped scheme in which the I/O devices are treated as if they were memory and data are simply moved to or from them in the same way as for memory operations. It is necessary to provide external logic for address decoding.

For serial data transfer one bit at a time the CRU channel may be used. This allows individual bits to be set or reset and addressed for transfer via the CRU input and output lines.

It is relatively easy to provide direct memory access operations on the 9995, since there is a hold input facility which will cause the CPU to release the address and data bus lines for use by external devices.

Interrupt facilities

Five levels of interrupt priority are provided on the 9995. Each interrupt uses a vectored addressing scheme, with the vectors held in the first 64 words of the data memory. A non-maskable interrupt is provided and there are also facilities for software interrupt operations. Reset is treated as an interrupt and occupies the highest priority level.

Instruction set

The TMS9995 has basically the same instruction set as the 9900 and other members of the 9900 family, with some enhancements to improve efficiency.

Arithmetic and logic

Any of the registers in the currently selected workspace set may be used as accumulators and may perform 16-bit addition, subtraction, multiplication and division. Whereas on the other 9900 types only unsigned multiply and divide are provided, the 9995 has two new instructions allowing signed multiplication and division.

Logical functions provided are AND, OR and EX-CLUSIVE OR, as well as the usual shift and rotate operations. Data may be incremented, decremented, complemented, negated and compared, and there are also bit manipulation facilities.

Data transfer

A full range of data transfer instructions is provided for moving data between the registers and memory or directly from memory to memory. Individual bits may be manipulated using the CRU facility. New features not included in the standard 9900 instruction set are the instructions for loading the workspace and status registers from memory.

Branch and jump

Twelve conditional branch operations are provided, and there are two unconditional branches. There are two subroutine branches, one of which causes a new bank of working registers to be selected.

Two new features are software interrupts actuated by an arithmetic overflow or an unrecognised instruction. The latter is used for detecting macro instructions.

Addressing modes

Eight basic addressing modes are available on the TMS9995. They are register, register indirect, register indexed, direct, indirect, immediate, relative and relative to the CRU for I/O operations.

Timing

An on-chip clock oscillator is provided which uses an external crystal for timing and runs at 6 MHz. Instruction execution is very fast and a typical multiply or divide instruction is performed in about 10 μs.

Support chips

The TMS9995 can be used with support chips designed for the 9900 family of processors, among which are:

TMS9901	Programmable I/O and interrupt controller
TMS9902	Serial I/O controller (asynchronous)
TMS9903	Synchronous serial I/O controller
TMS9909	Floppy disk controller
TMS9911	Direct memory access controller
TMS9914	IEEE488 GPIB adapter
TMS9918	Colour video display and graphics generator
TMS9927	Video timer/controller
TIM99600	Dynamic memory refresh controller
TIM99630	Error detection and correction logic

Development aids

For prototype evaluation and simple hardware and software development capability an evaluation module is available for the TMS9995. This provides communications facilities for a control terminal and for connection to a host computer to allow programs to be down loaded. There is also an area of board available for breadboarding of custom interfaces, etc.

For full development facilities in both hardware and software the Texas Instruments AMPL development system may be used. This system uses either a floppy or hard disk for the operating system and provides assemblers, linkers and debug facilities for software development, as well as full in-circuit emulation for testing prototype hardware systems. Facilities are also available for high level languages and for programming PROMs and EPROMs as required.

WESTERN DIGITAL PASCAL MICROENGINE

Western Digital have introduced the WD9000, which is a 5-chip microcomputer set designed to execute directly the PASCAL P code. The CPU is based on the Western Digital MCP1600 series and uses two chips. In the WD9000 set 3 ROM chips provide the P code interpreter. Microengine is a trade mark of the Western Digital Corporation.

In addition to the PASCAL Microengine Western Digital have also developed a microcomputer set designed to execute the high level ADA language system. This system has been given the general type number ME1600.

Prime manufacturer

Western Digital Corporation.

Devices available

CP1611B   CPU chip
CP1612B   Control chip

There are also 3 preprogrammed MICROM ROM chips for the PASCAL P code. They are 512 × 22 bits each.

Alternative source devices

National is licensed to produce chip set.

Architecture

The CPU is a 16-bit type with stack oriented hardware. A 16-bit multiplexed data and address bus is provided, giving access to 128 kbyte of memory.

Internally the CPU has a group of 26 8-bit general purpose registers which may be grouped in pairs to form 16-bit registers. There is an 8-bit flag register for status flags.

The control chip contains a programmed logic array and control logic to interpret macro instructions called from the interpreter ROMs.

For high speed arithmetic the processor has hardware multiply and divide and floating point arithmetic functions.

Package

All five devices use 40-pin dual in line packages.

Pin connections

CPU chip

1	$\phi 3$	21	$\phi 2$
2	V_{bb}	22	WAIT
3	DAL00	23	MIB15
4	DAL01	24	MIB14
5	DAL02	25	MIB13
6	DAL03	26	MIB12
7	DAL04	27	MIB11
8	DAL05	28	MIB10
9	DAL06	29	MIB9
10	DAL07	30	MIB8
11	DAL08	31	MIB7
12	DAL09	32	MIB6
13	DAL10	33	MIB5
14	DAL11	34	MIB4
15	DAL12	35	MIB3
16	DAL13	36	MIB2
17	DAL14	37	MIB1
18	DAL15	38	MIB0
19	V_{ss}	39	V_{dd}
20	$\phi 4$	40	$\phi 1$

Control chip

1	$\phi 3$	21	$\phi 2$
2	V_{bb}	22	V_{cc}
3	I3	23	MIB15
4	I2	24	MIB14
5	I1	25	MIB13
6	I0	26	MIB12
7	MIB17	27	MIB11
8	BUSY	28	MIB10
9	COMPUTE	29	MIB9
10	RESET	30	MIB8
11	MIB16	31	MIB7
12	REPLY	32	MIB6
13	WAIT	33	MIB5
14	D_{OUT}	34	MIB4
15	R/W	35	MIB3
16	IACK	36	MIB2
17	SYNC	37	MIB1
18	D_{IN}	38	MIB0
19	V_{ss}	39	V_{dd}
20	$\phi 4$	40	$\phi 1$

Signal functions

DAL00 – DAL15	Multiplexed data/address I/O tri-state
MIB00 – MIB17	Micro instruction bus (active low) bits 16 and 17 used by the ROMs
D_{IN}, D_{OUT}	Data bus control lines
$\phi 1, \phi 2, \phi 3, \phi 4$	Four-phase clock inputs
I0 – I3	Hardware interrupt inputs
REPLY	Memory I/O acknowledge output
IACK	Interrupt acknowledge output
W/R	Read–write control output (read low)
$V_{bb}, V_{cc}, V_{dd}, V_{ss}$	Power supply inputs

All logic signals are TTL compatible.

Power requirements

V_{cc} +5 V ± 5%
V_{bb} −5 V ± 5%
V_{dd} +12 V ± 5%

Input–output

All input–output devices are memory mapped and treated as memory locations.

Interrupt facilities

Four levels of hardware interrupt are provides using the lines I0 – I3.

Instruction set

Unlike other processors which operate with a machine code instruction set, the Western Digital PASCAL Microengine will directly execute PASCAL P code as produced by the UCSD PASCAL compiler. Other types of microprocessor, when used with the PASCAL language, use an interpreter program to convert the P code into machine language and then execute the machine code instructions.

The ADA Microengine will be similarly designed to deal with programs written using the new ADA software system.

Development aids

Western Digital produce a single board microcomputer based on the WD9000 chip set with the type number WD900. This unit provides 64 kbyte of on-board memory, a floppy disk controller for up to 4 drives, two full duplex serial input–output channels and 2 parallel input–output ports. An expansion card is also available to allow memory to be increased to 128 kbyte. A PASCAL compiler to UCSD level III.0 is available for use with this microcomputer system. The system can also be obtained packaged as a complete desktop computer with the type number WD90.

For the ADA Microengine a completely packaged system will be available with the type number ME1675. It will include 2 floppy disk drives, 128 kbyte of memory, VDU, printer and 10-slot chassis with power supply. Alternatively a selection of individual cards and system components will be available with type numbers in the ME1600 series.

ZILOG Z8000 SERIES

The Zilog Z8000 series of microprocessors, like many of the other recent 16-bit designs, has the type of architecture and computing power normally associated with medium to large size minicomputers and even some mainframe machines. By using VLSI techniques Zilog have managed to pack an extremely powerful 16-bit microprocessor onto a single nMOS silicon chip. At the present time only one other 16-bit microprocessor, the Motorola 68000, appears to offer more power or complexity, but other microprocessors currently being developed may well alter this situation.

Two basic versions of the Z8000 type processor are being produced. One provides a segmented addressing system allowing access to a 23-bit address bus and permitting up to 8 million 16-bit words, or 16 megabytes, of memory to be used. By using an external memory management chip the memory space can be made relocatable so that the physical address in the memory need not concern the programmer and is automatically taken care of by the hardware. This is in some ways similar to the virtual addressing schemes used by large minicomputers. The system can also allocate different address spaces to the system and user and to program and data.

Zilog have also developed a series of support devices specifically for the 16-bit Z8000 series, rather than rely on upward compatibility of the 8-bit Z8 or Z80 support chips. It is also possible to use the Z8000 in multiple processor type systems.

This processor, like the Intel 8086 and Motorola 68000, is designed for those applications where a medium size minicomputer might normally be employed. The Z8000 provides very efficient program execution and high throughput of data, thus making it ideal for real time simulation work, complex system control and signal analysis. Of course the Z8000 is also very effective in simpler applications and will show a considerable speed advantage over say an 8-bit processor.

Prime manufacturer

Zilog Inc.

Devices available

Z8001	Segmented address version for 16 megabyte memory
Z8002	Non-segmented version 64 kbyte memory
Z8003	As Z8001 but with virtual memory facility
Z8004	As Z8002 but with virtual memory facility

Alternative source devices

SGS/ATES

Z8001	Segmented processor
Z8002	Non-segmented version

Advanced Micro Devices

Am8001	Segmented version
Am8002	Non-segmented version

Architecture

For simplicity fig. 4.12 shows only the programmable registers of the processor.

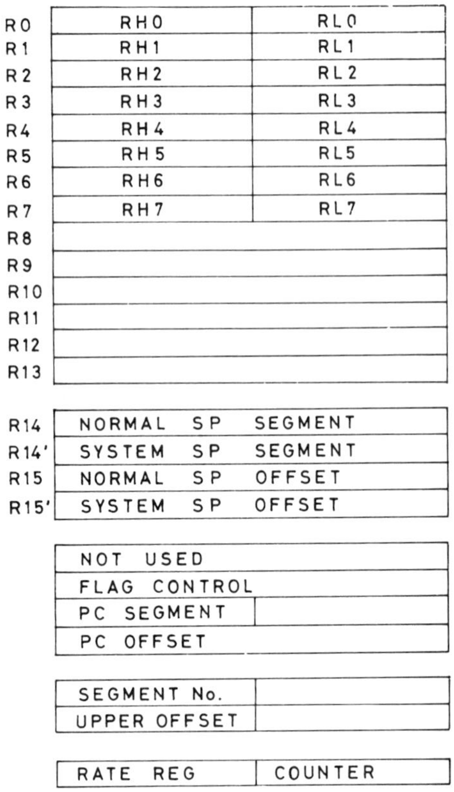

R0	RH0	RL0
R1	RH1	RL1
R2	RH2	RL2
R3	RH3	RL3
R4	RH4	RL4
R5	RH5	RL5
R6	RH6	RL6
R7	RH7	RL7
R8		
R9		
R10		
R11		
R12		
R13		

R14	NORMAL	SP	SEGMENT
R14'	SYSTEM	SP	SEGMENT
R15	NORMAL	SP	OFFSET
R15'	SYSTEM	SP	OFFSET

NOT USED
FLAG CONTROL
PC SEGMENT
PC OFFSET

SEGMENT No.
UPPER OFFSET

RATE REG	COUNTER

Fig. 4.12

Unlike the 8-bit processors the Z8000 does not have a dedicated register for use as the accumulator. Instead it uses a bank of sixteen general purpose 16-bit registers, any of which may be used as an accumulator as required. All but register R0 may also be used as index registers as well.

The main 16-bit registers are designated as R0 – R15, but the first 8 of these may also be used as pairs of 8-bit registers, defined as registers RH0 – RH7 and RL0 – RL7. For double length operations the registers may be used in pairs as 32-bit registers (RR0, RR2, RR4 – RR14), and for some operations four 64-bit quad registers may be set up (RQ0, RQ4, RQ8 and RQ12). This system allows the CPU to handle a wide variety of data types.

Registers R14 and R15 operate as the stack pointer. In this case R14 provides a memory segment number and the offset is contained in register R15. The Z8000 supports two stacks, one for the user and one for the system. There are in fact two registers for both R14 and R15, although only one of these will be operational at any given time. In the Z8002 only R15 is used for the stack pointer, since this chip does not allow segmented memory addressing.

Two registers are used for the program counter, one for the segment address and one for the offset. These registers are independent of the main register array. In the Z8002 only one 16-bit program counter is provided. For program control purposes there is a 16-bit status register which provides a wide range of control and status flags. There are two more registers used as pointers to a program status area in the memory which will contain vectors for interrupt processing. Finally there is a register for the control of refreshing of dynamic memory.

Memory in the Z8000 system may be divided into areas for system and user, and also into separate data and program areas which are all defined by status control lines from the processor. Thus the same address from the processor may refer to different areas of the physical memory and it would be possible to have up to 48 million words of physical memory on a Z8000 segmented system, since there are six possible address spaces: system program, system data, system stack, user program, user data and user stack. Each of these may be 8 million words in size.

Address and data are multiplexed over a common 16-bit bus system in the Z8000.

Package

Z8001   48-pin dual in line ceramic
Z8002   40-pin dual in line ceramic
Z8003   48-pin dual in line ceramic
Z8004   40-pin dual in line ceramic

Pin connections

Z8001   48-pin version

1	AD0	25	SN1
2	AD9	26	SN0
3	AD10	27	BUSRQ
4	AD11	28	WAIT
5	AD12	29	BUSAK
6	AD13	30	R/W
7	STOP	31	N/S
8	MI	32	B/W
9	AD15	33	DECOUPLE
10	AD14	34	AS
11	V_{cc}	35	CLOCK
12	VI	36	GND
13	NVI	37	SN2
14	SEGT	38	AD1
15	NMI	39	AD2
16	RESET	40	AD3
17	MO	41	AD5
18	MREQ	42	SN4
19	DS	43	AD4
20	ST3	44	AD6
21	ST2	45	AD7
22	ST1	46	SN5
23	ST0	47	SN6
24	SN3	48	AD8

Z8002 40-pin version

1	AD9	21	ST0
2	AD10	22	BUSRQ
3	AD11	23	WAIT
4	AD12	24	BUSAK
5	AD13	25	R/W
6	STOP	26	N/S
7	MI	27	B/W
8	AD15	28	DECOUPLE
9	AD14	29	AS
10	V_{cc}	30	CLOCK
11	VI	31	GND
12	NVI	32	AD1
13	NMI	33	AD2
14	RESET	34	AD3
15	MO	35	AD5
16	MREQ	36	AD4
17	DS	37	AD6
18	ST3	38	AD7
19	ST2	39	AD8
20	ST3	40	AD0

Signal functions

AD0 – AD15	Multiplexed address/data bus tri-state
VI, NVI, NMI	Interrupt inputs (active low)
ST0 – ST3	Processor status outputs (active high)
R/W	Read–write output (write low)
B/W	Byte/word mode output (word low)
SN0 – SN6	Segment number outputs tri-state
SEGT	Segmentation trap input
RESET	Reset input (active low)
CLOCK	Single-phase clock input
MI, MO	Multiple processor input, output (active low)
MREQ	Memory request (active low, tri-state) output
DS	Data strobe output (active low)
BUSRQ	Bus request input (active low)
BUSAK	Bus acknowledge output (active low)
AS	Address strobe output (active low)
STOP	Stop input for single step (active low)
N/S	Normal/system mode output (system low)
WAIT	Wait input (active low)
DECOUPLE	Not used at present
V_{cc}, GND	Power supply inputs

Power requirements

Supply current   +5 V ± 5%
GND   0 V
Supply current   300 mA

Temperature range

All devices 0°C to +70°C

Input–output

Input–output instructions provide a 16-bit address to define the selected input–output device. Data are then transferred via the 16-bit data bus. CPU status outputs indicate that an input–output data transfer is being executed. Appropriate logic will be needed externally to select and control the input–output peripheral device.

Interrupt facilities

Interrupts may be non-maskable, vectored or non-vectored via the appropriate input lines. Reset overrides all other types of interrupt. There are also trap operations and a segment trap triggered by an external signal.

On any interrupt or trap condition the program status information is pushed onto the system stack, together with a word indicating the reason for the interrupt.

ZILOG Z8000 SERIES

Appropriate program action must then be taken to service the interrupt or trap condition. Interrupt vectors are held in a program status area of the system memory.

Instruction set

There are 110 basic instruction types, which may be executed in various modes to give over 400 different types of operation. Instructions are usually one or two words for the operation, followed by one or two words for addressing if needed.

Arithmetic and logic
Addition, subtraction, multiplication and division are all provided and may be executed on bytes, words or double length words as required. Facilities are provided for BCD arithmetic.
Logical AND, OR and EXCLUSIVE OR are available, as well as a selection of shift, rotate, compare, complement and clear operations. These operations may be carried out in all data format modes.

Data manipulation
A wide range of data transfer and exchange operations can be carried out between registers and memory. Instructions are included for block data moves and for string manipulation, as well as for individual bit manipulation within words.

Branch and jump
Conditional jump instructions are provided for both short relative addressing and long addressing within the memory space. Subroutine call routines are provided with relative or direct addressing.

Input–output
Data transfers to input and output devices may be by any of the data formats, byte, word, etc., or block transfers may be carried out as desired. Input–output devices may be addressed individually.

System control
A number of instructions are provided for system control and include operations for use with multiple microprocessor type systems.

Addressing modes
The main addressing modes provided by the Z8000 are register, indirect register, direct, immediate, indexed, relative, base address and base indexed.
When a memory management unit and segmented addressing are used the physical address of a word in the actual memory may have no direct relation to the logical address generated by the Z8000 program, since the memory management unit will relocate memory areas within the actual hardware memory.

Timing

The maximum clock frequency for the Z8000 is 4 MHz and the clock signal is single phase.
With a 4 MHz clock the instruction execution time for most of the instructions will be between 1 and 4 μs, but multiply and divide operations, carried out by an internal software routine, take 20 – 70 μs, depending upon the actual data and whether single or double length words are in use.

Support devices

Z8010 (Z-MMU) Memory management unit
This device provides control of up to 8 megabytes of memory and performs dynamic relocation and segmentation of the data. It also permits various forms of memory protection.

Z8030 (Z-SIO) Serial communications controller
Two independent full duplex channels of serial input–output using either asynchronous or synchronous transmission modes.

Z8036 (Z-CIO) Counter/timer and parallel I/O unit
This device contains three 16-bit counter/timers and a pair of 8-bit parallel I/O ports which may be linked to form a single 16-bit port.

Z8038 (Z-MBU) FIFO input–output interface unit
First in first out buffer with 128 bytes acting as a buffered 8-bit I/O port.

Z8034 (Z-UPC) universal peripheral controller
Basically a Z8 microcomputer operating as a universal input–output controller for peripheral devices.

Z8060 (Z-FIFO) FIFO buffer unit
Expansion unit for 8038 and for use as a general FIFO buffer between peripherals and the Z8000 bus or between two or more Z8000 processors.

Z8016	Direct memory access controller
Z8052	CRT controller for visual displays
Z8068	Data encryption unit
AmZ8073	System timing controller
AmZ8127	Clock generator and controller
Z8065	Burst error processor

There are also several memory devices designed to suit the Z8000 Z bus system bus.

Development aids

From Zilog the PDS 8000 series of development systems provides both software and hardware development facilities for the Z8000 series microprocessors. The smaller systems are based on floppy disk operating systems, whilst the larger versions use hard disks for program and data storage. The systems provide text editor, assembler, debug and emulation facilities and may also use high level languages such as BASIC and FORTRAN.

From AMD the SYS 8 development system may be used for the Z8000 series and provides full hardware and software development capability. It is based on a twin floppy disk operating system and can use high level languages such as BASIC, FORTRAN and PASCAL. An evaluation board system for the Z8000 series is also available from AMD. This contains a Z8002 CPU, 8 kbyte of RAM and sockets for up to 12k of ROM. There are serial and parallel input and output ports and a keyboard/display unit may be added, or the system may be linked to a host computer as desired.

Futuredata provide development facilities for the Z8000 series microprocessors in their 2300 series universal microprocessor development systems. These are floppy disk based systems providing full software development and some hardware emulation facilities.

Tektronix support the Z8000 series devices with their 8540 Integration unit. It may be linked to a host computer to provide full software development and hardware emulation facilities.

5 OTHER MICROPROCESSOR TYPES

INTEL 2920 ANALOGUE SIGNAL PROCESSOR

The Intel 2920 analogue signal processor is a unique and unconventional form of microprocessor, designed to accept analogue signal inputs, emulate an analogue system using digital logic and finally produce a series of analogue signal outputs.

This microprocessor cannot readily be compared with the conventional digital microcomputer systems, although its basic function can be performed by using conventional microprocessor devices together with A/D and D/A conversion circuits. The major advantage of the 2920 in such applications is that the required circuitry is contained on a single chip.

Typical applications of the 2920 might be as filters, wave shapers, servo systems and many other types of analogue system. Major advantages of using a digital emulation over a conventional analogue circuit are ease of design and stability of operation. In some cases it is possible to design systems which would be impracticable using analogue techniques, but readily achieved by a digital emulation. However, it must be remembered that this device uses a sampled data technique which can produce problems not normally encountered when a conventional analogue circuit is used.

An on-chip UV eraseable PROM is provided on the 2920 for storage of program instructions. It makes the processor very convenient for experimentation, since the user is able to alter his program and system parameters until the desired result is achieved.

Prime manufacturer

Intel Corporation.

Devices available

2920-10	400 ns	cycle time
2920-16	600 ns	cycle time
2920-18	800 ns	cycle time

Architecture

As will be seen from fig. 5.1 the architecture of the 2920 is rather unusual when compared with other processors.

A 25-bit ALU is used for arithmetic and logic functions, but there is no accumulator as such as there would be in the conventional digital microprocessors. Digital data are stored in a 40-word RAM with 25 bits for each data word. The two inputs to the ALU are fed from two locations A and B in the RAM, and the result from the ALU is written into location B in the RAM. Locations A and B are specified by a pair of 6-bit address fields in the instruction and may in fact both be the same location in the RAM.

Data from the A location pass through a scaler on their way to the ALU. This scaler effectively shifts the data to the left or right by a selected number of bits to produce a binary scaling of the original data before they enter the ALU.

Analogue signals from 4 separate inputs are passed through a multiplexer and sample-hold circuit. The selected signal is then passed to one input of a comparator. Analogue–digital conversion is carried out by successive approximation, where the input signal is

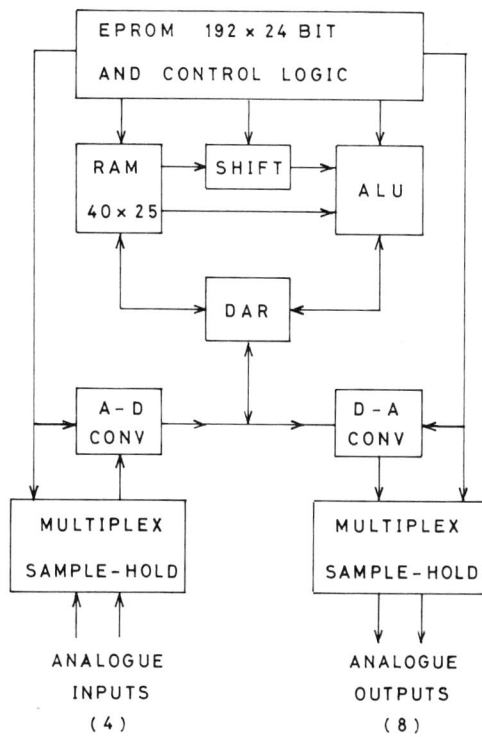

Fig. 5.1

compared with an analogue signal from a D/A converter driven from data derived from the RAM.

Nine-bit digital data from a selected RAM location may be passed via the D/A register (DAR) to a D/A converter. The analogue output from the converter is switched to one of eight sample hold circuits via an 8-way multiplexer. The resultant analogue signal is fed to the output pins via one of the eight buffer stages. Control of the input–output multiplexers and the A/D or D/A conversions is by an analogue control logic block.

Program instructions are stored in an EPROM, with 192 words of 25 bits each. Instructions are divided into five fields which control the analogue function, ALU operation, A and B RAM addresses and the scaler function. Instructions are executed in sequence, starting at location 0 of the EPROM and continuing until location 191 or an end of program instruction is reached. After location 191 or the end of program instruction the program sequence begins again at location 0 and repeats indefinitely. There are no branch or jump operations.

Timing is governed by an on-chip clock controlled by an external quartz crystal or by an external clock oscillator. Analogue stability and accuracy are governed by an external analogue reference voltage.

Package

The 2920 uses a 28-pin dual in line package.

Pin connections

The 2920 has two major modes of operation and the function of many of the package pins is different according to the mode being used. It is convenient therefore to deal with the pin layouts for the two modes separately.

Program mode is used to program the on-chip ROM and the pin layout is:

INTEL 2920 ANALOGUE SIGNAL PROCESSOR

1	D3	15	–
2	–	16	–
3	–	17	V_s
4	V_b	18	V_s
5	–	19	–
6	–	20	RUN/PROG
7	–	21	RST
8	V_b	22	INCR
9	–	23	VSP
10	–	24	PROG/VER
11	–	25	V_s
12	V_b	26	D0
13	–	27	D1
14	–	28	D2

In the alternative RUN mode the pin functions of the 2920 change and become:

1	OUT3	15	X1/CLK
2	OUT4	16	X2
3	OUT5	17	GRDD
4	GRDA	18	V_{cc}
5	OUT6	19	CCLK
6	OUT7	20	RUN/PROG
7	CAP1	21	RST/EOP
8	V_{REF}	22	OF
9	CAP2	23	VSP
10	IN0	24	M2
11	IN3	25	M1
12	V_{ss}	26	OUT0
13	IN2	27	OUT1
14	IN1	28	OUT2

Signal functions

Program mode

D0 – D3	EPROM data I/O
V_b	Digital ground
V_s	–5 V
INCR	Input pulse to increment ROM address counter
VSP	–5 V for verify mode or –25 V for programming
RST	Input pulse to reset address counter
RUN/PROG	Tied to V_{bb} for programming ROM
PROG/VER	High to program ROM or low for verify

Run mode

IN0 – IN3	Analogue signal inputs
OUT0 – OUT7	Analogue signal outputs
GRDA	Analogue signal ground
GRDD	Digital signal ground
CAP1, CAP2	Input sample/hold capacitors (external)
X1, X2	Timing crystal (external)
X1/CLK	Input for external clock
V_{REF}	Analogue reference voltage
OF	Overflow flag output (active low)
VSP	PROM power pin, 0 V for run mode
M1, M2	Mode select for analogue outputs
RST/EOP	Reset input (active low) End of program output (active low)
RUN/PROG	Tied to GRDD for run mode
CCLK	Output pulse at start of new instruction
V_{cc}, V_{bb}	Power supply inputs

Power requirements

V_{cc} +5 V ± 5% at 25 mA
V_{bb} –5 V ± 5% at 120 mA

Input–output

Four analogue inputs are provided with input voltage range of $-V_{REF}$ to $+V_{REF}$ where V_{REF} is from 1V to 2 V. Impedance at the input during signal acquisition is about 1000 Ω, in series with the storage capacitor of the sample/hold circuit.

Signal outputs may be selected as all analogue, all digital or a combination of 4 analogue and 4 digital outputs. analogue outputs provide a voltage swing between $+V_{REF}$ and $-V_{REF}$ with a drive current of about 0.5 mA. The digital outputs are TTL level compatible and will drive one TTL load. Other digital outputs have similar characteristics.

Instruction set

The instruction set of the 2920 is rather unusual, since it is possible to carry out several operations simultaneously using just one instruction. Each instruction from the PROM consists of a 24-bit code, divided into a series of fields as shown:

ALU function code 3 bits
RAM address A 6 bits
RAM address B 6 bits
Scaler ratio 4 bits
Anal. function code 5 bits

For the arithmetic (ALU) section there are addition and subtraction operations carried out on the 25-bit data from RAM locations A and B, with the results returned to location B. Note that addresses A and B may be the same. Absolute values of A may be transferred to B or added to the data in B.

Logical AND and EXCLUSIVE OR operations may be carried out between the A and B data. There is also a limit instruction which sets B to either the + or – limit value according to the sign of the A data.

Apart from the normal addition and subtraction modes there are also conditional addition and subtraction functions, used during A/D conversion and for multiplication or division. Other instructions deal with the overflow conditions in the ALU. It should be noted that the 2920 has no branch or jump operations and all instructions are carried out in sequence.

The fourth field of the instruction code determines the scaler setting, which effectively shifts the A data to either the right or left by a number of bits before it is applied to the ALU. This provides a binary scaling of the A value. The function may also be used when scaling numbers from the input or to the output.

Analogue operations are controlled by the final 5-bit field of the instruction code. Two bits select the function and the other three act as an address to select input or output channels. An input function allows the signal from a selected channel to be sampled and stored in the sample/hold circuit. Output instructions allow digital data to be passed through the D/A and the resultant analogue signal is routed to one of the output sample/hold circuits.

Other analogue operations allow individual A/D comparisons to be carried out on data bits for the successive

INTEL 2920 ANALOGUE SIGNAL PROCESSOR

approximation process, and also select individual bits for test purposes during conditional arithmetic operations. One instruction resets the program counter to zero to allow the instruction cycle to be repeated. There is also a no operation code for instructions which involve only digital operations.

Timing

The clock signal may be generated by a quartz crystal wired between pins 15 and 16, or may be an external clock pulse fed to pin 15. For the 2920-10 a clock frequency of 10 MHz is used.

Each instruction is carried out during 4 successive clock cycles, so with a 10 MHz clock the instruction cycle time is 400 ns. All instructions take the same time. Sample timing for the analogue inputs and outputs is governed by the sequence of instructions used.

Two slower versions of the 2920 are the 2920-16 with an instruction cycle time of 600 ns, and the 2920-18 which has a cycle of 800 ns.

Instructions are fetched and executed in groups of four, using a pipelining technique. The pulse at the output CCLK indicates the start of each new PROM fetch cycle.

PROM programming

The internal PROM is programmed by selecting the PROG mode on pins 20 and 24. For programming the PROM is organised as a 4-bit wide device. The data address is governed by a counter on the chip which may be reset by a signal to pin 21 and then incremented by pulses applied to pin 22. During programming the voltage on pin 23 is set at -25 V.

Once programmed the contents of the ROM may be verified by switching the signal to pin 24 to the verify mode, when the 4-bit data may be read out from D0 to D1 as the internal counter is incremented.

The PROM can be erased by the normal UV light method via the quartz window on the chip.

Support chips

None.

Development aids

There is a development support package which will operate on the Intel Intellec microprocessor development systems. It provides a 2920 assembler and also a simulator facility using a 2920 personality card.

The internal PROM may be programmed on the Intel PROM programmer system by using a suitable 2920 personality card.

INTERSIL IM6100

The IM6100, originally developed by Intersil, is one of the few 12-bit microprocessors to have been produced. It makes use of CMOS technology. When the 6100 was initially made available an important factor in its favour was that Intersil had designed the 6100 architecture and instruction set to emulate the PDP8E minicomputer. In its day this minicomputer was perhaps the most popular in the world, and hence a vast library of software had been built up for use with it. Users of the 6100 microcomputer could, in theory at least, take advantage of this software and use it directly on the 6100, thus saving system development time.

Since the 6100 is fabricated in CMOS it has an extremely low power consumption of some 12 mW at 5 V and is also tolerant of wide supply voltage variations. Both of these attributes make it highly suitable for use in battery powered or portable equipment. Its wide operating temperature range also makes it suitable for military applications.

The 12-bit word length has some advantages in industrial control applications, where it is common practice to use 12-bit data. An 8-bit processor has to deal with such data as two 8-bit bytes, thus taking more instructions and more time than the 12-bit processor.

It is now some 25 years since the PDP8E was designed and over the years it has become virtually obsolete, superseded by more powerful and flexible 16-bit machines. The 6100 shares the relatively primitive design of the PDP8E and today many of the newer 8-bit and certainly all of the 16-bit processors can easily outperform it. Thus unless some advantage can be gained by using the PDP8E software or the 12-bit data word length then the most likely applications of the 6100 will be in battery operated portable equipment. For other applications not requiring these features of the 6100 it would seem that a modern 8-bit or 16-bit microprocessor might be a more suitable choice.

Prime manufacturer

Intersil.

Devices available

IM6100	basic type, 4 MHz clock
IM6100A	8 MHz clock version
IM6100-1	3.33 MHz clock version

There are also military temperature range types which carry the suffix M, e.g. IM6100AM.

Alternative source devices

Harris Semiconductor

HM6100	equivalent to IM6100
HM6100A	equivalent to IM6100A
HM6100C	equivalent to IM6100-1

Harris also produce a military temperature type with the designation HM6100-2.

Architecture

As will be seen from fig. 5.2, the architecture of the 6100

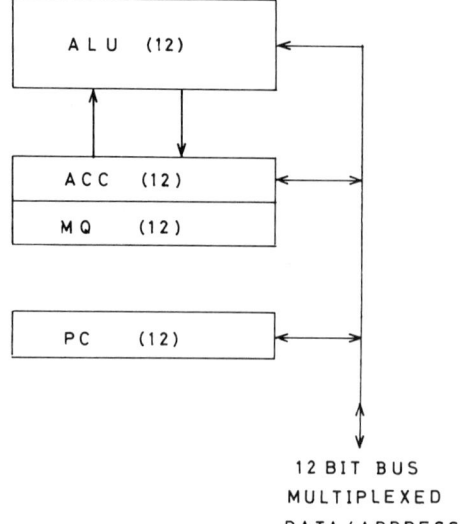

Fig. 5.2

is, like that of the PDP8E, very primitive in comparison with that of modern 8-bit processors.

There are in fact only three specific registers that can be directly operated upon by the programmer. These are the accumulator, the MQ register and the program counter, all 12 bits in length. Virtually all of the processing is carried out in the accumulator, whilst the MQ register seems to be rather limited in its use.

The 12-bit program counter allows direct addressing of up to 4096 bytes of memory, but it is possible to expand this to 32k by using external hardware. The memory is divided into pages of 128 bytes each, and in many single-byte instructions a 7-bit address is used to access memory within the current program page or within page 0 of the memory. Page 0 may be used as a set of 128 global registers. Of these locations 8 – 15 may be automatically incremented for use as indexing registers.

No distinction is made between program and data memory, so if program instructions are to be stored in ROM then each page of the memory space will need to be a mixture of both RAM and ROM. This can lead to complications, particularly when subroutines are being used. In subroutine operation the 6100 uses the first byte of the subroutine to store its return address.

Input and output devices can be controlled by the 6100 and may be allocated their own control codes if desired, these being decoded by external hardware. A selection of control and timing signals are provided to separate address and data which share a common 12-bit bus and to control external devices.

Package

40-pin dual in line either plastic or ceramic
Intersil use suffix P for plastic and D for ceramic
Harris use prefix HM3 for plastic and HM1 for ceramic

Pin connections

1	V_{cc}	21	DX5
2	RUN	22	DX6
3	DMAGNT	23	DX7
4	DMAREQ	24	DX8
5	CPREQ	25	DX9

6	RUN/HLT	26	DX10 GND
7	RESET	27	DX10
8	INTREQ	28	DX11
9	XTA	29	LINK
10	LXMAR	30	DEVSEL
11	WAIT	31	SWSEL
12	XTB	32	C0
13	XTC	33	C1
14	OSC OUT	34	C2
15	OSC IN	35	SKIP
16	DX0	36	IFETCH
17	DX1	37	MEMSEL
18	DX2	38	CPSEL
19	DX3	39	INTGNT
20	DX4	40	DATAF

Signal functions

DX0 – DX11	Data/address bus bidirectional
XTA, XTB, XTC, LXMAR	Timing pulse outputs
DEVSEL, SWSEL, MEMSEL and CPSEL	Active low outputs for I/O devices, memory and control panel operation
RUN/IILT, RUN	Control and status signals for CPU run/stop
RESET, WAIT	CPU control inputs active low
C0, C1, C2, SKIP	I/O transfer control outputs
LINK	Acc. carry bit output
DATAF	Indirect address flag
IFETCH	Instruction fetch cycle pulse
OSC	Clock oscillator connections
V_{cc}, GND	Power inputs
DMAREQ, INTREQ	Active low inputs for DMA and interrupt
DMAGNT, INTGNT	Grant status outputs for DMA and interrupt

Power requirements

IM6100 and IM6100-1	$V_{cc} = +5$ V, GND = 0 V
IM6100A	$V_{cc} = +10$ V, GND = 0 V
Supply current	2.5 mA (5 V), 10 mA (10 V)

Input–output

Input–output devices can be controlled by using the DEVSEL control output and data bus signals in conjunction with I/O instructions, in which the least significant 8 bits of the instruction code can be used to provide a control word for the I/O device. This is decoded by external hardware to give the desired operation.

Interrupt facilities

There is a basic single-level interrupt facility, triggered by an input at INTREQ which causes a jump to page zero location 1. The interrupt service routine will start at location 1 and the return address will be placed into location 0. By using the IM6101 it is possible to provide multilevel interrupt facilities for the 6100 CPU.

A second interrupt facility is provided for use with a control panel if desired.

Instruction set

The instruction set for the 6100 is the same as that of the PDP8E minicomputer. It consists of 63 different instructions.

Arithmetic and logic

Only a simple ADD operation is provided for the accumulator. Subtraction is achieved by complementing and adding. There is also a negate instruction.

Logically the accumulator can be ANDed with memory and ORed with the MQ register. There is no EXCLUSIVE OR function. Left and right shift or rotate operations are possible with the accumulator.

There are also various set and clear instructions for the accumulator.

All operations use 12-bit data words.

Branch and jump

There are no conditional branch instructions as such, these being achieved by using conditional skip instructions and unconditional jumps. There are a variety of skip conditions covering accumulator zero, negative, carry, and combinations giving less than, higher than zero, etc. It should be quite possible to produce all required test conditions using the available instructions.

Subroutine jump goes to the second location within the subroutine instruction area. The first location of memory allocated to a subroutine is used to store the address for the return to main program.

Address modes

The 6100 allows direct addressing within the current page or to page 0. Indirect addressing may also be via the current page of memory or through page 0. Locations in page 0 may be used as registers, and locations 8 – 15 may be used as index registers with auto indexing.

Timing

For on-chip oscillator operation a crystal is connected to the pins OSC IN and OSC OUT. When an external clock is used it is applied to OSC OUT whilst OSC IN is connected to 0 V. Maximum clock frequencies are 3.3 MHz for 6100-1, 4 MHz for 8100 and 8 MHz for 6100A (at 10 V). Internal logic is static, so clock can be reduced to zero with no ill effects.

With a 4 MHz clock frequency the instruction execution times will range from 5 to 11 μs according to the type of instruction being executed. Note that all of the 6100 instructions use only one memory word.

Support devices

A number of support devices are available for the 6100 type microprocessor:

6101 Programmable interface element (PIE)
This provides the control logic to allow external

peripherals to be interfaced to the 6100 and also contains logic for a multilevel interrupt facility.

6102   Memory extension, DMA and timer
Provides the memory expansion logic, DMA control and a real time clock

6103	Parallel input–output port (PIO)
IM6402, IM6403	UARTs for serial I/O
HD1-0165-5	Keyboard encoder (Harris)
6653, 6654	1k × 4 and 512 × 8 EPROMs CMOS
6312	1k × 12 bit ROM CMOS
6504/14, 6508/18 and 6551/61	4k and 1k RAM CMOS

All circuits are CMOS and most are available in versions for either 5 V or 10 V operation.

Development aids

Intersil

INTERCEPT junior. This is an evaluation type unit with a keypad and 8-digit LED display. It has 256 words of RAM and resident ROM based monitor. Can be expanded with additional modules.

INTERCEPT II. This is an expandable system with floppy disk, and can be used for full scale development of 6100 microprocessor projects. The system supports DEC software.

Harris HB0-61000 Micro 12 evaluation board

There are also development programs in FORTRAN to be used on the PDP8 minicomputer.

6 PARALLEL I/O DEVICES

PRINCIPLES

Data within the processor system are normally organised in a parallel format of 4, 8 or 16-bits wide. For many input–output operations it is convenient to transmit the data in this form to the peripheral device over 4, 8 or 16 parallel wires. However, data on the processor data bus are continually changing and will be a multiplexed stream of instruction codes, address data, processor data and input–output data. A peripheral device will generally require static data input so that it can accept the data and use it when convenient. Similarly peripheral devices may present data for input to the processor at times when the processor is busy and therefore unable to accept them. These problems are overcome by the use of input–output port devices.

An input–output port is basically a latched register or pair of registers. They can accept data from either the microprocessor or the external peripheral device and will store the data until the device being communicated with is ready to accept them.

Most of the available peripheral data port devices can be programmed so that selected lines may be set up as either outputs or inputs. In such a device there will usually be a data direction register. It can be accessed by the processor and will determine the direction of transfer of data on individual lines of the data port. Usually a 1 in the data direction register will set the corresponding data line as an output. In some types all 8 lines of the port must be set as either input or output. Other schemes may allow the port to be set up as two groups of 4 lines.

In a few cases a quasi-bidirectional system may be used. Here the port lines are normally outputs, but any line set at 1 may be used as an input. This technique is however generally used for single-chip microcomputer parallel ports.

Most data ports will provide either 8 or 4-bit wide data paths. In addition it is usual to provide some handshake lines. Normally two are used for each data path, one indicating to the remote device that data are ready at the output, the other being an input from the remote device to indicate that it has data ready to be accepted by the processor. These lines are often linked to flip flops within the port which may be used to request interrupt operation from the processor. In some of the port devices the interrupt facilities inside the port may be masked as required, rather than using the masking facilities of the processor itself.

To the processor a programmable parallel input–output port will usually appear as a series of registers or memory locations, and data are transferred to or from the port via the microprocessor data bus.

IEEE488 INTERFACE BUS

One form of parallel communications which may be regarded as a special case is the IEEE488 General Purpose Interface Bus (GPIB), based on the Hewlett Packard Instrument Bus. This system allows a number of peripheral devices to be joined to a common parallel bus system and to communicate both with one another and with the processor system.

In the GPIB system individual devices may be defined as *listeners* or *talkers*, and usually there will be one device which acts as the master bus controller. This master controller is normally the processor itself. Only one talker may be used at a time and it will place data on the bus, whereas there may be many listener devices which can accept data from the bus.

An 8-line bus is used for data transfers between the devices. A 3-line control bus governs these transfers. In addition there is a 5-line management bus which controls the general operation of the system.

The connectors used on the GPIB are 24-pin Cinch series 57 or equivalent with side contact pins. Each connector has a plug and socket in parallel so that further devices can be added to the bus system in a daisy chain fashion. The basic pin connections and signals are:

Pin	Signal
1	Data bit 1 LSB (DIO1)
2	Data bit 2 (DIO2)
3	Data bit 3 (DIO3)
4	Data bit 4 (DIO4)
5	End or identify (EOI)
6	Data valid (DAV)
7	Not ready for data (NRFD)
8	Not data accepted (NDAC)
9	Interface clear (IFC)
10	Service request (SRQ)
11	Attention (ATN)
12	Shield
13	Data bit 5 (DIO5)
14	Data bit 6 (DIO6)
15	Data bit 7 (DIO7)
16	Data bit 8 (MSB) (DIO8)
17	Remote enable (REN)
18	DAV ground
19	NRFD ground
20	NDAC ground
21	IFC ground
22	SRQ ground
23	ATN ground
24	LOGIC ground

DAV	Indicates that the data on the DIO lines are valid
NDAC	Indicates that data has not been accepted by the devices to which they were addressed. This line goes high when all devices have accepted data
NRFD	This line when low indicates that one or more of the devices that are to receive data is not ready. When high all devices are ready for data transfer
ATN	This line is activated by the bus controller to show that the data on the bus are an interface message.
EOI	This line indicates that the last byte of a data transfer has been completed. If combined with an ATN signal it starts a polling routine to discover which device on the bus has requested service
IFC	This is basically a reset signal for the bus
REN	This line causes devices on the bus to switch from local mode to remote mode
SRQ	Service requests from devices are wire ORed to this line to indicate to the controller that one of the devices requires servicing

The data lines may be used either for sending messages in ASCII or ISO character code format, or for identifying the device to be operated upon, or for command messages from the controller to the bus.

Detailed operation of the GPIB is relatively complex and will not be considered fully here. Data sheets for the specialised GPIB interface chips will normally provide these details and explain the operation of the interface device and the signal levels and timing required.

INTEL 8255 PPI

The Intel 8255 Programmable Peripheral Interface provides 24 programmable input–output lines which are interfaced to an 8-bit microprocessor data bus. Although this device is designed for the 8080, 8085 and 8086 series microprocessors, it can also be used with other 8-bit microprocessors.

Prime manufacturer

Intel Corporation.

Alternative source devices

Advanced Micro Devices

Am8255A, Am9555A

Mitsubishi

M5L8255

National

INS8255

N.E.C.

μPD8255, μPD8255A

OKI

MSM8255A

Siemens

SAB8255A

Signetics

8255A

Architecture

The 8255 provides three 8-bit input–output ports which may be programmed as either inputs or outputs. Port C may be set up as two 4-bit ports and may also be used as handshake lines for the A and B ports. Two mode control registers are used, one for port A and half of port C and the second for port B and the second part of port C. A wide range of programming combinations of the ports is possible. Interrupt can be controlled via port C.

Package

40-pin dual in line plastic or ceramic
Intel use prefix C or D for ceramic and P for plastic
Other types use C or D for ceramic and P for plastic

Pin connections

1	PA3	21	PB3
2	PA2	22	PB4
3	PA1	23	PB5
4	PA0	24	PB6
5	RD	25	PB7
6	CS	26	V_{cc}
7	GND	27	D7
8	A1	28	D6
9	A0	29	D5
10	PC7	30	D4
11	PC6	31	D3
12	PC5	32	D2
13	PC4	33	D1
14	PC0	34	D0
15	PC1	35	RESET
16	PC2	36	WR
17	PC3	37	PA7
18	PB0	38	PA6
19	PB1	39	PA5
20	PB2	40	PA4

Signal functions

D0 – D7	Data bus bidirectional
PA0 – PA7	Port A programmable I/O lines
PB0 – PB7	Port B programmable I/O lines
PC0 – PC7	Port C programmable I/O lines
WR	Write control input (active low)
RD	Read control input (active low)
CS	Chip select (active low)
A1, A0	Address lines for control and data registers
RESET	Reset input
V_{cc}, GND	Power supply inputs

All inputs and outputs are TTL compatible

Power requirements

V_{cc}	+5 V $\pm$ 5%
GND	0 V
Supply current	120 mA

Temperature range

Standard part   0°C to +70°C
Military part   −55°C to +125°C,
          Intel M8255 AMD Am9555

Timing

The 8255 operates with a data bus rate of approximately 1 MHz maximum to match the 8080 and 8085 processors.

MOTOROLA MC6821 PIA

The Motorola MC6821 Peripheral Interface Adapter provides two fully programmable 8-bit input–output ports from an 8-bit data bus. It is primarily designed to operate with 6800 and 6809 type processors, but can also be used with other 8-bit types with some minor interface logic.

Prime manufacturer

Motorola Semiconductors Inc.

MC6821, MC68A21, MC68B21

Alternative source devices

American Microsystems Inc.

S6821, S68A21, S68B21, S68H21

Fairchild

F6821, F68A21, F68B21

Hitachi

HD46821

Fujitsu

MBL6821E, MBL6821H, MBL6821N

Synertek

SY6821, SY68B21, SY6521, SY6521A

Thomson EFCIS

EF6821, EF68A21, EF68B21

Architecture

The 6821 contains 6 programmable registers, 2 for input–output data, 2 control registers and 2 data direction registers, with one set of three registers for each port. The data direction registers determine which lines are inputs and which are outputs. A '1' bit in this register sets the line corresponding to that bit as an output. Data direction registers and data registers share an address and are selected by a bit in the control register. Two handshake lines are provided for each 8-bit port and their functions are programmable. There is an interrupt facility for each port which may be inhibited.

Package

40-pin dual in line plastic or ceramic
Suffix P usually indicates plastic type
Suffix L or D may be used for ceramic types

Pin connections

1	V_{ss}	21	R/W
2	PA0	22	CS0
3	PA1	23	CS2
4	PA2	24	CS1
5	PA3	25	E
6	PA4	26	D7
7	PA5	27	D6
8	PA6	28	D5
9	PA7	29	D4
10	PB0	30	D3
11	PB1	31	D2
12	PB2	32	D1
13	PB3	33	D0
14	PB4	34	RESET
15	PB5	35	RS1
16	PB6	36	RS0
17	PB7	37	IRQB
18	CB1	38	IRQA
19	CB2	39	CA2
20	V_{cc}	40	CA1

Signal functions

D0 – D7	Data bus bidirectional
PA0 – PA7	Port A programmable input or output lines
PB0 – PB7	Port B programmable input or output lines
CA1, CA2	Port A handshake lines programmable
CB1, CB2	Port B handshake lines programmable
IRQA, IRQB	Interrupt output lines (active low)
CS0, CS1, CS2	Chip select inputs (CS2 active low)
RS0, RS1	Register select inputs
R/W	Read–write control input (write low)
E	Data bus enable and data strobe input
RESET	Reset input (active low)
V_{cc}, V_{ss},	Power supply inputs

All signals are TTL compatible. Port B outputs drive 2 TTL loads, other outputs drive one TTL load.

Power requirements

V_{cc}	+5 V ± 5%
V_{ss}	0 V
Supply current	100 mA

Temperature range

Standard part	0°C to +70°C
MC6821C types	−40°C to +95°C
Military parts (suffix Q or M)	−55°C to +125°C

Timing

Data are clocked to and from the data bus by the E input, which is usually based on $\phi 2$ or the CPU clock. Standard parts work at 1 MHz clock rate. The 68A21 and 68B21 parts run at 1.5 MHz and 2 MHz. AMI make a 68H21 part for 2.5 MHz operation.

ZILOG Z80-PIO

The Z80 Parallel Input–Output interface chip provides two 8-bit parallel I/O ports from an 8-bit microprocessor data bus. The I/O lines are programmable as inputs or outputs. Although designed primarily for use with the Z80 processor this unit may also be used with other 8-bit microprocessors if suitable interface signals are provided.

Prime manufacturer

Zilog

Z80-PIO

Alternative source devices

SGS-ATES

Z80-PIO

Mostek

MK3881

Architecture

The Z80-PIO contains two 8-bit I/O ports, each having a data register and a control register. The ports may be programmed in four different modes. One mode sets up the port as inputs whilst a second mode allows the port to be an output. There are two handshake lines associated with each port and their action depends upon the port programming. In the third mode the ports may be used as control ports, with individual lines set as inputs or outputs. Finally port A may be used as a bidirectional port whilst port B acts as a control port. Facilities are provided for interrupt from each port and an interrupt priority scheme can be arranged.

Package

40-pin dual in line plastic or ceramic
Ceramic type suffix C or R plastic type suffix P or Z

Pin connections

1	D2	21	BRDY
2	D7	22	IEO
3	D6	23	INT
4	CE	24	IEI
5	C/D	25	ϕ
6	B/A	26	V_{cc}
7	A7	27	B0
8	A6	28	B1
9	A5	29	B2
10	A4	30	B3
11	V_{ss}	31	B4
12	A3	32	B5
13	A2	33	B6
14	A1	34	B7
15	A0	35	RD
16	ASTB	36	IORQ
17	BSTB	37	M1
18	ARDY	38	D5
19	D0	39	D4
20	D1	40	D3

Signal functions

A0 – A7	Port A programmable I/O lines
B0 – B7	Port B programmable I/O lines
D0 – D7	Data bus bidirectional
ARDY, BRDY	Register A, B ready outputs
ASTB, BSTB	Port A, B strobe pulse inputs
IEI, IEO	Interrupt enable in/out for daisy chaining
IORQ	I/O request from CPU (active low)
A/B	Port A, B select input (A low)
C/D	Control/data select input (data low)
M1	M1 CPU cycle (Z80) input
RD	Read control input (active low)
CE	Chip enable (active low)
INT	Interrupt request output (active low)
ϕ	CPU and system clock input
V_{cc}, V_{ss}	Power supply inputs

Power requirements

V_{cc}	+5 V ± 5%
V_{ss}	0 V
Supply current	70 mA

Temperature range

0°C to +70°C	standard type
−40°C to +85°C	type suffix E
−55°C to +125°C	type suffix M

General

There is a higher speed version with the type number Z80A-PIO to operate with the faster Z80A processor. Mostek part number is MK3881A for this type.

INTEL 8291 GPIB LISTENER-TALKER

The Intel 8291 provides the functions of a listener-talker for the IEEE488 interface bus system when used with the 8080, 8085 or 8086 series of microprocessors. It should be noted that this device will not allow the microprocessor to take control of the interface bus. If the controller function is required the 8291 will need to be used in conjunction with an 8292 GPIB controller. Although primarily designed for use with the Intel series of processors, this device could be used with other types of microprocessor provided that its control bus signals are made compatible with those of the Intel type.

Prime manufacturer

Intel Corporation
8291

Alternative source devices

None.

Package

40-pin dual in line type

Pin connections

1	TR1	21	RS0
2	TR2	22	RS1
3	CLK	23	RS2
4	RESET	24	IFC
5	TRIG	25	REN
6	DMAR	26	ATN
7	DMAA	27	SRQ
8	CS	28	DIO1
9	RD	29	DIO2
10	WR	30	DIO3
11	INT	31	DIO4
12	D0	32	DIO5
13	D1	33	DIO6
14	D2	34	DIO7
15	D3	35	DIO8
16	D4	36	DAV
17	D5	37	NRFD
18	D6	38	NDAC
19	D7	39	EOI
20	V_{ss}	40	V_{cc}

Signal functions

D0 – D7	Data bus to processor bidirectional tri-state
DIO1 – DIO8	Data bus for GPIB bidirectional
INT	Interrupt request output to processor
RD, WR	Read–write control inputs (active low)
TR1, TR2	Control outputs to GPIB transceivers
CS	Chip select (active low)
RESET	Reset input
DMAR	DMA request output
DMAA	DMA acknowledge input
CLK	Clock input for internal timing circuits
TRIG	Trigger output pulse
DAV, NRFD, NDAC	GPIB data control lines
ATN, SRQ, IFC, REN, EOI	Management bus control signals
V_{cc}, V_{ss}	Power supply inputs

All logical inputs and outputs are TTL compatible and outputs will drive one standard TTL load. TR1 output drives two loads.

Power requirements

V_{cc} $+5 \pm 5\%$
V_{ss} 0 V
Supply current   180 mA

Temperature range

0°C to +70°C

General

The CLK input is used for internal time delays, and the frequency used may be any convenient value in the range 1 – 8 MHz. Data timing from the microprocessor bus will be equivalent to a memory with 250 ns access time.

The 8291 contains a total of sixteen 8-bit registers, which may be selected by using the RS0, RS1 and RS2 select inputs in conjunction with the RD and WR control lines. Eight registers are read only and eight write only.

Sixteen interrupt conditions may be produced, and of these fourteen may be masked by internal logic. Only one interrupt request line is used to the main processor.

Three status registers handle interrupt mask, polling and address functions. Three registers are used for address control and one for address mode. Data on the interface bus use a pair of registers.

INTEL 8292 GPIB CONTROLLER

The Intel 8292 General Purpose Interface Bus controller is designed to provide the interface between the data bus of 8080, 8085 or 8086 series microprocessors and an IEEE488 bus. Unlike the 8291 this device provides only the functions for bus control and data transfer control. Although primarily designed for use with the Intel series of microprocessors, it may be used with other processors if suitable signal conditioning is supplied.

Prime manufacturer

Intel Corporation

8292

Alternative source devices

None.

Package

40-pin dual in line type

Pin connections

1	IFCR	21	SRQ
2	X1	22	ATNI
3	X2	23	IFC
4	RESET	24	SYC
5	–	25	–
6	CS	26	–
7	V_{ss}	27	CLTH
8	RD	28	–
9	A0	29	ATNO
10	WR	30	–
11	SYNC	31	CIC
12	D0	32	TCI
13	D1	33	SPI
14	D2	34	EOI
15	D3	35	OBFI
16	D4	36	IBFI
17	D5	37	DAV
18	D6	38	REN
19	D7	39	COUNT
20	V_{ss}	40	V_{cc}

Signal functions

D0 – D7	Data bus to main processor data bus
A0	Used to select control or status registers within the 8292 or the main data bus of the 8292
CS	Chip select input (active low)
RD, WR	Read–write control inputs (active low)
X1, X2	Timing crystal for internal clock
RESET	Reset input (active low)
SYNC	Output clock for synchronisation purposes
IFCR	IFC input from GPIB line
ATNI, ATNO, SRQ, EOI, REN, IFC	GPIB bus control lines
TCI, SPI, OBFI, IBFI	Interrupt output lines
DAV	Data available GPIB line
COUNT	Counter input
CLTH	Clear latch output used for IFCR
CIC	Controller in charge output used for SRQ line
V_{cc}, V_{ss}	Power supply inputs

Power requirements

V_{cc} +5 V ± 5%
V_{ss} 0 V

Temperature range

0°C to +70°C

General

The 8292 is in fact a specially programmed 8041A microcomputer and is intended to be used with the 8291 GPIB listener–talker device. The 8292 in fact produces only the management bus control signals and monitors the DAV line, but does not deal with the GPIB data bus lines.

When used in a system its outputs to the GPIB bus will need to be buffered through an Intel 8293 GPIB bus transceiver to give the correct bus signals.

MOTOROLA MC68488 GPIB INTERFACE

The Motorola MC68488 is an interface chip for the IEEE488 bus system to processors of the 6800 and 6909 series. It may also be used with the 68000 type processor and can be adapted for use by other 8-bit microprocessor types if desired.

Prime manufacturer

Motorola Semiconductor Inc.

MC68488, MC68A488, MC68B488

Alternative source devices

American Microsystems Inc.

S68488

Fairchild
F68488

Fujitsu
MBL68488

Thomson EFCIS
EF68488

Package

40-pin dual in line ceramic or plastic type
Suffix L indicates ceramic type and P for plastic type

Pin connections

1	V_{ss}	21	IFC
2	DMAG	22	REN
3	CS	23	SRQ
4	ASE	24	TRIG
5	R/W	25	EOI
6	$\phi 2$	26	ATN
7	D0	27	TR2
8	D1	28	TR1
9	D2	29	IB7
10	D3	30	IB6
11	D4	31	IB5
12	D5	32	IB4
13	D6	33	IB3
14	D7	34	IB2
15	DMAR	35	IB1
16	DAV	36	IB0
17	DAC	37	RS0
18	RFD	38	RS1
19	RESET	39	RS2
20	V_{dd}	40	IRQ

Signal functions

D0 – D7	Data bus from MPU bidirectional
IB0– IB7	GPIB data bidirectional (inverted logic)
RESET	Reset input (active low)
DMAR	DMA request output
DMAG	DMA grant input
IRQ	Interrupt request output
RS0, RS1, RS2	Register select inputs
TR1, TR2	Control outputs to bus transceivers on GPIB
CS	Chip select (active low) input
R/W	Read–write control input (write low)
ASE	Address switch enable output (active low) used to place device address from GPIB on to the microprocessor bus
DAC, RFD, DAV ATN, SRQ, EOI, REN,	GPIB control lines
IFC	GPIB management control lines
TRIG	Trigger pulse output
V_{dd}, V_{ss}	Power supply inputs

All inputs and outputs are TTL compatible. The outputs will drive one TTL load, with the exception of the IRQ output which can drive two TTL loads.

The outputs to the GPIB lines will normally be coupled to the bus via MC3448A bus transceivers, each of which will handle 4 lines. These transceivers incorporate the required termination for a GPIB bus line and will not load the bus if power is removed.

Power requirements

V_{dd}	+5 V ± 5%
V_{ss}	0 V
Power consumption	600 mW

Temperature range

0°C to +70°C

Operation

Internally the MC68488 has a total of 15 registers which are selected by using the RS0, RS1 and RS2 lines in conjunction with the R/W control line. Two registers are used for GPIB data, whilst the others perform control and status functions.

As with most 6800 peripherals the $\phi 2$ processor clock is used for strobing data to and from the processor data bus. If used with other types of processor a suitable strobe pulse will be required to suit the processor system concerned.

Seven operations may generate interrupts. They may be individually masked by an interrupt mask register and may be identified by bits in an interrupt status register.

For detailed operational notes refer to data sheet.

TEXAS INSTRUMENTS TMS9914 GPIB ADAPTER

The Texas Instruments 9914 is an IEEE488 Interface Bus device primarily intended for use with the TMS9900 series of microprocessors. It provides both the normal listener–talker function and the master control function for such a bus. It may also be possible to use this device with other types of microprocessor.

Prime manufacturer

Texas Instruments Inc.
TMS9914

Alternative source devices

None.

Package

40-pin dual in line type

Pin connections

1	DMAR	21	TE
2	DMAG	22	REN
3	CE	23	IFC
4	WE	24	NDAC
5	DB$_{IN}$	25	NRFD
6	RS0	26	DAV
7	RS1	27	EOI
8	RS2	28	ATN
9	INT	29	SRQ
10	D7	30	CONT
11	D6	31	DIO8
12	D5	32	DIO7
13	D4	33	DIO6
14	D3	34	DIO5
15	D2	35	DIO4
16	D1	36	DIO3
17	D0	37	DIO2
18	ϕ	38	DIO1
19	RESET	39	TRIGGER
20	V$_{ss}$	40	V$_{cc}$

Signal functions

D0 – D7	Data bus to processor bidirectional
DIO1 – DIO8	Data lines for GPIB bidirectional
DMAR	DMA request output (active low)
DMAG	DMA grant input (active low)
CE	Chip enable (active low)
WE	Write enable control input (active low)
DB$_{IN}$	Data bus input enable input from MPU
RS0, RS1, RS2	Register select inputs
INT	Interrupt request output (active low)
RESET	Reset input (active low)
ϕ	Clock input for internal timing
CONT	Control output for bus transceivers
TRIG	Trigger output pulse
TE	Talk enable output control for line transceivers
DAV, NDAC, NRFD	Bus data control lines
ATN, REN, SRQ, EOI, IFC	Bus management controls
V$_{cc}$, V$_{ss}$	Power supply inputs

All signals are TTL compatible and outputs will generally drive one standard TTL load.

Power requirements

V$_{cc}$	+5 V ± 5%
V$_{ss}$	0 V
Supply current	150 mA

Temperature range

0°C to +70°C

General

This device is designed to be used with 75160 non-inverting bus buffers for the drive to the DIO lines of the IEEE bus, and 75162 non-inverting buffers for the control lines to the bus. The CONTROL and TE lines are used to control the data direction through the buffers.

The ϕ clock signal is used for internal timing and need not be the processor system bus. Any convenient frequency up to 5 MHz may be used for this clock.

There are 16 internal registers used to control the operation of the 9914. They are selected by using RS0, RS1 and RS2 in conjunction with the WE line. Four registers are used for status signals, with two acting as interrupt registers allowing 16 different interrupt conditions. Fourteen of these interrupts may be masked using a pair of mask registers. Both serial and parallel polling of bus devices are provided via a pair of registers. Data are handled by two registers, one for read and one for write. The remaining 4 registers are used for address and command functions.

7 SERIAL I/O DEVICES

PRINCIPLES

Although parallel data transfers may be convenient and fast for local transmission to displays or a keyboard, this method of transmission requires a relatively large number of wires and is not particularly suited to applications where distances involved are longer than a few metres. For data transmission to remote terminals and other computer systems the serial method of transmission is normally employed. In serial transmission the bits of data are sent in sequence over a single wire, either as logic signals or as a tone modulated signal.

Half and full duplex

In its simplest form serial transmission may be on a single wire plus a return line. Data are sent in either one or other direction at a time. This mode is known as *half duplex* and is often used where transmission is generally made in one direction, such as in outputs to a remote printer or VDU.

The alternative mode of operation uses two separate data lines, one for transmitted data and the second for received data, with a common ground return line. With this arrangement data may be transmitted in both directions simultaneously. It is normally used for communication with a control terminal or a remote computer, and is known as *full duplex*.

Transmission mode

Two modes of transmission may be used, namely *asynchronous* and *synchronous*. The asynchronous mode deals with each byte or character separately, sending it as a single packet of data. Synchronisation between transmitter and receiver is established at the start of each character code and individual characters may be sent at a varying rate with the system idling between successive character data. This method of transmission is particularly suited for use with control terminals, where the human operators will press the keys of the keyboard at uneven time intervals. The mode is also useful with remote sensors where a byte of data may be transmitted at infrequent intervals. The asynchronous mode is also known as start-stop transmission and is used for telex and teletype systems as well as for computers.

One disadvantage of asynchronous transmission is that it includes a number of redundant data bits and will become less efficient where large quantities of data need to be sent at high speed. In the alternative synchronous mode data are sent in blocks of perhaps 256 bytes at a time, and synchronisation is established only at the start of a data block. In this mode the transmit and receive clocks must be maintained in synchronism throughout the data block, either by using phase lock loop techniques or by transmitting a clock signal along with the data on a separate wire. In some cases the clock may be derived from the received signal itself for synchronisation purposes. There are two basic forms of synchronous operation. In one type, usually referred to as *bi-sync*, data are in the form of bytes or words, whilst in some other systems, such as SDLC and HDLC, data are simply treated as a bit stream.

Both asynchronous and synchronous modes usually include some form of error detection. In asynchronous mode this is usually a parity bit included as part of each character or data byte, whilst in the synchronous mode some form of cyclic redundancy check (CRC) system is normally used.

Asynchronous data format

In the asynchronous mode the transmitted signal is normally held at the '1' or mark level when no data are being sent. At the beginning of each character or byte of data a start bit is transmitted. This is a '0' or space level, lasting for one bit period, and is used as a synchronisation signal by the receiver device. Having detected a start bit the receiver logic will examine the following n bit periods of signal and decode from them the transmitted data. The sequence of data for a typical asynchronous signal is shown in fig. 7.1.

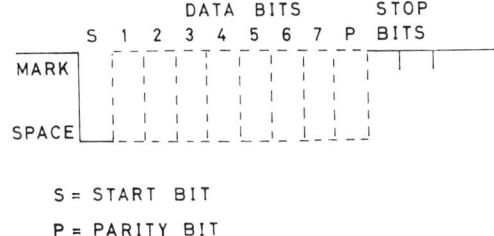

S = START BIT

P = PARITY BIT

Fig. 7.1

The number of data bits may be selected from 5 to 8 bits. For computer applications 7 or 8 bits will usually be chosen, since data will generally be either binary in the form of 8-bit bytes, or text in the form of 7-bit character codes. Following the data there may be an optional parity error check bit. The parity check may be selected as either even or odd. If even parity is selected then the state of the parity bit is chosen to make the total number of '1' bits in the word (data + parity bit) even. For odd parity the extra bit will be set so as to make the total number of '1' bits odd. In some systems the parity bit may be set permanently to either a '0' or '1' level, or alternatively it may be omitted altogether.

At the end of the transmitted word there will be a number of stop bits at the mark level. These stop bits act as separators between adjacent words in the stream to ensure that the receiver will always be able to detect the start bit of the next word when data are being transmitted as a continuous stream. The number of stop bits is usually one for high speed transmission or two for low speed transmission. When a 5-bit word length is selected, however, there will usually be 1½ stop bits to match the standards used for teletype transmission.

Baud rate

The rate of data transmission is referred to as the *baud rate*. For a binary coded data signal this will be the number of bits per second. Commonly used transmission rates are 50, 75, 110, 150, 300, 600, 1200, 1800, 2400, 4800, 9600 and 19200 baud. Note that this rate refers to the bit transmission rate and does not take into account any idling periods between individual words. The actual word rate will depend upon the number of bits used. For a typical terminal system operating at 1200 baud with 8-bit data plus parity and start-stop bits (11 bits) the word rate with continuous transmission will be approximately 110 words per second. Baud rates up to perhaps 64k baud may be used in synchronous transmission systems.

Modems

When data are to be transmitted over long lines (greater than 10 – 20 m) the normal logic signals may be distorted, giving rise to errors. This is particularly true where the public telephone network is used, since the lines are intended for use by audio signals. To overcome these problems it is usual to employ a tone modulated system of transmission over such paths. At the transmitting end the mark level signal is converted to an audio tone of say 1200 Hz, whilst the space level is translated into a tone of perhaps 2400 Hz. These tones are sent along the line. At the receiving end a frequency demodulator is used to convert the tone signals back to the appropriate logic levels. For normal full duplex transmission a modulator–demodulator (modem) unit is used at each end of the line. Actual carrier frequencies used will be governed by the specifications of the transmission line network and may vary from one system to another.

Control signals

For proper operation of a remote serial transmission system, several handshake control signals are normally used to ensure that the devices at the transmitting and receiving ends are ready when transmission commences.

A *request to send* (RTS) signal is normally sent along a separate wire from the data by the transmitting device to indicate that it wishes to send data. This is acknowledged by a *clear to send* (CTS) signal from the remote receiver if the remote device is ready to accept new data. If the remote device has not completed processing of previous data it will send a '0' on the CTS line to inhibit transmission until it is ready.

Two further control signals are used to indicate that the transmit or receive equipment is turned on and ready to operate. These are DTR (*data terminal ready*) which is output from the device, and DSR (*data set ready*) which is the signal from the remote device indicating that it is ready. When a modem is used a further signal is normally used, which is DCD (*data carrier detect*). This indicates that the line is connected and operational.

In many cases for local communication, especially if a modem is not used, the RTS and CTS lines are joined at the local terminal and the DCD and DTR lines may also be linked. In such a system only the transmit and receive data lines and the common return line are actually connected between the two communicating devices.

RS232 (V24) interface

The usual standard adopted for serial communications is known as the EIA RS232 or CCIT V24 system, which are basically the same. This standard defines the signal levels for the serial data and control signals and the type of connector and pin allocation of the various signals.

Signal levels are normally -6 V for data mark and $+6$ V for data space. Control signals are defined as off when the -6 V level is present and on for a $+6$ V level. The minimum signal level is normally $+3$ V or -3 V and maximum signal levels may extend to $+12$ V or -12 V. Signal tolerances on the V24 standard are generally tighter than those on the RS232 standard.

The connectors used at each end of the cable are D type 25 pin, and the pin allocations relevant to a microprocessor system are:

Pin	Function
1	Ground
2	Transmitted data (TXD) output
3	Received data (RXD) input
4	Request to send (RTS) output
5	Clear to send (CTS) input
6	Data set ready (DSR) input
7	Signal ground
8	Data carrier detect (DCD) input
20	Data terminal ready (DTR) output

Other pins are allocated to functions which are not normally used in a microprocessor system.

Note that these connections are those normally used for a control terminal. Often the microprocessor will have its RXD and TXD signals transposed so that a simple pin to pin cable connection can be used, with TX of the terminal joining to RX at the microprocessor end and *vice versa*. The control signals RTS and CTS are similarly transposed. Arrangements for the DTR, DSR and DCD lines may vary from one system to another. In many cases the control signals are not in fact connected between the two devices, but appropriate links are made at each end to override the control functions. In such cases the systems at both ends of the line are assumed to be ready at all times.

Synchronous data formats

Synchronous transmission may be either byte or bit orientated. In the byte oriented protocol, such as bi-sync, the message transmission starts with synchronisation signals. They may consist of clock synchronising signals, usually alternate '1' and '0' patterns followed by one or two synchronisation words, which may have some predefined code pattern that the receiver system will recognise. This sync pattern is used to determine the start points of the following data bytes. After the sync word there will be a stream of perhaps 256 bytes of data which may be ended by a parity check (CRC) word for error detection.

In the bit oriented protocols, such as SDLC (synchronous data length control) and HDLC (high level data link control) the data commences with an address field and a control field, and is followed by a bit field with any number of data bits up to the capacity of the receiver memory. The address field is used to identify individual devices in the system where several communicating devices are connected to a common line or network.

INTEL 8251A PCI

The Intel 8251 Programmable Communications Interface provides both asynchronous and synchronous serial communications from an 8-bit microprocessor bus system. Although primarily built for use with the 8080 and 8085 series microprocessors, it can also be used with other 8-bit microprocessors.

Prime manufacturer

Intel Corporation

8251A

Alternative source devices

Advanced Micro Devices

Am8251A, Am9551A

National Semiconductor

INS8251A

N.E.C.

µPD8261A

Siemens A.G.

SAB8251A

Mitsubishi

M5L8251A

Package

28-pin dual in line type plastic or ceramic

Pin connections

1	D2	15	TXRDY
2	D3	16	SYD
3	RXD	17	CTS
4	GND	18	TXE
5	D4	19	TXD
6	D5	20	CLK
7	D6	21	RESET
8	D7	22	DSR
9	TXC	23	RTS
10	WR	24	DTR
11	CS	25	RXC
12	C/D	26	V_{cc}
13	RD	27	D0
14	RXRDY	28	D1

Signal functions

D0 – D7	Data bus bi-directional
WR	Write control input (active low)
RD	Read control input (active low)
RXD	Receive data input
TXD	Transmit data output
RTS	Request to send output (active low)
CTS	Clear to send input (active low)
DTR	Data terminal ready output (active low)
DSR	Data set ready input (active low)
C/D	Control or data select input (data low)
RXC, TXC	Receive and transmit clock inputs
TXE	Transmit empty output
SYD	Sync. detect bidirectional
CLK	Clock pulse input
RXRDY, TXRDY	Receiver, transmitter ready outputs
CS	Chip enable input
RESET	Reset input
V_{cc}, GND	Power supply inputs

Power requirements

V_{cc}	+5 V ± 5%
GND	0 V
Supply current	100 mA

Temperature range

Standard part	0°C to +70°C
Intel M8251A and AMD 9551A	−55°C to +125°C

Data formats

Asynchronous mode

Programmable word length of 5 – 8 bits
Stop bits programmable for 1, 1½ or 2 bits
Parity may be even, odd or none

Synchronous mode

Word length and parity as asynchronous
Internal or external character sync
Single or double SYN characters
Automatic sync insertion

Both modes will run either full or half duplex.

Baud rate

External baud rate generator is required, but internal system may be programmed for 16× and 64× clocks in the asynchronous mode.

Baud rate range   0 – 19 200 baud asynchronous
                  0 – 64k baud synchronous

INTEL 8273 PDLC

The Intel 8273 Programmable HDLC/SDLC controller is designed to provide serial communication with the HDLC or SDLC protocol for microprocessors in the 8080, 8085 and 8086 series. This device may also be used with other types of microprocessor.

Prime manufacturer

Intel Corporation

8273

Alternative source devices

None at present.

Package

40-pin dual in line type

Pin connections

1	FD	21	A0
2	TXI	22	A1
3	CLK	23	DPLL
4	RESET	24	CS
5	TXDA	25	32×C
6	TXDR	26	RXD
7	RXDA	27	RXC
8	RXDR	28	TXC
9	RD	29	TXD
10	WR	30	CTS
11	RXI	31	CD
12	DB0	32	PA2
13	DB1	33	PA3
14	DB2	34	PA4
15	DB3	35	RTS
16	DB4	36	PB1
17	DB5	37	PB2
18	DB6	38	PB3
19	DB7	39	PB4
20	V_{ss}	40	V_{cc}

Signal functions

DB0 – DB7	Data bus bidirectional
PA2 – PA4	Input port lines for modem control
PB1 – PB4	Output port lines for modem control
TXDR, RXDR	TX/RX data request outputs for DMA (active low)
TXDA, RXDA	DMA data acknowledge inputs (active low)
TXC, RXC	TX, RX clock inputs
TXD	Transmit data output
RXD	Receive data input
FD	Flag detect output (active low)
CTS	Clear to send input (active low)
RTS	Ready to send output (active low)
RD, WR	Read–write control inputs (active low)
RXI, TXI	Receive, transmit interrupt outputs
A0, A1	Register select inputs
CD	Carrier detect input (active low)
CLK, 32×C	Clock and 32× clock inputs
DPLL	Digital phase lock loop output (active low)
CS	Chip select input (active low)
V_{cc}, V_{ss}	Power supply inputs

Signals are all TTL compatible.

Power requirements

V_{cc} +5 V ± 5%
V_{ss} 0 V
Supply current   180 mA

Temperature range

0°C to +70°C

Data format

Supports SDLC and HDLC protocols
Data words programmable for 5 – 8 bits
Full or half duplex or SDLC loop operation
Automatic CRC generate and check
NRZ or NRZI coding
Zero bit insertion and deletion

Data rate

This is controlled by external receive and transmit clocks and may operate at up to 64k baud. There is a phase lock loop included for clock recovery from received data.

General

There are 7 internal registers for data, control and status. They are selected by combinations of A0, A1, CS, RD and WR plus the RXDA and TXDA signals.

Two small parallel input and output ports are provided. They may be user programmed for control of the modem or other devices attached to the serial output channel.

For full details of programming and operation refer to manufacturer's data sheet.

INTERSIL IM6402 UART

The Intersil IM6402 Universal Asynchronous Receiver Transmitter device is a general purpose CMOS serial data communications chip. It may be used with any microprocessor or as a stand alone device for parallel to serial communication.

Prime manufacturer

Intersil.

Alternative source devices

Harris Semiconductor

HD6402

Package

40-pin dual in line type   ceramic or plastic
Suffix P in type number denotes plastic package

Pin connections

1	V_{cc}	21	MR
2	–	22	TBRE
3	GND	23	TBRL
4	RRD	24	TRE
5	RBR8	25	TRO
6	RBR7	26	TBR1
7	RBR6	27	TBR2
8	RBR5	28	TBR3
9	RBR4	29	TBR4
10	RBR3	30	TBR5
11	RBR2	31	TBR6
12	RBR1	32	TBR7
13	PE	33	TBR8
14	FE	34	CRL
15	OE	35	PI
16	SFD	36	SBS
17	RRC	37	CLS2
18	DRR	38	CLS1
19	DR	39	EPE
20	RRI	40	TRC

Signal functions

RBR1 – RBR8	Receiver buffer register outputs
TBR1 – TBR8	Transmitter buffer register inputs
RRD	Receiver register disable
RRC	Receiver register clock
RRI	Receiver register input
DR	Data received flag output
DRR	Data received reset input
SFD	Status flag disable input
PE	Parity error output
OE	Overrun error status output
FE	Framing error status output
MR	Master reset input
TRE	Transmit register empty output
TBRE	Transmit buffer register empty output
TBRL	Load transmit buffer input
TRO	Transmitter data output
PI	Parity inhibit input
SBS	Stop bit select input
CLS1, CLS2	Character length select inputs
EPE	Even parity select input
TRC	Transmit clock input
CRL	Control register load input

Power requirements

V_{cc}	(6402A) +4 V to +11 V
	(6402) +4 V to +6.5 V
GND	0 V
Supply current	5 mA approx. max.

Data format

Asynchronous mode only
Word length programmable 5 – 8 bits
Stop bits programmable for 1, 1½ or 2 bits
Parity odd, even or none

Baud rate

An external clock generator is required and will determine the baud rate. Baud rates vary from 0 to 62.5k baud for standard type and to 250k baud for 6402A operating with +10 V supply.

General

The 6402 has separate receive and transmit data buses, which may be paralleled together when used with a microprocessor.

Input and output signals are CMOS compatible and will also operate with TTL signals when a +5 V supply is used.

MOTOROLA MC6850 ACIA

Introduced by Motorola for use with their 6800 and 6809 series microprocessors, the MC6800 ACIA (Asynchronous Communications Interface Adapter) provides a serial input–output channel from an 8-bit processor bus system. Although primarily designed for the 6800 microprocessor it can readily be adapted to work with other types, such as the 6502 series and the 2650.

Two higher speed versions, the MC68A50 and MC68B50, have been produced to work at 1.5 MHz and 2 MHz with the 68A00 and 68B00 microprocessors.

Prime manufacturer

Motorola Semiconductors Inc.

MC6850, MC68A50 and MC68B50

Alternative source devices

American Microsystems Inc.

S6850, S68A50 and S68B50

Fairchild

F6850, F68A50 and F68B50

Hitachi

HD46850

Thomson EFCIS

EF6850, EF58A50 and EF68B50

Package

24-pin dual in line type
Ceramic type indicated by suffix L (D for Fairchild)
Plastic type by suffix P

Pin connections

1	V_{ss}	13	R/W
2	RXD	14	E
3	RXC	15	D7
4	TXC	16	D6
5	RTS	17	D5
6	TXD	18	D4
7	IRQ	19	D3
8	CS0	20	D2
9	CS2	21	D1
10	CS1	22	D0
11	RS	23	DCD
12	V_{cc}	24	CTS

Signal functions

D0 – D7	Bidirectional data bus tri-state
RXD	Receive data input
RXC	Receive clock input
TXD	Transmit data output
TXC	Transmit clock input
CS0, CS1	Chip select inputs (active high)
CS2	Chip select input (active low)
RTS	Request to send output (active low)
CTS	Clear to send input (active low)
DCD	Data carrier detect input (active low)
IRQ	Interrupt request output (active low)
RS	Register select input
R/W	Read–write control input (write low)
E	Enable input usually derived from $\phi 2$ CPU clock

All signals to and from the device are TTL compatible and the output and bus lines will drive one TTL load. Inputs are high impedance and are protected against static by diodes. The IRQ output has open drain with no pull up resistor and is suitable for wired OR operation.

Power requirements

V_{cc}	+5 V ± 5%
V_{ss}	0 V
Supply current	60 mA

Temperature range

6850	0°C to +70°C
6850L	−40°C to +85°C
MC6850BJ, MC6850CJ and F6850M	−55°C to +125°C

Transmission formats

Asynchronous start-stop serial mode only
Programmable bit format with 8 or 9 data bits
One or two stop bits
Odd, even or no parity bit
Programmable clock division by 1, 16 or 64

Baud rate

Baud rate is determined by external transmit and receive clocks. Maximum clock frequency is 500 kHz in divide by one mode, and 800 kHz for divide by 16 or 64 mode.

Architecture

The 6850 contains 4 registers which are accessible via the data bus. These are the transmit data, receive data, control and status registers. Selection is by a combination of the states of the R/W and RS lines, as follows:

R/W	RS	Register selected
0	0	Control
0	1	Transmit data
1	0	Status
1	1	Receive data

The registers will appear as two memory locations to a 6800 microprocessor. Chip select lines CS0, CS1 and CS2 may be used to form part of the address decoding scheme.

Transmit and receive circuits are double buffered with separate shift registers for transmission and reception of data.

The enable input is used internally for clocking data to and from the data bus and also to enable the data bus buffers on the chip. This signal is normally derived from the phase 2 clock of the CPU. With other types of processor some suitable strobe signals will be needed here.

Operation

The contents of the control register will govern the operation of the transmitter and receiver sections and control the state of the interrupt logic.

Bits 0 and 1 govern the clock division ratio. When set with both bits at '0' a reset function is performed. It is essential that this operation be carried out before the 6850 is used for data handling.

Bits 2, 3 and 4 of the control register select the data format, whilst bits 5, 6 and 7 control the interrupt facility. Bits 5 and 6 control the state of the RTS output line and also enable or disable interrupts generated by the transmit section. Bit 7 controls the masking of interrupts from the receive section.

The status register provides a number of flags to show the status of the transmission link. Bits 0 and 1 indicate receive register full and transmit register empty. Flags are provided for the state of the CTS and DCD inputs and 3 bits are used for framing, overrun and parity errors during reception. Bit 7 is an interrupt flag which indicates that an interrupt condition exists. This bit is cleared by reading the receive data register or writing to the transmit data register.

MOTOROLA MC6852 SSDA

The Motorola MC6852 Synchronous Serial Communications Adapter provides a serial data channel from an 8-bit data bus. It is primarily designed for use with the 6800 series microprocessors, although it can be used with other processor types. Only the synchronous mode of data transmission is supported by this device.

Prime manufacturer

Motorola Semiconductors Inc.

MC6852, MC68A52, MC68B52

Alternative source devices

American Microsystems Inc.

S6852, S68A52, S68B52

Fairchild

F6852, F68A52, F68B52

Fujitsu

MBL6852E, MBL6852H, MBL6852N

Hitachi

HD46852

Thomson EFCIS

EF6852, EF68A52, EF68B52

Package

24-pin dual in line   plastic or ceramic
Plastic type MC6852P   Ceramic types MC6852L

Pin connections

1	V_{ss}	13	R/W
2	RXD	14	E
3	RXC	15	D7
4	TXC	16	D6
5	SM/DTR	17	D5
6	TXD	18	D4
7	IRQ	19	D3
8	TUF	20	D2
9	RESET	21	D1
10	CS	22	D0
11	RS	23	DCD
12	V_{cc}	24	CTS

Signal functions

D0 – D7	Data bus bidirectional
RXD	Receive data input
TXD	Transmit data output
RXC	Receive clock input
TXC	Transmit clock input
RESET	Reset input (active low)
IRQ	Interrupt request output (active low)
E	Enable input also used to strobe data in
R/W	Read–write control input (write low)
CS	Chip select input (active low)
TUF	Transmitter underflow output
SM/DTR	Sync match, data terminal ready output
RS	Register select input
DCD	Data carrier detect input (active low)
CTS	Clear to send input (active low)
V_{cc}, V_{ss}	Power supply inputs

All signals are TTL compatible.

Power requirements

V_{cc}	+5 V ± 5%
V_{ss}	0 V
Power dissipation	850 mW max.

Temperature range

MC6852	0°C to +70°C
MC6852C	−40°C to +85°C
MC6852Q	−55°C to +125°C

Data format

Word length 7, 8 or 9 bits
Odd, even or no parity
Programmable sync code format
One or two SYN code operation
Synchronous mode only

Baud rate

An external baud rate generator is required to produce the transmit and receive clocks. Rates up to 600kb.p.s. are possible.

General

Two high speed versions, the 68A52 and 68B52, are available to operate with the higher speed 6800 processors. The A type allows 1.5 MHz data bus speed, and the B type goes to 2 MHz.

MOTOROLA MC6854 ADLC

The Motorola MC6854 Advanced Data Link Controller is a serial input–output device designed to provide serial communication using the SDLC or HDLC protocol from an 8-bit microprocessor bus system. It is primarily designed for use with the 6800 or 6809 series microprocessors, but can no doubt be used with other 8-bit microprocessors.

Prime manufacturer

Motorola Semiconductors Inc.

MC6854, MC68A54, MC68B54

Alternative source devices

American Microsystems Inc.

S6854, S68A54, S68B54

Fairchild

F6854, F68A54, F68B54

Fujitsu

MBL6854

Thomson EFCIS

EF6854, EF68A54, EF68B54

Package

28-pin dual in line type   plastic or ceramic
Suffix L for ceramic type suffix P for plastic

Pin connections

1	V_{ss}	15	D7
2	RTS	16	D6
3	RXD	17	D5
4	RXC	18	D4
5	TXC	19	D3
6	TXD	20	D2
7	IRQ	21	D1
8	RESET	22	D0
9	CS	23	RDSR
10	RS0	24	TDSR
11	RS1	25	FLAG DET
12	R/W	26	LOLC/DTR
13	E	27	DCD
14	V_{cc}	28	CTS

Signal functions

D0 – D7	Data bus bidirectional
RXD	Receive data input
RXC	Receiver clock input
TXD	Transmit data output
TXC	Transmit clock input
IRQ	Interrupt request output (active low)
RESET	Reset input (active low)
CS	Chip select input (active low)
RS0, RS1	Register select inputs
R/W	Read–write control input (write low)
E	Data bus enable and strobe input
RDSR	Rx data service request output for DMA mode
TDSR	Tx data service request output for DMA mode
FLAG DET	Flag detect output (active low)
LOLC	Loop on line control output (active low)
DTR	Data terminal ready (non-loop mode) (active low)
DCD	Data carrier detect input (active low)
CTS	Clear to send input (active low)
RTS	Ready to send output (active low)
V_{cc}, V_{ss}	Power supply inputs

All signals are TTL compatible.

Power requirements

V_{cc}	+5 V ± 5%
V_{ss}	0 V
Power dissipation	850 mW max.

Temperature range

Standard part	0°C to +70°C
Suffix L	−40°C to +85°C
Suffix Q	−55°C to +125°C

Data format

Supports HDLC and SDLC formats
Information data 5 – 8 bits
NRZ or NRZI modes
Zero insertion and deletion
Automatic flag detection and sync

Data rate

Externally controlled by transmit and receive clock inputs. Maximum clock frequency is 650 kHz for standard part, 1 MHz for 68A54 and 1.5 MHz for 68B54.

General

The 6854 contains 2 status registers, 4 control registers, 2 transmit data registers and a receive data register. These are selected by the RS0, RS1 lines in conjunction with R/W and bit 0 of control register 1.

N.E.C. µPD379 USRT

The N.E.C. µPD379 is a Universal Synchronous Receiver Transmitter device, designed to handle both bit and byte oriented serial data communications from an 8-bit microprocessor data bus.

Prime manufacturer

Nippon Electric Co.

µPD379

Alternative source devices

None.

Package

42-pin dual in line type package

Pin connections

1	–	22	V_{ss}
2	V_{dd}	23	TCBE
3	CS	24	SYN/ABT
4	RR	25	TXD
5	DRR	26	TD0
6	RXC	27	TD1
7	RXD	28	TD2
8	CFR	29	TD3
9	ABTR	30	TD4
10	SYNR/IDLR	31	TD5
11	RD7	32	TD6
12	RD6	33	TD7
13	RD5	34	SYNC/ZIP
14	RD4	35	SNTR/CFT
15	RD3	36	TCBL
16	RD2	37	TXC
17	RD1	38	MS2
18	RD0	39	MS1
19	DR	40	MRL
20	OE	41	V_{cc}
21	V_{bb}	42	–

Signal functions

RD0 – RD7	Receiver data outputs
TD0 – TD7	Transmitter data inputs
RXC, TXC	Receive/transmit clock inputs
RXD	Receive data input (serial)
TXD	Transmit data output (serial)
RR	Receive logic reset (active low) input
CS	Chip select input (active low)
DRR	DR reset input (active low)
DR	Rx buffer full flag output
MS1, MS2	Mode select inputs
MRL	Mode select strobe input
SYN/ABT	Sync/abort flag output
TCBE	Transmit buffer empty
SYNC/ZIP	Sync/zero insertion control input
OE	Overrun error output
SYNR/IDLR	Sync/idle received flag output
CFR	Closing flag received output
ABTR	Abort code received output
SNTR/CFT	Sync/closing flag transmit control input
V_{bb}, V_{cc}, V_{dd}, V_{ss}	Power supply inputs

Power requirements

V_{dd}	+12 V ± 5%
V_{cc}	+5 V ± 5%
V_{bb}	−5 V ± 5%
V_{ss}	0 V
Power dissipation	380 mW max.

Temperature range

0°C to +70°C

Data format

Device can handle only SDLC bit oriented protocol
In standard sync byte oriented mode all data are 8 bits
Bi-sync must be controlled by external logic
Sync pattern can be preset to any desired code
No automatic sync insertion and deletion

Baud rate

This is determined by external transmit and receive clocks.

General

This device is not as versatile as other newer types such as the Intel 8273 or the Z80–SIO, and may well require quite a few external logic devices for full operation. Note that the transmit and receive data buses are separate, as with some other types of early serial controllers, and this may require the use of two parallel data ports from the microprocessor.

SIGNETIC 2651 PCI

The Signetic 2651 Programmable Communications Interface gives both asynchronous and synchronous serial data communications from an 8-bit data bus. Although originally designed for use with the 2650 microprocessor, it is readily adapted for use by other 8-bit microprocessors.

Prime manufacturer

Signetics Inc.
2651

Alternative source devices

Standard Microsystems Corporation
COM2651

Package

28-pin dual in line

Pin connections

1	D2	15	TXRDY
2	D3	16	DCD
3	RXD	17	CTS
4	GND	18	TXE/DSC
5	D4	19	TXD
6	D5	20	BRCLK
7	D6	21	RESET
8	D7	22	DSR
9	TXC	23	RTS
10	A1	24	DTR
11	CE	25	RXC
12	A0	26	V_{cc}
13	R/W	27	D0
14	RXRDY	28	D1

Signal functions

D0 – D7	Bidirectional data bus
A0, A1	Internal register select inputs
RXRDY, TXRDY	Receiver, transmitter ready outputs
RTS	Request to send output (active low)
DTR	Data terminal ready output (active low)
CTS	Clear to send input (active low)
DSR	Data set ready input (active low)
DCD	Data carrier detect input (active low)
CE	Chip enable input (active low)
TXD	Transmit data output
RXD	Receive data input
RXC, TXC	Receive and transmit clocks bidirectional
TXE/DSC	Transmitter empty or data set change output
BRCLK	Baud rate generator clock input
R/W	Read–write control input (read low)
RESET	Reset input
V_{cc}, GND	Power supply inputs

Power requirements

V_{cc} +5 V ± 5%
GND   0 V

Temperature range

0°C to +70°C

Data format

Asynchronous mode
   Programmable word length 5 – 8 bits
   Stop bits programmable for 1, 1½ or 2 bits
   Parity may be even, odd or none

Synchronous mode
   Supports bi-sync mode with words of 5 – 8 bits and parity
   Single or double SYN operation
   Internal or external sync

Baud rate

There is an internal programmable baud rate generator driven by the BRCLK input clock. Internally selectable rates are from 50 to 19200 baud with 16 steps.

External clock may be used for baud rates up to 1 Mb/s. Internal options available for 16× and 64× receive clock.

General

No system clock is required by the 2651 device.

SYNERTEK SY6551 ACIA

Designed primarily to work with the 6500 range of processors, the 6551 provides asynchronous serial communication from a parallel 8-bit data bus system. It can readily be used with other 8-bit microprocessors. This devices appears to the main processor as four memory locations.

Prime manufacturer

Synertek Inc.
SY6551

Alternative source devices

Rockwell
R6551

Package

28-pin dual in line type   plastic or ceramic

Pin connections

1	GND	15	V_{cc}
2	CS0	16	DCD
3	CS1	17	DSR
4	RES	18	DB0
5	RXC	19	DB1
6	XTAL1	20	DB2
7	XTAL2	21	DB3
8	RTS	22	DB4
9	CTS	23	DB5
10	TXD	24	DB6
11	DTR	25	DB7
12	RXD	26	IRQ
13	RS0	27	$\phi2$
14	RS1	28	R/W

Signal functions

DB0 – DB7	Data bus bidirectional
CS0, CS1	Chip select inputs (CS1 active low)
XTAL1, XTAL2	Timing crystal for baud rate clock
RS0, RS1	Register select inputs
IRQ	Interrupt request output (active low)
TXD	Transmit data output
RXD	Receive data input
RXC	Receive clock bidirectional
RTS	Request to send output (active low)
CTS	Clear to send input (active low)
DTR	Data terminal ready output (active low)
DSR	Data set ready input (active low)
DCD	Data carrier detect input (active low)

All signals are TTL compatible. Outputs drive one TTL load.

Power requirements

V_{cc}	+5 V ± 5%
GND	0 V
Supply current	65 mA

Temperature range

Standard type	0°C to +70°C
SYE6551	−40°C to +85°C

Data format

Asynchronous mode only with half or full duplex
Word length programmable from 5 to 9 bits
Parity programmable odd, even or none
Stop bits programmable for 1, 1½ or 2 bits

Baud rate

Internal baud rate generator is programmable for 15 baud rates from 50 to 19200 baud. This clock uses an external 1.832 MHz timing crystal. External 16× clock may be used for other rates up to 125k baud.

General

The 6551 can generate interrupt suitable for use with most processors, particularly the 6500 and 6800 types.

A timing strobe is required for data timing over the data bus, and this is normally the $\phi2$ clock from a 6500 or 6800 processor system.

SIGNETICS 2661

The Signetics 2661 Enhanced Programmable Communications Interface device provides either synchronous or asynchronous serial data communications from an 8-bit data bus system. It is primarily designed for use with the 6500 series of 8-bit microprocessors, but could readily be interfaced to most other 8-bit processors.

Prime manufacturer

Signetics Inc.

Alternative source devices

Synertek Inc. SY2661

Package

28-pin dual in line type
SYC2661 ceramic, SYP2661 plastic

Pin connections

1	D2	15	TXRDY
2	D3	16	DCD
3	RXD	17	CTS
4	GND	18	TXE/DSC
5	D4	19	TXD
6	D5	20	BRCLK
7	D6	21	RESET
8	D7	22	DSR
9	TXC/XSY	23	RTS
10	A1	24	DTR
11	CE	25	RXC/BKD
12	A0	26	V_{cc}
13	R/W	27	D0
14	RXRDY	28	D1

Signal functions

D0–D7	Data bus bidirectional
RESET	Reset input
A0, A1	Register address lines
R/W	Read–write control input (read low)
CE	Chip enable (active low)
RTS	Request to send output (active low)
CTS	Clear to send input (active low)
DTR	Data terminal ready output (active low)
DSR	Data set ready input (active low)
DCD	Data carrier detect input (active low)
TXC, RXC	Transmit and receive clock inputs
TXD	Transmit data output
RXD	Receive data input
DSC	Data set change output
XSYNC	External sync.
BKD	Break detect
BRCLK	Baud rate generator clock
TXRDY, RXRDY	Transmit, receiver ready outputs
V_{cc}, GND	Power supply inputs

Power requirements

V_{cc} +5 V ± 5%
GND 0 V

Temperature range

0°C to +70°C

Data formats

Asynchronous mode
  Programmable word length 5–8 bits plus parity
  Programmable stop bits for 1, 1½ or 2 bits
  Parity odd, even or none

Synchronous mode
  Word length and parity as for asynchronous mode
  Single or double SYN operation
  Internal or external character sync.
  Transparent or non-transparent mode

Baud rate

There are 16 internally selectable baud rates. Three versions of the chip with suffix −1, −2 or −3 provide different baud rate sets. An internal or external baud rate clock may be used. Maximum baud rate is 1M baud. Asynchronous mode allows baud rates to 62.5k baud when a 16× clock is used.

General

No system clock is required by the 2661.

TEXAS INSTRUMENTS TMS9902 ACC

Designed for use with the 9900 series of microprocessors, the TMS9902 is an Asynchronous Serial Communications Controller providing a single serial I/O channel and a programmable timer on the same chip. It should be noted that the 9902 interfaces with the CRU channel of the 9900 processor rather than with a parallel data bus. Therefore it will not be easy to use with other types of processor.

Prime manufacturer

Texas Instruments Inc.
TMS9902

Alternative source devices

American Microsystems Inc.
S9902

Package

18-pin dual in line type
TMS9902NL plastic, TMS9902JL ceramic

Pin connections

1	INT	10	S4
2	X_{OUT}	11	S3
3	R_{IN}	12	S2
4	CRU_{IN}	13	S1
5	RTS	14	S0
6	CTS	15	CRUCLK
7	DSR	16	ϕ
8	CRU_{OUT}	17	CE
9	V_{ss}	18	V_{cc}

Signal functions

S0 – S4	Bit address inputs from 9900 CPU
CRU_{IN}	Output to CRU channel of 9900
CRU_{OUT}	Input from CRU channel of 9900
CRUCLK	Input from CRU clock line of 9900
X_{OUT}	Transmitter serial data output
R_{IN}	Receiver serial data input
INT	Interrupt request output (active low)
RTS	Request to send output (active low)
CTS	Clear to send input (active low)
DSR	Data set ready input (active low)
ϕ	TTL clock input
CE	Chip enable (active low)
V_{cc}, V_{ss}	Power inputs

Power requirements

V_{cc}	+5 V ± 5%
V_{ss}	0 V
Supply current	100 mA

Temperature range

0°C to +70°C

Data format

Asynchronous serial format only
Programmable bit format from 5 to 8 bits
Programmable stop bits 1, 1½ or 2 bits
Even, odd or no parity check

Baud rate

The 9902 includes on-chip generation of transmit and receive data rates, which are independently programmed and therefore may be different if desired. Range from 75 to 500k baud.

Interval timer

An 8-bit on-chip interval timer is provided which can be programmed for delays of from 64 µs to 16.32 ms using a 1 MHz clock input ϕ.

TEXAS INSTRUMENTS TMS9903 SCC

The TMS9903 is a Synchronous Communications Controller, designed specifically for use with the Texas 9900 series of microprocessors. It makes use of the special CRU channel of the 9900, and is not readily interfaced to other types of microprocessor. The device can handle both synchronous and asynchronous serial data communications and also contains a programmable interval timer, giving delays of 64 μs to 16.32 ms.

Prime manufacturer

Texas Instruments Inc.
TMS9903

Alternative source devices

American Microsystems Inc.
S9903

Package

20-pin dual in line type
TMS9903NL plastic, TMS9903JL ceramic

Pin connections

1	INT	11	SCR
2	X_{OUT}	12	S4
3	R_{IN}	13	S3
4	CRU_{IN}	14	S2
5	RTS	15	S1
6	CTS	16	S0
7	DSR	17	CRUCLK
8	CRU_{OUT}	18	ϕ
9	V_{ss}	19	CE
10	SCT	20	V_{cc}

Signal functions

S0 – S4	Bit address inputs from 9900
RTS	Request to send output (active low)
CTS	Clear to send input (active low)
DSR	Data set ready input (active low)
X_{OUT}	Transmitter data output
R_{IN}	Receiver data input
ϕ	TTL clock input
CRU_{IN}	Output to CRU_{IN} line of 9900
CRU_{OUT}	Input from CRU_{OUT} line of 9900
CRUCLK	Input from CRUCLK on 9900
INT	Interrupt request output (active low)
CE	Chip enable input (active low)
SCR	Serial receive clock input
SCT	Serial transmit clock input
V_{cc}, V_{ss}	Power supply inputs

All signals are TTL compatible.

Power requirements

V_{cc}	+5 V ± 5%
V_{ss}	0 V
Supply current	100 mA

Temperature range

0°C to +70°C

Data formats

Asynchronous mode
  Number of bits programmable from 5 to 9
  Stop bits programmable for 1, 1½ or 2
  Parity may be odd, even or none

Synchronous mode
  SDLC, HDLC and bi-sync line protocols
  Programmable character length 5 – 9 bits
  Programmable CRC generation and detection
  Automatic zero insert and delete for HDLC and SDLC
  Two programmable sync characters
  Odd, even or no parity

Baud rate

Internally programmable from 0 to 250k baud, with either full or half duplex operation.

Timer

An on-chip programmable interval timer is provided, giving interval times from 64 μs to 16.32 ms.

Interrupts may be generated by either the timer or the serial data channel.

ZILOG Z80-SIO

Designed primarily for use with the Zilog Z80 microprocessor, the Z80-SIO Serial Input–Output device has the capability of handling both synchronous and asynchronous communication. It can also deal with some advanced communications protocols such as HDLC and SDLC.

Two completely independent serial input–output channels are provided with full duplex capability. Data are passed to the microprocessor via an 8-bit data bus. This device may also be used with other microprocessors, if suitable interface logic is provided, to give Z80 type control signals.

Prime manufacturer

Zilog Inc.
  Z80-SIO

Alternative source devices

Mostek
  MK3884, MK3885 and MK3887

SGS-ATES
  Z80-SIO

Package

40-pin dual in line type   ceramic or plastic
Ceramic type suffix D (Zilog)
Plastic type suffix B or P

Pin connections

1	D1	21	RESET
2	D3	22	DCDB
3	D5	23	CTSB
4	D7	24	RTSB
5	INT	25	DTRB
6	IEI	26	TXDB
7	IEO	27	RXTXCB
8	M1	28	RXDB
9	V_{cc}	29	SYNCB
10	W/RDYA	30	W/RDYB
11	SYNCA	31	V_{ss}
12	RXDA	32	RD
13	RXCA	33	C/D
14	TXCA	34	B/A
15	TXDA	35	CE
16	DTRA	36	IORQ
17	RTSA	37	D6
18	CTSA	38	D4
19	DCDA	39	D2
20	CLK	40	D0

Signal functions

D0 – D7	Data bus bidirectional tri-state
RTSA, RTSB	Ready to send outputs (active low)
CTSA, CTSB	Clear to send inputs (active low)
DCDA, DCDB	Data carrier detect inputs (active low)
TXDA, TXDB	Transmit data outputs (active high)
RXDA, RXDB	Receive data inputs
W/RDYA, W/RDYB	Wait/ready status outputs (active low)
B/A	Channel A or B select (A low) input
C/D	Control/data select input (D low)
CE	Chip enable input (active low)
M1	Machine cycle M1 input from Z80 (active low)
IORQ	I/O request input from Z80 CPU (active low)
RD	Read status from Z80 CPU (active low)
SYNCA, SYNCB	External sync I/O (active low)
DTRA, DTRB	Data terminal ready outputs (active low)
RXCA, RXCB	Receive clock inputs
TXCA, TXCB	Transmit clock inputs
INT	Interrupt request output (wire OR active low)
IEI, IEO	Interrupt enable I/O for daisy chaining
RESET	Reset input (active low)
CLK	System clock input from CPU
V_{cc}, V_{ss}	Power supply inputs

Power requirements

V_{cc}	+5 V ± 5%
V_{ss}	0 V
Supply current	140 mA max.

Temperature range

0°C to +70°C

Data formats

Asynchronous mode

  Number of data bits programmable for 5, 6, 7 or 8 bits
  Parity bit programmable for odd, even or no parity
  Stop bits programmable for 1, 1½ or 2 stop bits
  Channels A and B may have different formats

Synchronous modes
  Monosync mode uses 8-bit sync word internally formatted
  Bi-sync mode uses 16-bit internally generated sync word
  External sync mode uses external sync generate and check
  HDLC and SDLC formats may be supported

Baud rate

Set by external clock generator.

8 MEMORY DEVICES

INTRODUCTION

One of the most important support devices for a microprocessor is the memory, used to store the program instructions and the data being processed. In a single-chip microcomputer the memory will normally be included on the same chip as the central processor unit. For most applications of this type of device no external memory will be required. For a normal microprocessor system, however, the memory will be external to the microprocessor chip itself.

Two types of memory may be used with a processor system. The first is a read–write memory, generally referred to as a RAM (*random access memory*). This is normally used as a data store and as storage for intermediate calculations or results. In systems where general computing is carried out, such as in a personal or business computer, the RAM may also be used to store the program instructions, since these will vary from one task to the next.

One problem with the RAM type of memory is that if the power is removed the stored data will be lost. This type of memory is called a *volatile* memory. Where the applications make use of the same program at all times it is desirable that the program memory should retain its contents, even when the computer is switched off, so that the program does not need to be loaded into the machine each time it is switched on. To achieve this a second type of memory device, known as a *read only memory* or ROM is generally used. The data stored in a ROM are permanent, although some types do have a facility for data erasure and reprogramming, and will be retained even when power is removed from the memory device. This type of memory is called a *non-volatile* memory.

Random access memories

A typical random access read–write memory contains a large array of memory cells, each of which is used to store one bit of data. An addressing system is also included on the chip, which will allow individual cells or groups of cells to be selected and have data written into or read from them. Normally the cells are arranged in rows and columns, and the addressing system is used to select one row and one column to identify a particular cell. The cell when selected is connected to a data bus which transfers data to or from that cell.

Two basic modes of internal operation are available in RAM type memories. These are *static* and *dynamic*. Each type has advantages and disadvantages, which will now be considered.

Static memories
In a static RAM each cell contains a latching circuit similar to a logic flip flop, which once set to a logic state will retain that state until it is reprogrammed. Thus once data have been written into the memory they will be retained indefinitely provided that the memory remains in a powered up condition. To read data from such a memory the appropriate address is applied and after a short delay the stored data will appear on the data output lines. The delay between the application of the address and output of stable data is known as the *access time*.

Typical static memories will have capacities varying from as little as 16 bits up to some 8192 bits. Earlier types were arranged with only a single cell selected at a time, to give say a 1024×1 bit memory. In a microprocessor system it is usual to have a data bus perhaps 8 or 16-bits wide and to deal with this 8 or 16 memories might be addressed in parallel, so that each memory provides one bit for the data bus. Later types of memory have been organised so that when an address is applied 4 or 8 bits of data are input or output in parallel. A typical memory of this type is the Mostek MK4118, which has an internal organisation of 1024×8 bit words. A single memory of this type conveniently provides 1024 bytes of scratchpad or data memory for a small microprocessor system.

Dynamic memories
One problem with the static type of memory is that the cell uses a relatively complicated circuit and in the early days of memory production it was difficult to produce a large size static memory on a silicon chip.

An alternative type of cell makes use of the stored charge in a capacitor as a memory. This type of memory cell is simpler than a static type, but due to leakage the charge on the cell slowly dies away and eventually the data are lost. To overcome this problem the data in the cell are 'refreshed' from time to time by simply being read out and written back into the cell, effectively to restore the charge on the capacitor. This type of memory is known as a dynamic memory due to the continual refreshing action needed to retain the data. During a refresh cycle all of the cells in the memory need to be read and rewritten. In most modern dynamic memories it is arranged that a whole row or column of cells is refreshed simultaneously, so that the number of refresh operations in a cycle is reduced. Typical dynamic memories will need to be refreshed every 2 ms, although some newer types may extend this time to 4 ms.

Because of the smaller cell size, dynamic memories will generally provide much larger capacity than static types. A typical dynamic memory may have from 4k to 64k bits and is normally only one bit wide. Some 256k bit dynamic memories are being developed.

The large capacity of the dynamic memory implies the use of a large number of address lines. A 64k bit memory will need 16 address lines to enable individual bits to be selected. In order to keep down the size of the package it is normal for the address of the memory to be multiplexed so that the row and column addresses are applied in succession to the same set of package pins. When the row address is applied an RAS (Row Address Strobe) pulse is also applied to the chip and the row address is latched into an internal register. The column address is then applied to the same set of pins and is accompanied by a CAS (Column Address Strobe) pulse which latches it into a register and also causes the desired cell to be selected for reading or writing. Normally data will appear at the output whilst the CAS line is held low after an address has been applied. Refresh operations require only the address for the row and the RAS pulse to be applied when the whole row will be refreshed automatically.

Read Only Memories

Two basic types of read only memory are generally available. In one type, known as a *mask programmed*

ROM, the data pattern is built into the memory when it is manufactured and cannot be altered. The alternative type is known as a *programmable read only memory* or PROM, and when manufactured it will have all of its cells set to the same state which may be either a '0' or '1' according to the type of device. The data are programmed into the memory by selecting cells and applying a large pulse of electrical energy to set them to a new state. Once the memory is programmed it will retain the data indefinitely even when its power supply is removed.

The normal type of PROM has fusible wire links or diodes in each of its cells. During programming these links will be selectively fused to alter the state of the cells and thus enter the desired data pattern into the memory. Once it has been programmed a PROM is very much like a mask programmed ROM and cannot readily be altered, although unprogrammed cells may still be altered.

Several types of PROM are now available which are erasable. One type, generally referred to as an EPROM, may be erased by exposing the chip to short wave ultraviolet light, and usually has a quartz window in the lid of the package to allow light to fall on the chip. After exposure for perhaps 10–20 minutes all of the cells in the chip will be restored to their original state. In this type of memory the data are stored as an electrical charge within the cell, but unlike a dynamic type RAM the storage time for an EPROM is many years. A second type of erasable PROM uses an electrical signal to erase the data, and this type is normally referred to as an EEPROM (*electrically erasable* PROM).

PROMs and EPROMs are convenient for use in prototype development and small production runs, where the expense of the manufacture of a special mask programmed ROM is not justified. For large production projects a mask type ROM will generally be more economical, since it is cheaper to make than an EPROM and does not need to be individually programmed. The cost of the mask design, however, makes a mask ROM unattractive unless some thousands are to be produced.

A further type of non-volatile memory is the *electrically alterable ROM* or EAROM, which like a PROM or EPROM uses electrical programming. In this device, however, it is possible to use the memory in much the same way as a RAM, except that it is slower in operation in the writing mode. The difference from a RAM is that the data will be retained, in much the same way as for a PROM, when the power is removed. At present EAROMs require a number of different supply rails and tend to be less easy to use than PROMs or EPROMs. The EAROM also tends to be more expensive than the popular EPROM types. There are applications, however, where an EAROM is useful, particularly in adaptive type systems where program parameters may need to be varied but a non-volatile memory is essential.

CCD and bubble memories

Two types of memory developed for mass storage of data are the *charge coupled device* (CCD) type and the *magnetic bubble* type memory.

In the CCD memory the storage cells are connected in a long chain, which is effectively a shift register. The data are circulated in serial fashion through the memory. Whilst this type of memory can provide large capacity of 64k bits or more, it has relatively slow access to the data, since they are in the form of a continuously circulating serial stream.

The magnetic bubble memory has some similarities to a charge coupled type, since it too uses a serial stream of data. In this case tiny magnetic bubbles are circulated through the memory using magnetic fields. Data are stored by changing the state of individual bubbles which act as single-bit cells. A typical bubble memory module may have perhaps 1 million bit capacity and is non-volatile, since the magnetic pattern is retained in a power down condition. With increasing sizes of RAM becoming available the bubble memory is losing some of its attractiveness and some manufacturers have now withdrawn from production of these devices.

CMOS and TTL types

Most of the popular RAM, ROM and EPROM devices use the *n*MOS construction process, providing medium speed and medium power operation. For low power application, however, these devices can be obtained with CMOS fabrication. In general the CMOS types available have lower memory capacity than *n*MOS types, but their capacity is steadily being improved.

For high speed operation bipolar techniques such as TTL and ECL may be used for memories. As with CMOS, these types generally have lower capacity than the *n*MOS types, and tend to use rather more power. The TTL types are also available in small capacities of perhaps 32 or 64 bits, and may be convenient for use as scratchpad registers in a small system where a larger *n*MOS memory may not be justified.

2101/11/12 SERIES 1024 BIT STATIC RAM

Originally introduced by Intel, the 2101, 2111 and 2112 series of static memories are now manufactured by several sources. These memories are all organised as 256 words of 4 bits each. The main differences between the three types are concerned with the arrangement of input and output data lines and the chip select facilities provided.

Of the three types only the 2101 has separate input and output lines. It is best suited to systems where continuous availability of output signals is required or where the data source driving the input cannot readily be disabled. Both the 2111 and 2112 are suited to bus orientated systems where the data source can readily be operated in a tri-state mode.

The 2101 and 2111 each have two chip select inputs, and this may simplify the organisation of larger memories since the amount of external chip selection logic will be reduced. This would be useful in small memories where up to four of the memory chips are operating in parallel. In such systems the output lines are wire ORed in parallel.

Some manufacturers also produce low power versions of these memories. The type number will usually take the form 21L01 or 2101L for the low power version of the 2101 and so on.

A range of operating speeds, usually faster than that of the standard device, is also available from some makers. All types use nMOS technology, although there are some TTL types available which are pin and function compatible with the 2101.

Device type codes

Advanced Micro Devices

Am9101, Am9111, Am9112, Am2111 Standard type
Am91L01, Am01L11, Am91L12, Am21L11 Low power

Intel Corporation

2101, 2111, 2112, 8101, 8111, 8112
2101L, 2111L, 2112L Low power

Mitsubishi

M5L2101, M5L2111, M5L2112

N.E.C.

μPD2101A, μPD2111A, μPD2112A

Signetics

2101, 2111, 2112

Synertek

SY21101A, SY2111A, SY2112A

Toshiba

TMM311 (2111), TMM312 (2112)

Package

2101 22-pin dual in line type
2111 18-pin dual in line type
2112 16-pin dual in line type

Ceramic type package is denoted by a prefix C or D for Intel devices and suffix D for AMD types (e.g. C2101, Am9111D).

Plastic package is denoted by prefix P or by suffix P or N.

Pin connections

Type 2101 22-pin DIL

1	A3	12	OP2
2	A2	13	IP3
3	A1	14	OP3
4	A0	15	IP4
5	A5	16	OP4
6	A6	17	CE2
7	A7	18	OD
8	V_{ss}	19	CE1
9	IP1	20	WE
10	OP1	21	A4
11	IN2	22	V_{cc}

Type 2111 18-pin DIL

1	A3	10	CE2
2	A2	11	IO1
3	A1	12	IO2
4	A0	13	IO3
5	A5	14	IO4
6	A6	15	CE1
7	A7	16	WE
8	V_{ss}	17	A4
9	OD	18	V_{cc}

2112 type 16-pin DIL

1	A3	9	IO1
2	A2	10	IO2
3	A3	11	IO3
4	A0	12	IO4
5	A5	13	CE
6	A6	14	WE
7	A7	15	A4
8	V_{ss}	16	V_{cc}

Signal functions

A0 – A7	Address inputs
IP1 – IP4	Data inputs
OP1 – OP4	Data outputs
IO1 – IO4	Multiplexed data I/O
OD	Output disable (low for enable)
WE	Write enable (active low)
CE	Chip enable (active low)
CE1	Active low, but on the 2101 CE2 is active high
V_{ss}, V_{cc}	Power supply inputs

On multiplexed I/O versions the write enable (WE) input is taken low to disconnect the outputs and allow data to be written into the memory.

All inputs and outputs are TTL compatible and the outputs will normally drive two TTL loads. All inputs are protected against static by diodes.

2101/11/12 SERIES 1024 BIT STATIC RAM

Power requirements

V_{cc} +5 V ± 5%
V_{ss} 0 V
Supply current   35 mA   standard type 2101/11/12
    20 mA   low power versions

Note that the AMD versions 9101, 9111 and 9112 can retain memory contents with the supply reduced to about 1.5 V. The standby current may be as low as 7 mA under these conditions.

Temperature range

Standard version has a range of 0°C to +70°C.

AMD and Intel produce military temperature range devices covering the range −55°C to +125°C, and these are denoted by a prefix or suffix M in the type number.

Timing

For the standard parts the access time for reading or writing data in the memory is 1 μs.

A variety of alternative versions of the part are now available, with access times ranging from 175 ns to 650 ns. Some of these types are:

175 ns types

    Synertek   SY21H01, SY21H11 and SY21H12

200 ns types

    Synertek   SY21H01-2, SY21H11-2 and SY21H12-2
    AMD   Am9101E, Am9111E and Am9112E

250 ns types

    AMD   Am9101D, Am9111D and Am9112D
    Other makes   2101A-2, 2111A-2 and 2112A-2

300 ns types

    AMD   Am9101C, AM9111C and Am9112C

350 ns types

    All makes   2101A, 2111A and 2112A

400 ns types

    AMD   Am9101B, Am9111B and Am9112B

450 ns types

    All makes   2101A-4, 2111A-4 and 2112A-4

500 ns types

    AMD   Am9101A, Am9111A and Am9112A

650 ns types

    All makes   2101-2, 2111-2 and 2112-2

2102 SERIES 1024 BIT STATIC RAM

Originally introduced by Intel, the 2102 is an *n*MOS type static RAM with a 1024 × 1 bit internal organisation. A wide range of types based on the original 2102 is now available, and these devices have become extremely popular. They are widely accepted as an industry wide standard for this size of memory chip.

The 2102 is designed primarily for use in small to medium size memories. Typical applications are in the screen refresh memory for VDUs and buffer memories for printers and other peripheral devices. The 2102 is also widely used to provide a small amount of RAM for microprocessor systems in control applications, where perhaps 1 or 2 kbyte of memory are required. In the past the 2102 has been used for medium size memories for small microcomputer systems, but with the arrival of much larger 8-bit wide memory devices it is now less attractive for this purpose.

Most manufacturers produce a low power version of the 2102 which is generally given a code number of the type 21L02 or 2102L. These versions typically consume about half the power of a standard 2102.

Although the early 2102 was a relatively slow device there are now versions which provide a wide range of access times, from 200 ns up to the 1 μs standard speed.

Device type codes

Advanced Micro Devices

Am9102, Am91L02

Hitachi

HM452102

National Semiconductor

NM2102A, NM2102AL

N.E.C.

μPD2102AL

Texas Instruments

TMS4035

Most other makes use the basic 2102, 21L02 and 2102L coding.

Package

16-pin dual in line   plastic or ceramic
Ceramic has prefix C or D for Intel, and suffix D for AMD or J for Texas types
Plastic types have prefix P or suffix P or N

Pin connections

1	A6	9	V_{ss}
2	A5	10	V_{cc}
3	WE	11	D_{IN}
4	A1	12	D_{OUT}
5	A2	13	CE
6	A3	14	A9
7	A4	15	A8
8	A0	16	A7

Signal functions

A0 – A9	Address inputs
D_{IN}	Data input
D_{OUT}	Data output
CE	Chip enable (active low)
WE	Write enable (write low)
V_{ss}, V_{cc}	Power supply inputs

When write enable goes low data are accepted and written into the memory. Address must be stable before the write pulse and data must remain stable during write pulse.

The output line is tri-state and will go high impedance when CE is high, thus allowing devices to be paralleled in a wired-OR arrangement.

All signals are TTL compatible and the output line can drive two standard TTL loads. Inputs are diode protected for static.

Power requirements

V_{cc}	+5 V ± 5%
V_{ss}	0 V
Supply current	Standard version 45 mA
	Low power version 33 mA

Note that devices coded 21L02 are simple low power versions, whereas the 2102L and 2102AL also have a standby power mode. In the standby mode the supply may be allowed to fall to 1.5 V without loss of stored data and the standby current may typically be about 15 mA. This standby feature is included on the AMD9102 types.

Temperature range

Standard 2102 type devices normally have an operating range of 0°C to +70°C.

Some manufacturers also produce −40°C to +85°C versions for industrial use, whilst Intel and AMD produce full military temperature range (−55°C to +125°C) versions, denoted by an M as prefix or suffix to the type number.

Timing

The standard 2102 has a read or write access time of 1 μs, which by modern memory device standards is relatively slow. Most microprocessors will require memory access in some 500 ns or less, so that special arrangements will be required if a standard 2102 is to be used.

All manufacturers now produce a range of faster 2102 devices, with access times down to 200 ns. Many produce the 2102A, which in its standard version gives 350 ns access time.

Some of the available types are listed below:

200 ns types

Fairchild 2102R

250 ns types

General type no. 2102A-2
AMD 9102D
Fairchild 2102H
Toshiba TMM313-1

2102 SERIES 1024 BIT STATIC RAM

350 ns types
    General type no. 2102A
    Fairchild 2102F

450 ns types
    General type no. 2102A-4
    Fairchild 21021
    Toshiba TMM313-4

650 ns types
    General type no. 2102-2
    AMD 9102
    National 2102A-6

Note that low power types include L in type number in the form 21L02 or as the last letter.

256 × 4 BIT CMOS STATIC RAM

The most popular type of 256 × 4 bit CMOS RAM available is the RCA MWS5101 and equivalent types from other manufacturers. From Harris and Intersil there are some variants with other package sizes or slightly different pin layout.

This type of memory is particularly useful with CMOS type processors or for any system where low power consumption is important. These memories are also very tolerant of power supply vaiations, which makes them very suitable for battery operated portable equipment.

Suppliers and device type codes

American Microsystems
  S5101L

Harris Semiconductor
  HM6551
  HM6501 different pin layout
  HM6561, HM6562, different package

Hitachi
  HM435101

Intersil
  IM6551

Mitsubishi
  M5L5101L

Motorola
  MCM5101

N.E.C.
  µPD5101L

Solid State Scientific
  SCM5101L

RCA
  MWS5101L

Synertek
  SY5101L

Sharp
  LH5101L

Toshiba
  TC5501

Package

5101, 6551	22-pin dual in line type
6501	22-pin dual in line type
6561	18-pin dual in line type
6562	16-pin dual in line type

Pin connections

5101 and 6551 type

1	A3	12	Q1
2	A2	13	D2
3	A1	14	Q2
4	A0	15	D3
5	A5	16	Q3
6	A6	17	CS2
7	A7	18	CE
8	V_{ss}	19	CS1
9	D0	20	W
10	Q0	21	A4
11	D1	22	V_{cc}

6501 type

1	A3	12	Q1
2	A2	13	D2
3	A1	14	Q2
4	A0	15	D3
5	A5	16	Q3
6	A6	17	CS
7	A7	18	OE
8	V_{ss}	19	CE
9	D0	20	W
10	Q0	21	A4
11	D1	22	V_{cc}

6561 type

1	A3	10	CS2
2	A2	11	I/O 1
3	A1	12	I/O 2
4	A0	13	I/O 3
5	A5	14	I/O 4
6	A6	15	CS1
7	A7	16	W
8	V_{ss}	17	A4
9	CE	18	V_{cc}

6562 type

1	A3	9	I/O 1
2	A2	10	I/O 2
3	A1	11	I/O 3
4	A0	12	I/O 4
5	A5	13	CE
6	A6	14	W
7	A7	15	A4
8	V_{ss}	16	V_{cc}

Signal functions

A0 – A7	Address inputs
D0 – D4	Data inputs
Q0 – Q4	Data outputs tri-state
I/O 1 – I/O 4	Data bus I/O tri-state
CS1, CS2	Chip select inputs (active low)
CE	Chip enable input (active low)
W	Write enable (write low)
V_{cc}, V_{ss}	Power supply inputs

Note that the connection arrangements are compatible with the 2101, 2111 and 2112 type *n*MOS RAMs.

All inputs and outputs are TTL compatible and outputs will drive two standard TTL loads.

256 × 4 BIT CMOS STATIC RAM

Power requirements

V_{cc} +5 V ± 0.5 V
V_{ss} 0 V
Supply current   1.5 – 25 mA according to speed of operation
Standby current   1 μA maximum

Temperature range

RCA5101E   −40°C to +85°C (Harris 6551-9)
RCA5101D   −55°C to +125°C (Harris 6551-2)
Harris 6551-5   0°C to +75°C

Most of the standard types have the −40°C to +85°C range.

Timing

The 5101 series of CMOS RAMs are all static in operation, and application of the appropriate address will cause the data to appear at the outputs when the W line is held at '1'. When W is taken to '0' the data applied at the data inputs will be written into the selected memory location. The CE and CS inputs must all be at '0' for either read or write operations. When CE is taken high the outputs go to high impedance and the memory goes into a standby power down mode. Memory data will normally be retained provided V_{cc} does not fall below +2 V.

After the address is applied there is an access delay time before data at the outputs are valid or data are ready to be accepted by the memory. A range of access times from 150 ns to 800 ns is available, and details of these are:

150 ns

    National   NMC6551B-9

180 ns

    Intersil   IM6551A, IM6561A

200 ns

    Harris   HM6501B, HM6551B, HM6561B, HM6562B

250 ns

    RCA   MWS5101L1, MWS5101L2

300 ns

    Harris   HM6501, HM6551, HM6561, HM6562
    Sharp   LH5101S

350 ns

    RCA   MWS5101L3
    Intersil   IM6551

450 ns

    Various makes   5101L-1
    Toshiba   TC5501
    RCA   MWS5101L8

650 ns

    Various makes   standard 5101 version

800 ns

    Various makes   5101L-8 version

2114 SERIES 1k × 4 BIT STATIC RAM

The 2114 type static RAM has become an industry wide standard type and is now produced by most of the major semiconductor memory manufacturers. It is organised as 1024 words which are 4 bits wide. This makes it very convenient for use with 4, 8 and 16-bit microcomputer systems. Typical applications are for small to medium size read–write memories, screen buffers for VDUs and printer buffer memories. There is a wide range of speed options available and low power versions are also produced.

Device type codes (Standard version)

Advanced Micro Devices
9114

American Microsystems
S2114

Electronic Arrays
EA21142

EMM-SEMI
2114

Fairchild
2114

Hitachi
472114-4

Intel
2114

Mitsubishi
M5L2114L

MOS Technology
MPS2114-45

Motorola
MCM2114-45

National Semiconductor
MM2114

N.E.C.
µPD2114

OKI Semiconductor
MSM2114

Panasonic
MN2114

Rockwell
R2114

Siemens
SAB2114

Synertek
SY2114

Texas Instruments
TMS4045-45

Thomson EFCIS
EF2114

Toshiba
TMM314A

Package

18-pin dual in line type   ceramic or plastic
Ceramic type denoted by prefix C or D for Intel.
Other makes use suffix C or D (Fairchild) or J (Texas)
Plastic types usually have prefix or suffix P or N

Pin connections

1	A6	10	WE
2	A5	11	I/O 4
3	A4	12	I/O 3
4	A3	13	I/O 2
5	A0	14	I/O 1
6	A1	15	A9
7	A2	16	A8
8	CS	17	A7
9	V_{ss}	18	V_{cc}

Signal functions

A0 – A9   Address inputs
I/O 1 – I/O 4 Data I/O pins
WE   Write enable (active low)
CS   Chip select (active low)
V_{ss}, V_{ss} Power supply input

Power requirements

V_{cc} +5 V ± 5%
V_{ss} 0 V
Supply current   130 mA max.
Most manufacturers also produce a low power version of the 2114 which is generally coded as a 21L14 or 2114L
Supply current for L version   65mA max.

Temperature range

Commercial part   0°C to +70°C
Industrial part   −40°C to +85°C
Military part   −55°C to +125°C suffix or prefix M

Signal levels

Input and output signals are TTL compatible and for the 2114 the outputs can drive 2 TTL loads.

Data input and output are multiplexed via common lines and input is selected when the WE line goes low. Chip select line CS when set high causes I/O lines to go to tri-state high impedance condition.

Timing

The standard 2114 has an access time of 450 ns maximum. The write pulse must have a minimum length of 250 ns.

256 × 8 BIT ERASABLE nMOS PROM

In this size of erasable nMOS programmable read only memory there are two popular types. One is the Intel 1702 and its derivatives. The other is the National MM5203 type. Both types are static memories and require no clock signals for their operation.

This type of memory is useful for small prototype microprocessor systems as a program memory, since the device can easily be erased using UV light and then reprogrammed with a modified computer program for further tests.

The two types are not pin compatible and have slightly different operating characteristics. Both are suitable for similar applications.

Device type codes

Intel Corporation

1702A, 1702AL, low power version

Advanced Micro Devices

Am1702, Am1702A and Am9702A

Mitsubishi

M5L1702A

National Semiconductor

MM4203, MM5203
MM1702A

Package

All types   24-pin dual in line with quartz window

Pin connections

1702 types

1	A2	13	P
2	A1	14	CS
3	A0	15	V_{bb}
4	D1	16	V_{gg}
5	D2	17	A7
6	D3	18	A6
7	D4	19	A5
8	D5	20	A4
9	D6	21	A3
10	D7	22	V_{cc}
11	D8	23	V_{cc}
12	V_{cc}	24	V_{dd}

MM5203 type

1	A3	13	A9
2	A2	14	CS
3	A1	15	MODE
4	D1	16	V_{dd}
5	D2	17	A8
6	D3	18	A7
7	D4	19	A6
8	D5	20	A5
9	D6	21	A4
10	D7	22	PROG
11	D8	23	V_{bb}
12	V_{ss}	24	V_{ll}

Signal functions

A0 – A8	Address inputs
A9	MSB address for 5203 type in 512 × 4 mode
D1 – D8	Data outputs in read mode
	Data inputs in programming mode
CS	Chip select input (active low)
PROG	Programming pulse input
MODE	5203 type selects 256 × 8 or 512 × 4 addressing. In the 512 × 4 bit mode the address line A9 selects odd data lines (D1, D3, D5, D7) when high, and even data lines (D2, D4, D6, D8) when low. In 256 × 4 mode A9 is held low
V_{bb}, V_{cc}, V_{dd}, V_{ll}, V_{ss}	Power supply inputs

Power requirements

1702 types   Read mode

V_{cc}	+5 V ± 5%
V_{bb}	+5 V ± 5%
V_{gg}	−9 V ± 5%
V_{dd}	−5 V ± 5%
V_{ss}	0 V
Supply current I_{dd}	40 mA
Supply current low power 1702AL	7 – 35 mA

In the low power version the V_{gg} line is clocked so that power is drawn during read cycles and falls to a standby level at other times.

5203 types   Read mode

V_{ss}	+5 V ± 5%
V_{bb}	+5 V ± 5%
V_{dd}	−12 V ± 5%
V_{ll}	−12 V ± 5%
Supply current	35 mA

Temperature range

Standard type 1702A and MM5203
   0°C to +70°C

Am9702 and MM4203 types
   −55°C to +85°C

Signal levels

In the normal read mode of operation both types of device are TTL compatible for address input and data output signals. The data outputs will drive at least one TTL load.

Erasure

Both types of device are designed to be erased by UV light and have a quartz window in the top of the package for this purpose. Erasure of the MM5203 type causes all bits to be set to '1'. In the 1702A all bits will be erased to the '0'. The AMD type Am1702 resets all bits to the '1' state, but the Am1702A operates in the same way as other 1702A types.

Read operation

Intel 1702A type

For reading the PROG input is set at V_{cc} and the CS input at V_{ss}. Operation is completely static and when an address is applied the appropriate data will be output on the data lines after a short access time. For the standard 1702A the access time is 1 μs. The 1702A-6 gives a slower access time of 1.5 μs, whilst the 1702A-2 has an access time of 650 ns.

National MM5203 type

With MODE set at '1' and A9 set at '0' the memory operates as a 256 ×8 system. If MODE is set at '0' and A9 is used as an address the organisation is 512 × 4 with odd and even addresses selected by A9. Operation is static and the read access time is 1 μs maximum. Note that a '1' level is V_{ss} and a '0' level is 0 V or V_{dd}. The PROG pin should be tied to V_{ss} and CS must be low for the read mode.

Programming

1702A type

For the 1702A the V_{gg}, V_{dd} supplies and the address and data inputs are pulsed with signals of −40 V to −48 V. The maximum V_{gg} level is in fact −40 V. Data use −48 V for '1' level and 0 V for a '0' level. Program pulse width is 2 – 3 ms and some 32 complete cycles through the memory will be needed to program the data fully. One pulse is applied for each successive address.

5203 type

During programming V_{ss} is set at 0 V and V_{bb} at +12 V. V_{ll} is not required but may be tied to V_{dd}. Address and data inputs will be about 0 V for a '1' level and −48 V for a '0' level. The data operate with negative logic so that a '0' level input will cause a '1' to be programmed and *vice versa*. Both V_{dd} and the PROG line are pulsed with a −48 V pulse for each data word.

512 × 8 BIT nMOS ERASABLE PROM

There are two basic versions of nMOS UV erasable programmable ROMs with a 512 × 8 bit internal organisation. One type comes originally from Intel with the type number 2704. The second type is the National Semiconductor MM5204Q. These two types are neither compatible nor interchangeable.

This size of PROM is useful for small lock up tables for data conversion and also for small program memory for a microprocessor based control system. Programming is by a sequence of pulses and erasure makes use of short wave UV light.

With the advent of the larger 2708 and 2516 PROMs with capacities of 1k or 2 kbyte the smaller 512 byte memories may become less attractive. Because of the very high volume production of the larger memories it may well be cheaper to use say half of the capacity of a 2708 rather than use one of the smaller memories. Some of the newer 1k and 2k memories also have the advantage of requiring only one power supply rail.

Device type codes

American Microsystems

S5204A

Intel Corporation

2704

National Semiconductor

MM5204Q

SGS-ATES

M2704

Package

Both types
24-pin dual in line ceramic type with quartz window

Pin connections

Intel 2704 types

1	A7	13	D3
2	A6	14	D4
3	A5	15	D5
4	A4	16	D6
5	A3	17	D7 (MSB)
6	A2	18	PROG
7	A1	19	V_{dd}
8	A0 (LSB)	20	CS/WE
9	D0 (LSB)	21	V_{bb}
10	D1	22	V_{ss}
11	D2	23	A8 (MSB)
12	V_{ss}	24	V_{cc}

National MM5204Q types

1	V_{cc}	13	A7
2	R/W	14	A8
3	CS	15	D0 (LSB)
4	PROG	16	D1
5	A0 (LSB)	17	D2
6	A1	18	D3
7	A2	19	D4
8	A3	20	D5
9	A4	21	D6
10	A5	22	D7 (MSB)
11	A6	23	V_{gg}
12	V_{cc}	24	V_{ss}

Signal functions

A0 – A8	Address inputs
D0 – D7	Data outputs (used as inputs for programming)
CS	Chip select (active low)
R/W	Read–write control input (read mode low)
WE	Write enable input (active high)
PROG	Programming pulse input
V_{bb}, V_{cc}, V_{dd}, V_{gg}, V_{ss}	Power supply inputs

Power requirements

Intel 2704 type (Read mode)

V_{dd}	+12 V ± 5%
V_{cc}	+5 V ± 5%
V_{bb}	−5 V ± 5%
V_{ss}	0 V
Power dissipation	800 mW max.

National MM5204Q type (Read mode)

V_{cc}	+5 V ± 5%
V_{gg}	−12 V ± 5%
V_{ss}	0 V
Power dissipation	750 mW max.

Temperature range

Intel 2704	0°C to +70°C
National MM5204Q	0°C to +70°C

Erasure

Both types are erased by using short wave UV light exposure through the quartz window in the lid of the package.

Read mode operation

Intel 2704 type

For the reading mode the PROG pin is connected to V_{ss} and the CE input is set at '0' logic level. Normal logic level address signals are applied to lines A0 – A8 and data will be output on lines D0 – D7. The memory is static in operation and when an address has been applied the corresponding data output will appear after a short access delay time. For the 2704 memory the access time is a maximum of 450 ns.

National MM5204Q type

For reading with a 5204 type the PROG pin is connected to V_{cc} and both the R/W and CE inputs are set to the '0' level. The operation of the 5204 is completely static so

512 × 8 BIT nMOS ERASABLE PROM

that when an address is applied to lines A0 – A8 the corresponding data will appear at the D0 – D7 outputs after an access time of 750 ns maximum.

Programming

Intel 2704 type

Initially, or after erasure by UV light, all of the bits in the memory will be set in the '1' state. During the programming process selected bits will be set to the '0' state.

For programming the CE/WS pin must be connected to the +12 V line and a series of +26 V amplitude pulses will be fed into the PROG input. Each location is addressed in sequence and the desired data are set up on the data lines D0 – D7, which now become inputs. A single programming pulse is then applied. This process is repeated for all addresses with one pulse per step. Each complete pass through the memory is called a loop and a number of passes will be needed to fully program the memory. The number of passes needed depends on the width of the program pulse and can be calculated from $n = 100/t$, where t is pulse width in ms. Thus for a 1 ms wide pulse 100 passes will be required.

National MM5204Q type

Initially and after an erasure all of the bits in a 5204 are set at the '0' state. During programming a '1' state will be selectively programmed into the desired bits of the memory.

For programming the R/W line is set at V_{cc} and −50 V pulses are applied to the PROG input. Data and addresses are applied as normal logic level signals. The number of pulses needed for each data word is given by $n = 60/t$, where t is the width of the program pulse in ms.

2708 SERIES 8192 BIT nMOS ERASABLE PROM

Possibly the most widely used erasable read only memory is the 2708 type, which is organised as 1024 words each 8 bits wide. This arrangement is particularly convenient for use in microcomputer systems with 8 or 16 bit wide data buses. The 2708 device may be erased by using UV light.

The standard version of the 2708 requires 3 power supply rails. This may be inconvenient in many systems where the microprocessor itself requires only a +5 V supply. Several manufacturers now produce a version of the 2708 which will operate from a single +5 V supply rail, and the Intel 2758 is typical of these devices. The single supply versions, although pin compatible with the 2708 for address and data signals, are not a direct replacement for the standard 2708 since the other pins are used slightly differently. With some minor wiring modifications, however, a standard 2708 may be replaced by the single supply version.

Typical applications of the 2708 are as program memory for a microcomputer system and as a look up table memory or data conversion device. The 2708 is particularly useful for prototype development of microprocessor based systems and for small scale production where it would be uneconomical to use a mask programmed memory.

Device type codes

Advanced Micro Devices
  Am2708, Am9708

Electronic Arrays
  EA2708

Fairchild
  2708, F68708

Hitachi
  HN462708

Intel Corporation
  2708, 2708L, 8708
  2758 single supply type

Fujitsu
  MB8518

Mitsubishi
  M5L2708

Motorola
  MCM2708, MCM68708

National
  MM2708
  MM2758 single supply type

OKI Semiconductor
  MSM2708AS
  MSM2758AS single supply

SGS-ATES
  M2708

Signetic
  2708

Texas Instruments
  TMS2708, TMS27L08
  TMS2508 single supply

Toshiba
  TMM322

Package

24-pin dual in line with quartz window
May be plastic or ceramic
Some AMD types have sapphire lids

Pin connections

Standard 2708

1	A7	13	D4
2	A6	14	D5
3	A5	15	D6
4	A4	16	D7
5	A3	17	D8
6	A2	18	PROG
7	A1	19	V_{dd}
8	A0	20	CS
9	D1	21	V_{bb}
10	D2	22	A9
11	D3	23	A8
12	V_{ss}	24	V_{cc}

2758 Single supply type

1	A7	13	D4
2	A6	14	D5
3	A5	15	D6
4	A4	16	D7
5	A3	17	D8
6	A2	18	CE
7	A1	19	AR
8	A0	20	OE
9	D1	21	V_{pp}
10	D2	22	A9
11	D3	23	A8
12	V_{ss}	24	V_{cc}

Signal functions

A0 – A9	Address inputs
D1 – D8	Data outputs (inputs for programming)
PROG	Program pulse input
CE	Chip enable/program pulse input
OE	Output enable (active low)
AR	Input selects input reference level
CS	Chip select input (active low)
V_{bb}, V_{cc}, V_{dd}, V_{ss}	Power supply inputs

All logical signals inputs and outputs of the devices in the normal read mode are TTL compatible and data outputs will drive one standard TTL load.

Power requirements

Standard 2708 type

V_{cc}	+5 V ± 5%
V_{dd}	+12 V ± 5%
V_{bb}	−5 V ± 5%
Supply current I_{dd}	50 mA
I_{bb}	30 mA
I_{cc}	6 mA

The low power versions 2708L and 27L08 take approximately one third of the supply current values for the 2708.

Single supply type

V_{cc}	+5 V ± 5%
V_{ss}	0 V
Supply current	50 – 60 mA

This type has a power down mode selected by setting the CE input at V_{cc}. In this mode typical current is 10 mA.

Temperature range

Standard types	0°C to +70°C
Military types	−55°C to +125°C

These devices are normally coded with an M as either a suffix or prefix to the type number, e.g. Intel MD2708, Motorola MCM2708M and National MM2708M.

Programming

The 2708 or 2758 device will initially, or after erasure, have all bits of the memory set at the '1' state. During programming selected cells are set to the '0' state by the application of high voltage pulses. When set at the '0' state the memory cell holds an electrical charge which will be retained indefinitely under normal conditions.

The technique required for programming varies from one manufacturer to another, although all follow basically the same pattern. Although a common programming technique may be used, in some PROM programmer systems it may not be totally effective with some makes of device and the manufacturer's data sheet should be consulted regarding programming requirements. As a guide details are given for the Intel type devices.

2708 type programming

The CS input is set at +12 V. Address and data information are then applied in sequence to the appropriate pins and whilst the address and data for each word are stable a +25 V programming pulse is applied to the PROG input line.

The programming pulse width may be from 100 μs to 1 ms. For a 1 ms pulse the complete memory must be scanned at least 100 times. For a 100 μs wide pulse at least 1000 scans will be required to ensure complete programming. In microprocessor based programming systems it is common practice to use a 400 μs wide programming pulse and 256 scans through the memory. Note that with the 2708 it is not possible to program individual cells or words.

2758 single supply types

For this type of PROM the OE line is set at +5 V and V_{pp} is set at +25 V ± 1 V. Data and address signals are applied to the appropriate pins to select the word to be programmed and a 50 ms wide TTL level pulse is applied to the CE input. This pulse goes from the '0' level to the '1' level. Individual words may be programmed in any sequence, with one program pulse being applied to enter the data into the memory. To prevent damage to the device it is essential that V_{cc} should be present before the V_{pp} level is raised to +25 V and remain on until after the V_{pp} level has been reduced to 0 V. Data and address must be stable during the programming pulse and typical address set up time is 2 μs.

Timing

The 2708 and 2758 are static memories and therefore during the read mode no clock signals are required. The address is set up and after an access time period the output data will be stable. For the standard 2708 the access time is 450 ns. Access time for the single supply types is also 450 ns. Some higher speed versions of the 2708 and 2758 are available:

Standard 2708 types

300 ns access time
Motorola   MCM27A08, MCM68A708

350 ns access time
Intel   2708-1
National   MM2708-1
Texas   TMS2708-35

Single supply types

175 ns access time
Texas   TMS2508-20

250 ns access time
Texas   TMS2508-25

300 ns access time
Texas   TMS2508-30

2716 SERIES 16k BIT ERASABLE PROM

The 2716 type ROM is organised as 2048 × 8 bit words and is well suited for use with microprocessor systems having 8 or 16-bit data bus systems. The 2716 memory may be erased by using UV light and may be electrically programmed in the field.

Although the standard version of the 2716 operates from a single +5 V power supply there are some versions which need 3 separate power rails similar to those for the 2708 type. Texas Instruments use the type number 2516 for their single supply version and 2716 for the triple supply type. It seems likely that the older triple supply types will slowly disappear, leaving the single supply type as standard for all manufacturers.

Typical applications for the 2716 are as the program memory for small microcomputer systems and as a large look up table or code conversion device such as a custom character generator. It is particularly useful for prototype systems and for custom equipment where only small numbers are produced and a mask programmed ROM would be uneconomical. Some types of single-chip microcomputer device have a piggyback socket on the device package to accept a 2716 type PROM.

Device type codes

Advanced Micro Devices
  Am2716

American Microsystems
  S2716

Electronic Arrays
  EA2716, EA2716M

Fairchild
  F2716

Fujitsu
  MBM2716

Hitachi
  HN462716

Intel Corporation
  2716, M2716

ITT Semiconductors
  2716

Mitsubishi
  M5L2716

Mostek
  MK2716

Motorola
  MCM2716
  TM2716 triple supply type

National
  MM2716, MM2716M

N.E.C
  μPD2716

OKI Semiconductor
  MSM2716

Panasonic
  MN2716

Signetics
  2716

Synertek
  SY2716

Texas Instruments
  TMS2516
  TMS2716 triple supply type

Toshiba
  TMM323

Thomson EFCIS
  EF2716

Package

24-pin dual in line type with quartz window in the lid for UV erasure. Usually ceramic type

Pin connections

Standard 2716 type

1	A7	13	D3
2	A6	14	D4
3	A5	15	D5
4	A4	16	D6
5	A3	17	D7
6	A2	18	CE
7	A1	19	A10
8	A0	20	OE
9	D0	21	V_{pp}
10	D1	22	A9
11	D2	23	A8
12	V_{ss}	24	V_{cc}

TMS2716 triple supply type

1	A7	13	D3
2	A6	14	D4
3	A5	15	D5
4	A4	16	D6
5	A3	17	D7
6	A2	18	CS
7	A1	19	V_{dd}
8	A0	20	A10
9	D0	21	V_{bb}
10	D1	22	A9
11	D2	23	A8
12	V_{ss}	24	V_{cc}

2716 SERIES 16k BIT ERASABLE PROM

Signal functions

A0 – A10	Address inputs
D0 – D7	Data outputs for read – tri-state
	Data inputs for programming
CE	Chip enable (active low)
OE	Output enable (active low)
V_{pp}	Programming voltage input
CS	Chip select (active low)
V_{bb}, V_{cc}, V_{dd}, V_{ss}	Power supply inputs

Power requirements

Standard 2716
V_{cc}	+5 V ± 5%
V_{ss}	0 V
Supply current	60 mA
Standby mode supply current (CE='1')	10 mA

Triple supply type
V_{cc}	+5 V ± 5%
V_{bb}	−5 V ± 5%
V_{dd}	+12 V ± 5%
V_{ss}	0 V
Power consumption	720 mW max.

Temperature range

Standard type 0°C to +70°C
Types for military temperature range −55°C to +125°C are available with prefix or suffix M in type number, e.g. M2716

Signal levels

All inputs and outputs are TTL compatible signals. The output lines are tri-state with a capability of driving one standard TTL load.

Programming

For the standard 2716 the programming system is similar to that for the 2758 type. The OE line is set at +5 V and V_{pp} is raised to +25 V ± 1 V. Data and address signals are applied to the appropriate pins to select the word data that are to be programmed and a 50 ms wide pulse is applied to the CE input. This pulse has standard TTL levels and goes from '0' to '1'. Words may be programmed in any sequence, with a single programming pulse being used to enter each data word.

Precautions must be taken to ensure that V_{cc} is always applied before V_{pp} and held on until V_{pp} has been removed or set to 0 V. Data and address must be stable during the period of the program pulse, and typically the address and data set up delays are 2 μs.

The triple supply version is programmed in a similar way to the 2708, and manufacturer's data sheets should be consulted for details of this procedure.

Timing

The 2716 type memory is static operation and requires only that the address for the desired data be applied. Typical access time before data becomes valid after an address is set up will be 450 ns.

Some manufacturers also produce higher speed versions of the 2716. Details are:

350 ns access time

Intel 2716-1
Mostek 2716-6
Motorola MCM27A16
Texas TMS2516-35
Other makes use the 2716-1 designation

390 ns access time

Hitachi HN462716-2
Intel 2716-2
Mostek MK2716-7
Other makes use the 2716-2 designation

2532/2732 TYPE 32k BIT ERASABLE PROM

The 2532 and 2732 read only memories are arranged as 4096 words of 8 bits each. The two types are not pin compatible with one another, although both are in the same size package and both types are erasable by UV light.

Typical applications for these devices are as program memory for microprocessor systems and as large size data look up tables such as character or pattern generators. Both types are pin compatible with their suppliers' mask ROMs, and may be used as prototyping devices before the production of a mask programmed ROM.

Device type codes

Advanced Micro Devices
  Am2732

Fujitsu
  MBM2732

Hitachi
  HN462532
  HN462732

Intel Corporation
  2732

Motorola
  MCM2532

National
  MM2532

N.E.C.
  µPD2732

OKI Semiconductor
  MSM2532AS
  MSM2732AS

Texas
  TMS2532

Toshiba
  TMM2732

Package

24-pin dual in line with quartz window in lid for erasure

Pin connections

2532 type

1	A7	13	D3
2	A6	14	D4
3	A5	15	D5
4	A4	16	D6
5	A3	17	D7
6	A2	18	A11
7	A1	19	A10
8	A0	20	CE/PROG
9	D0	21	V_{pp}
10	D1	22	A9
11	D2	23	A8
12	V_{ss}	24	V_{cc}

2732 type

1	A7	13	D3
2	A6	14	D4
3	A5	15	D5
4	A4	16	D6
5	A3	17	D7
6	A2	18	CE/PROG
7	A1	19	A10
8	A0	20	OE/V_{pp}
9	D0	21	A11
10	D1	22	A9
11	D2	23	A8
12	V_{ss}	24	V_{cc}

Signal functions

A0 – A11	Address inputs
D0 – D7	Data outputs (read mode) tri-state
	Data inputs (programming mode)
CE	Chip enable (active low) input when $V_{pp} = 0$ V
PROG	Programming pulse (active low) when $V_{pp} = +25$ V
OE	Output enable (active low)
V_{pp}	Programming supply (0 V read mode) (+25 V program mode)
V_{cc}, V_{ss}	Power supply inputs

When CE is high and V_{pp} is at 0 V the chip operates in a low power standby mode with high impedance outputs.

All input and output signals are TTL compatible and the output lines will drive one standard TTL load.

Power requirements

Both types

V_{cc}	+5 V ± 5%
V_{ss}	0 V
Supply current	85 mA
Standby mode supply current	15 mA

Temperature range

All types   0°C to +70°C

Programming

When erased the 2532 or 2732 device will have all bits set at the '1' state. During programming bits may be set to '0', but once set may only be changed by complete erasure of the device.

For programming a +25 V supply is applied to V_{pp} and normal address and data signals are applied to select the memory location and desired data pattern. A programming pulse going from the high to low logic levels and having a length of approximately 50 ms is then applied to the CE/PROG input to enter the data word into the memory. Words may be written into the memory in any sequence as desired and one program pulse will be required for each word entered. The V_{cc} supply must be present before application of the +25 V to V_{pp} and must remain present until after the V voltage is removed or reduced to +5 V.

For the normal read mode of operation V_{pp} is set at +5 V for the 2532 and at the low logic level (logic '0') for the 2732.

Timing

The 2532 and 2732 type memories are of static type and will require only the application of an address to produce the selected data output. Typical access time for stable output data after an address has been applied is 450 ns.

64k BIT DYNAMIC RAM

A number of manufacturers now produce a 64k bit RAM, using dynamic memory cells and nMOS fabrication. Unlike some of the smaller memories a more or less standard package and pin layout have been adopted. Some manufacturers such as Mostek and Motorola, however, make use of pin 1 for a refresh function, whilst other types generally leave this pin open to ensure compatibility with possible future 256k bit types in a similar size package. All types use a multiplexed addressing system similar to that adopted for standard 16k bit dynamic RAMs.

Device type codes

Inmos
  IMS2600

Hitachi
  HM4864

Motorola
  MCM6664

National
  NMC4164

N.E.C.
  µPD4164

Texas
  TMS4164

Toshiba
  TMM4164

Package

16-pin dual in line type

Pin connections

1	*	9	A7
2	D_{in}	10	A5
3	WR	11	A4
4	RAS	12	A3
5	A0	13	A6
6	A2	14	D_{out}
7	A1	15	CAS
8	V_{cc}	16	V_{ss}

Signal functions

A0 – A7	Multiplexed address inputs
D_{in}	Data input
D_{out}	Data output
WR	Read–write control input (write low)
CAS	Column address strobe input (active low)
RAS	Row address strobe input (active low)
*	Pin 1 is used by some makers for a refresh function
V_{cc}, V_{ss}	Power supply inputs

All inputs and outputs are TTL compatible and are diode protected against static charges.

Power requirements

V_{cc}	+5 V ± 10%
V_{ss}	0 V
Power dissipation	300 mW approx.
Low power standby mode	20 mW

Temperature range

0°C to +70°C

Addressing

The address for these 64k bit dynamic RAMs is applied in much the same way as the multiplexed address for a 16k dynamic RAM. The row address is applied first and is latched into the memory by a falling edge on the RAS line. Then the column address is applied and latched in by the falling edge of the CAS line. Data will be output shortly after the falling edge of the CAS signal, and may be maintained by holding CAS low. During write operations data must be stable before the CAS signal goes low.

Refresh

This type of memory will normally need to be refreshed every 2 ms and requires 128 refresh cycles. Refreshing is achieved by either reading or writing to all row addresses or by just applying the RAS strobes with an incrementing address.

Timing

Access times of some of the available types are:
  100 ns µPD4164-2, TMS4164-10, MK4164-10
  150 ns HM4864-2, NMC4164, MCM6664-15, µPD4164-1, TMS4164-15, TMM4164
  200 ns HM4864-3, MCM6664-20
  250 ns MCM6664-25

9 PERIPHERAL DEVICE CONTROLLERS

VISUAL DISPLAY CONTROLLERS

Visual display systems for use with microcomputers generally make use of video techniques where the text, or graphics, data are presented on a raster scan display similar to that used for television pictures. Fig. 9.1 shows a block diagram of the basic logic used to generate such a display.

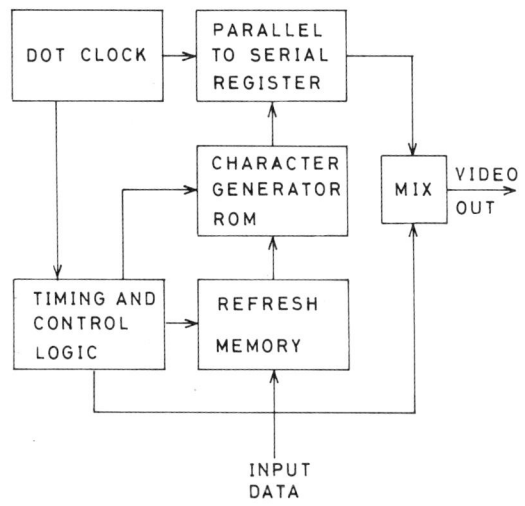

Fig. 9.1

The display area on the television screen is divided up into an array of rectangular segments arranged in columns and rows. Each segment contains one displayed text symbol. In order to produce a stable and flicker free display the entire area of the screen is scanned some 50 or 60 times every second. Data representing the entire display, with one data byte for each text symbol, are held in a display memory and read out in sequence as the display on the screen is traced out.

For text each symbol is built up from a matrix of illuminated dots, the individual dot patterns being held in a read only memory (ROM) and called up as required during the display scan. The dot pattern for each symbol is output one line at a time in parallel and is transferred to a shift register to be converted into a serial stream of pulses which will form the video signal. The video pulses are then combined with synchronisation pulses to produce a composite television video signal which may be used to drive a normal television monitor.

Apart from text displays some systems also provide high resolution graphics displays and may also present information in colour. The logic system required for a video display is quite complex, but several special integrated circuits have been developed to provide some or all of the logic needed for generating such a display.

For broadcast colour television the R, G and B signals are encoded to form a luminance (Y) or brightness component and two colour difference or chrominance signals (R–Y and B–Y), thus giving compatibility with monochrome receivers. Three different encoding standards are in common use.

The North American 525 line system uses NTSC coding. In this the chrominance signals are quadrature amplitude modulated onto a 3.58 MHz subcarrier which is added to the Y signal. For Europe the French system is SECAM, in which the chrominance signals are frequency modulated onto a 4.43 MHz subcarrier and multiplexed on alternate scan lines. Thus one scan carries the R–Y signal and the next the B–Y and so on. In the other European system, called PAL, the chrominance is dealt with in a similar fashion to that of NTSC, but the phase of the R–Y signal is reversed on alternate scan lines. Both PAL and SECAM are designed to overcome colour errors in NTSC which can be caused by phase shifts in the chrominance signals.

Some types of video display processor chips can produce the encoded luminance and chrominance signals, and will often be designed for either NTSC or PAL type coding. Colour can of course be added to any display system by the addition of some extra video processing circuitry.

Page format

One of the more popular display layouts has 24 or 25 rows of 40 characters and is commonly used for teletext and videotex systems. Other frequently used screen formats are 24 × 80, 16 × 64 and 16 × 32. Many video display controllers have a programmable page format allowing a wide range of row and column combinations to be selected.

Character generation

For text displays the symbols are built up by selectively lighting up dots in a small matrix which fills the character space on the screen. Typical dot formats are 5 wide by 7 or 8 lines high, 7 × 9, 6 × 10 or 7 × 16.

The dot patterns for the set of displayable symbols are stored in a ROM called a *character generator*. It is usual to apply the binary code representing the symbol as an address to the ROM to select the desired pattern of dots. By applying a row address a set of dots for one row of the symbol matrix will be output in parallel from the ROM. This dot pattern is then loaded into a shift register and converted into a serial stream of pulses for the video signal. Symbols are selected one after another as the scan progresses across the screen and then the whole process is repeated over the next few scans to build up the row of text.

Some display controllers contain a character generator ROM and a few have serial dot output, although most types will require a shift register to produce the serial pulses for the video signal. Other types will merely provide the row address for the character generator ROM whilst the symbol data will come from the display memory.

Character generators provide either a 64-character set with upper case letters only, or a 96-character set including the lower case letters. Some types may also include special symbols, Greek letters and graphics patterns.

Display memory

The data for a complete screenful of text or graphics must be readily available as the image is traced out. To achieve this it is stored in a fast read–write memory (RAM). Address and control signals for this memory are provided by the video display controller. The memory itself will sometimes be part of the main memory of the microprocessor system and will be multiplexed between the processor and display as required. In this way the display system normally controls the memory, but the processor can take control in order to insert new data.

For a typical 40 × 24 display the display memory will have 960 bytes for the displayed page. Some controllers can handle several pages of memory and will effectively display a page from the complete memory.

Graphics displays

Three basic approaches may be adopted for displaying graphics on the screen. For low resolution displays the mosaic graphics technique may be used. Here each text character space is divided up into 4 or 6 segments arranged as two columns with two or three rows. The segment patterns are stored in a ROM in the same way as text symbol dot patterns and displayed by the same process as for text symbols. In many cases the mosaic graphics patterns are merely treated as extra symbols in the displayable character set.

For high resolution graphics the screen area is divided up into a large array of dots, with perhaps 256 rows and 256 dots per row. Each dot may be individually selected and set on or off. In a typical system each byte in the display memory would represent 8 successive dots along a scan line. For a 256 × 256 dot display the memory would need to have 8 kbyte. In a typical system successive bytes would be called up from memory and passed in parallel to a shift register for conversion to a serial video pattern. For colour, or multilevel brightness, a set of perhaps 2–4 bits might be allocated to each dot. In this case either a lower resolution is used or a larger memory will be needed. Colour may, of course, be achieved by using three separate display memories for R, G and B.

A third approach which can give high resolution with a smaller memory requirement is to store small graphics patterns of perhaps the size of a text symbol and to call these up in much the same way as a text symbol is called up. With such a scheme it may be possible to display the pattern at any point on the screen, but memory is required only for that pattern. A variation on this theme is the *sprite technique* used in the TMS9918. Here the memory is divided into a series of planes, each of which may contain a small pattern. These patterns are called up and superimposed to form the final video signal. Such a system readily allows various animation schemes, since the location of a sprite can readily be moved around the screen.

In graphics displays using luminance and chrominance coding schemes the resolution in colour may be limited by the bandwidth of the encoding scheme. For most high resolution colour graphics direct R, G, B, video drive is normally used.

Some graphics devices, such as the Thomson EF9365, have facilities for drawing lines between two points on the screen, with internal logic selecting the dots to be lit to produce the desired line. This type of device may also draw text symbols rotated through 45° or 90° from normal.

Cursor

In virtually all video displays a cursor may be used to show where the next symbol to be inserted into the memory will be displayed on the screen. The cursor may be a flashing block, an underline or a symbol in reverse video. Normally a cursor will move automatically to the next position as each symbol is inserted. Provision may be made for moving the cursor up, down, left and right by using control codes. Cursor location is stored as the address in display memory where the next input data will be written. Control codes may also be used to turn the cursor display on or off as desired.

Scrolling

Simple controllers provide a single page display in which the input data written after the end of the bottom line of the display will often be written over old data at the top of the display. This is referred to as *wrap around*.

Many systems provide scrolling, where when the data run off the bottom of the display the existing data are moved up by one row and the new data written into the bottom row. Thus the display acts like a paper scroll and this technique is called *scrolling*. In simple systems data pushed off the top of the screen will be lost. Where the system supports a number of pages it may be possible to scroll both up and down through the available pages of memory, thus providing a window into the complete display memory.

Apart from scrolling the multipage systems may allow page turning to an earlier or later page in the memory.

Scan standards

Since television display units are readily available the scan standards used for video display units are normally based upon existing television broadcast standards. Two such standards are in common use.

For North America and Japan the U.S. television system uses 525 horizontal scan lines to build up the picture and has 30 complete pictures per second using interlaced scanning. In order to reduce flicker in the display image the complete scan is divided into two successive field scans. During the first field the odd numbered scan lines are traced out and spread apart to fill the screen. On the following scan the even lines are traced out in the spaces between the lines of the first field. This gives 60 field scans per second, reducing flicker without increasing video signal bandwidth.

The alternative scan system used by most other countries is the international CCIR standard. This has 625 scan lines and 50 fields per second, with interlaced scanning, to give a total of 25 complete pictures or frames per second.

Some special types of display may use up to 1000 lines to provide very large amounts of text information. There are a few types in which the scan lines are traced out in a vertical direction.

Video output

The video signal needed to produce a television display has white represented by 100% signal level and black by 30%. The signal below the black level is used for synchronisation pulses, which extend down to the 0% level. A synchronisation pulse is inserted at the start of each scan line and a wider pulse or a group of pulses is used for field synchronisation at the start of each vertical scan. These pulses ensure a stable display on the screen.

The text or graphics video signal is a series of pulses, which are combined with the synchronisation pulses to produce a composite video signal. In some cases this video signal is used to modulate a radio frequency carrier signal, so that a standard television receiver may be used as a video display.

All video display controller devices will generate the sync pulse pattern and the basic system timing and control logic will also be provided. Some types may also produce the dot patterns representing text or graphics and simply require a combiner circuit to produce video output. Most types will require separate video logic to produce the dot pattern and the composite video. In some more advanced types the timing of the scanning and number of lines are programmable.

Colour displays

For colour displays 3 separate signals for red, blue and green are generated and used to drive the 3 electron guns of a colour television tube. In some systems 3 separate display memories, one for each colour, may be used with 3 video signal circuits to produce R, G and B outputs. In other arrangements 3 extra data bits may be added to the data for each text or graphics symbol, one for each colour, and these are used to switch the video signal through to the R, G and B outputs as required to select the colour for each text symbol.

Video attributes

In many display systems it is possible to allocate attributes such as inverse video, flashing symbols or double height, to individual characters or groups of characters on the screen. Typical attributes are, flashing, inverse video, double width, double height, half brilliance, highlight (extra bright) and protected. Protected areas do not allow new text to be written into the memory unless the protection attribute is removed.

Attributes may be encoded serially or in parallel. In the serial mode a control code is input in front of the text to which the attribute applies and a second control code may be used to reset the attribute. In such cases the control code may occupy one character space on the screen. In the parallel mode extra bits are allocated to each symbol code in the memory and these bits will define the attributes of the symbol with which they are associated.

Other features

Some types of video display controller provide facilities for using a light pen. In this type of system the light pen is a photocell which is placed on the screen so that it picks up light from part of the display. A pulse from the photocell is used to store the current display memory address at that point in the display scan, which will indicate the point in memory corresponding to the position of the light pen.

Controllers for video game applications may include a sound generator and moving object logic.

MOTOROLA MC6845

The Motorola MC6845 is a CRT display controller which provides the control and timing logic for a VDU, but it does require an external character generator ROM, screen refresh memory and video signal circuits. Although designed primarily for use with processors such as the 6800 and 6500 series, it could also be used with other microprocessors by using suitable interface circuits.

Prime manufacturer

Motorola Semiconductor Inc. MC6845

Alternative source devices

American Microsystems
  S6845, S68045

Fairchild
  F6845

Hitachi
  HD46505

Rockwell
  R6545

Synertek
  SY6545

Thomson EFCIS
  EF6845

Package

40-pin dual in line ceramic or plastic
Suffix L is ceramic suffix P for plastic

Pin connections

1	V_{ss}	21	CLK
2	RESET	22	R/W
3	LPST	23	E
4	MA0	24	RS
5	MA1	25	CS
6	MA2	26	D7
7	MA3	27	D6
8	MA4	28	D5
9	MA5	29	D4
10	MA6	30	D3
11	MA7	31	D2
12	MA8	32	D1
13	MA9	33	D0
14	MA10	34	RA4
15	MA11	35	RA3
16	MA12	36	RA2
17	MA13	37	RA1
18	DE	38	RA0
19	CSR	39	HS
20	V_{cc}	40	VS

Signal functions

D0 – D7	Data bus bidirectional
MA0 – MA13	Memory address outputs
DE	Display enable output
CSR	Cursor output
LPST	Light pen strobe input
RESET	Reset input (Active low)
RA0–RA4	Row address outputs to character generator
HS	Horizontal sync output
VS	Vertical sync output
R/W	Read–write control input (write low)
CLK	Character clock input
E	System clock input ($\phi 2$ from 6800 CPU)
RS	Register select
CS	Chip select (active low)
V_{cc}, V_{ss}	Power supply inputs

All inputs and outputs are TTL compatible and the outputs will drive one TTL load. Inputs are high impedance MOS type, and are diode protected.

Power requirements

V_{cc}	+5 V ± 5%
V_{ss}	0 V
Supply current	120 mA approx.

Temperature range

0°C to +70°C

Scan standard

The MC6845 is fully programmable for number of lines and the timing of each line. It will handle both 525 and 625 line standards by suitable programming. Either interlaced or non-interlaced scanning may be programmed.

Video output

Not provided. External circuits must be used to produce the video signal, but horizontal and vertical sync timing pulses are provided.

Colour

Not available.

Page format

The MC6845 is fully programmable for up to 128 rows of text, with up to 256 characters in each row. This permits up to 16384 characters to be displayed on the screen area. The number of scan lines for each row of text is also programmable, up to a total of 32 lines.

Character generation

An external character generator ROM is required. Five address outputs RA0 – RA4 permit row selection in the character ROM matrix.

Refresh memory

An external refresh memory of up to 16k words may be used. A 14-line address output is provided for the refresh memory. Part of this total memory may be used for the screen display if desired.

Cursor

An output is provided which goes high when the scan passes through the cursor position. This may be used to control the generation of the cursor video signal in external logic. The cursor address within the memory space is held in two of the internal registers of the 6845, and may be programmed as desired.

Scrolling

In the 6845 scrolling is controlled by software and may be by character or row, either up or down through the memory. This is achieved by manipulating the start address for the display on the screen.

Other features

A facility is provided for an external light pen. A pulse from the light pen is applied at the LPST input and the current screen memory address is stored within a register pair on the chip to indicate the position of the light pen on the screen.

General

The AMI S68045 is a low cost version of the 6845, in which the internal control registers are mask programmed to give two optional display mode formats. The Synertek and Rockwell type 6545 is basically the same as the 6845, but includes an extra register for status. This is read when the address register has been selected and provides status flags for the light pen, update and vertical blanking logic.

The 6845 contains 32 control registers, which may be selected via a 5-bit address register. The input RS when low allows the address register to be loaded by the CPU, whilst when RS is high the register selected by this address register is accessible for reading or writing by the CPU. In the 6545 when RS is low the status register can be read by the CPU.

The control registers are:

R0 Total character spaces per line
R1 Number of displayed characters per line
R2 Horizontal sync position
R3 Horizontal sync pulse width

These four registers determine number of characters per row and the horizontal scan and sync pulse timing. All are set up as a number of character spaces.

R4	Vertical total. Number of text rows in vertical scan
R5	Vertical adjust. Number of extra scan lines after last text row to make up complete scan
R6	Number of displayed rows of text
R7	Vertical sync position as number of rows from start of scan
R8	Interlace control for interlaced or non-interlaced scan
R9	Number of scan lines per row of text up to 32
R10	Cursor control allows cursor on/off and blinking. Also controls character scan line for start of cursor display
R11	End of cursor display scan line in character row
R12, R13	Start address in memory for displayed text
R14, R15	Cursor position address in refresh memory
R16, R17	Light pen address register

The Synertek 6545 has an additional register pair R18, R19. They are used to indicate the point in the refresh memory that is currently being addressed. This is automatically incremented as data are written into or read from the refresh memory.

The remaining register addresses are not used.

When used in a system the memory address from the 6845 must be multiplexed with the processor address bus before it is used to address the refresh memory. To the CPU this memory appears as part of the main processor memory. Priority may be given to the processor, or the 6845 may be allowed access during $\phi1$ of the CPU clock, thus giving transparent operation.

Graphics using the mosaic technique can be provided by using a suitable character generator ROM.

MOTOROLA MC6847

The Motorola MC6847 Video Display Generator (VDG) provides a complete video display controller for both text and graphics type displays. It provides both luminance and chrominance outputs for colour displays and incorporates a character generator ROM for text symbols. Although primarily designed for use with the 6800 and related processors, it may also be used with other types such as the 6500 series.

Prime manufacturer

Motorola Semiconductor Sync. MC6847, MC6847Y

Alternative source devices

American Microsystems

S68047

Package

40-pin dual in line type plastic or ceramic
Suffix L indicates ceramic and P indicates plastic

Pin connections

1	V_{ss}	21	DA12
2	DD6	22	DA0
3	DD0	23	DA1
4	DD1	24	DA2
5	DD2	25	DA3
6	DD3	26	DA4
7	DD4	27	GM2
8	DD5	28	Y
9	CHB	29	GM1
10	ϕB	30	GM0
11	ϕA	31	INT/EXT
12	MS	32	INV
13	DA5	33	CLK
14	DA6	34	A/S
15	DA7	35	A/G
16	DA8	36	RP
17	V_{cc}	37	FS
18	DA9	38	HS
19	DA10	39	CSS
20	DA11	40	DD7 (MSB)

Signal functions

DD0 – DD7	Data inputs from display memory
DA0 – DA12	Address outputs to display memory
GM0, GM1, GM2	Graphics mode select inputs
MS	Memory select input tri-state control for DA0 – DA12
Y	Luminance output signal
ϕA, ϕB	Chrominance output signals
CLK	Colour subcarrier clock input
CHB	Reference bias output for chroma signals
INV	Inverse text video control input
INT/EXT	Select input for internal/external char. ROM
A/G	Alpha/graphics select input (graphics low)
A/S	Alpha/semigraphics mode input (semigraphics low)
CSS	Colour set select input
HS, FS	Horizontal and field sync outputs
RP	Row preset timing output
V_{cc}, V_{ss}	Power supply inputs

All logical signals into and out of the 6847 are TTL compatible and outputs will drive one TTL load. Inputs are protected by diodes against static.

Power requirements

V_{cc} +5 V ± 5%
V_{ss} 0 V

Temperature range

0°C to +70°C

Scan standard

The MC6847 is designed for the U.S. 525-line TV standard using a non-interlaced display mode. The MC6847Y version provides a fully interlaced display mode.

Video output

A composite luminance output signal with sync pulses of about 0.6 V p–p is provided with sync positive. Chrominance outputs ϕA and ϕB are at matching levels and the CHB output is the nominal mean level of the chrominance signals. Outputs are designed to drive an MC1372 modulator circuit.

Colour

To U.S. NTSC colour standard with 525 lines and 3.38 MHz sub-carrier. Eight colours are available in the semigraphics modes, whilst in the full graphics mode sets of either 2 or 4 colours are available. Text is in one of two alternative colours.

Page format

Alphanumeric format is 16 rows, with 32 symbols per row.

Character generation

An internal character generator ROM provides a set of 64 text symbols, using a 5 × 7 dot matrix within an 8 dot by 12 line display area on the screen. An external character generator may also be used by setting the INT/EXT line high.

Refresh memory

An external refresh memory is required. For alphanumeric mode and semigraphics a 512 byte memory is required. In the full graphics mode a memory of between 1 kbyte and 6 kbyte will be required according to the graphics resolution selected. The 256 × 192 element graphics mode requires 6 kbyte of memory. A multiplexer system will be required for memory address and data lines, to allow the processor to write data to memory and later to allow the VDG to read data from memory to produce a display. Writing may be made transparent by using the FS line output to ensure that all write operations by the CPU occur during field blanking on the display.

Cursor

Not provided.

Scrolling

Not provided.

Other features

The video may be inverted by using the INV input to the 6847 in the alphanumeric mode. This may be controlled by data from the display memory to allow individual symbols to be presented in inverse video.

Graphics modes

The MC6847 provides two semigraphics modes for relatively low resolution graphics, and 8 modes of medium and high resolution graphics.

In the semigraphs 4 mode the character box of a text format display is divided into 4 equal quadrants to give a 2×2 graphics element. Colours are the same as for text and the colour of all elements in each character box is the same. Mode is selected by setting A/S at 1 and INT/EXT at 0.

The semigraphics 6 modes divides each text space into 6 elements, arranged as 3 rows of 2 elements each. This gives an overall graphics resolution on the screen of 64×48. Four colours may be used and two alternative sets of colours may be selected by using the CSS control input. This mode is selected by setting A/S to 1 and INT/EXT to 1.

Four high resolution modes are provided for graphics using a single colour. These are:

Mode 1R 128×64 elements, needs 1k memory
Mode 2R 128×96 elements, needs 1.5k memory
Mode 3R 128×192 elements, needs 3k memory
Mode 4R 256×192 elements, needs 6k memory

Two alternative colours may be selected by using the CSS line.

Four modes of graphics are provided with muticolour capability. They are:

Mode 1C 64×64 elements, needs 1k memory
Mode 2C 128×64 elements, needs 2k memory
Mode 3C 128×96 elements, needs 3k memory
Mode 4C 128×192 elements, needs 6k memory

Two alternative sets of 4 colours may be selected by the CSS input.

High resolution graphics modes are selected by setting A/G at 1 and using GM0, GM1 and GM2 to set the desired mode. GM0 selects colour modes when at 1 and mono modes when at 0. GM1 and GM2 select the mode number with GM1 least significant.

In the graphics modes a border may be set up around the display area and will be in the same colour as the graphics elements.

Note that in the graphics modes the INV, EXT/INT and A/S inputs have no effect.

THOMSON EFCIS EF9365/6

The Thomson EFCIS EF9365 and EF9366 devices are graphics display processors designed to provide both alphanumeric text and high resolution graphics displays on a television screen. An unusual feature of these devices is the provision of a high speed vector plotting ability, and the display of various sizes and orientations of the text symbols.

The 9365/6 devices can be used with any type of microprocessor that will provide 8-bit data.

Prime manufacturer

Thomson EFCIS   EF9365, EF9366

Alternative source devices

None.

Package

40-pin dual in line type
Suffix C indicates ceramic and P indicates plastic

Pin connections

1	CLK	21	LPCK
2	DAD5	22	ALL
3	DAD4	23	WO
4	DAD3	24	WH
5	DAD6	25	BLK
6	MSL0	26	D7
7	MSL2	27	D6
8	FMAT	28	D5
9	A0	29	D4
10	A1	30	D3
11	A2	31	D2
12	A3	32	D1
13	IRQ	33	D0
14	DW	34	SYNC
15	D_{IN}	35	MSL3
16	VB	36	MSL1
17	E	27	DAD0
18	R/W	38	DAD2
19	MFRE	39	DAD1
20	V_{ss}	40	V_{cc}

Signal functions

DAD0 – DAD6	Display memory address outputs
MSL0 – MSL3	Display address outputs
ALL	Display memory address control output
CLK	1.75 MHz clock input
FMAT, WO	Function control inputs
SYNC, BLK, VB	Sync and blanking outputs
D0 – D7	Data inputs
A0 – A3	Register address inputs
D_{IN}, DW, MFRE	Display memory control outputs
R/W	Read–write control (W low)
E	System clock from CPU
IRQ	Interrupt request output
WH, LPCK	Light pen control signals
V_{cc}, V_{ss}	Power supply inputs

All signals are LS/TTL compatible.

Power requirements

V_{cc} +5 V ± 5%
V_{ss} 0 V

Temperature range

0°C to +70°C

Scan standard

This device operates with the CCIR 625-line 50 field per second standard. The EF9365 provides an interlaced scan with up to 512 × 512 graphics elements. The 9366 operates with non-interlaced scanning.

Video output

Not provided. The system will require a parallel-to-serial high speed shift register to convert the display memory output into video signals. The 9365 will provide synchronisation signals for the video processing circuits.

Colour

Not provided.

Page format

Text is treated as graphics symbols, with characters based on a 6 × 8 matrix space. Character size may be programmed over a wide range. Maximum text density on the screen for the EF9365 is 57 rows, with 85 characters per row.

Character generation

Internal character ROM will generate a 96-character set using 7 × 5 dot matrix. Characters may also be displayed tilted through 45° or 90° in either direction. Character size may also be programmed from 1 to 16 times the normal in both the X and Y directions, with independent control of X and Y magnification. Symbols may be placed at any point on the high resolution graphics matrix.

Refresh memory

The display memory is external to the device. For a 512 × 512 graphics display 32 kbyte of memory will be required.

Cursor

Not provided.

Scrolling

Not provided.

Graphics facilities

In the high resolution mode the 9365 has a capability of 512 × 512 elements, whilst the 9366 provides 512 × 256 elements.

Position of the graphics element is governed by X and

Y address registers, which point to the current drawing point on the screen.

Lines are drawn by vector technique, using two registers to indicate the relative X and Y position of the end of the vector to be drawn. Control functions allow the vector to be drawn, left alone or erased. Four types of line may be drawn: solid, dotted, dashed or dot-dash alternately.

For high speed plotting of small vectors an alternative drawing mode may be used. Here the direction of the vector is specified in 45° increments and the length of the line may be specified as one, two or three units.

Text symbols are dealt with using a technique similar to the small vector system, but are governed by the internal character generator so that the data simply specify the desired character code. Text is drawn at the current X, Y writing position on the graphics area. At the end of drawing a text symbol the X, Y position is adjusted automatically to a point ready for another text symbol on the same horizontal or vertical line.

Other facilities

The devices provide facilities for using a light pen.

General

Internally the graphics display processor contains an array of 13 control and data registers which are addressed by a 4-bit register address code. The registers are:

R0   Status (read) Command (write)
R1   Draw/erase control and interrupt control
R2   Line type and symbol orientation control
R3   Character size control
R4   Not used
R5   DELTA X vector drawing control
R6   Not used
R7   DELTA Y vector drawing control
R8   X address most significant bits
R9   X address least significant bits
R10   Y address most significant bits
R11   Y address least significant bits
R12   Light pen X position
R13   Light pen Y position

Registers R14 and R15 are not used.

Text symbols are specified by writing data into the R0 command register.

THOMSON EFCIS 96364

The Thomson EFCIS 96364 is a video display controller which provides the display logic and timing for a text display on a television screen. It may be used with any type of microprocessor system using an 8-bit data bus.

Prime manufacturer

Thomson EFCIS   96364A, 96364B

Alternative source devices

Standard Microsystems
  CRT96364

Package

28-pin dual in line type

Pin connections

1	Q1	15	PT
2	Q0	16	ST
3	RS	17	W
4	A9	18	A0
5	A8	19	A1
6	A7	20	A2
7	A6	21	A3
8	A5	22	A4
9	$\phi 1$	23	C0
10	INI	24	C1
11	RO0	25	C2
12	RO1	26	SYNC
13	RO2	27	RP
14	V_{ss}	28	V_{cc}

Signal functions

A0 – A9	Display memory address outputs
QO0, QO1	Timing crystal inputs
RO0 – RO2	Dot row address output to character generator
C0 – C2	Cursor control inputs
SYNC	Composite line and field sync output
$\phi 1$	Character clock timing input
PT	Cursor output
RS, RP	Page control outputs
W	Memory write control output
INI	End of line clock output
V_{cc}, V_{ss}	Power supply inputs

All signals are TTL compatible.

Power requirements

V_{cc}	+5 V ± 5%
V_{ss}	0 V
Supply current	120 mA

Temperature range

0°C to +70°C

Scan standard

96364A   625 lines, 50 Hz
96364B   525 lines, 60 Hz

Video output

Needs external video logic to produce video signal, but sync signal is output.

Colour

Not provided.

Page format

Displayed page format is 16 lines of 64 characters each. The device can handle up to 4 pages of text stored in the memory, although only one set of 16 lines is displayed.

Character generator

Device needs an external character generator ROM which should have a 5×7 or 6×8 dot matrix.

Refresh memory

Device supports several pages of memory, with each page using 1 kbyte of memory. An external page addressing scheme will be required which is incremented or decremented by the RP and RS control lines.

Cursor

Device provides a cursor position control output and allows full control of cursor position with automatic advance as a character is written into memory.

Scrolling

Device provides automatic scrolling up or down through the complete refresh memory system.

Graphics

Not provided except for mosaic type graphics which may be set up in the external character generator ROM if desired.

General

Refresh memory devices must have an access time of less than 450 ns for proper opration with the 96364.

FLOPPY DISK CONTROLLERS

Perhaps the most popular form of mass data storage for use in microcomputer systems is the floppy disk. The storage medium is a flexible plastic disk coated on one or both sides with a magnetic oxide and enclosed in a cardboard or plastic envelope for protection. The disk remains inside the envelope when in use and access for the read–write heads is provided by a slot in each face of the envelope.

When mounted in its drive unit the disk is rotated at high speed inside its envelope. A magnetic pick up head is brought into contact with it to read or write data in the form of changes in magnetisation of the oxide along a series of concentric tracks. The head is mounted on a carriage so that it can be stepped radially across the disk to move from track to track. When not being used for reading or writing the head is lifted clear of the disk to reduce disk surface wear.

Two popular sizes of floppy disk are available. The 8 in diameter disk is standard and is often referred to as an 8 in diskette. A smaller minifloppy disk, sometimes referred to as a mini-diskette, uses a 5¼ in diameter disk, but gives a smaller storage capacity. This type is commonly used for personal computer systems. The standard 8 in disk normally carries 77 data tracks on its surface, whilst the minifloppy type has 35 tracks. Some disk drives can however record 40 tracks on the minifloppy and 80 on the standard diskette. For more data capacity disks may be recorded on both sides using a special disk drive with twin heads. In fact all diskettes are usually coated on both sides, but those for double sided use are specially prepared and both sides are checked for errors.

Each track on the disk is divided up into a number of sets of data called *sectors*. Two alternative techniques are used to locate individual sectors on a track. First there is the *hard sector system*, which uses a special diskette having a ring of equally spaced small holes punched in it. These holes are sensed by a photocell and lamp system which produces a pulse as each sector starts to pass under the magnetic head. A single separate index hole is used to identify sector 1 on the track and a counter in the disk controller logic may then locate any desired sector on that track by counting pulses from the sector marker holes.

Although hard sector disks are still used, the more common system is the *soft sectored disk* where the sectors are located by using information stored on the data track. This scheme has the advantage that the number of sectors can be programmed by writing the appropriate signals on the track before the disk is used. Once again a single index hole punched through the disk is used to locate the first sector on the track. For a standard diskette there will normally be 15 sectors along a track and each sector will contain 256 bytes of useable data. Alternative formats are 26 sectors of 128 bytes each, or 8 sectors of 512 bytes each. It is also possible to treat the track as a single sector of 4096 bytes. For mini-diskettes it is usual to have 10 sectors of 256 bytes, but alternative data formats are 18 sectors of 128 bytes, 5 sectors of 512 bytes or a single sector of 2048 bytes.

Each sector in a soft sectored disk consists of two sets of information separated by a gap. The first set comprises the identification field which gives the track and sector numbers and the sector length in bytes. The second set of data is the data field, containing the recorded data for that sector. As well as data each of these fields also contains a marker to show which type of record it is (ID or data), and some error check data for error detection and possibly correction. Each sector is separated from the next by a gap containing timing pulses. On the larger disks there is a short block of data called the *index address mark* written at the start of the track just after the index hole has been detected. This is used to prevent possible erasure of data on the first sector of a track when the last sector of the track is being written. This mark is not included on the mini-diskette.

Data are written on the track as a serial stream of pulses using a phase encoded technique. Some disk systems are designed to record double density data using a modified FM signal and will give double capacity from the disk. Most controllers can handle single density only, but newer designs can be switched for either single or double density and may also handle single or double sided disks. Amplification and signal conditioning of the recorded data are normally carried out in the disk drive unit and the controller system merely handles logic level signals.

The logic required to control a floppy disk system is complex. Early controllers consisted of a large array of discrete logic or even a microcomputer system. In fact the CPU of the computer system could handle disk control, but it is usual to offload this task to a specialised controller chip, of which a number of types are now available. Because of the complex operation of such chips it is recommended that the manufacturer's data sheet be consulted for detailed information. Here we give brief details of a number of available types to assist in choosing a potentially suitable type.

DISK CONTROLLER DATA

Intel 8271
Also made by Siemens (SAB8271). Soft sector single density (FM) for single or double side disks with one or two drives. Supply +5 V. 40-pin DIL package. Matched to 8085 and similar bus system.

Motorola MC6843
Also made by Hitachi (HD46503), Fairchild (F6843), EFCIS (EF6843). Soft sector single density (FM) for single side disks with one drive. Up to 4 drives with external multiplexer. Supply +5 V. Package 40-pin DIL. Matched to 6800 type microprocessor bus.

Motorola MC6849
Soft sector dual density (FM/MFM) for single or double side disks with one drive. Supply +5 V. 40-pin DIL package. Matched to 6800 type microprocessor bus system.

N.E.C. µPD372
Soft sector single density (FM) for single side disks with up to 4 drives. Package 42-pin DIL. Supply +5 V, +12 V. Designed for use with 8080 microprocessor or similar bus system.

N.E.C. µPD765
Soft sector dual density (FM/MFM) for single or double side disks with up to 4 drives. Multi-sector and multi-track data transfers. Package 40-pin DIL. Supply +5 V. Designed for 8080, 8085, Z80 or similar bus systems.

National INS82891 and INS82893
Soft sector dual density (FM/MFM) for single or dual side disks with one drive. Package 40-pin DIL. Supply +5 V. This device is similar to the Western Digital WD1791. Data on bus are inverted. INS82893 has non-inverted bus data.

Standard Microsystems SMC3400HSDH
Hard sector dual density (FM/MFM) for up to 2 drives. Package 40-pin DIL. Supply +5 V, −12 V.

Standard Microsystems SMC7003
Soft sector dual density (FM/MFM) for up to 4 drives. Package 40-pin DIL. Supply +5 V.

Signetics 8X330
Soft sector dual density (FM/MFM) for up to 4 drives. Designed for use with the 8X300 microprocessor.

Texas Instruments TMS9909
Soft or hard sector single density (FM) for up to 4 drives. Package 40-pin DIL. Supply +5 V. Designed for use with the 9900 series microprocessors and microcomputers.

Western Digital WD1771
Also made by National (INS1771). Soft sector single density (FM) for up to 4 disk drives. Package 40-pin DIL. Supply +5 V, +12 V. Designed for use with 8080 and similar microprocessors.

Western Digital WD1790 series
Also made by Synertek (SY1791, SY6591). WD1791 and WD1793 are soft sector dual density (FM/MFM) for single or double side disks with a single drive. The 1791 has inverted data on the bus lines, whilst the 1793 has normal data. Package 40-pin DIL. Supply +5 V. Designed to work with any microprocessor system.

The Synertek SY6591 is a version of the 1791 which has been matched to the 6500 series microprocessor bus system.

WD1792 and WD1794 are soft sector single density (FM) types for single or double side disks with one drive. Supply +5 V. Package 40-pin DIL. Designed to work with any bus system. The 1794 has normal data and the 1792 has inverted data.

10 OTHER SUPPORT DEVICES

Apart from the peripheral device controllers and memory chips there are a number of other types of support device used in building up a microcomputer system. Among these are timers, event counters and various combination devices which may contain RAM, ROM, input–output ports and perhaps a timer. These combination chips are designed to be used with a basic CPU chip to form a 2-chip computer system. A typical case is the 6802 CPU and the 6846 combination chip. There are many applications where analogue input and output are required and suitable conversion devices are available for this purpose. Various clock generator devices, bus buffer circuits and a few special bus control circuits may also be used. These have been listed under the support chips for the individual types of microprocessor and will not be dealt with here. In recent years speech synthesis devices have been produced which allow the computer system to produce a limited vocabulary of speech output.

Timers and counters

One function that is frequently required in a microprocessor system is that of timing or event counting. A typical timer function is achieved by presetting a counter to a specified count, then allowing it to be clocked down to zero. At this point it produces an output to indicate the end of the time period. Of course the CPU itself could perform this function, but this would prevent it from carrying out any other data processing. The technique can of course be used if the CPU has nothing to do during the time delay.

If an external counter or timer is used it can operate independently of the CPU, thus allowing the latter to continue executing the program. Normally the external counter causes an interrupt when it reaches zero. The time delay produced may be programmed by setting the desired value into the counter and choosing a suitable clock for the counter input. Often the counter clock is derived from the computer system clock and may be prescaled by a fixed frequency division before its use with the counter.

Various modes of operation are possible. In a simple one-shot delay mode the counter is loaded with a preset value and allowed to count down to zero to give a time delay. Some types have a frequency division mode. Here the preset count is held in a separate register. Each time the counter reaches the zero point its output line is complemented and the counter again preset to the stored value. This produces a square wave output whose frequency is the input clock frequency divided by the preset count value.

For event counting the counter is driven by a clock which is derived from the event to be counted. Some counters also have an input gate circuit which allows the clock input to be switched on and off. This arrangement can be used to measure the width of an input pulse by counting the number of clock pulses occuring whilst the input gate is held open by the pulse being measured.

Many of the devices available contain two or three counters which may be operated independently or in conjunction with one another. Thus two 8-bit counters may be linked to form a 16-bit count, or one may be used as a variable prescaler whilst the other acts as the main 8-bit counter. Sometimes the counter may be arranged to produce a single clock pulse at its output as the count passes through zero, thus giving a delayed strobe pulse facility. The possibilities for programming some of the available counter devices are considerable and can only be fully explored by careful study of the device data sheet.

Digital to analogue converters

In the real world most of the signals encountered are analogue in form. For many applications the digital output signals from a microprocessor will need to be converted into analogue form before they can be used. This is achieved by using a digital to analogue (D/A) converter.

The typical D/A converter arrangement consists of a set of switches, a resistance ladder network and a precise voltage reference, as shown in fig. 10.1. Each

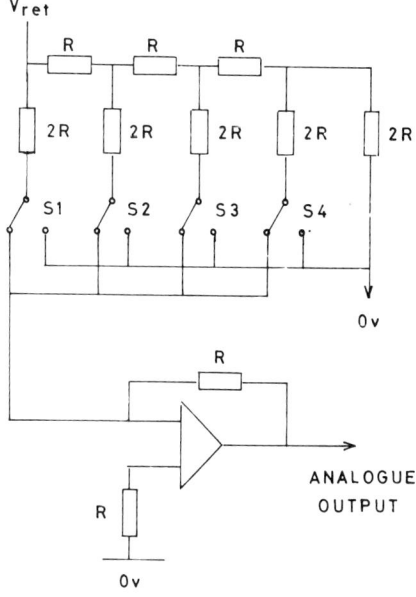

Fig. 10.1

stage of the ladder network produces an attenuation by a factor of two, and the binary weighted output current from each leg may be routed either to the amplifier input or to ground according to the state of switches S1 to S4 which are controlled by the data input. Switch S1 produces an amplifier output of $V_{r/2}$ or 0 V. Switches S2, S3 and S4 produce contributions of $V_{r/4}$, $V_{r/8}$ and $V_{r/16}$ respectively. The resultant output is an analogue voltage proportional to the binary digital number fed into the switches.

The reference voltage for the converter is generated by a precision Zener diode, which in some cases may be built into the D/A converter device. Other types will require an external reference voltage.

The switches used in the ladder network are solid state types which may be driven by signals from the processor data bus. In order to maintain a steady analogue output the data must be continuously applied to the switches and often the D/A converter will contain a buffer register into which the data may be latched. If there is no buffer register then the D/A converter will need to be driven from an input–output port of the microprocessor system which can provide a latched data output.

The resolution of the analogue output is dependent upon the number of data bits used for the converter. Thus an 8-bit converter will provide 256 discrete output steps to give an analogue resolution of slightly better than 0.4% of full scale. Many industrial systems use 12 bits of data to give 4096 steps and a resolution of about 0.025% full scale. This is about as good as the analogue side of the system is capable of handling.

Accuracy depends primarily upon the precision of the voltage reference and the temperature characteristics of the ladder network. Linearity is the deviation from a straight line transfer characteristic and is governed largely by the buffer amplifier which normally follows the network. An important characteristic is the consistency of step size as the various bits of data are switched in. This is sometimes referred to as *monotonicity* or as differential linearity.

Most converters will use pure binary coded inputs, but a few types are arranged to accept BCD data, in which groups of 4 bits are used for each decade. Three forms of binary coding may be used: straight binary, offset binary or twos complement binary. The corresponding data must be provided by the processor for correct analogue output.

The output of the D/A network is normally unipolar and runs from 0 V to V_r. When a bipolar output is required this is produced by adding an offset voltage to the buffer amplifier so that the output will be zero at half scale and will swing positive and negative about that value.

Two dynamic parameters for D/A converters are the *slew rate* and the *settling time*. The slew rate is the rate at which the output level can change. The settling time is the time taken for the output to stabilise to within 1 bit of the final value. These factors are largely influenced by the buffer amplifier used.

Analogue to digital converters

Two techniques are used for converting analogue input signals into digital form for entry into a microcomputer system. One approach uses an integration technique, generally where relatively slow conversion of data is required. The other is successive approximation, for fast conversion.

The arrangement of a dual slope integrating converter is shown in fig. 10.2. At the start of conversion the input to the integrator is at zero. The input voltage is then fed to the integrator input, causing the integrator output to rise slowly at a rate dependent upon the value of the input signal. The integrator is allowed to operate whilst a counter counts off a fixed time period, usually governed by the full scale count of the counter. At the end of this period the input is removed and a fixed reference voltage is applied to the input of the integrator, with polarity such that the integrator output falls at a fixed rate governed by the reference signal. The counter continues to count up from zero and when the output of the integrator reaches zero the counter is stopped. At this point the counter reading will be proportional to the ratio between the input voltage and the reference voltage. The counter reading may now be used as the digital output signal.

The conversion time of the dual slope converter will

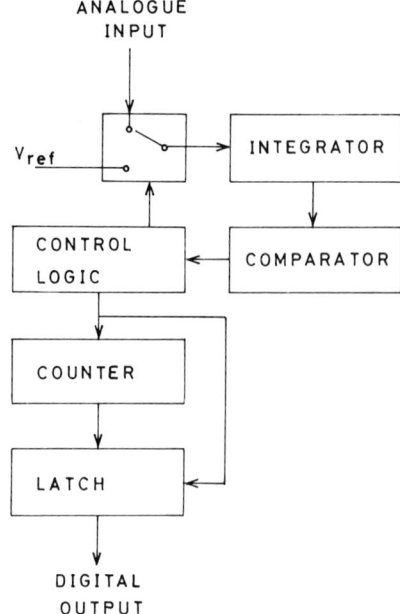

Fig. 10.2

be governed by the size of the counter and the clock rate used to drive it. Typically a conversion time of 16.6 ms or 20 ms or a multiple of these would be used since these are the period times of the common 60 Hz and 50 Hz supply systems. If the integration is carried out over a period of one power supply cycle then any power line noise picked up at the input will integrate out to zero in the converter. Faster conversion is of course possible, but will usually be in the order of several milliseconds.

In the alternative scheme the arrangement shown in fig. 10.3 is used. Here the successive approximation

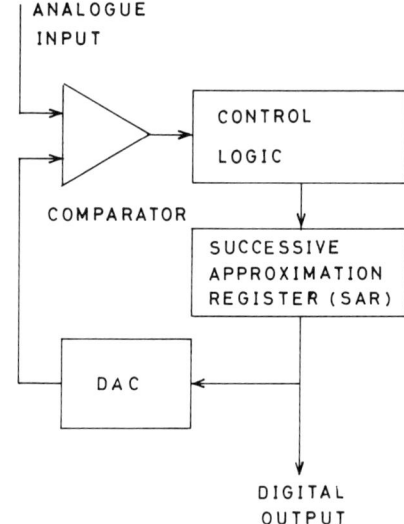

Fig. 10.3

register SAR is initially set to zero. The output of the SAR is fed to a D/A converter to produce an analogue signal. This is then compared with the input signal in a comparator stage. The most significant bit of the SAR is now set at 1, giving a half scale output from the D/A converter. If the input is greater than this level the bit remains set, but if the input is less then the bit is reset to 0. The next lower bit of the SAR is then set to 1 and the comparison process is repeated. This process continues until the output of the D/A converter and the input voltage are matched. Then the contents of the SAR will be the digital equivalent of the analogue input. This process is similar to that used when using weights on a pair of scales.

Since there will only be a number of steps equal to the number of bits in the digital data this type of conversion is very fast and typical conversion times are in the order of a few microseconds or tens or microseconds, being limited only by the settling times of the comparator and D/A converter at each step of the approximation process.

As with D/A converters the popular resolution levels will be 8 and 12 bits. Coding of the digital output may be either in binary or BCD, and for binary it may be simple, offset or twos complement format. Unlike the D/A converter, which is basically a static device which converts whatever data are fed to the input of the ladder network, the A/D converter needs a trigger pulse to start the conversion process. It will produce an output signal which indicates that it has completed the conversion process and data are ready to be read out. Because the converter takes a finite time to carry out the conversion the input signal just be held steady during the conversion process. Often the converter unit may have a sample and hold amplifier included at its analogue input. This device takes a sample of the incoming signal just before conversion commences and holds this signal steady during the conversion process.

INTEL 8252 TIMER

The Intel 8252 Programmable Interval Timer provides 3 independent fully programmable timer/counters in one package. It is designed primarily for use with processors of the 8080 and 8085 families, but may also be used with other processors with suitable interfacing.

Prime manufacturer
Intel Corporation   8253, 8253-5

Alternative source devices
Advanced Micro Devices
Am8253, Am8253-5

National Semiconductor
INS8253

N.E.C.
μPD8253, μPD8253-5

Siemens
SAB8253

Package
24-pin dual in line   plastic or ceramic

Pin connections

1	D7	13	OUT1
2	D6	14	GATE1
3	D5	15	CLK1
4	D4	16	GATE2
5	D3	17	OUT2
6	D2	18	CLK2
7	D1	19	A0
8	D0	20	A1
9	CLK0	21	CS
10	OUT0	22	RD
11	GATE0	23	WR
12	V_{ss}	24	V_{cc}

Signal functions

D0 – D7	Data bus bidirectional
OUT0 – OUT2	Timer outputs
CLK0 – CLK2	Timer clock inputs
GATE0 – GATE2	Timer gate inputs
A0, A1	Counter select inputs
CS	Chip select input (active low)
RD	Read control input (active low)
WR	Write control input (active low)
V_{cc}, V_{ss}	Power supply inputs

All inputs and outputs are TTL compatible and outputs will drive one TTL load. Note that on the 8253-5 version the output lines can sink 2.2 mA, compared with 1.6 mA for the 8253.

Power requirements

V_{cc}	+5 V $\pm$ 5%
V_{ss}	0 V
Power supply current	140 mA

Temperature range
Standard   0°C to +70°C

Count rate
Maximum   2 MHz

General

Each of the three counters has a 16-bit counter register. Programming is achieved by selecting the desired counter by using the A0 and A1 address lines. The binary number applied is the number of the selected counter. Binary 3 applied to A0, A1 selects a mode control register which allows the mode of operations for each counter to be set up.

Data may be written into a counter register to set them up for counting, when it will decrement down to zero using its CLK input as a clock. The 16 bits of data are loaded as two bytes written in succession to the counter address. Mode selection allows either 8 or 16 bits to be loaded. It will also allow the counter to be operated in decimal mode, when it will count in BCD giving 4 decades.

Six modes of operation are available for each counter. In mode 0 the counter acts a simple down counter, producing an output pulse when it reaches zero but continuing to count. In the second mode the counter operates as a one shot, producing a delayed pulse at its output and then stopping. The third mode is as a pulse rate generator, where the ocunter will output a pulse every n pulses where n is the preset count value. A variation on this is the square wave mode, where the counter stays high for half the count and remains low for the rest of the count during each count cycle. The final modes are used to generate delayed strobe pulses, one being triggered by a software operation of loading the counter, whilst the other is triggered by a pulse applied at the gate input.

Note that the 8253-5 is designed to be compatible with the 8085 type microprocessor.

MOTOROLA MC6840

The Motorola MC6840 Programmable Timer Module (PTM) provides three independent and full programmable 16-bit counters or timers in a single package. Designed primarily for the 6800 series processors it can also be used with other types.

Prime manufacturer

Motorola Semiconductor   MC6840, MC68A40, MC68B40

Alternative source devices

American Microsystems

S6840, S68A40, S68B40

Fairchild

F6840, F68A40, F68B40

Fujitsu

MBL6840

Thomson EFCIS

EF6840, EF68A40, EF68B40

Package

28-pin dual in line type   plastic or ceramic

Pin connections

1	V_{ss}	15	CS0
2	G2	16	CS1
3	O2	17	E
4	C2	18	D7
5	G3	19	D6
6	O3	20	D5
7	C3	21	D4
8	RESET	22	D3
9	IRQ	23	D2
10	RS0	24	D1
11	RS1	25	D0
12	RS2	26	G1
13	R/W	27	O1
14	V_{cc}	28	C1

Pin functions

D0 – D7	Data bus bidirectional
RS0 – RS2	Register select inputs
CS0, CS1	Chip select inputs (note CS0 is active low)
R/W	Read–write control input (write low)
RESET	External reset input (active low)
E	Enable (system clock input usually CPU $\phi 2$)
IRQ	Interrupt request output active low
C1, C2, C3	Timer clock inputs
G1, G2, G3,	Timer/counter gate inputs (active low)
O1, O2, O3	Timer outputs
V_{cc}, V_{ss}	Power supply inputs

All inputs and outputs are TTL compatible and outputs will generally drive one TTL load. Timer outputs and interrupt will drive two TTL loads. Inputs are diode protected.

Power requirements

V_{cc}	+5 V ± 5%
V_{ss}	0 V
Power dissipation	330 mW

Temperature range

Standard part	0°C to +70°C
Suffix C (Motorola)	−40°C to +85°C
Suffix JCS (Motorola)	−55°C to +125°C

General

Three completely independent 16-bit counters or timers are provided and their count state may be monitored by reading the counter registers if desired. All counters count down and will generate a time out pulse at the output when they reach zero. They may also be programmed to generate an interrupt request if desired.

Timer number 3 has a selectable prescaler counter with a count ratio of 8 which may operate at up to 4 MHz for the standard 6840 and up to 6 or 8 MHz for 68A40 and the 68B40 respectively.

To the microprocessor system the device will appear as a set of 8 registers which may be selected by the RS0 – RS2 input lines. In some cases two registers may share the same address, one being selected by a read instruction and the other by a write instruction. A total of sixteen 8-bit registers is included on the chip.

Each counter has two 8-bit registers for its count and a control register to determine the mode of operation. There is also an 8-bit status register. This contains 4 flag bits to allow determination of which counter caused an interrupt.

Timers may be run in either a continuous mode or in a single shot mode. There is provision for pulse width or delay measurement by using the gate inputs. In the continuous mode the counters may be treated as a single 16-bit counter or as two 8-bit counters.

ZILOG Z80 CTC

The Zilog Z80-CTC Clock Timer Circuit provides four separate 8-bit programmable timers or counters for use with a Z80 type processor system. This device may also be used with other types of CPU, although its interrupt system is designed specifically for the Z80 type.

Prime manufacturer

Zilog Inc.   Z80-CTC, Z80A-CTC

Alternative source devices

Mostek

MK3882, MK3882-4

SGS-ATES

Z80-CTC, Z80A-CTC

Package

28-pin dual in line type   plastic or ceramic

Pin connections

1	D4	15	ϕ
2	D5	16	CE
3	D6	17	RESET
4	D7	18	CS0
5	V_{ss}	19	CS1
6	RD	20	CLK/TRG3
7	ZC0	21	CLK/TRG2
8	ZC1	22	CLK/TRG1
9	ZC2	23	CLK/TRG0
10	IORQ	24	V_{cc}
11	IEO	25	D0
12	INT	26	D1
13	IEI	27	D2
14	M1	28	D3

Pin functions

D0 – D7	Data bus bidirectional
CS0, CS1	Register select inputs
CE	Chip enable (active low) input
RESET	Reset input (active low)
M1	Instruction fetch cycle pulse input (active low)
CLK/TRG0-3	External clock or trigger inputs
ZC0 – ZC2	Zero count or timeout output
IEI, IEO	Interrupt daisy chain lines
INT	Interrupt request output (active low)
RD	Read cycle signal from CPU (active low)
IORQ	I/O request from CPU input (active low)
ϕ	System clock from CPU
V_{cc}, V_{ss}	Power supply inputs

All signals are TTL compatible.

Power requirements

V_{cc}	$+5$ V $\pm 5\%$
V_{ss}	0 V
Supply current	120 mA max.

Temperature range

Standard	0°C to +70°C
Commercial	−40°C to +85°C, suffix E or −10
Military	−55°C to +125°C, suffix M or −20

General

The Z80-CTC contains four separate 8-bit timer/counters which may be decremented by either the system clock or an external clock signal. Each timer has 3 registers, one for control, one for the time constant and one counter register. The time constant and control registers can be written to and the down counter register can be read. Registers are selected by the CS0 and CS1 inputs. They select a control register and count register for one of the 4 timers. The time constant will be loaded by setting a flag bit in the control register for the counter when the following byte of data written to the control register address will be transferred into the time constant register.

Timers may be set to act as simple down counters with a clock derived from the system clock ϕ. A division ratio of either 16 or 256 may be selected in this mode. An external clock may be used to drive the counter via the CLK/TRG input. When the counter times out by reaching zero count an output is produced on its ZC line, except in the case of counter 3 which has no ZC output.

All counters may be used to generate an interrupt request output via the INT line. Highest priority will be timer 0 with timer 3 at the lowest priority level. Interrupt vector logic is incorporated into counter 0 and an interrupt vector address will need to be set up in this logic when the Z80-CTC is initialised. Refer to manufacturer's data sheet for details of this operation. Timers will produce interrupts as they count to zero, and this is the only way to access timer 3.

ANALOGUE CONVERTER DEVICE DATA

There are many types of A/D and D/A converter device available and no attempt will be made here to provide data on all of them. Brief data on some of the more popular types follow, and will perhaps give some guidance to the range of devices available.

Most A/D converters are of the successive approximation type, but where the integration technique is used this will be indicated. The conversion time is given after the resolution and scaling data, e.g. 12-bit binary 20 μs. Some types of D/A converter require an external reference voltage and perhaps an external buffer amplifier. These points are noted in the data. On many types of converter the scale may be selected as offset binary, complemented binary or BCD by appropriate connection of links on the converter device. The voltage range may also be selectable by links on some types.

Analogue to digital converters

Beckman 7555 and 7556 series
CMOS low power type. 12-bit binary 50 μs with either serial or parallel output data. Package 7555 32-pin DIL, 7556 36-pin DIL. Voltage input range 0 – +10 V or +10 V. Note the 7555 has no internal reference or comparator.

Burr Brown ADC80 series
Hybrid modules. 8 to 12-bit binary 10 – 20 μs with input range selectable from +2.5 V to +10 V.

Datel Intersil ADC-HS12 series
Hybrid module. 12-bit binary 9 μs with serial or parallel data outputs. Input voltage range selectable ±2.5 V to ±10 V.

Datel Intersil ICL ICL7109
CMOS integrating type converter. 12-bit binary at 7.5 conversions per second for 60 Hz integration. Max. rate is 30 per second. Input range up to ± 5 V. Package 40-pin DIL.

Ferranti ZN427E
Bipolar successive approx. type. 8-bit binary 10 μs. Package 18-pin DIL.

Signetics NE5034
Successive approx. type. 8-bit binary 17 μs. Package 22-pin DIL. Parallel data output suitable for microprocessor operation.

Teledyne 8703
CMOS low power type using charge balancing technique. 8-bit binary 1250 μs with parallel output. Package 24-pin DIL.

Digital to analogue converters

Analog Devices AD7524
CMOS low power type. 8-bit binary with latched inputs. Needs external reference. Package 16-pin DIL.

Beckman 7545, 7546
CMOS types. 12-bit binary with serial or parallel inputs and latch. 7545 needs external reference and buffer amplifier. Package 30-pin DIL (7545), 36-pin DIL (7546).

Burr Brown DAC85
12-bit binary or 3-digit BCD. Needs input latches for interface to microprocessor bus. Output range ±2.5 V to ±10 V. Package DIL type.

Datel AD7541
12-bit binary 4 quadrant multiplying type. Needs input latches, voltage reference and output buffer amplifier. Package 18-pin DIL type.

Ferranti ZN425E
8-bit binary input. Contains input latch and reference but needs an output amplifier. Package 16-pin DIL.

National Semiconductor DAC0800
8-bit binary type which may be used as multiplying DAC. Package 16-pin DIL. Needs external reference and input latches.

Signetics NEC5018
8-bit binary type with on-chip reference, input latches and output buffer amplifier. Package 22-pin DIL. Matches most microprocessor bus systems.

Signetics NE5118
8-bit binary type similar to NE5108 but with current output and no buffer amplifier.

ANALOGUE DEVICE MANUFACTURERS

In general, analogue interface devices such as analogue to digital and digital to analogue converters are produced by specialist manufacturers rather than by the microprocessor suppliers. A list of the more popular analogue device suppliers, together with their addresses, follows. All of these suppliers produce digital to analogue converters and most of them also provide analogue to digital converters.

Analog Devices Inc.

Analog Devices Inc.,
Route One Industrial Park,
P.O. Box 280,
NORWOOD,
Ma. 02062, U.S.A.
Tel 617 329 4700

Analog Devices Ltd.,
Central Avenue
EAST MOLESEY,
Surrey, England
Tel 01-941 0466

Analog Devices GMBH,
8000 MUNCHEN 2,
Mozartstrasse 17,
West Germany
Tel 089 53 03 19

Beckman

Beckman Instruments Inc.,
Advanced Electro Products Div.,
2500 Harbor Blvd.,
FULLERTON,
Ca. 92634, U.S.A.
Tel 714 871 4848

Beckman Instruments Ltd.,
Queensway,
GLENROTHES,
Fife KY7 5PU, Scotland
Tel 0592 753811

Burr Brown

Burr Brown Research Corp.,
Intl. Airport Industrial Park,
TUCSON,
Arizona 85734, U.S.A.
Tel 602 746 1111

Burr Brown International Ltd.,
25A King Street,
WATFORD,
Herts WD1 8BT, England
Tel 0923 33837

Datel-Intersil

Datel-Intersil,
11 Cabot Blvd.,
MANSFIELD,
Ma. 02048, U.S.A.
Tel 617 828 8000

Datel-Intersil (UK) Ltd.,
9th Floor,
Snamprogetti House,
Basing View,
BASINGSTOKE,
Hants, England
Tel 0256 57361

Ferranti

Ferranti Electronics Ltd.,
Fields New Road,
Chadderton,
OLDHAM,
Lancs. OL9 8NP, England
Tel 061 624 0515

Ferranti Electric Inc.,
87 Modular Avenue,
COMMACK,
N.Y. 11725, U.S.A.
Tel 516 543 0200

Ferranti GMBH,
Widenmayerstrasse 5,
D8000 MUNICH 22,
West Germany
Tel 089 29 38 71

Harris

Harris Semiconductor,
P.O. Box 883,
MELBOURNE,
Florida 32901, U.S.A.
Tel 305 724 7000

Harris Systems Ltd.,
P.O. Box 27,
145 Farnham Road,
SLOUGH,
Berks. SL1 4XD, England
Tel 0753 34666

Hybrid Systems

Hybrid Systems,
Crosby Drive,
Bedford Research Park,
BEDFORD,
Ma. 01730, U.S.A.
Tel 617 275 1570

Hybrid Systems,
12a Park Street,
CAMBERLEY,
Surrey, England
Tel 0276 28128

Micro Networks

Micro Networks Corp.,
324 Clark Street,
WORCESTER,
Ma. 01606, U.S.A.
Tel 617 852 5400

Pascall Electronics Ltd.,
Hawke House,
Green Street,
SUNBURY ON THAMES,
Middx. TW16 6RA, England
Tel 09327 87418

Precision Monolithics

Precision Monolithics Inc.,
1500 Space Park Drive,
SANTA CLARA,
Ca. 95050, U.S.A.
Tel 408 246 9222

Bourns (Trimpot) Ltd.,
Hodford House,
17 – 27 High Street,
HOUNSLOW
Middx. TW3 1TE, England
Tel 01-572 6531

Teledyne Philbrick

Teledyne Philbrick,
Allied Drive at Route 128,
DEDHAM,
Ma. 02026, U.S.A.
Tel 710 348 6726

Teledyne Philbrick,
Heathrow House,
Bath Road,
CRANFORD,
Middx. TW5 9QQ, England
Tel 01-897 2501

11 DEVELOPMENT AIDS

In order to produce any microprocessor based system some form of development aid will be required to allow the program to be written and tested and the hardware to be checked. Two levels of equipment are available, namely the evaluation boards and the full scale development system.

EVALUATION BOARDS

For simple projects and for training purposes the evaluation board can be a useful piece of equipment. Normally it will consist of a small microprocessor system built up on perhaps one or two circuit boards. There will usually be some form of keypad or keyboard to allow data to be entered into memory and to allow commands to be entered into the system. Some form of digital display, usually of the LED 7-segment type, is provided to allow data to be displayed and examined by the user. There may also be input–output channels for an external printer or terminal, and possibly some facilities for breadboarding custom circuits for interfacing external devices. Apart from the processor the board will usually contain some read–write memory and also a ROM, which will contain some form of monitor and debug program to govern the operation of the board.

With this type of system the program data are entered into memory from the keyboard as hexadecimal or binary data. Contents of the memory and the CPU registers may usually be examined and altered by the user. There will also be facilities for stepping through a program one instruction at a time to allow faults in the program logic to be traced. The program may also be executed at normal speed if desired.

One disadvantage of this type of system is that it requires considerable time and effort on the part of the user to evaluate even a simple program, since all instructions must first be converted into machine code for entry into the system. With anything other than a simple program this could lead to errors which may be very difficult to trace. Nevertheless such systems have been used successfully to develop working microprocessor systems.

Typical evaluation systems

Intel SDK85
Single board based on 8085 microprocessor with 256-byte RAM, 24-key keypad, 6-digit LED display and facility for using external TTY terminal.

Intel SDK86
Similar to SDK85 but based on 8086 16-bit microprocessor. 2 kbyte memory, 48 parallel I/O lines and serial RS232 interface for external terminal.

Motorola MEK6800D2
Two-board system for 6800 family microprocessors. 256-byte RAM, 24-key keypad, 6-digit LED display and cassette interface for program storage.

Motorola MEK6802D5
Similar to D2 kit but based on the 6802 type processor.

Motorola MEK68kDM
Single-board system for the MC68000 16-bit processor, with 32 kbyte RAM, three timers and 32 I/O lines plus serial RS232 terminal port. Can be used in EXORCISER system to download programs developed by Cross Assembler in that system.

Harris MICRO-12
Single-board system for the 6100 12-bit microprocessor with 256-word RAM, 16-key keypad, 8-digit LED display and terminal/audio cassette interfaces.

Intersil INTERCEPT Junior
Single-board system for the 6100, with similar facilities to he Harris MICRO 12.

Rockwell AIM65
Two-board system for the 6502 microprocessor with 1 kbyte RAM, keyboard and small thermal printer on the CPU card. Can also use external terminal.

CBM KIM 1
Single-board system for the 6502 with 1 kbyte RAM, 23-key keypad, 6-digit display and cassette interface for program storage. Also from Synertek as the SYM-1.

Fairchild SPARK 16
Single-board system for the Microflame 16-bit devices. Needs external control terminal.

Signetics INSTRUCTOR 50
Cabinet based system for evaluation of 2650 microprocessor. Keypad and LED displays with audio cassette interface for program storage.

Intel PROMPT 48
Desktop system for 8048/8748 devices with keypad input and LED displays, plus facilities for programming 8748 on-chip PROM.

There are many other simple systems available, but the above list will give some guidance to the type of facilities likely to be offered with such systems.

FULL DEVELOPMENT SYSTEMS

For serious work with microprocessors it is essential that a fully comprehensive hardware and software development system for the processor being used should be available. This will provide program assembler facilities, a text editor, program loader and debug facilities and often a hardware emulation capability. Many systems are also capable of operating with high level computer languages such as BASIC, FORTRAN and PASCAL. The operating system will normally be based upon the use of a floppy disk for file handling, although some simpler systems may use magnetic tape cassette storage for data files. The main disadvantage of the cassette based systems is that they are very much slower in operation than a floppy disk. Communication with the development system will usually be via a VDU type computer terminal, and provision is usually made for the addition of a line printer for hard copy output. This is ideal for obtaining permanent listings of programs. There may also be provision for programming of PROM devices.

At the lowest level, programs will be generated by using an *assembler*. This allows the instructions to be written as mnemonics, and data variables and program labels may be given symbolic names of perhaps 5 or 6 alphanumeric characters. The assembler program will convert this *source code* symbolic program language into hexadecimal or binary machine code. It will automatically allocate addresses and values to variables and constants, and will generate the required opcode data for the microprocessor program. Branch and jump addresses will be calculated automatically, and where necessary alphanumeric data may be converted to the appropriate binary code form. At the end of the assembly process the assembler program will produce a machine code *object file* which is ready to be loaded and run in the microprocessor system. It is also possible to obtain a full listing of the program, giving source and object codes as well as all address information, showing exactly where each of the instructions will be located in the program memory. The assembler itself will also have directive instructions which allow areas of memory to be allocated for variables and to permit the generation of interger constants within the memory. It is also possible to specify where the program will reside in the computer memory map.

In order to generate the source code file a text editor program will normally be provided. Editors may vary from a simple line by line editor to full scale screen editors, which allow data to be changed and inserted merely by moving the cursor around the screen and keying in simple control codes. The text editor will generate a text file which may be stored on the floppy disk and later used as the data input for the assembler program.

A loader program may be used to load the object code file produced by the assembler into the memory ready for the program to be executed. With the simpler systems the program will be loaded into memory at a point specified in the source code file. More advanced assemblers may generate relocatable programs, where the load address is determined at the time of loading the program. This scheme has the advantage that the program can be assembled as small modules which are linked together as required by a linker loader program just before the program is to be loaded. If changes are made to a module the linker will automatically adjust any addresses in other modules that may have been affected by the program change, so that it is not necessary to modify any of the other modules. Thus programs may make use of a range of standard modules to provide frequently required functions such as input–output routines.

In assembly language programming each program line will correspond to one instruction in the final machine code object program. A simpler approach to programming is to use one of the high level languages such as BASIC, FORTRAN or PASCAL, where the program consists of a series of statements which may be in the form of commands such as INPUT or PRINT, or in the form of equations such as $Y = A + B - C$. A special program known as a *compiler* or *interpreter* is then used to convert this source file of statements into an assembler source file or a machine code object file.

In an interpreter the source statements are translated as the program is executed. This is the technique normally used for BASIC programs. A disadvantage of the interpreter is that because of the translation process the execution speed of the program is much slower than for an equivalent program in machine code produced by an assembler.

With a compiler the source code is translated into an object file in machine code which can later be loaded and run in the same way as the object program produced by an assembler. Because the compiler has to cope with all possible combinations of data and operations it may produce rather less efficient object code than a specially tailored assembler generated program. However, most compilers can permit the insertion of special assembly code sections to deal with any critical functions where maximum speed or efficiency is desired. FORTRAN normally uses the compiler technique and some systems may also provide compilers for BASIC programs.

PASCAL source programs normally are translated into an intermediate form called P code, which is theoretically able to be run on any machine which handles PASCAL. The P code is then interpreted during execution of the program, or sometimes may be compiled to produce a machine code program file.

There are a number of other high level languages which may be provided, such as PL/M, MPL, CORAL, APL and FORTH. They are usually designed to be suited for particular applications, but generally follow similar patterns to languages such as FORTRAN and PASCAL.

Debug facilities for software usually include trace facilities, where the program may be halted at points known as *breakpoints* so that the state of the CPU registers or memory contents may be examined. Sometimes the program may be run one instruction at a time with status print out between steps to allow the flow of data to be examined.

For hardware testing an *in-circuit emulator* may be used. Here the development system is used to replace and emulate the operation of the CPU in the prototype hardware system. The actual CPU chip is removed and replaced by a special probe unit connected to the development system. Such a system may also provide logic analyser facilities which will allow the waveforms and logic states of the target hardware system to be examined as the program is run. An in-circuit emulator also allows the full debug facilities of the development

DEVELOPMENT AIDS

system to be used on the prototype hardware unit.

Most development systems are designed to handle one manufacturer's products, but there are some systems which can handle processors from several different manufacturers. When several processors can be handled by a system it is usual to have to change the CPU and debug parts of the system by inserting different cards for each processor. In some types, however, one processor is used to emulate the operation of other types of device and only the software need be changed.

Where full debug and emulation facilities are not needed the development system may provide a *cross assembler* for the desired processor type. This is an assembler which will accept source code for one processor type and compile it using a system based upon a different type of processor. Thus programs for a 6502 processor may be cross assembled on a system which uses a Z80 processor. The resultant object code will be that required to run the program on a 6502 system, but usually it is not possible to run or debug the program on the development system which runs the cross assembler. In some cases a cross assembler will be designed to run on a minicomputer system such as the DEC PDP11.

A list of some of the available development systems follows. This indicates the type of filing system, processors handled and languages available for each type of system.

Intel Corporation   Intellec series II
Floppy disk based system for 8048, 8049, 8051 series, 8080A, 8085A and 8086 processors. Hardware emulator. Languages PL/M, BASIC, FORTRAN IV. PROM programmer. User library.

Hughes Microelectronics   H800 system
Floppy disk based system for 8080, 8085, 8048, 6800, 6809, 6502, 1802, 1804, Z80 processors. Supports CP/M operating system programs. In-circuit debug and logic analyser facilities. PROM programmer. Screen editor.

Mostek   SYS-80FT
Floppy disk based system for Z80 and MK3870 series. Languages BASIC, FORTRAN. In-circuit emulation and PROM programmer.

Motorola   EXORCISER II
Floppy disk based system for 3870, 6800, 6801, 6802, 6805, 6809 and 2900 series. Also 68000 by using the MEX68KDM board. Languages MPL, BASIC, FORTRAN, PASCAL. In-circuit emulation. PROM programmer.

Motorola   EXORSET
Floppy disk based system for the 6809, providing software development and debugging.

Motorola   EXORMACS
Newly introduced floppy disk based system for the MC68000 16-bit processor. Languages PASCAL.

National Semiconductor   STARPLEX
Floppy disk based system for 8080, 8085, 8048, 8070, NSC800 and eventually NS16000 series. Languages BASIC and FORTRAN for 8080 series.

RCA   COSMAC system
Floppy disk system for 1802/1804 processors. Languages PLM1800. PROM programmer.

Thomson EFCIS   THEMIS system
Floppy disk based system for the 6800 series microprocessors. Primarily for software development.

Texas Instruments   AMPL system
Floppy disk based system for 9900 series devices. Languages BASIC, FORTRAN, CORAL and PASCAL. Has hardware emulator facilities and logic analyser.

Zilog   ZDS system
Floppy disk based system for the Z80 processor. Languages PLZ, FORTRAN, BASIC and COBOL. In-circuit hardware emulation.

Gen Rad Futuredata   AMDS 2300 series
A universal system with floppy disks and capable of either single user or multistation operation. Can support wide range of processor types including Z80, 8080/85, 6800 series, 6809, 6500 series, 68000, 1802 and others. Languages include BASIC and FORTRAN or PASCAL. Provides in-circuit emulation for many types and logic analyser facilities.

Available from:

Gen Rad Futuredata,
6151 West Century Blvd.,
Suite 1124,
LOS ANGELES,
Ca. 90045, U.S.A.
Tel 213 641 7200

ISG Data Sales Ltd.,
Unit 9,
Fairacres Industrial Estate,
Dedworth Road,
WINDSOR, Berks., England
Tel 07535 57955

Tektronix   8002 and 8500 series Development Labs.
Universal microprocessor development systems with floppy disk based operating systems. Designed to handle a wide range of types, including the AMI S2000 series, 8080/8085, 8086, 6800 series, 6500 series, 8048 series and others. Provides hardware emulation for most types. Languages include BASIC, FORTRAN and PASCAL.

Available from

Tektronix Inc.,
P.O. Box 1700,
BEAVERTON,
Oregon 97075, U.S.A.
Tel 503 644 0161

Tektronix UK Ltd.,
P.O. Box 69,
Coldharbour Lane,
HARPENDEN,
Herts. AL5 4UP, England
Tel Harpenden 63141

12 DIRECTORY OF MANUFACTURERS

DIRECTORY OF MANUFACTURERS

Advanced Micro Devices
Advanced Micro Devices Inc.,
901 Thompson Place,
SUNNYVALE,
Ca. 94086, U.S.A,
Tel 408 732 2400

Advanced Micro Devices (UK) Ltd.,
AMD House,
Goldsworth Road,
WOKING,
Surrey GU21 1JT, England
Tel Woking 22121

American Microsystems
American Microsystems Inc.,
3800 Homestead Road,
SANTA CLARA,
Ca. 95051, U.S.A.
Tel 408 246 0330

AMI Microsystems Ltd.,
Princes House,
Princes Street,
SWINDON SN1 2HU, England
Tel Swindon 37852

AMI Microsystems GMBH,
Rosenheimer Str, 30–32,
Suite 237,
MUNICH 80, W. Germany
Tel 89 483081

AEG Telefunken
AEG Telefunken,
Semiconductor Division,
Postfach 1109,
7100 HEILBRONN,
W. Germany
Tel 17131 8821

AEG Telefunken (UK) Ltd.,
217 Bath Road,
SLOUGH, Berks SL1 4AW, England
Tel 0753 872101

AEG Telefunken,
570 Sylvan Avenue,
ENGLEWOOD CLIFFS,
N. J. 07632, U.S.A.
Tel 201 568 8570

Electronic Arrays
Electronic Arrays Inc.,
550 E. Middlefield Road,
MOUNTAIN VIEW,
Ca. 94043, U.S.A.
Tel 415 964 4321

Electronic Arrays,
Analog Devices Ltd.,
Central Avenue,
E. MOLESEY,
Surrey, England
Tel 01-941 0466

EMM Semi
EMM-Semi,
2000 W.14th Street,
TEMPE,
Arizona 85281, U.S.A.
Tel 602 968 4431

EMM Electronic Memories Ltd,
92 The Centre,
FELTHAM,
Middx. TW13 4BH, England
Tel 01-751 1213

Fairchild Semiconductor
Fairchild Semiconductor,
PO Box 880A,
MOUNTAIN VIEW,
Ca. 94042, U.S.A.
Tel 415 962 3941

Fairchild Camera and Instrument (UK) Ltd.,
230 High Street,
POTTERS BAR,
Herts. EN6 5BU, England
Tel 0707 51111

Fairchild Semiconductor GMBH,
6200 WEISBADEN 12,
Postfach 9549,
Hagenauer Str,
W. Germany
Tel 06121 2051

Ferranti
Ferranti Ltd.,
Western Road,
BRACKNELL,
Berks RG12 1RA, England
Tel 0344 3232

Ferranti Electric,
E. Bethpage Road,
PLAINVIEW,
N.Y. 11803, U.S.A.
Tel 516 293 8383

Fujitsu
Fujitsu Ltd.,
Syuwa Onarimon Building 1–1,
Shinbashi 6 chome,
TOKYO 105,
Japan
Tel 103 437 2111

Fujitsu America Inc.,
2945 Kifer Road,
SANTA CLARA,
Ca. 95051, U.S.A.
Tel 408 727 1700

General Instrument
General Instrument Microelectronics Ltd.,
Regency House,
1–4 Warwick Street,
LONDON W1R 5WB, England
Tel 01-439 1891

General Instrument Corp.,
Microelectronics Division,
600 W. John Street,
HICKSVILLE,
N.Y. 11802, U.S.A.
Tel 516 733 3107

Harris
Harris Semiconductor Division,
P.O. Box 883,
MELBOURNE,
Florida 32901, U.S.A.
Tel 305 724 7400

Thame Components, Ltd.,
Thame Park Industrial Estate,
THAME,
Oxon. OX9 3RS, England
Tel 084 421 3146

Hitachi
Hitachi Ltd.,
6-2 Otemachi 2-Chome,
Chiyoda-ku,
TOKYO 1 00, Japan
Tel 03 270 2111

Hitachi America Ltd.,
707 W. Algonquin Road,
ARLINGTON HEIGHTS,
Ill. 60005, U.S.A.
Tel 312 593 7660

Hitachi Electronic Components (UK) Ltd.,
P.I.E. Building,
2 Rubastic Road,
SOUTHALL,
Middx. UB2 5LL, England
Tel 01-574 0732

Hughes
Hughes Aircraft Co.,
Solid State Products Div.,
500 Superior Ave.,
NEWPORT BEACH,
Ca. 92663, U.S.A.
Tel 714 759 2942

Hughes Microelectronics Ltd.,
Clive House,
12-18 Queens Road,
WEYBRIDGE,
Surrey KT13 9XD, England
Tel Weybridge 47262

Intel Corporation
Intel Corporation,
3065 Bowers Ave.,
SANTA CLARA,
Ca. 95051, U.S.A.
Tel 408 987 8080

Intel Corporation (UK) Ltd.,
Dorcan House,
Eldene Drive,
SWINDON,
Wilts. SN3 3TU, England
Tel 0793 26101

Inmos
Inmos Corp.,
P.O. Box 16000,
COLORADO SPRINGS,
Col. 80935, U.S.A.
Tel 303 630 4000

Inmos Ltd.,
Whitefriars,
Lewins Mead,
BRISTOL BS1 2NP, England
Tel 0272 290861

Intersil
Intersil Inc.,
10900 N. Tantau Ave.,
CUPERTINO,
Ca. 95041, U.S.A.
Tel 408 996 5000

Intersil-Datel (UK) Ltd.,
Snamprogetti House,
Basing View,
BASINGSTOKE,
Hants. RG21 2YS, England
Tel 0256 57361

ITT
ITT Semiconductors,
500 Broadway,
LAWRENCE,
Ma. 01841, U.S.A.
Tel 617 688 1881

ITT Semiconductors,
Maidstone Road,
Footscray,
SIDCUP,
Kent DA14 5HT, England
Tel 01-300 3333

Matsushita (Panasonic)
Matsushita Electronics Corp.,
1-1 Saiwa cho,
Takatsuki-shi,
OSAKA 569, Japan
Tel 0726 82 5521

Panasonic,
1 Panasonic Way,
SECAUSUS,
N. J. 07094, U.S.A.
Tel 201 348 1276

National Panasonic (UK) Ltd.,
300-318 Bath Road,
SLOUGH,
Berks. SL1 6JB, England
Tel 0753 34522

Mitel
Mitel Semiconductor,
P.O. Box 13089,
KANATA,
Ontario K2K 1X3, Canada
Tel 613 592 2122

DIRECTORY OF MANUFACTURERS

Mitel Semiconductor,
2321 Morena Blvd.,
Suite M,
SAN DIEGO,
Ca. 92110, U.S.A.
Tel 714 276 3421

Mitel Semiconductor,
Hamilton Road,
SLOUGH,
Berks. SL1 4QY, England
Tel 0752 76126

Mitsubishi
Mitsubishi Electric Corp.,
Mitsubishi Denki Building,
Marunouchi,
TOKYO 100, Japan
Tel 03 218 3473

Melco Sales Inc.,
3030 E. Victoria Street,
COMPTON,
Ca. 90221, U.S.A.
Tel 213 537 7132

Mitsubishi Semiconductors,
Mitsubishi Electric (UK) Ltd.,
Otterspool Way,
WATFORD,
Herts. WD2 8LD, England
Tel 0293 40566

Monolithic Memories (MMI),
Monolithic Memories Inc.,
1165 East Arques Ave.,
SUNNYVALE,
Ca. 94086, U.S.A.
Tel 408 739 3535

Memory Devices Ltd.,
Central Avenue,
EAST MOLESEY,
Surrey KT8 0SN, England
Tel 01-941 1066

MOS Technology
MOS Technology Inc.,
950 Rittenhouse Road,
NORRISTOWN,
Penn. 19401, U.S.A.
Tel 215 666 7950

Mostek
Mostek Corp.,
1215 West Crosby Road,
CAROLLTON,
Texas 75006, U.S.A.
Tel 214 323 1829

Mostek UK Ltd.,
Masons House,
1-3 Valley Drive,
Kingsbury Road,
LONDON NW9, England
Tel 01-204 9322

Mostek International,
150 Chaussee de la Hulpe,
BRUSSELS, Belgium
Tel 02 660 2568

Motorola
Motorola Semiconductors,
3501 Ed Bluestein Blvd.
AUSTIN,
Texas 78721, U.S.A.
Tel 512 928 2600

Motorola Ltd.,
York House,
Empire Way,
WEMBLEY,
Middx. HA9 0PR, England
Tel 01-902 8836

Motorola Inc.,
16 Chemin de la Vole Creuse,
P.O. Box 8,
1211 GENEVE 20, Switzerland
Tel 022 99 11 11

Mullard
Mullard Ltd.,
Mullard House,
Torrington Place,
LONDON WC1E 7HG, England
Tel 01-580 6633

National
National Semiconductor Corp.,
2900 Semiconductor Drive,
SANTA CLARA,
Ca. 95051, U.S.A.
Tel 408 737 5000

National Semiconductor (UK) Ltd.,
301 Harpur Centre,
Horne Lane,
BEDFORD MK40 1TR, England
Tel 0234 47147

National Semiconductor GMBH,
808 Fuerstenfeld-Bruck,
Industriestrasse 10,
W. Germany
Tel 081 41 13 71

Nippon Electric Co. (N.E.C.)
Nippon Electric Co. Ltd.,
N.E.C. Building,
33-1 Shibba Gochome,
Minato-ku,
TOKYO 108, Japan
Tokyo 454 1111

N.E.C. Microcomputers Inc.,
173 Worcester Street,
WELLESLEY,
Ma. 02181, U.S.A.
Tel 617 237 1901

N.E.C. Electronics UK,
116 Stevenston Street,
NEW STEVENSTON ML1 4LT, Scotland
Tel 0698 732221

OKI Semiconductor
Oki Electric Industry Co. Ltd.,
10-3 Shibaura 4-chome,
Minato-ku,
TOKYO 108, Japan
Tel 03 454 2111

Oki Semiconductor Inc.,
1333 Lawrence Expressway,
Suite 401,
SANTA CLARA,
Ca. 95051, U.S.A.
Tel 408 984 4842

Oki Electric Europe GMBH,
Emanuel Leutze Str. 8,
4000 DUSSELDORF 11,
W. Germany
Tel 0049 211 592031

Plessey
Plessey Microsystems Ltd.,
Water Lane,
TOWCESTER,
Northants NN12 7JN, England
Tel 0327 50312

Plessey Microsystems,
1641 Kaiser Ave.,
IRVINE,
Ca. 92714, U.S.A.
Tel 714 540 9931

Raytheon
Raytheon Co.,
Semiconductor Division,
350 Ellis Street,
MOUNTAIN VIEW,
Ca. 94042, U.S.A.
Tel 415 968 9211

Raytheon Semiconductor,
The Pinnacles,
HARLOW,
Essex CM19 5BB, England
Tel 0279 419310

Raytheon Halbleiter GMBH,
Thalkirchnerstrasse 74,
D8000 MUNICH 2, W. Germany
Tel 089 539693

Radio Corp. of America (RCA)
RCA Solid State Div.,
Box 3200, Route 202,
SOMERVILLE,
N.J. 08876, U.S.A.
Tel 201 685 6000

RCA Ltd.,
Solid State Europe,
Windmill Road,
SUNBURY ON THAMES,
Middx. TW16 7HW, England
Tel 04106 2001

Rockwell
Rockwell International,
Electronic Devices Division,
3310 Miraloma Avenue,
P.O. Box 3669,
ANAHEIM,
Ca. 92803, U.S.A.
Tel 714 632 3729

Electronic Devices Division,
Rockwell-Collins,
Heathrow House,
Bath Road,
Cranford,
HOUNSLOW,
Middx., England
Tel 01-759 9911

Electronic Devices Div.,
Rockwell International GMBH,
Fraunhoferstrasse 11,
C8033 Munchen-Martinsried,
W. Germany
Tel 069 859 9575

SGS-ATES
SGS-ATES Componenti Elettronica SpA,
Via C. Olivetti 2,
20041 AGRATE BRIANZA, Italy
Tel 039 650 3414

SGS-ATES (United Kingdom) Ltd.,
Planar House,
Walton Street,
AYLESBURY,
Bucks., England
Tel 0296 5977

SGS-ATES Semiconductor Corp.,
240 Bear Hill Road,
WALTHAM,
Ma. 02154, U.S.A.
Tel 617 890 6688

Siemens
Siemens AG,
Richard Strauss Strasse 76,
Postfach 20219,
8000 Munchen 2, W. Germany
Tel 089 92211

Siemens Ltd.,
Siemens House,
Windmill Road,
SUNBURY ON THAMES,
Middx. TW16 7HS, England
Tel 09327 85691

Siemens Corp.,
186 Wood Ave.,
SOUTH ISELIN,
N.J. 08830, U.S.A.
Tel 201 494 1000

Signetics (Phillips)
Signetics Corp.,
811 E. Arques Ave.,
SUNNYVALE,
Ca. 94086, U.S.A.
Tel 408 739 7700

Signetics Mullard Ltd.,
Mullard House,
Torrington Place,
LONDON WC1E 7HD, England
Tel 01-580 6633

Signetics GMBH,
D7 STUTTGART 80,
Ernsthaldenstrasse 17, W. Germany
Tel 0711 73 50 61

Solid State Scientific
Solid State Scientific Inc.,
Montgomeryville Ind. Park,
MONTGOMERYVILLE,
Pa. 18936, U.S.A.
Tel 215 855 8400

Standard Microsystems (SMC)
Standard Microsystems Corp.,
35 Marcus Boulevard,
HAUPPAGE,
N.Y. 11787, U.S.A.
Tel 516 273 3100

Rastra Electronics Ltd.,
275–281 King Street,
Hammersmith,
LONDON W6 9NF, England
Tel 01-748 3143

Synertek
Synertek Inc.,
3001 Stender Way,
SANTA CLARA,
Ca. 95051, U.S.A.
Tel 408 988 5600

Synertek,
Honeywell House,
Charles House,
BRACKNELL,
Berks. RG12 1EB, England
Tel 0344 24555

Texas Instruments
Texas Instruments Inc.,
MOS Products Div.,
HOUSTON,
Texas 77001, U.S.A.
Tel 713 776 6617

Texas Instruments Ltd.,
Manton Lane,
BEDFORD,
Beds. MK41 7PA, England
Tel 0234 67466

Texas Instruments Deutschland GMBH,
Haggertystrasse 1,
8080 FREISLING, W. Germany
Tel 08161 80-1

Thomson EFCIS
Thomson EFCIS,
B.P. 5,
92403 COURBEVOIE, France
Tel 01-788 5001

Thomson EFCIS,
B.P. 217,
38019 GRENOBLE, France
Tel 76 97 41 11

Thomson CSF Ltd.,
Ringway House,
Bell Road,
Daneshill,
BASINGSTOKE,
Hants. RG24 0QG, England
Tel 0256 29155

Toshiba
Tokyo Shibaura Ltd.,
Semiconductor Division
2 Iginza 5 Chome,
Chou-ku, Japan
Tel 571 5711

Toshiba America Inc.,
2151 Michelson Drive,
Suite 190,
IRVINE,
Ca. 92715, U.S.A.
Tel 714 955 1155

Toshiba (UK) Ltd.,
Toshiba House,
Frimley Road,
Frimley,
CAMBERLEY,
Surrey GU16 5JJ, England
Tel Camberley 62222

Western Digital
Western Digital Corp.,
3128 Red Hill Ave.,
P.O. Box 2180,
NEWPORT BEACH,
Ca. 92663, U.S.A.
Tel 714 557 3550

Zilog
Zilog Inc.,
10340 Bubb Road,
CUPERTINO,
Ca. 90514, U.S.A.
Tel 408 446 4666

MICROPROCESSOR DATA BOOK

Zilog (UK) Ltd.,
Babbage House,
King Street,
MAIDENHEAD,
Berks. SL6 1DU, England
Tel 628 36131

Zilog GMBH,
Zugspitzstrasse 2a,
D8011 Vaterstetten,
MUNICH, W. Germany
Tel 08106 4035

13 GLOSSARY OF MICROPROCESSOR TERMS

GLOSSARY OF TERMS

Accumulator A temporary storage register used in conjunction with the arithmetic and logic unit (ALU) for execution of arithmetic and logical operations.

ALU Arithmetic and logic unit. A section of the CPU logic that performs the arithmetic and logical operations. The result of such an operation is placed in the accumulator.

Architecture The internal organisation of a microprocessor system.

ASCII American Standard Code for Information Interchange. A popular coding scheme for alphanumeric data in which each character is represented by a 7-bit data word. The code is basically the same as the ISO7 data code apart from a few characters.

Assembler A program used to translate an assembly language form of program coding (source code) into the machine code data which will be executed by the processor. The assembly language uses mnemonics for the instructions and symbolic names for data, making it easy to understand.

Basic Beginners All purpose Symbolic Instruction Code. This is a high level language which is easy to learn and is generally used for personal computer systems. It uses English words as instructions and symbolic names for data. Most versions of BASIC are interpretive programs, but it is also possible to obtain BASIC compilers.

Baud Measure of data rate in a serial transmission system. In a binary system the baud rate is the same as the number of bits per second.

Benchmark A short program designed to compare the speed and performance of different types of microprocessor for a particular application.

Bit Binary digit. The basic data unit in a microprocessor. A bit may have the values 0 or 1.

Bootstrap A short program, usually stored in ROM, used to get the processor to load its operating system into memory ready for use. Generally used to start up a disk based operating system.

Branch An instruction which causes the processor to jump to a new point in the sequence of instructions instead of executing the next instruction in sequence. Generally used after a conditional test to provide two alternative routes through the program.

Breakpoint A point in a program where the CPU can be made to stop program execution and display the contents of its registers and the CPU status. Used for debugging software and generally implemented by a software interrupt.

Bus Group of wires, common to various units in the system, and used to carry data between them. Examples are the data bus and the address bus.

Byte An 8-bit binary data word.

CPU Central Processor Unit. The part of a microprocessor system that controls operations, interprets instruction codes and executed the instructions. Contains the ALU, accumulator, program counter and possibly other data registers.

Character One of a set of alphanumeric symbols which may be represented by a unique binary code pattern.

Chip Popular name for an integrated circuit device.

Clock A regular train of pulses used to provide the timing control in a microprocessor system.

Compiler A computer program used to translate an application program written in a high level language, such as FORTRAN, into machine form.

Cross assembler An assembler program for a microprocessor which is designed to be executed on a computer using a different type of processor, or by a minicomputer. Often used in universal development systems to allow software to be developed for any processor without the need to change the hardware system.

CRC Cyclic redundancy check. A form of error checking in which a check pattern is written at the end of each block of data. Commonly used for magnetic tape and disk systems. The check pattern is based upon the data that have been written in the data block.

Data buffer A register or small memory in the processor or a peripheral device which is used temporarily to hold data when the peripheral device and the CPU are operating at different data rates. In a printer system the buffer may hold a complete line of text or perhaps a complete page.

Data bus Series of wires common to all units of a microcomputer system, through which data may be transferred between the various units.

Data pointer A register used to hold the memory address of data to be processed.

Debugging The process of detecting and correcting errors in operation of a program.

Development system A computer system designed specifically to allow development of the software and testing of the hardware of a prototype microprocessor system.

Diagnostic A special program designed to test a computer system and indicate any faults in its operation.

DIL Dual in line. The most common form of package for a microprocessor or related device. It has a row of pins at each side of the package for connections.

Disk A magnetically coated disk used for mass storage of data in a computer system. Disks may be of the hard type, such as the Winchester disk, or may be of flexible plastic in a protective envelope, as in the case of the floppy disk.

Diskette An alternative name for an 8 in diameter floppy disk.

DMA Direct memory access. A technique by which a peripheral device is allowed to take control of the address and data buses instead of the CPU, and transfer data directly into the computer memory.

Dynamic memory A memory in which data are stored as a charge on a capacitor. Since the charge can leak away such a memory must be continually refreshed by rewriting the data to maintain the storage.

EAROM Electronically Alterable Read Only Memory. A memory device in which the data can be altered electrically, but will be retained in the memory when power is removed.

Editor A program which allows text data to be entered into a data file and manipulated as desired to produce a final stored file of text data.

EEPROM Electrically Erasable Programmable Read

Only Memory. A read only memory that can be erased by applying an electrical signal to it.

Emulator A program, or hardware logic system, which allows the instruction set of a microprocessor to be executed on a computer system based upon a different type of microprocessor. Frequently used in universal development systems to allow a wide range of processor types to be handled without changing the system hardware.

EPROM Erasable Programmable Read Only Memory. A read only memory that can be erased by using UV light or by applying an electrical signal.

Fetch cycle A CPU timing cycle during which the instruction code data are loaded from memory.

File A collection of related data stored in memory. Files may be held on floppy disk or on magnetic tape.

Firmware A set of programs, such as a monitor or compiler, permanently held on a ROM ready for use in a microprocessor system.

Flag A data bit used to indicate the state of a device or the result of an operation. A flag bit might for instance indicate whether the result of the previous operation was zero or non-zero.

Flat pack An alternative form of integrated circuit package in which the leads are brought out in the same plane as the package. Often used where there are many leads required and the package is required to be small.

Floppy disk A magnetically coated plastic disk mounted in a protective envelope and used to provide mass storage of data. Standard size is 8 in diameter, whilst a mini-floppy disk is 5¼ in in diameter.

FORTRAN FORmula TRANslator. A high level computer language intended for use in scientific applications.

Hardware The electronic and mechanical equipment that makes up a computer system.

Hard disk A rigid magnetically coated disk for mass data storage, such as the Winchester disk.

High level language A computer programming language which uses English words as instructions and symbolic names for variables. Programs written in this langrage are translated into machine code by a compiler. Typical high level languages are BASIC, FORTRAN and PASCAL.

Half duplex Serial transmission system in which data may only travel in one direction at any time, as compared with *full duplex*, where data are transmitted in both directions simultaneously.

Instruction A code or expression which defines what the CPU is to do and which data it shall use during the execution of the instruction. Instructions are made up of one or more bytes of data which are interpreted by the CPU before execution.

Instruction cycle The sequence of events when the processor executes one instruction. This will be several clock or machine cycles according to the type of instruction.

Instruction set The set of instructions which a processor is able to execute.

Interpreter A program which translates instructions from a high level language to machine code as the program is being executed. BASIC is typically handled by an interpreter.

Interrupt A process by which the normal sequence of program execution may be interrupted, either by a signal from external hardware or by a software instruction. At this point the program branches to a service routine to deal with the interrupting device before resuming the main program sequence.

Interrupt mask Technique by which external interrupts may be ignored by setting a mask bit in the CPU.

Interrupt vector A location in memory which contains the address to which the program must jump to start the interrupt service routine.

ISO7 A code system for text data being interchanged between different computers. Similar to ASCII, but this is an international standard.

Jump Similar to a branch. Branch is often used for short jumps were the address is specified as relative to the program counter. Jump is used to describe this type of operation with an absolute or indexed address.

Kilobyte Term used for 1024 bytes. Thus a 4 kbyte memory will contain 4096 byes. Kilo prefix may also be used in the same sense with bits and words.

Library A set of programs, usually stored on disk, for common functions and operations. These programs are selected and inserted into the main program as required during the compilation and loading processes.

Linker A special program used to link together sections of assembly code program to form an executable program. It is particularly used where assembly code modules are relocatable.

Loader A program which calls up the machine code program from disk or cassette and loads it into the computer memory ready for execution.

LSI Large scale integration. Method of fabrication of integrated circuits which places a large amount of logic onto a single silicon chip. All microprocessors use LSI.

Machine code The sets of data which the processor interprets as instructions to be executed. Processors can be programmed at this level by writing the appropriate codes into the memory directly, and this is done in some of the simpler microprocessor evaluation boards.

Macro A sequence of instructions which can be treated as a single instruction by the assembler and used to save programming time, where a similar operation has to be used many times during a program. Unlike a subroutine, a macro produces the appropriate set of machine code in the program sequence each time it is used.

Macro-assembler An assembler program that can handle macro type instructions.

Memory Data storage hardware associated with the CPU. The memory may be RAM or ROM and may be used to store the program, or data being processed.

Microcomputer Term used to describe a complete computer system on a chip comprising the CPU, program memory, data memory and possibly several input–output ports. Also used for a complete microcomputer system made up from separate components.

Microprocessor The central processor (CPU) section of a microcomputer system.

Mini floppy name used to describe a 5¼ in diameter floppy disk. Also called a mini-diskette.

Mnemonic code Type of coding, as used in an assembler, in which a mnemonic is used to represent the instruction and is chosen to indicate its action. Typical codes are ADD, SUB, LDA (load A) and STA (store A).

Modem Modulator–demodulator. Device used to convert logic level signals into two audio tones for transmission over long distances and to restore the logic levels at the receiving end.

Monitor A program, normally resident in ROM, which provides a series of basic utility routines for operating a microprocessor system.

Multiplexing Process by which several different signals may be switched in sequence over a common set of wires. An example is where the data and address are multiplexed over a common bus system to reduce the number of wires needed.

Microprocessor system A system in which a number of microprocessors share the same bus system, peripherals and possibly the same memory. Enables processors to work in parallel to speed up throughput of processed data.

Nibble (nybble) Term used for a 4-bit data word.

Non-volatile memory Memory system which does not lose its data contents if the power is removed. Examples are the various forms of ROM and the magnetic bubble memory.

Object program The output from an assembler or compiler. It will usually be in machine code but may need to be linked and loaded before it can be executed by the CPU.

Of code The binary or hexadecimal code representing one of the instructions to be executed by the processor. As an example a load accumulator op code might be 96 (hex.).

Operating system The set of programs, usually stored on a disk, which govern the operations of the computer and includes assemblers, loaders, input–output utilities and file handling facilities.

Page A subdivision of the complete memory system which may be selected by higher order address bits. In an 8-bit system the 4 page is usually 256 bytes.

Parity A method of error checking in which an extra bit is added to the data element. For odd parity the bit is set so that the total number of '1' bits in the data word is odd. It is also possible to use even parity.

Peripheral A device external to the processor, such as a printer, floppy disk unit or visual display unit which is controlled by and communicates with the CPU.

Pointer Name given to a register which contains the address in memory of data or program instructions.

Polling Technique in which several peripheral devices are checked in sequence at regular intervals to see if they need attention. May also be used to find out which of the peripherals caused an interrupt.

Port An input–output channel between the CPU and external devices such as keyboards, displays, etc.

Program The sequence of instructions to be followed by the CPU in order to carry out the desired operations.

Program counter A pointer register controlled by the CPU which contains the address of the next instruction that is to be executed. Normally the program counter will be automatically incremented as the instruction is decoded.

PROM Programmable Read Only memory. Any read only memory that can be programmed in the field, but the term is normally reserved for the fusible link types.

RALU Register Arithmetic and Logic Unit. An ALU which also contains some registers.

RAM Random Access Memory. Term used to describe read–write memory which is normally used for data storage in a processor system.

Refresh Process required with dynamic memories to ensure retention of the data. Usually achieved by reading data at regular intervals, when the memory will automatically rewrite the stored data. Most memories refresh a row or column at a time, thus reducing the amount of time used for the refresh operation.

Read Process of taking data from a memory device without altering the contents of the memory location.

Register A single word memory location, either in the CPU or in the main memory, used to hold temporary data during the execution of the program. Using the internal CPU registers gives faster execution, since there are no memory accesses required.

ROM Read Only Memory. A memory which has a permanent data pattern written into it. Generally used for firmware and monitor programs. PROMs are programmed by the use of links in the mask used when fabricating the chip.

Scratchpad A small memory or section of memory used for storage of intermediate results during the execution of a program.

Serial Mode of data handling in which individual bits of the data word are dealt with in succession rather than simultaneously.

Service routine A short program which is run when one of the peripheral devices causes an interrupt. Similar in some ways to a *subroutine*, but activated by hardware rather than software.

Slice Type of processor in which a section of the CPU is provided with a limited word size, but arranged so that several slices can be operated in parallel to provided the desired word length. Generally used for very fast bipolar technology processor systems.

Software The program used for a computer system.

Source program A program written in a high level language such as BASIC or FORTRAN which needs to be translated or interpreted before it can be executed.

Stack A series of registers or a section of memory used to hold addresses or data, in particular for holding the return address and processor status during interrupt or subroutine operations. Operates as a first in last out memory.

Stack pointer A register used to hold the address of the current top location of the stack.

Statement An instruction line in a high level language such as BASIC or FORTRAN.

Static memory A memory system which does not need clocking or refreshing operations. Data are presented or may be accepted a short time after the address is applied.

String A sequence of alphanumeric data which will be held in memory as a group of character codes but may be dealt with as a single entity in terms of programming.

GLOSSARY OF TERMS

Subroutine A section of frequently used operations in a program which are treated as a small separate program. The execution may be made to jump to the subroutine at any desired point in the main program and on completion of the subroutine execution is returned to the main program at the next instruction in sequence after the subroutine call.

Terminal A remote control console, usually a visual display unit (VDU) from which programs can be entered and run.

Text editor A program which allows alphanumeric text to be entered into memory and manipulated eventually to produce a file in the memory or on disk. Generally used for entering and amending high level language programs.

Trace Technique by which the processor can be made to step through the program one instruction at a time, giving a display of register contents and status after each step. Used for debugging programs.

UART Universal Asynchronous Receiver Transmitter. A device used to control serial data transmission using the asynchronous start stop method of coding.

USRT Universal Synchronous Receiver Transmitter. Similar to a UART but designed for synchronous mode of data transmission.

VDU Visual Display Unit. Terminal where the display is presented on a television type screen.

Vector Memory location used to store the address of the service routine for an interrupting device.

Volatile memory Memory, such as a conventional RAM device, where the memory contents will be lost if the power is removed.

Word A unit of data in a computer systems which consists of a number of bits treated as a single entity. Normal word lengths are 4, 8, 12, 16 and 32 bits.

Write The process of transferring data into a memory or other device such as a peripheral.

LIBRARY OF DAVIDSON COLLEGE